THE

PUBLICATIONS

OF THE

SURTEES SOCIETY

VOL. 209

Hon. General Editors

R. H. BRITNELL and M. M. HARVEY

THE

PUBLICATIONS

OF THE

SURTEES SOCIETY

ESTABLISHED IN THE YEAR
M.DCCC.XXXIV

VOL. CCIX

SIR THOMAS GRAY

SCALACRONICA
1272–1363

EDITED AND TRANSLATED AND
WITH AN INTRODUCTION
BY
ANDY KING

THE SURTEES SOCIETY

THE BOYDELL PRESS

First published 2005
Paperback edition 2019

A Surtees Society Publication
published by The Boydell Press
an imprint of Boydell & Brewer Ltd
PO Box 9, Woodbridge, Suffolk IP12 3DF, UK
and of Boydell & Brewer Inc.
668 Mt Hope Avenue, Rochester, NY 14620–2731, USA
website: www.boydellandbrewer.com

ISBN 978-0-85444-064-1 hardback
ISBN 978-0-85444-079-5 paperback

ISSN 0307–5362

A catalogue record for this book is available
from the British Library

Details of other Surtees Society volumes are available
from Boydell & Brewer Ltd

The publisher has no responsibility for the continued existence or accuracy
of URLs for external or third-party internet websites referred to in this book,
and does not guarantee that any content on such websites is, or will remain,
accurate or appropriate

This publication is printed on acid-free paper

CONTENTS

For Lewis and Freya

PREFACE

The present volume contains the text of Thomas Gray's *Scalacronica* covering the period 1272 until 1363, where it ends. As Gray's French is sometimes somewhat obscure, a facing-page translation has also been provided. A further volume will provide the text for the rest of Gray's work, covering the period from the Creation until 1272.

ACKNOWLEDGEMENTS

At a time when a Labour government is doing its best to foist the 'values' of the market upon the British university system, it is a great pleasure to be able record the unstintingly generous assistance and encouragement that I have received from numerous academic colleagues and friends, many of whom have been subjected to my musings on the *Scalacronica* at inordinate length. In particular – and at the risk of sounding like an Oscar acceptance speech – I have to thank Richard Barber for initiating the whole project, and Caroline Palmer for bringing it to press with such enthusiasm; Michael Prestwich for supervising it; Margaret Harvey and Richard Britnell for acting in an editorial capacity for the Surtees Society, with great sympathy; Gill Cannell, sub-librarian at the Parker Library, Corpus Christi College, Cambridge, and Frances Willmoth, the archivist at the Old Library, Jesus College Cambridge, who were both very welcoming and provided microfilms; Matt Holford for checking the manuscript of Leland's abstract at the Bodleian, and for various references; Françoise Le Saux and Jane Taylor for providing invaluable help with the more intractable parts of Thomas Gray's 'Frenssh after the scole of the New Castel on the Tyne'; Alan Piper for elucidating various problems of paleography, and numerous other miscellaneous queries; Richard Moll for advice and references to the provenance of the MS; Julia Marvin for advice on the Anglo-Norman prose *Brut* chronicle; Andrew Ayton for supplying numerous manuscript references for the Grays' military careers; James Carley for advice on John Leland; Corinne Saunders for identifying medieval books; Michael Penman

for providing a perspective from the other side of the border; Len Scales for help on Teutonic affairs; and Margaret Harvey, again, for help on ecclesiastical matters; and Sarah Layfield, Liz Evershed, Melanie Devine, Andrea Ruddick, Mike Huxtable, Julian Harrison, Alistair Tebbit, Jon Boniface, Geoff Carter, Keith Waters and P.J. Everty for providing references and/or advice. Last, but by no means least, I have to thank Claire Etty, for detailed comment on the introduction, and for helping to shape my views of Thomas Gray's border society over the *longue durée*. Of course, none of the above can be held responsible for the numerous errors which undoubtedly remain, and which are all my own unaided work.

I would also like to acknowledge gratefully the Masters of Corpus Christi College, Cambridge, for granting me access to the only surviving MS of the *Scalacronica*; and the Arts and Humanities Research Board, who provided the generous funding for the project, without which the current volume would not have appeared.

On a more personal note, many thanks to Claire, Sarah and Jeff, for providing very welcome distraction, of a stuporifically mundane nature, including 'Tea and Sympathy', and 'Retail Therapy'; to my parents, Beth King and Ted Hutchinson, without whose unstinting support, both financial and moral, I'd never have been in a position to start this edition, let alone finish it; and to Lewis and Freya who put up with being dragged round every site of medieval historical interest in northern England.

Durham, Wednesday before the Translation of St Thomas, 53 Elizabeth II

ABBREVIATIONS

Ailred of Rievaulx	Ailred of Rievaulx, 'Vita sancti Edwardi regis', *Patrologiæ cursus completus: Patrologia Latina*, ed. J.P. Migne, cxcv.
Anonimalle, 1307–34	The *Anonimalle Chronicle, 1307–1334*, ed. W.R. Childs and J. Taylor, Yorkshire Archaeological Society Record Series cxlvii (1991).
Anonimalle, 1333–81	The *Anonimalle Chronicle, 1333–81*, ed. V.H. Galbraith (Manchester, 1927).
Avesbury	'Robertus de Avesbury de gestis mirabilibus regis Edwardi Tertii', *Chronica A. Murimuth et R. de Avesbury*, ed. E.M. Thompson, Rolls Series 93 (1889).
Baker	*Chronicon Galfridi le Baker de Swynebroke*, ed. E.M. Thompson (Oxford, 1889).
Barbour	*Barbour's Bruce*, ed. M.P. McDiarmid and J.A.C. Stevenson, 3 vols., Scottish Text Society, 4th ser., xii, xiii, xv (1980–5). References are by book and line, according to the divisions of the original text.
BL	British Library.
Bower	*Bower's Scotichronicon*, ed. D.E.R. Watt, *et al.* (9 vols., Aberdeen and Edinburgh, 1987–98).
Bridlington	'Gesta Edwardi de Carnarvon auctore canonico Bridlingtoniensi', *Chronicles of the Reigns of Edward I and Edward II*, ed. W. Stubbs, Rolls Series 76 (2 vols., 1882–3), vol. ii.
Bruce, ed. Duncan	The *Bruce*, ed. A.A.M. Duncan (Edinburgh, 1997).
Brut, ed. Brie	The *Brut*, ed. F.W.D. Brie, Early English Text Society, 1st ser., 131, 136 (2 vols., 1906, 1908).
Capgrave, *Chronicle*	John Capgrave, *The Chronicle of England*, ed. F.C. Hingeston, Rolls Series 1 (1858).

Capgrave, *De illustribus Henricis*	John Capgrave, *Liber de illustribus Henricis*, ed. F.C. Hingeston, Rolls Series 7 (1858).
CCR	*Calendar of Close Rolls.*
CDS	*Calendar of Documents Relating to Scotland*, ed. J. Bain (4 vols., Edinburgh, 1881–8), corrected with reference to *Calendar of Documents Relating to Scotland*, vol. v: *Supplementary*, ed. G.G. Simpson and J.B. Galbraith (Edinburgh, 1988).
CFR	*Calendar of Fine Rolls.*
'Chancery Enrolments, Bury'	'Durham Records, Calendar of the Cursitor's Records, Chancery Enrolments. Roll of Richard de Bury, Bishop of Durham', *The Thirty-First Annual Report of the Deputy Keeper of the Public Records* (London, 1870), app. ii.
'Chancery Enrolments, Hatfield'	'Durham Records, Calendar of the Cursitor's Records, Chancery Enrolments. Roll of Thomas de Hatfield, Bishop of Durham', *The Thirty-Second Annual Report of the Deputy Keeper of the Public Records* (1871), app.
Chandos Herald	*La Vie du Prince Noir by Chandos Herald*, ed. D.B. Tyson (Tübingen, 1975).
CIM	*Calendar of Inquisitions Miscellaneous.*
CIPM	*Calendar of Inquisitions Post Mortem.*
Cleopatra D.iii	British Library, Cotton MS Cleopatra D.iii.
CP	G.E. Cockayne, *et al.* (eds.), *The Complete Peerage*, rev. and ed. V. Gibbs (12 vols., London, 1910–59).
CPR	*Calendar of Patent Rolls.*
DCM	Durham Cathedral Muniments.
Documents, ed. Palgrave	*Documents and Records Illustrating the History of Scotland, Preserved in the Treasury*, ed. F. Palgrave (Record Commission, 1837).
Documents, ed. Stevenson	*Documents Illustrative of the History of Scotland, 1286–1306*, ed. J. Stevenson (2 vols., London, 1870).
Eulogium	*Eulogium historiarum*, ed. F.S. Haydon, Rolls Series 9 (3 vols., 1858–63).
Flores	*Flores historiarum*, ed. H.R. Luard, Rolls Series 95 (3 vols, 1890).

Fœdera	*Fœdera, conventiones, litteræ, et cujuscunque generis public acta*, etc., ed. T. Rymer (4 vols. in 7 parts, Record Commission edn, 1816–69).
Fordun	*Johannis de Fordun. Chronica gentis Scotorum*, ed. W.F. Skene (Edinburgh, 1871).
Froissart	Jean Froissart, *Chroniques*, ed. S. Luce, *et al.* (15 vols., Paris, 1869–1975).
Gransden, *Historical Writing*, i	Gransden, A., *Historical Writing in England, c.550 to c.1307* (London, 1974).
Gransden, *Historical Writing*, ii	Gransden, A., *Historical Writing in England, c.1307 to the Early Sixteenth Century* (London, 1982).
Great Cause	*Edward I and the Throne of Scotland, 1290–1296: An Edition of the Record Sources for the Great Cause*, ed. E.L.G. Stones and G.G. Simpson (2 vols., Oxford, 1978).
Guisborough	*The Chronicle of Walter of Guisborough*, ed. H. Rothwell, Camden Society, 3rd ser., lxxxix (1957).
Hemingburgh	*Chronicon domini Walteri de Hemingburgh*, ed. H.C. Hamilton, English Historical Society Publications (2 vols., 1849).
Huntingdon	Henry of Huntingdon, *Historia Anglorum*, ed. D. Greenway (Oxford, 1996).
'Inquests Post Mortem, Hatfield'	'Durham Records, Calendar of the Cursitor's Records, Inquisitions Post Mortem. Pontificate of Thomas de Hatfield', *The Forty-Fifth Annual Report of the Deputy Keeper of the Public Records* (London, 1885), app. i.
Knighton, ed. Lumby	*Chronicon Henrici Knighton*, ed. J.R. Lumby, Rolls Series 92 (2 vols., 1889–95).
Knighton, ed. Martin	*Knighton's Chronicle, 1337–96*, ed. G.H. Martin (Oxford, 1995).
Lambeth	Lambeth Palace, London, MS 12.
Lanercost	*Chronicon de Lanercost*, ed. J. Stevenson, Bannatyne Club lxv (Edinburgh, 1839).
Langtoft	*Pierre de Langtoft, le règne d'Edouard Ier*, ed. J.C. Thiolier (Créteil, 1989).
Le Bel	*Chronique de Jean le Bel*, ed. J. Viard and E. Déprez (2 vols., 1904–5).

Louth Park Chronicle	*Chronicon de Abbatie de Parco Lude. The Chronicle of Louth Park Abbey*, ed. E. Venables, tr. A.R. Maddison, Publications of the Lincolnshire Record Society i (1891).
Manning	Robert Manning of Brunne, *The Story of England*, Rolls Series 87 (2 vols., 1887).
Marlborough	Thomas of Marlborough, *History of the Abbey of Evesham*, ed. J. Sayers and Leslie Watkiss (Oxford, 2003).
Melsa	*Chronica monasterii de Melsa*, ed. E.A. Bond, Rolls Series 43 (3 vols., 1866–8).
Monmouth	Geoffrey of Monmouth, *Historia regum Britannie, I: Bern Ms*, ed. N. Wright (Woodbridge, 1985).
Murimuth	'Adæ Murimuth continuatio chronicarum', *Chronica A. Murimuth et R. de Avesbury*, ed. E.M. Thompson, Rolls Series 93 (1889).
NCH	*Northumberland County History* (15 vols., Newcastle upon Tyne, 1893–1940).
NCMH	*The New Cambridge Medieval History VI, c.1300–c.1415*, ed. Michael Jones (Cambridge, 2000).
NRO	Northumberland Record Office, Gosforth.
Polychronicon	*Polychronicon Ranulphi Higden monachi Cestrensis*, ed. C. Babington and J.R. Lumby, Rolls Series 41 (9 vols. 1865–86)
PRO	The National Archive: Public Record Office, Kew.
Reading	*Cronica Johannis de Reading et Anonymi Cantuariensis, 1346–67*, ed. J. Tait (Manchester, 1914).
Rishanger	*Willelmi Rishanger, chronica et annales*, ed. M.T. Riley, Rolls Series 28/ii (1865).
Rot. Parl.	*Rotuli Parliamentorum* (6 vols., London, 1767–77.
Rot. Scot.	*Rotuli Scotiæ*, ed. D. Macpherson (2 vols., Record Commission, 1814–19).
RPD	*Registrum palatinum Dunelmense*, ed. T.D. Hardy, Rolls Series lxii (4 vols., 1873–8).

RRS, David II	*Regesta Regum Scottorum VI: The Acts of David II, 1329–71*, ed. Bruce Webster (Edinburgh, 1982).
RRS, Robert I	*Regesta Regum Scottorum V: The Acts of Robert I, 1306–29*, ed. A.A.M. Duncan (Edinburgh, 1988).
SAL	Society of Antiquaries of London.
Scalacronica, Maxwell	*Scalacronica. The Reigns of Edward I, Edward II and Edward III*, tr. H. Maxwell (Glasgow, 1907).
Scalacronica, Stevenson	*Scalacronica, by Sir Thomas Gray of Heton, Knight*, ed. J. Stevenson (Edinburgh, 1836).
Scrope and Grosvenor	*The Controversy between Sir Richard Scrope and Sir Robert Grosvenor*, ed. N.H. Nicholas (2 vols., London, 1832).
Sempringham	'Chroniques de Sempringham', *Le Livre de Reis de Brittanie*, ed. J. Glover, Rolls Series 42 (1865).
SP	J.B. Paul (ed.), *The Scots Peerage* (9 vols., Edinburgh, 1904–14).
Trivet annales	*Nicholai Triveti annales*, ed. Thomas Hog, English Historical Society (1845).
Trivet continuatio	*Nicolai Triveti annalium continuatio*, ed. Anthony Hall (Oxford, 1722).
Trokelowe	'Johannis de Trokelowe Annales', *Johannis de Trokelowe et Henrici de Blaneforde chronica et annales*, ed. H.T. Riley, Rolls Series xxviii (1866).
Venette	*The Chronicle of Jean de Venette*, tr. J. Birdsall and R.A. Newhall (New York, 1953).
Vita Edwardi	*Vita Edwardi Secundi*, ed. Noel Denholm-Young (London, 1957).
Walsingham	*Thomæ Walsingham, historia Anglicana*, ed. H.T. Riley, Rolls Series 28/i (2 vols., 1863).
Wyntoun	*The Original Chronicle of Andrew of Wyntoun*, ed. F.J. Amours, Scottish Text Society (6 vols., 1903–14).

Outline Genealogy of the Gray Family

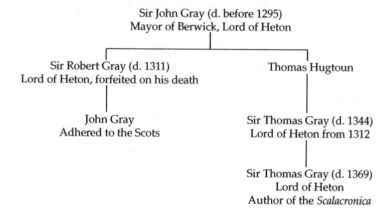

Sir John Gray (d. before 1295)
Mayor of Berwick, Lord of Heton

Sir Robert Gray (d. 1311)
Lord of Heton, forfeited on his death

Thomas Hugtoun

John Gray
Adhered to the Scots

Sir Thomas Gray (d. 1344)
Lord of Heton from 1312

Sir Thomas Gray (d. 1369)
Lord of Heton
Author of the *Scalacronica*

INTRODUCTION

AUTHORSHIP AND DATE: A LITERARY PRISONER

The author of the *Scalacronica* commences his *opus magnum* by claiming that, 'he who wrote this chronicle does not wish to reveal his name plainly'. However, he *is* willing to reveal that he was a prisoner of war when he started to write the work, and that he was of 'that order which is enlightened by good customs, a support for the old, for maidens and for Holy Church' – by which it would appear that he means the 'order' of knighthood. He then appends a rhymed verse which drops some heavy hints as to his identity.[1] First of all, he tells us that his 'proper attire' would be a coat of the same colour as the cloak of a cordelier (*i.e.* a Greyfriar). He then describes his 'other' coat which bears 'the status of his order', *i.e.*, a surcoat bearing his heraldic arms, and proceeds to give a somewhat cryptic description of these arms:[2] a 'hardy beast' on a background the 'colour of fire' (which must mean *gules*, or red), quartered with his mother's arms, with a border. Just to make quite sure, he goes on to give his name in the form of an alphabetical puzzle, which spells out 'Thomas Gray'; and he adds that his father had the same name. He continues by describing how he came to write the book, again mentioning his imprisonment, this time adding the detail that he was held in Edinburgh castle. Later, he adds that he started to write in 1355.[3] The author of the *Scalacronica* was therefore a knight named Thomas Gray, the son of another Thomas Gray, who was captive in Edinburgh in 1355, and who was alive in 1363, when the book ends. These criteria are all filled by Sir Thomas Gray, the constable of Norham castle who

---

1 Below, p. 3.
2 Thus, in his introduction, Stevenson comments rather sniffily that 'the account which is here given of his armorial bearings is too indefinite to be reduced, with certainty, to the terms of modern heraldry', *Scalacronica*, Stevenson, p. xxxv, n.
3 Below, p. 7.

was captured by the Scots in 1355.[4] Furthermore, the Gray family arms were a silver lion on a red background, with an engrailed silver border;[5] and his father was the constable of Norham of that name whose exploits dominate the *Scalacronica*'s account of the reign of Edward II. Given these correlations, and the close match between Gray's known career and the interests of the chronicle's author, there are few medieval works whose authorship can be more securely established.[6] The alphabetical puzzle was doubtless inspired by the example of the chronicler Ranulf Higden (whom Gray alludes to as one of his sources), who altered the initial capital letters of the sixty chapters of Book I of his *Polychronicon* to produce an acrostic which read: 'Presentem cronicam compilavit Frater Ranulphus Cestrensis monachus'.[7] In an age when texts were often copied as continuations

---

4   The toponym 'de Heton', often used by modern historians to describe the chronicler, was not actually used by him. It was first adopted by his son, another Thomas, to distinguish him from Thomas Gray de Horton, who (unlike his like-named forebears) was active in Northumbrian affairs, during the reign of Richard II; see, *e.g.*, *Rot. Scot.*, ii, 84 (1386). It should also be noted that Gray spelt his surname with an 'a', not an 'e'. This is how it is spelt in the alphabetical puzzle by which he identifies himself as the author of the *Scalacronica*; where he refers to his father, he consistently uses the spelling 'Gray', more often than not with the prefix 'de'; and his seal bears the legend 'LE : SEEL THOMAS : GRAY . CHEVALIER' (Greenwell and Blair, 'Durham Seals', 79, no. 1112 and pl. iv). However, documentary references to the author and his father use the spellings 'Gray' and 'Grey' indifferently, with or without the 'de'.

5   *Gules a lion within a border engrailed silver*, Blair, 'North Country Arms', 259–60. An indenture of 1359 still retains Gray's seal, which shows him on horseback bearing a shield with a lion rampant within an engrailed border. It is not quartered, but this may be because it would not have been possible to reproduce legibly a quartered coat of arms on a seal of this size. DCM, 3.14.Spec.17; Greenwell and Blair, 'Durham Seals', 79, no. 1112 and pl. iv – where it is misdated to 1346. The seal of Gray's grandson, Sir Thomas Gray, also shows a shield with a lion rampant, without any quartering; *ibid.*, no. 1113.

6   It is, for instance, interesting to note that there is actually no hard evidence to link Geoffrey Chaucer the poet with Geoffrey Chaucer the courtier and servant of Richard II's government, though the identification is obvious and universally accepted.

7   Gransden, *Historical Writing*, ii, 44, 47, and plate II (a); Taylor, *Historical Literature*, 101. Henry Knighton also copied Higden, employing an acrostic to identify himself as the author of his chronicle (*Knighton*, ed. Martin, xvii). By a strange coincidence, Gray's own grandson (the Sir Thomas Gray who was involved in the Southampton plot of 1415) was to be alluded to by a cryptogram in Thomas Elmham's metrical Life of Henry V. This fifteenth-century

of other books, it was easy for an author's name to become detached from his work; incorporating that name into the body of the text in this way was one means of preventing this from happening. It is, of course, possible that the *Scalacronica* is actually the work of a clerk writing in Gray's name.[8] However, Gray was clearly directly involved in its compilation; he is the only plausible source for the reminisences of his father that provide the basis for much of the more contemporary sections of the work, and was himself the source of some of the material. Therefore, in the absence of any actual evidence of the involvement of a 'ghost writer', there seems to be no good reason not to take Gray's claim to authorship at face value.

The idea of the literary prisoner was well known in England long before the career of Sir Thomas Malory; the obvious example would have been Boethius, who wrote his vastly influential *Consolation of Philosophy* while awaiting execution in 524. There were rather more contemporary examples, such as *Le Mireur a Justices* ('The Mirror of Justices'), a curious and mendacious legal tract written *circa* 1290. Its author claimed to be a 'prosecutor of false judges', by whom he had been maliciously imprisoned. He further claimed that whilst imprisoned, he had searched treasury records and charters to discover the laws of England.[9] Aside from the unlikelihood of a prisoner being allowed access to royal records, the whole work is of a highly inventive nature, and we may assume that, in the case of *Le Mireur a Justices*, the claim of its author to being a prisoner was merely a literary device. The author of the *Scalacronica* was certainly not incapable of using similar literary artifice, as his opening vision of the Sibyl demonstrates. However, as Thomas Gray actually was a prisoner, there is no good reason to doubt his own account that he started to write his book while he was captive in Edinburgh castle, particularly as he made use of Scottish sources unknown to most other English chroniclers. Gray was captured in mid-October 1355, which

---

work included many such cryptograms, one of which spelled out Gray's name backwards (Given-Wilson, *Chronicles*, 147; Gransden, *Historical Writing*, ii, 207–8). The use of crpytograms by English chroniclers to identify themselves is discussed by Given-Wilson, *Chronicles*, 147–52.

8 I have to thank Craig Taylor for pointing out this possibility to me.

9 *Mirror of Justices*, ed. Whitaker and Maitland, pp. 2, xxii–xxiv. The attribution of the *Fleta* to a prisoner in the Fleet gaol was an invention of the seventeenth-century lawyer and polemicist Sir Edward Coke; there is no such claim in the work itself (*Fleta*, ed. Sayles, pp. xxiv–xxv).

provides a starting date for his literary endeavours.[10] Obviously, he cannot have completed it before 1363, where the narrative ends. However, he was back in England by the end of November 1356 at the latest, and could have spent little more than a year in captivity. Furthermore, he made extensive use of the *Historia aurea* of John of Tynemouth. This was not a common work, being some seven times longer than the *Polychronicon*, and only three complete manuscripts have survived.[11] However, one of these belonged to the library at Durham Priory; it is recorded in a catalogue made in 1395, and its narrative for the years 1328 to 1338 was used as a source for a continuation of a short Latin chronicle. The continuation ends in 1347, and was presumably compiled soon after then, probably at Durham, suggesting that the priory had already acquired its copy of the *Historia aurea* by the time that Gray started work on his *Scalacronica*. The Durham monks evidently had a high regard for the work; another Durham manuscript, containing excerpts from it, describes it as 'the mother of all histories'.[12] In all probability, it was Durham's copy that was used by Gray; and he could hardly have made use of it while he was incarcerated in Edinburgh. The fact that this work is alluded to in his prologue, and is used in conjunction with Scottish sources without any obvious trace of interpolation, suggests that the material he wrote in captivity was subsequently rewritten after his release. On the other hand, Gray's claim that he was totally ignorant of history, until his imprisonment gave him the chance to improve his knowledge, is almost certainly merely a modesty *topos*, typical of

---

10 The date and length of Gray's captivity are discussed below, xl–xli. It should be noticed that Gray states only that he started his work while a prisoner, not that he finished it.
11 Taylor, *Historical Literature*, 103–5; Gransden, *Historical Writing*, ii, 56. The *Historia*'s narrative of the reign of Edward III was used to provide continuations for a number of other chronicles, including Guisborough and the *Polychronicon* (Galbraith, 'Historia Aurea', 385–7), but Gray implies that he had access to a copy going back at least as far as 1066, so he is likely to have been using the complete work.
12 *Catalogi veteres*, 56; Jesus College, Cambridge, MS Q.B.7; Offler, 'Franciscan Chronicle', 47. The complete Durham copy describes its author as John of the diocese of York (Galbraith, 'Historia Aurea', 385). It should be noted that if Gray did use the Durham copy of the *Historia aurea*, this seems to have been the only work the monks were willing to lend him. He does not seem to have had access to works such as *Lanercost*, which the monks certainly knew, nor Robert Graystanes' history of the priory itself, completed in 1336 and which covered events up to 1334 (Offler, *Medieval Historians*, 14–15).

medieval authors. He specifically states that he started to write in 1355; however, he was not captured until the October of that year, and it hardly seems likely that he was able to acquire, from scratch, enough knowledge to contemplate writing a universal history from the Creation, in the five months before the Feast of the Annunciation, the usual date for starting the new year.

Towards the end of his book, after recounting the risings in Paris and the activities of the King of Navarre in 1358, Gray pauses in his narrative, before going on to describe the French expedition of 1359, an expedition on which he was present himself.[13] He writes that, 'as some notable battles were omitted from the writing at the time they occurred in the narrative of this book, which had already been written, so it is only right that they should be described in another part'.[14] There follows a series of vivid accounts of *mêlées* and skirmishes, dating as far back as the battle at the Benedictine abbey of Guitres, Gascony, in 1341.[15] The obvious explanation for these interpolations is that Gray heard these tales from his fellow English knights and esquires, while on campaign in France; and indeed, many of them read like tales told round the campfire. It would appear that Gray put aside his work almost in mid-paragraph, to answer his king's summons to war. All of which indicates that the main body of the *Scalacronica*, dealing with events up to 1358, was written between Gray's release in or before November 1356 and his departure on the royal expedition to France of 1359, which sailed at the end of that October.

In chapter 54, Gray refers to events in Spain taking place at 'around that time' when the unfortunate Katherine de Mortimer was killed, in June 1360. The peace agreement between Castile and Aragon which he refers to must be the peace treaty sealed at Terrer in May 1361; as he also refers to the renewal of the war, he must have written this chapter after the breakdown of this treaty in June 1362. As he makes no allusion to Pedro's dethronement in March 1366, or to the Black Prince's invasion of Castile on his behalf in 1367, it seems likely that this chapter was written before 1366. It would appear that the last part of the chronicle, from 1359 to 1363, was written up within a couple of years of the events it describes. Quite why Gray decided to stop writing at the marriage of David II, in spring 1363, is not clear,

---

13 See below, xliii.
14 Below, 159.
15 Below, 159. Note however that the text erroneously dates this battle to 1333.

as he lived until 1369, some six years later, and does not appear to have been in particularly poor health before then. However, it is not inconceivable that the murder of his close associate John de Coupland, in December 1363, brought recent history uncomfortably close to to home. Coupland had made a speciality of dredging up old accusations of adhering to the Scots during Edward II's reign, and holding the sons and grandsons of those accused to account for the alleged treachery of their forebears.[16] Given that the affair split Northumbrian society, leaving a legacy of bitter antagonism, Coupland's murder might well have have been rather too sensitive a matter to be put into the *Scalacronica*; but equally, it would have been difficult to gloss over it completely.[17] The whole business may have sapped Gray's enthusiasm for contemporary history. However, this can be only be speculation, and there may well have been rather more mundane, and unknowable, factors behind his decision to stop at 1363.

SIR THOMAS GRAY'S CAREER AND BACKGROUND

The *Scalacronica* is unusual in that its author was personally involved in many of the events he describes. Since there are many direct connections between the contents of the chronicle and the experiences of Sir Thomas Gray and his father, an account of their careers provides a useful context for the chronicle. They saw extensive service in the king's wars, and played an important part in both the royal administration in Northumberland, and that of the bishops of Durham in the palatinate. It is therefore possible to trace both their careers in considerable detail – indeed, there are few medieval chroniclers whose careers are so well documented as that of Thomas Gray.

Thomas Gray came from a family which had straddled the Anglo-Scottish border, until the outbreak of war in 1296 made this position untenable. He was probably the grandson of one Thomas Hugtoun, who the 'Lanercost' Chronicle records as experiencing a vision, in 1295.[18] In this vision, Hugtoun's long-dead father, Sir John

---

16 For Coupland's nefarious activities and his subsequent murder, see King, 'War, Politics and Landed Society', 154–73; for Gray's association with him, below, xlii–xliii.
17 At least two contemporary chroniclers refer to the affair; *Knighton*, ed. Martin, 186; Reading, 162.
18 See 'Outline Genealogy of the Gray Family', above, xvi.

Gray, appeared to him in the habit of a Greyfriar, to warn his son that his neighbours in Berwick had been neglecting the charitable donations which he had begun in honour of St Francis; if they did not mend their ways, they would swiftly experience the loss of their worldly goods and the dishonour of their bodies. Unfortunately, the good citizens of Berwick did not heed this this timely warning, and so duly lost their worldly goods – and in many cases, their lives – when Edward I sacked the town with the utmost ferocity the following year.[19] John Gray was mayor of Berwick in 1253, but seems to have had a rather more belligerent career than this implies, for 'Lanercost' comments that he was 'as much a knight as a burgess' (*tam miles quam burgensis*) and the surviving portion of the Hundred Rolls for Northumberland records that a John Gray forfeited lands there after the battle of Evesham.[20] Presumably, like other disinherited northern Montfortians such as John de Vesci, John Gray was able to make his peace with the crown, for his manor of Heton (near the Tweed, in the Bishop of Durham's liberty of Norhamshire) was later said to have been inherited by Sir Robert Gray in accordance with the law of England. However, on Robert's death, it was seized by Anthony Bek, Bishop of Durham, as a forfeiture of war, for Robert had died in Scotland as an opponent of the king, and his son remained in rebellion.[21] While John had been active in politics in both Scotland and England and, in a more forgiving age, had been able to recover from backing the wrong side, Robert was forced to choose his allegiance, and as a result, lost his inheritance. By October 1312, Sir Thomas Gray, father of the chronicler, held Heton of the bishops of Durham. His precise relationship to Robert is not specified; however, a Thomas Gray of Heton mentioned in the Hundred Rolls for Northumberland should perhaps be identified with Thomas Hugtoun, the younger son of John Gray.[22] Thus assuming the chronicler's father was Thomas Hugtoun's son, and that Robert Gray was therefore his uncle, he benefited from his uncle's forfeiture in a war that split many families, across a border line which, until 1296, had had very little practical significance.

---

19 *Lanercost*, 185–6; see also Little, 'Authorship of Lanercost'. For the fall of Berwick, see below, 37.

20 *Lanercost*, 186; *Scalacronica*, Stevenson, p. xiii; Scott, *Berwick-upon-Tweed*, 478; *Rotuli hundredorum*, ii, 27.

21 *RPD*, i, 77–8; *CPR 1307–13*, 337; Knowles, 'Resettlement of England'.

22 *Rotuli hundredorum*, ii, 23; *Scalacronica*, Stevenson, pp. xiii–xiv; *RPD*, ii, 1170–1.

Thomas Gray *le piere*

Thomas Gray, the chronicler's father, made his fortune through military service in Scotland. The benefits which father and son derived from their war service were the basis for their rapid rise in social standing;[23] and this coloured the chronicler's attitudes to warfare, as the *Scalacronica* reveals. However, the elder Gray's career was almost finished before it had begun, for in May 1297, he had the misfortune to be in the company of William de Heselrigg, sheriff of Clydesdale, when the latter was killed by William Wallace, along with most of his companions. Gray himself was stripped and left for dead, surviving only because he happened to be left between two burning buildings, the warmth of which kept him alive until help arrived in the morning.[24] He recovered quickly enough, for in June he was serving in the retinue of John de Warenne, Earl of Surrey, who had just been given the custody of Scotland. He served with Warenne again in 1298; and the following January, he was in the garrison of Berwick under Robert fitz Roger, lord of Warkworth.[25]

In September 1301, Gray was fighting in Selkirk forest with Patrick of Dunbar, Earl of March, and Hugh de Audley; and he was still with the earl in September 1302. The *Scalacronica* gives a fairly detailed account of the night time battle at Roslin in February 1303, at which the English suffered defeat. The account mentions Dunbar's presence, so Gray may well have been there himself. If so, he managed to escape, but was not so lucky that spring, when he accompanied Edward's Scottish expedition, in Hugh de Audley's company of 60 men-at-arms. While comfortably – and rashly – quartered at Melrose Abbey, in advance of the main army, Hugh and his men suffered another surprise night attack, and all were killed or captured. Gray was forced to surrender when the house he was defending burnt down over his head.[26]

Despite this setback, Edward was able to push his forces right into the north of Scotland, and most of the Scots came to terms early in 1304. Gray was evidently released fairly quickly, for that July, he was free to serve at the siege of Stirling castle, held by Sir William Oliphant. Here, Gray was in the retinue of the French *emigré* Henry de

---

23 King, 'Scaling the Ladder'.
24 Below, 41.
25 *Rot. Scot.*, i, 47; *Scotland in 1298*, ed. Gough, 44; *CDS*, v, no. 2198.
26 *CDS*, ii, no. 1230; *CDS*, v, no. 272; *Rot. Scot.*, i, 52; below, 47.

Beaumont. Beaumont had entered Edward's service in 1297, becoming a knight of the royal household at about the same time Gray began his career in arms. Beaumont's sister Isabella was the widow of John de Vesci, lord of Alnwick, and in November 1304, she was appointed custodian of Bamburgh castle. The Beaumonts evidently had ambitions to extend their influence in Northumberland, and so it is hardly surprising that Henry should have employed a Northumbrian knight such as Gray.[27] The *Scalacronica* has a dramatic account of Gray's rescue of his lord, who had been caught by a hook thrown from a Scottish siege engine. As he dragged Beaumont back to safety, Gray was hit in the head by a bolt from a springald. Not surprisingly, it was assumed that he had been killed, and he had the unusual experience of witnessing his own funeral, for he revived just as he was about to be buried.[28]

From this point Gray seems to have enjoyed Henry de Beaumont's confidence, and it is not unreasonable to assume that this stemmed at least partly from gratitude for Gray's prompt action at Stirling. A mark of this confidence was his appointment as Isabella de Vesci's attorney, along with Henry himself, in an inquiry concerning her rights in the barony of Crail, in Scotland, taken at Perth in May 1305.[29] Gray's association with Beaumont also opened up an avenue to royal patronage. In 1306, in the aftermath of the collapse of Edward's settlement of Scotland, he was able to petition the king for various lands of Walter de Bickerton of Kincraig, and Alexander Fraser, son of Andrew Fraser, although if these petitions were indeed granted, the deteriorating situation in Scotland would have prevented their effective implementation.[30]

The rebellion of Robert Bruce ensured continued employment for Gray, and he received a protection for service in Berwick in 1306, after which he rejoined Henry de Beaumont's company. In October, he was employed to take some money to the royal household at Lanercost Priory in Cumberland, where Edward was lying 'gravely ill'; it may have been on this occasion that the king promised him land at

---

27 Prestwich, 'Isabella de Vescy', 148–9. Beaumont's career is summarised in *CP*, ii, 59–60.
28 Below, 47. For the siege, see Prestwich, *Edward I*, 497–500. I have to thank Dr P.J. Everty for shedding valuable light on this episode.
29 *CDS*, ii, no. 1670.
30 *Documents*, ed. Palgrave, i, 303–4, 313; Prestwich, 'Colonial Scotland', 10–11.

Ughtrotherestrother.[31] Edward's death did not hinder Gray's burgeoning military career. In October 1307, he was amongst a group of earls, barons and knights who received orders to go to Scotland, 'with horse and arms and all your forces', for the defence of the realm and their own possessions; and the following October, he received a protection for service in Scotland until Easter next.[32] The accession of Edward II also brought Gray into closer contact with the court, for Henry de Beaumont was a favourite of the new king. In October 1307, Gray was able to obtain a grant of free warren for Henry de Ilderton of Northumberland; and in December, he stood as mainpernor for Christiana de Seton, who had been detained in Sixhills Convent, Lincolnshire, by reason of her husband's adherence to the Scots. The *Scalacronica* records – incidentally – that Gray attended the coronation of Edward II, in February 1308, presumably in Beaumont's retinue.[33] Clearly, Gray's social standing was now on the ascendant (indeed, he had probably been knighted by July 1302[34]), a mark of which was his appointment as constable of the castle of Cupar, Fife.[35] The *Scalacronica* describes how, on his way back from the coronation with a company of just twenty-six men-at-arms, he fought off an ambush of 400 Scotsmen (led by Walter de Bickerton, for whose lands Gray had recently petitioned), capturing 180 horses after their owners fled on foot through a peat bog. On another occasion, he had to fight his way back to the castle through the town of Cupar, after Alexander Fraser (the other Scot whose estates Gray coveted) had set an ambush for him there, on a market day.[36]

The castle of Cupar fell to the Scots by the middle of 1308, but Gray

31 *CDS*, v, nos. 415, 2621, 492 (p. 210), 510; *Documents*, ed. Palgrave, i, 313. It should be noted that despite the elder Gray's service in the borders, the *Scalacronica* still manages erroneously to record Edward as present in Dunfermline in 1306; below, 55.
32 *Rot. Scot.*, i, 58; others so ordered included Henry de Beaumont, and the prominent northern landowners Henry de Percy, Robert de Clifford and John fitz Marmaduke.
33 *Calendar of Chancery Rolls 1300–26*, 107; *CCR 1307–13*, 14; *CDS*, iii, no. 27; below, 69.
34 In that month, Sir Thomas Gray, knight, witnessed a deed (concerning Scottish lands) of the Northumbrian Sir Walter de Burghdon, also witnessed by Sir William Ridel and Sir William de Muschamp, both of whom were from north Northumberland; 'North Country Deeds', ed. Brown, 125–7.
35 Cupar had been recaptured from the Scots in June 1306; McNamee, *Wars of the Bruces*, 31.
36 Below, 69.

continued to serve in Scotland over the following years, both at the head of his own retinue and with Henry de Beaumont. It was at this time that Gray began to play a role in the affairs of the bishopric of Durham, witnessing a grant by Bishop Antony Bek of the manor of Crailing, in the sheriffdom of Roxburgh, to Sir William Dacre in August 1310.[37] He was fighting in Scotland when the crisis over Piers Gaveston reached its height. The Ordinances of 1311 demanded Beaumont's removal from the court, and Gray was thus aligned with the king, if only by default.[38] This worked to his advantage in October 1312, when he recovered his family's manor of Heton in Norhamshire, which had been granted by Edward II to Walter de Wodeham in 1311, during the vacancy after Bek's death, only to be seized back into the king's hands after Wodeham's death, in accordance with the resumption of royal grants demanded by the Ordainers. Naturally, the newly installed Bishop Kellaw objected strenuously to this seizure and his objections were presumably answered, for it was shortly after this that the manor was granted to Thomas.[39] Although Gray's acquisition of Heton may have been occasioned by political circumstances – for Bishop Kellaw was primarily concerned to re-establish his bishopric's rights over the manor, while Edward II would have been happy to circumvent the Ordainers – it was his continued loyal service in the Scottish wars that ensured that he was able to take advantage of these political circumstances to recover his family's lands, for this service made him acceptable to Edward. Nevertheless, this grant may have embroiled him and his son in a long-running dispute with Wodeham's heirs, for as late as 1354, Reynold son of Simon de Wodeham (presumably the grandson of Walter) quitclaimed all rights in the manor of Heton, which deed was enrolled in the chancery; clearly Gray's acquisition of the manor remained a contentious issue.[40]

At Bannockburn, Gray was again in the retinue of Henry de Beaumont. However, he fell out with Beaumont over tactics, during the skirmishing on the day before the main battle, and was captured

37 Barrow, *Bruce*, 190; *Rot. Scot.*, i, 58; *CCR 1307–13*, 166; *CDS*, v, nos. 2744, 2756, 2909, 2921, 2921; *CPR 1334–8*, 78.
38 *Rot. Parl.*, i, 284. Gray received letters of protection for service in Scotland on 31 March 1312, until Michaelmas (*CDS*, v, no. 2932).
39 *RPD*, i, 77–8, ii, 1170–1; *CPR 1307–13*, 337; *CFR 1307–19*, 243.
40 *CCR 1354–60*, 97.

when his horse was killed under him by Scottish spearmen.[41] By way of comparison, another Northumbrian captured at Bannockburn was Robert de Clifford, lord of Ellingham. He had to pay a ransom of £100 and lost horses and harness which he claimed to be worth 100 marks; and there is no reason to doubt that Gray's losses were just as heavy.[42] Nonetheless, Gray's capture does not seem to have impeded his career; he must have been free by April 1315 when he was appointed to a commission of oyer and terminer to deal with the killing of some Scots near Norham, who were travelling under a safe-conduct to arrange the ransom of William, Lord Latimer.[43] He remained in royal service; in March 1317, as a retainer of the Earl of Arundel, keeper of the Scottish March, he accompanied Arundel and Henry de Beaumont (with whom he seems to have repaired his relationship), on a raid into Jedwood forest, taking advantage of Robert Bruce's absence in Ireland. However, they were ambushed by James Douglas at Lintalee, and retreated without having achieved anything; Gray lost a horse, called 'Arselli', for which he received compensation of twenty marks.[44] He also served in the garrison of Berwick with fourteen esquires, and may have been there when the town fell to the Scots in April 1318.[45] His standing at court at this time is demonstrated by the fact that he was on Edward's Christmas present list, being one of the twenty-five knights recorded as receiving a gift of plate from the king at Westminster on 26 December 1316.[46] Another rather more practical reward followed in the wake of Gilbert de Middleton's notorious robbery of the Cardinals in September 1317. Gray petitioned for, and

---

41 Below, 75. Barrow, *Bruce*, 216–21. The *Scalacronica*'s account of Gray's capture is discussed by King, 'Helm with a Crest', 32.
42 *Northumberland Petitions*, ed. Fraser, 161–2. Clifford should not be confused with the like-named Cumbrian baron who was killed at the same battle.
43 *CPR 1313–17*, 250. Latimer had also been captured at Bannockburn. The ransoming and treatment of prisoners of war on the Scottish Marches is discussed by King, 'Prisoners and Casualties'.
44 *Calendar of Chancery Warrants 1244–1326*, 438; below, 77 (note that Gray's account omits to mention the presence of either Beaumont or his father); SAL, MS 120, f. 52v. Barbour, XX, lines 335–492, has a detailed account of the campaign; for the background, McNamee, *Wars of the Bruces*, 151.
45 *CCR 1318–23*, 43; this records that he was still owed £179 11s 4d in arrears of wages and compensation for lost horses in Dec.
46 SAL, MS 120, f. 67v. Gray is listed with two other Northumbrian knights, William Ridel and John Fenwick, and Ridel had been associated with Gray as a witness to various deeds of Bishops Kellaw and Beaumont (*RPD*, ii, 1170–1, 1178, 1179–80; DCM, Reg. II, f. 73).

received, an hereditary grant of lands in Howick, near Alnwick, forfeited by John Mautalent, an adherent of Walter de Selby, one of Middleton's most prominent allies.[47] The intended targets of Middleton's ambush were the newly elected Bishop of Durham, Louis de Beaumont, and his brother, Gray's patron. In 1319, after Louis' belated consecration, Gray was appointed as sheriff of Norham and Islandshire, and constable of Norham castle;[48] in the aftermath of Middleton's rising, Louis de Beaumont was badly in need of reliable supporters amongst the local gentry, and one of his brother's followers would have been an obvious starting point.

Norham castle overlooks a crossing of the Tweed, and the office of constable was no sinecure; but the appointment marked the degree of Gray's social advancement, for he retained a garrison that, in September 1322, numbered twenty men-at-arms and fifty hobelars, paid for by the crown, plus 'some men of the bishop of Durham'.[49] After Middleton's rising, the castle seems to have come under a more or less permanent state of siege. This set the scene for the best known incident of Gray's career, when Sir William Marmion arrived at the castle, determined to make famous the gold-crested helm presented to him by his beloved.[50] The Scots seem to have made every effort to take the castle; at one point, during Gray's absence in the South they managed to break into the outer ward due to the treachery of one of his men. However, the garrison held out in the inner ward, and on Gray's return three days later, the Scots fled.[51] The *Scalacronica* portrays Gray and his garrison as standing virtually alone during this period, so dispirited were the English. This may have been only a slight exaggeration; certainly, when Norham was besieged in 1322 (following the disastrous English defeat at Old Byland, Yorkshire in October), the king wrote to the constables of Bamburgh, Dunstanburgh, Warkworth and Alnwick castles to berate them for their failure to go to Gray's assistance.[52]

---

47 *CIM 1307–49*, nos. 366, 375; *CDS*, iii, nos. 610, 635; *CPR 1317–21*, 333–4; Middleton, *Gilbert de Middleton*, 93. The grant was made in May 1319; the lands were valued at £7 10s in time of peace, with the reversion of a further £6 worth of land, held by Mautalent's mother in dower. For Middleton's rebellion, see below, 79–81.

48 Raine, *North Durham*, 45.

49 *CDS*, iii, no. 772; *CCR 1330–3*, 367.

50 Below, 81–3.

51 Below, 85.

52 *CDS*, iii, nos. 783, 787; McNamee, *Wars of the Bruces*, 99. Gray himself received

The failure of the royal expedition to Scotland in 1322, followed by the rebellion of Andrew de Harcla, forced Edward to face his inability to impose a military solution. Meanwhile, Robert Bruce had his own problems – in the shape of the Soules conspiracy – and a thirteen year truce was duly sealed.[53] However, the outbreak of peace was not universally welcomed in northern England, for Thomas Gray was not the only northerner to have made a successful career from the war. His patron, Henry de Beaumont, was the Earl of Buchan, by right of his wife; as the truce abrogated English claims to Scottish lands, he stood to lose a great deal. On 30 May 1323, at a meeting of the royal council to ratify the treaty, Beaumont pointedly refused to support it, or to conceal his disaffection. As a result he was threatened with imprisonment, and Gray stood as mainpernor for him, along with prominent northern 'hawks' such as Henry Percy and Ralph de Neville, and William Ridel.[54]

Gray's interests and associations clearly aligned him with the northern faction which favoured the resumption of war with Scotland; in September 1323, he witnessed Gilbert Aton's confirmation of Antony Bek's grant of Alnwick to Henry de Percy, in the company of such prominent 'Disinherited' lords as Robert de Umfraville and, of course, Percy himself.[55] However, for those whose estates lay entirely in the Marches, continued prosperity depended largely on royal favour.[56] Gray had been able to obtain access to such favour, having been granted a pension of 6d a day, in February 1320, to be paid by the sheriff of York.[57] That others were not so fortunate is demonstrated by the fate of William de Beanley. He had served in the

letters from the king commending him for his continued resistance (*CDS*, iii, nos. 777, 787).
53 The Soules conspiracy is described by Gray, below, 79.
54 *CCR 1318–23*, 717; McNamee, *Wars of the Bruces*, 236–7; Fryde, *Tryanny and Fall*, 159. Ridel was an associate of Gray's, see above, n. 34. The *Scalacronica* makes no reference to Beaumont's fall from favour, despite the elder Gray's personal involvement as a mainpernor for him.
55 *Percy Chartulary*, ed. Martin, 232. Bek's grant of Alnwick to the Percys is described by Gray, below, 31.
56 Tuck, 'Northumbrian Society', 33.
57 *CCR 1323–7*, 202. This amounted to £9 2s 6d *per annum*, and was equivalent to the daily rate of pay for a hobelar – for a knight, on active service, the customary rate of pay was 2s a day: Prestwich, *Armies and Warfare*, 84. He also experienced considerable difficulty in getting the sheriff to pay up; *CCR 1318–23*, 452; *CCR 1323–7*, 202, 480. However, he presumably received additional renumeration from the Bishop of Durham.

garrison of Berwick (and so may have been known to Gray), and after
its fall had petitioned for relief from the rent of twelve marks he now
owed the king, following the forfeiture of Patrick, Earl of March,
citing the loss of his horse and despoiling of all his goods and chattels
by the Scots. Evidently, the petition fell on deaf ears, and by 1320, he
was reduced to selling off his land to John de Lilleburn. After this, he
adhered to the Scots; and in March 1326, his forfeited lands in
Howick were granted to Gray for life.[58] Unfortunately, after 1323,
Gray's chief patron, Henry de Beaumont, was in what amounted to
internal exile; nor was his brother Louis in much higher favour,
having been sent a sarcastic letter from the king, lambasting his
'default, negligence and laziness' in defending his bishopric.[59] His
patrons were no longer in a position to further his interests, and since
the battle of Boroughbridge, royal patronage had largely come under
the influence of the Despensers; so it is hardly surprising that by June
1325, Gray had become a lifetime retainer of the younger Hugh who
'wished above all else that the said Sir Thomas should remain with
him for the term of his life', and who procured for him a fee of 200
marks, paid from the royal Chamber.[60] Loyal subjects of the king
were in somewhat short supply in the Marches at this time, following
the rebellions of Gilbert de Middleton and Andrew de Harcla, and
the persistent disaffection of the Disinherited. As the constable of an
important castle, Gray would have been a particularly desirable
recruit for the Despensers, who were anxious to ensure that such
castles were held by their own supporters. This Despenser connection certainly bore fruit; on the same day as the grant of Howick, Gray
received the custody of the lands of the late John de Eure during the
minority of his son and heir. He was also awarded the heir's
marriage, in response to his petition reminding the king of his
promise to help arrange advantageous marriages for Gray's daughters. Another daughter was also married to a minor in royal custody,

<hr/>

58 *CPR 1324–27*, 254; *CDS*, iii, no. 881; *Northumberland Petitions*, 165–6; 'Woodman Charters', tr. Craster, 48.
59 *CCR 1318–23*, 697.
60 '. . . qe desirast sur toute rien qe le dit monsire Thomas demorast ouesque liu a terme de vie', SAL, MS 122, f. 29; Saul, 'The Despensers and Edward II', 28–9. Interestingly, the Chamber account refers to Gray as the king's constable of Norham, and not the bishop's, so it would appear that Edward had tired of Louis de Beaumont's 'negligence', and taken the castle into royal control.

the heir of the Yorkshire knight Sir Gerard Salvayn.[61] The previous July, Gray had been appointed to receive back into the king's peace those in Northumberland who joined the Scots 'through poverty or other urgent necessity'; and in August 1326, he was appointed, along with Ralph Neville, John de Fenwick and John de Lilleburn, to commandeer shipping from the ports of Northumberland and North Yorkshire for the fleet of John de Sturmy.[62] Despite the abundance of royal favour which it brought him, Gray's attachment to the Despensers appears to have been simply a marriage of convenience, and there is no evidence to suggest that he did anything whatsoever to prevent their fall from power. Certainly, if the *Scalacronica*'s disparaging comments on the Despensers reflect the elder Gray's opinions, he had no high regard for his new patrons; and indeed – perhaps predictably, given the Despensers' unpopularity – the *Scalacronica* entirely neglects to mention his connection to them.[63]

Gray had maintained his links with the Disinherited, witnessing Henry Percy's licence to Alnwick Abbey to receive some land from Robert Soppeth, in October 1325.[64] Nevertheless, it would appear that he was not regarded as entirely trustworthy by the Mortimer regime, for 'Lanercost' describes Robert de Manners as 'keeper' of the castle of Norham at the time of Edward III's coronation (1 February 1327). Gray's replacement was undoubtedly due to his association with the Despensers.[65] At the same time, however, Mortimer seems to have been anxious to buy his support. On 14 December 1326, the sheriff of York was ordered to pay the arrears of Gray's pension of 6d a day, by which point, although Edward II was still nominally king, Mortimer's authority was already well established.[66] In the following February, within a month of the deposition, Gray's pension was confirmed by the new king and three weeks later it was converted to an annuity of £20, which more than doubled its value.[67] These measures seem to have been successful in mollifying Gray, who does

61 *Northumberland Petitions*, 2, 10–11; CPR 1324–27, 254. For Salvayn, see King, 'Thomas of Lancaster's Quarrel', 36–44.
62 *CPR 1324–27*, 147, 311.
63 Below, 91; thus Saul's description of Gray as an 'important Despenser accomplice' ('The Despensers and Edward II', 29) rather overstates the case.
64 Tate, *Alnwick*, ii, app., p. xviii.
65 *Lanercost*, 258–9. This is confirmed by a deed of Nov. 1328 (concerning the manor of Murton near Norham) witnessed by Robert Manners, 'then constable of the castle of Norham' (printed in *NCH*, ii, 238n.).
66 *CCR 1323–7*, 627; Fryde, *Tyranny and Fall*, 195.

not seem to have resented his dismissal. Indeed, the *Scalacronica* singles out Manners for praise, for his successful defence of Norham against the Scots in 1328.[68]

In fact, Gray's Despenser connections do not seem to have resulted in any lasting harm to his prospects. He established new links with David of Strathbogie, the disinherited Earl of Atholl, witnessing a quitclaim in favour of the earl's steward in June 1333, and receiving a five year grant from the earl of the castle of Mitford.[69] Similarly, he witnessed Henry de Percy's grant of the manor of Newburn to Ralph Neville in 1332, and served as Percy's deputy when the latter was appointed warden of Berwick, after the town was recaptured from the Scots in 1333.[70] Although the *Scalacronica*'s account of events in Scotland at this time makes no reference to any exploits by its author's father at this time, his continuing royal service is indicated by the grant, in heredity, of a messuage in Berwick on Tweed, in June 1334. Another hereditary grant followed in January 1335, of a moiety of a carucate of land in Nesbit, Northumberland, which had escheated to Edward II by the rebellion of John de Trollope.[71] These were presumably rewards for service in Scotland; certainly, the elder Gray served as a commissioner of array for Northumberland in March 1333, and in September 1336 received a protection for service with Henry Percy.[72]

Miles nobilis: Thomas Gray *le fitz*

The younger Thomas Gray, author of the *Scalacronica*, makes his first, somewhat inglorious, appearence in the records in October 1331.[73]

---

67 *CPR 1327–30*, 15, 30.

68 Below, 101. The elder Gray was himself another of the witnesses to the deed concerning Murton, along with Manners.

69 *CPR 1338–40*, 213; *CIPM*, vii, no. 677. This was probably a lease at rent, intended to help cover Strathbogie's costs arising from the expedition of the Disinherited in 1332. Mitford Castle was in a ruinous state, having been burned to the ground when it was captured by the Scots in the aftermath of Gilbert de Middleton's rebellion.

70 *Percy Chartulary*, ed. Martin, 232; *CPR 1330–4*, 261; *Lanercost*, 275; *Anonimalle, 1333–81*, 1 (derived from the same source as *Lanercost*); *Rot. Scot.*, i, 256.

71 *Rot. Scot.*, i, 270; *CPR 1334–8*, 62; *NCH*, xiv, 138–40. The *messuage* in Berwick had been forfeited by one Ralph de More, for unspecified reasons.

72 *CPR 1330–4*, 416; *CDS*, v, no. 3525.

73 The nationwide survey of men-at-arms ordered by the king in May 1324 records for Northumberland (in addition to Thomas Gray, *miles*, obviously the

Described as 'son of Thomas Grey, knight', he was accused of being party to the poaching of deer in Gilbert de Umfraville's park at Birtley, where one of Umfraville's servants was assaulted. The ringleaders were William Felton and Robert de Ogle, both of whom appear in the pages of the *Scalacronica*.[74] In the following January, Thomas, son of Sir Thomas Gray, was one of the witnesses to an indenture between the sheriff of Norham, Robert de Manners, and the Prior of Durham.[75] Not long after, at some time before October 1332, one John de Raynton, a burgess of Berwick (and therefore, at this time, a Scot), was abducted near Holburn in Northumberland, contrary to the provisions of the recent peace. It was subsequently discovered that he had been imprisoned by Thomas Gray the younger and his men, and had been made to hand over his two sons as hostages for a ransom of 1000 marks. However, it appears that Gray was not acting alone, for it was Robert de Manners, in his capacity as constable of Norham, who was ordered to release the sons by a writ dated 28 July 1333 (by which time 360 marks had already been extracted from their father).[76] While Gray's involvement in poaching might be put down to youthful delinquency, his role in the abduction of Raynton demonstrates that he was now considered old enough – and responsible enough – to be put in charge of his own men, providing an indication of his age. In the Court of Chivalry, during the famous Scrope v. Grosvenor case of 1386, Sir John Bromwich claimed to have taken up arms in 1342 at the tender age of eleven. Much more typical were the marchers Sir Richard Tempest, armed at the age of fifteen, in 1371; Sir Matthew Redman, armed at the age of seventeen, in 1347; William Heselrigg, armed at the age of twenty, in 1336; and John Thirlwell, armed before the age of twenty-two, in *circa* 1354.[77] By comparison, we may therefore reason-

---

father of the chronicler), a *homo ad arma* called Thomas Gray (*Parliamentary Writs*, ed. Palgrave, II, ii, 649–50). Though it has been suggested that this was the chronicler himself (Blair, 'Knights of Northumberland', 170), this is more likely to be Thomas Gray of Horton, who died c. 1347, and was a knight by c. 1341 (*NCH*, xiv, 178–80).

74 *CPR 1330–4*, 202; for Felton and Ogle, below, 123, 149.
75 *Richard of Bury, Register*, 218. Quite why the younger Gray witnessed this agreement, instead of his father, is not apparent.
76 *CPR 1330–34*, 387; *CDS*, iii, no. 1083. It has been suggested that the affair was a heavy-handed exercise in debt collection (*NCH*, xiv, 136).
77 *Scrope and Grosvenor*, i, 205, 198, 194, 126, 181. It has to be said that these depositions are not totally reliable about ages; for instance, Thirlwell claimed that his

ably infer that if the younger Thomas Gray was bearing arms, and witnessing legal agreements, in 1332, he was probably born shortly after 1310. Thus from about the end of the reign of Edward II, his chronicle was based, at least partly, on personal experience.

Gray's first taste of real warfare was probably the campaign of the Disinherited which culminated in their overwhelming victory at Dupplin Moor in August 1332. This was a private expedition, and there are no records to indicate who served amongst the forces of the Disinherited, but the *Scalacronica* contains a particularly vivid account of the battle, and the events leading up to it. Not only does this read like an eyewitness report, but it includes details recorded by no other sources, notably Beaumont's pre-fight speech – and, unlike some medieval chroniclers, Gray does not appear to have been given to inventing speeches for his characters.[78] Of course, the *Scalacronica's* narrative may have been derived at second hand from the eyewitness reports of others, an authority claimed by the compiler of a short Latin chronicle owned by the monks of Durham.[79] Nevertheless, given the elder Gray's connections with Henry de Beaumont and David of Strathbogie, both prominent amongst the Disinherited, it is not unlikely that the younger Gray served with them on the expedition. Thomas Gray *le fitz* certainly served in Flanders, for in June 1338, he received a protection until the following Christmas to accompany William de Montague (newly created earl of Salisbury) across the sea, in the service of the king; and whilst there, he was recompensed for losing a horse valued at £20. Nor was Gray the only northerner to serve with Montague; John de Coupland received a similar protection at the same time, a figure who was later to wield a baleful influence in Marcher society, and with whom Gray was to become closely associated.[80] The king had granted Montague the castle of Wark on

---

father died at the advanced age of seven score years and five (though this may just have been a scribal error, for the father was said to have been armed for a slighlty less unbelievable sixty-nine years). It should be noted that William Heselrigg was one of the Heselriggs of Eslington, probably a cadet branch of the family of the William Heselrigg who was killed by William Wallace in 1297; below, 41.

78 Below, 109. Other detailed accounts of the battle include Bridlington, 103–7; *Brut*, ed. Brie, 274–9 (which quotes a different rousing speech, made by Fulk Fitzwarin instead of Beaumont); *Lanercost*, 267–8; and Bower, vii, 72–81.

79 Durham Cathedral Library, MS B.ii.35, f. 31v.; but cf. Offler, 'Franciscan Chronicle', 46.

80 *Fœdera*, II, ii, 1048; *Wardrobe Book of William de Norwell*, ed. Lyon, *et al.*, 311.

Tweed in 1329, in the face of rival claimants; and Montague's recruit-
ment of locals such as Gray and Coupland may have been an attempt
to buy local support for his lordship. If so, he was not very successful,
for Montague was one of those whose elevation to the nobility was
criticised in the *Scalacronica* as a waste of crown resources.[81] The
Scalacronica's description of how he and the Earl of Suffolk were
taken prisoner, 'through their own ill-judgement . . . surprised on a
foolhardy *chevauchée* before Lille', in 1340, does not suggest that Gray
was impressed by his *parvenu* commander.[82] Indeed, the Flanders
campaign is described in rather caustic terms: Edward is said to have
spent his time not in making war, but in jousting and living the fine
life.[83]

By 1340, Gray was back on the borders. Regrettably, it is at this
point in the narrative that several folios are missing from the sole
surviving manuscript of the *Scalacronica*.[84] However, John Leland's
abstract (made from a complete copy of the manuscript) records that
Gray repulsed a raid by the earls of March and Sutherland, carried
out, doubtless deliberately, at the time of the siege of Tournai. This is
corroborated by a letter describing the defeat of the two earls by the
garrison of Roxburgh, supported by Gray, Robert Manners and John
de Coupland.[85] Leland's abstract does not specify that this was Gray
the younger, but since his father was to be dead within four years,
and must have been well into his sixties by this stage, it is probably
safe to assume that the *Scalacronica* was relating the exploits of its
author.[86] Gray the elder may well have been experiencing intimations

---

Coupland also lost a horse, worth £12. For Coupland, see King, 'War, Politics
  and Landed Society', 154–73.
81 Below, 123. The grant of Wark to Montague, and the subsequent legal challenge, is discussed in *NCH*, xi, 39–41.
82 Below, 129.
83 Below, 127. Presumably however, Gray must have been involved in some fighting, otherwise he would not have been compensated for the loss of his horse.
84 Below, liii–liv. The missing section covers the years 1340–56.
85 Below, 133, 134; PRO, SC 1/54/30, printed in the appendix below. Manners,
  Coupland and the garrison of Roxburgh are all mentioned in Leland's abstract,
  but the exact context is not clear.
86 However, when describing the younger Gray's capture in 1355, Leland's
  abstract (below, 134) does refer to 'Thomas Gray (conestable of Norham, sunne
  to Thomas Gray that had beene 3. tymes besegid by the Scottes in Norham
  castel yn King Edwarde the secunde dayes)'. Assuming Leland is accurately
  reporting the text here, and that this is not just his interpolation, this detail

of mortality, for in February 1342, he obtained a licence to alienate six marks of rent from the manor of Eworth to provide a chaplain to celebrate masses at a chapel there.[87] This is one of very few recorded acts of piety by either him or his son.

In March 1344, custody of the manor of Middlemast Middleton in Coquetdale, worth 10 marks *per annum*, was granted to Thomas Gray, *le fitz*, 'in consideration of his good service beyond the seas as well as within'. Within a month, the same manor had been re-granted to him in fee.[88] By the time of the second grant, Gray was no longer distinguished as 'le fitz', for his father had died in the meanwhile. Gray received a pardon from Bishop Richard Bury of Durham, dated 10 April 1344, for minor breaches of the bishop's franchisal authority committed by his father 'now deceased'. At the same time, he was granted seisin of all the lands that his father had held in the bishop's liberty. These included the manor of Heton (held as half of a knight's fee); two thirds of the manor of Kyley; and five librates of land, another £5 8s worth of land formerly held by one Martin Byset, and six burgages, all in Norham. He also inherited his father's fishing rights on the Tweed.[89] The death of Bishop Bury in April 1345 enabled Gray to gain his father's erstwhile office as constable of Norham. Bury's replacement, Thomas Hatfield, initially confirmed Robert Manners in the post, but Manners was subsequently ordered to hand it over to Gray.[90] Gray also received further crown patronage

---

87 *CPR 1340–43*, 380. The licence was obtained jointly with a certain Alice, late the wife of John de Burghdon. The allowance of 6 marks for the chaplain compares with the stipends of 5 marks *per annum* paid to the Bishop of Durham's chaplains at Darlington, Auckland, Howden, Allerton and Norham, recorded in 1334; *CCR 1333–7*, 277.

88 *Scalacronica*, Stevenson, pp. liii–liv; *CPR 1343–5*, 220, 252, 275; *CDS*, iii, no. 1431; *CFR 1337–47*, 364–5; *CIM 1307–49*, no. 1893; Middleton, *Gilbert de Middleton*, 94–5. The manor was in the king's hand due to the defection to the Scots of the heir, William Middleton, at the end of Edward II's reign. This grant has been assigned to Thomas Gray of Horton (*NCH*, xiv, 300); however, the grantee is refered to as 'le fitz', and as Horton died at a fair age in 1347, leaving a son called David as his heir, this identification seems unlikely.

89 *Richard of Bury, Register*, 57–8; 'Chancery Enrolments, Bury', 72; *RPD*, iv, 310–11 (N.B., *RPD* is misdated to 1345; similarly, *Scalacronica*, Stevenson, pp. xxvii–xxviii, misdates Gray's death to 1343).

90 'Chancery Enrolments, Hatfield', 133, 146, 147.

might suggest that this was Gray's first mention of himself in his own chronicle; and therefore, that the reference to a Thomas Gray in 1340 is to his father

shortly after his father's death. In May 1344, he was granted joint custody, with his brother-in-law John de Eure, of Calverton Darras in Northumberland (forfeited by Robert Darreyns for debts incurred whilst he was sheriff); in May 1345, he was granted free warren in various of his demesnes and a licence to make a park; and in August, he was granted a burgage and dovecote in Newcastle forfeited by a felon.[91] This was clearly designed to secure his continued military service, and in the same year he took out letters of protection for the proposed expedition to Sluys, which came to nothing in the event.[92] He did, however, serve at the battle of Neville's Cross in October 1346, which ended so disastrously for the Scots with the capture of King David II. Here, Gray captured two prominent Scots, and was among the twelve who received letters from Edward thanking them for their good service.[93] Just before Christmas, Gray and fifteen other northern magnates (including all the other recipients except the Archbishop of York), were summoned to come to Westminster in January to discuss the defence of the realm and a proposed expedition to Scotland.[94]

Gray's military exploits also earned him an *entrée* to royal service of a more peaceful nature, for in April 1348, he was appointed to his first legal commission, to inquire into violations of the truce. Others followed; in May 1349, he was among those commisioned to inquire into the seizure of an English ship by Scottish pirates, off Holy Island; in July 1352, he was part of a commission of oyer and terminer concerning an assault on Bishop Hatfield at Morpeth, whilst he was travelling to Berwick to negotiate with the Scots for the release of David II. The following February, Gray was included on a similar commission dealing with an assault and maiming perpetrated in Benwell, near Newcastle; and in June 1355, just before his capture, he was inquiring into the abduction and robbery of Isabel de Eslington

---

91 *CFR 1337–47*, 381; *Calendar of Charter Rolls 1341–1417*, 38; *CPR 1343–5*, 537. Despite his criticism of Edward III's generosity to his newly created earls in 1337 (below, 123), Gray evidently did not consider royal patronage to be a waste of the 'appurtenances of the crown' when it applied to himself.

92 PRO, C 76/20, mm. 8, 13 (I have to thank Dr Andrew Ayton for this reference); *RPD*, iv, 312.

93 *Rot. Scot.*, i, 678, 675. Another who received such a letter was Robert de Ogle, Gray's erstwhile partner in crime.

94 *Rot. Scot.*, i, 679.

at North Gosforth.[95] He also served as a justice in the bishop's court at Durham at this time.[96]

Gray's involvement in local government took place against a background of continuing hostilities with Scotland. Even as the negotiations for the release of David II dragged on, the Scots were reconquering much of the territory they had lost after Neville's Cross. At some point around 1351, Gray stood as a pledge for Alan de Heton, lord of Chillingham in Northumberland, when Heton was captured by William Douglas. Unfortunately, de Heton defaulted on the agreement, leaving Gray bound to surrender himself to Scottish imprisonment. He petitioned the Earl of Northampton, the king's lieutenant on the Marches, for remedy; and if he did have to surrender himself to Douglas, he cannot have remained as a hostage for long.[97] In fact, as Leland's abstract notes, the Scottish magnates were hardly united in the absence of their king, a situation which John II of France sought to exploit by sending the Sire de Garencières with fifty men-at-arms and 40,000 *deniers d'or a l'escu* (10,000 marks by Gray's reckoning, £8,000 by Wyntoun's), in an attempt to persuade the Scots to attack England.[98] Garencières arrived in Scotland in March 1355; by September, he had obviously had some success, for according to French records, the money was handed over to a representative of 'the lords and barons of Scotland' at Bruges, on the 15th of that month. Evidently, these lords and barons did not include William Douglas, for Leland's abstract relates that the lords Percy and Neville, wardens of the march, agreed a truce with him, presumably on the strength of which Edward took many northern magnates with him to Calais in October, including William, Lord Greystoke, the keeper of Berwick. There was thus some justification for Gray's complaint – as related by Leland – that 'King Eduarde was so distressid with his afferes beyound the se, that he toke litle regard to the Scottisch matiers', for it soon became clear that Douglas could

---

95 *Rot. Scot.*, i, 713–14; *CPR 1348–50*, 317, 452; *CPR 1350–4*, 339, 446; *CPR 1354–8*, 291.

96 Hodgson, 'Manor of Offerton', 276 (mis-dated by the editor to 1241); *Greenwell Deeds*, ed. Walton, nos. 194, 199.

97 PRO, DL 34/1/21. As an example of a prose passage which was presumably composed by Gray himself, the letter is of some interest, and has been printed in the Appendix, below. For its date, see King, 'Prisoners and Casualties', 279. Chillingham is a few miles south of the Gray family *caput* at Heton. For Alan de Heton, see King, 'War, Politics and Landed Society', 173–85.

98 Below, 139.

only have been acting in a personal capacity. Patrick, Earl of March, was happy to accept Garencières' money and led a raid across the border. It was this raid, made shortly after Edward's departure, which led to Thomas Gray's capture on about 16 October; and in the absence of its keeper, Berwick was captured by the Earl of Angus on 6 November.[99] Thus, it may be said that we owe the *Scalacronica* to the machinations of the King of France, though this was a somewhat indirect form of royal literary patronage.

Ironically, Gray's account of his own capture survives only in outline, in Leland's abstract. Fortunately, the event is recounted in Andrew Wyntoun's chronicle, composed in an appropriately chivalric style *circa* 1420, and, rather more prosaically, by John Fordun, writing in the 1370s. According to Leland's abstract, the Earl of March set up an ambush on the Scottish side of the Tweed, and sent a banneret and 400 men to forage near Norham. Gray came out of the castle to intercept them, 'with few mo then 50 menne of the garnison, and a few of the communes', and was caught in the ambush. The English fought 'with a wonderful corage', but were outnumbered six to one; the 'communes' fled and Gray was taken prisoner. This accords with Fordun's account, which confirms that Gray was captured in an ambush by a superior force of Scots led by the Earl of March, whilst pursuing Scottish raiders who had fled back into Scotland (whose leader is named as William de Ramsay of Dalhousie).[100] Fordun's account is full of praise for the resistance of the English who 'took their lives in their hands and manfully resisted the Scots', rather than fleeing with dishonour, and describes Gray as a *miles nobilis*. It also states that Gray's 'son and heir' Thomas was taken in the same action and adds the detail that a number of Frenchmen were amongst Gray's captors. There are only a couple of major contradictions between Fordun and the *Scalacronica*. Fordun has William Douglas as one of the leaders of the Scots, whereas Leland's reading of the *Scalacronica* implies that Douglas was observing the truce. And, unsurprisingly, they disagree over the breakdown of that truce.

99   Below, 141; *Rot. Parl.*, iii, 11; Wyntoun, vi, 198–9; Avesbury, 427, 431; Campbell, 'England, Scotland and the Hundred Years War', 196–200; Nicholson, *Scotland*, 156–62. Gray states that he was captured twenty-one days before the fall of Berwick (an action in which Garencières and his men played a major part, according to Bower, vii, 282).
100 Fordun, 371, identifies him just as 'dominus de Ramsay'; Bower, vii, 278, as 'Willelmus Ramsey de Dalwolsi' (though most MSS of Bower have just 'Ramsey de Dalwolsi').

Fordun states that March had been provoked by English raiding; in contrast, Gray records that he had been unwilling to agree to a truce in the first place.[101] Fordun was copied, virtually *verbatim*, by Walter Bower (writing early in the fifteenth century), with the addition of a lurid anecdote concerning one of the French knights, who is said to have bought some of the English prisoners captured in the battle so that he could massacre them in revenge for the death of his father, killed by the English in France. Wyntoun's account is very similar to Fordun; the main differences are that Gray's men are numbered at eighty; a different son, William, is mentioned, who is knighted on the battlefield by his father; and Garencières is named among those present, which is entirely likely.[102]

It was during this captivity that Gray started work on the *Scalacronica*; however, while he found plenty of time to indulge his historical interests, he cannot have spent more than a year in captivity. He had presumably been freed by 28 November 1356, when he was appointed to a crown commission to inquire into the smuggling of English sheep into Scotland (to evade English customs) and to arrest those responsible. A couple of days previously, the king had granted him a licence to export 100 sacks of wool directly from Berwick (saving him the expense of carting them to Newcastle), by way of a contribution towards his ransom.[103] On 3 October 1357, he was entrusted with the custody of John Gray, one of the hostages for the ransom of King David, the agreement for which was finally sealed on the same day.[104] He soon returned to his employment as a royal justice; in February 1359, he was appointed to inquire into the

101 Below, 140; Fordun, 371–2. Fordun also mentions that one of the Scottish casualties was John de Haliburton, who had been captured by Gray at Neville's Cross (*Rot. Scot.*, I, 678). Gray's son may well have died in captivity for the inquest *post mortem* after Gray's death (in 1369) recorded that his heir was his son Thomas, aged just ten ('Inquests Post Mortem, Hatfield', 201–2). This Thomas would thus have been born *c.* 1359 and named after an elder brother who must have died before his birth.
102 Bower, vii, 278–81; Wyntoun, vi, 207–9. William was granted the keeping of certain forfeited lands in Northumberland by the king, in 1358, but he had died by Michaelmas 1362; *CFR 1356–68*, 74; PRO, CP 40/411, m. 218.
103 *CPR 1354–8*, 499; *CDS*, iii, no. 1625; *Fœdera*, III, i, 343; *Rot. Scot.*, i, 798. Prisoners of war were frequently released on parole before their ransoms had been paid; King, 'Prisoners and Casualties', 276–8.
104 *CDS*, iii, 434; Nicholson, *Scotland*, 163. John was a grandson of Andrew Gray, a supporter of Robert Bruce in 1306; the family was probably related to the Grays of Heton. *SP*, iv, 269–70.

misdoings of John Clifford, the constable of Berwick, who had imprisoned two Scotsmen in time of truce (one of his fellow commissioners was John de Coupland, captor of David II at Neville's Cross, destined to be murdered by Clifford and others in December 1363). In May, he was once again serving as a justice in Durham.[105] However, he continued to combine such judicial duties with his military career, going to war again in the autumn of 1359, crossing the Channel in the retinue of the Black Prince, with Edward III's expedition to France. To judge from the lively and detailed account of the expedition in the *Scalacronica*, the experience was rather more rewarding than his previous service overseas; and indeed, he seems to taken the opportunity to collect material for his work, which by this time he would appear to have brought up to the present.[106] In October 1361, perhaps as a reward for his service, he was appointed a warden of the march, along with Henry Percy, Ralph Neville, Richard Tempest and John de Coupland. This cannot have been an entirely harmonious association, for Tempest was one of those later accused of abetting Coupland's murderers.[107]

Before going to France, Gray had been employed by the Bishop of Durham in the latter's dispute with Patrick, Earl of March, over the vill of West Upsettlington, Berwickshire. He was to hold an inquiry into whether it lay within England, despite being to the north of the Tweed; unsurprisingly, this was found indeed to be the case. Aside from any rancour against his erstwhile captor, a degree of self interest may have coloured his judgement, for in November 1366, a fourth part of the manor was granted to him and his heirs by the king, for 'for free service to the king in the wars of Scotland and elsewhere, and for 10 marks paid by him to the king'.[108] This land had been forfeited by Nicholas de Hayden and his son for their involvement in Gilbert de Middleton's rebellion. One of the factors that led to John de

---

105 *CIM 1348–77*, no. 343; Tuck, 'Northumbrian Society', 36–7; King, 'War, Politics and Landed Society', 165, 170; 'North Country Deeds', ed. Walton, 118. Coupland's capture of David was described in the *Scalacronica* (according to Leland's abstract); below, 134.

106 *Fœdera*, III, i, 443. The expedition is described by Sumption, *Trial by Fire*, 405–54; Rogers, *War, Cruel and Sharp*, 385–422; Barber, *Black Prince*, 157–168. For Gray's progress on his work, see above, xxi.

107 *Rot. Scot.*, i, 857; King, 'War, Politics and Landed Society', 165; Tuck, 'Northumbrian Society', 37.

108 *CCR 1354–60*, 550; *CPR 1364–7*, 341; *CDS*, iv, no. 126. For the background of this longstanding dispute, see Neville, *Violence, Custom and Law*, 29, 49.

Coupland's murder was his unscrupulous exploitation of the Middleton rebellion to bring about retrospective forfeitures with which to harass his rivals in Northumbrian political society; and Gray may have been involved in similar practices. He was evidently one of Coupland's allies for he was prominent amongst those who joined with his widow, Joan, in suing against 'the evildoers who slew the said John or those who harboured them'.[109] Certainly, as a follower of Henry de Beaumont, Gray the elder could hardly have had much sympathy for Middleton's supporters, and the *Scalacronica*'s account of the rising suggests that his son was no more understanding. Indeed, Gray's grossly exaggerated claim that Middleton 'had almost all of Northumberland on his side, except just the castles of Bamburgh, Alnwick and Norham', and that the former two were treating with him, may well have been deliberately designed to provide some retrospective justification for the dubious activities of Coupland and his cronies, amongst whom Gray should clearly be counted.[110] Gray also seems to have made some enemies of his own, for in February 1366, he obtained a commission of oyer and terminer, 'touching those who have made conspiracies, collusions and alliances in the county of York, whereby Thomas de Gray . . . is damaged; and also touching falsities, losses, grievances and excesses done to [him]'.[111] Shortly after this, Gray and three others were commissioned – in strangely cryptic terms – to investigate a plot by certain unspecified Northumbrians to employ John de Clifford to capture Bamburgh castle, a plot said to be 'well known in the parts of Northumberland and not unknown to them'. However, most of Coupland's murderers were able to make their peace with the crown; Gray would have had to swallow whatever enmity he felt himself, for in September 1367, he was again serving as a warden of the East March, along with Gilbert de Umfraville, Henry Percy and his son (the future earl), Peter de Mauley, Roger Widdrington, John de Bolton and, once again, Richard Tempest.[112]

109 *CCR 1364–8*, 292; *CDS*, iv, no. 124. For Coupland's retrospective forfeitures, see King, 'War, Politics and Landed Society', 154–64.
110 Below, 81.
111 *CPR 1364–7*, 279–80.
112 *CPR 1364–7*, 371; Tuck, 'Northumbrian Society', 37; *Rot. Scot.*, i, 914, 915. The Widdringtons had been amongst the main victims of Coupland's sharp practices. Gray continued to serve as constable of Norham (*ibid.*, 920).

By now, Gray must have been well into his fifties, and he seems to have felt his age, for at about this time, he re-ordered his affairs, setting up a jointure with his wife and a string of entails.[113] This settlement proved a wise precaution, for he died just two years later, in October 1369, leaving a ten-year-old son as his heir. The legacy of a successful career in the king's wars included three manors and a moiety of another in Durham, along with other properties including 300 acres of land; three manors plus moieties of five others in Norhamshire, and various other tenements and fisheries on the Tweed; and considerable estates in Northumberland, including the four and a half manors he held of the Percy family in 1368.[114] But undoubtedly the greatest legacy of that career is the *Scalacronica*.

SOURCES[115]

According to his prologue, Gray based the fourth book of the *Scalacronica*, for the period 'from the first arrival of William the Conqueror here' up to the (then) present, on the *Historia aurea* of John of Tynemouth.[116] The *Historia aurea* is a monumental universal history going up to 1347 inspired by, and based on, Ranulf Higden's *Polychronicon* – although most of the material covering the 1340s consists of letters and other documents quoted *verbatim*, with little in the way of linking narrative.[117] The *Historia aurea* does indeed

---

113 'Chancery Enrolments, Hatfield', 279–80.
114 'Inquests Post Mortem, Hatfield', 201–2 (the first inquest *post mortem* was held at Durham on 22 Oct.); *CIPM*, xii, pp. 228–9. The settlement of 1367 mentioned several other properties, including two other manors, so the inquests *post mortem* appear to understate Gray's landed wealth; cf. previous note.
115 Note that detailed discussion of Gray's sources, where known, is generally provided in the endnotes accompanying each chapter.
116 In fact, Gray relied on a version of the Anglo-Norman prose *Brut* chronicle for much of his narrative for the period 1100–1272, though he makes no reference to this in his prologue; see King and Marvin, 'A Warning to the Incurious'.
117 Taylor, *Historical Literature*, 103–5; Gransden, *Historical Writing*, ii, 56. The text of *Historia aurea* from 1327 to 1346 was used to provide a continuation to Guisborough's chronicle; and the continuation is printed in *Hemingburgh*, ii, 297–426. This continuation 'may therefore be regarded as a rough-and-ready text of the *Historia aurea*' (Galbraith, 'Historia Aurea', 389). For ease of reference, citations to this part of the *Historia aurea* have therefore been given to *Hemingburgh*, rather than to Lambeth MS 12 (the copy of the *Historia aurea* owned by Durham Priory), which has been referenced for the period up to 1327.

provide the basic framework for Gray's narrative up to about 1340. However, he did not use it without discrimination. For instance, the *Historia aurea* includes material relating to the Papacy and the Empire (derived ultimately from Martin of Polonius and his continuators) scattered throughout its narrative. Gray compiled and condensed this material into separate thematic chapters.[118] Nor was he dependent solely on the *Historia aurea*. The *Scalacronica's* narrative for the reign of Edward I contains many details which appear to derive from a chronicle similar, though not identical, to Guisborough.[119] For instance, Gray's description of Robert Bruce's murder of John Comyn (chapter 39) is not dependent on the account in the *Historia aurea*:

> In this year on 29 January, at the town of Dumfries (where the justices of the King of England were then residing in the castle), Robert de Bruce, aspiring to the kingdom of Scotland, sacrilegiously killed the noble man John Comyn who was unwilling to agree to his treason, in the church of the Friars Minor.[120]

Instead, Gray's account is clearly derived from a source related to that used by Guisborough for these events, although he evidently relied on the *Historia aurea* for the date (in fact, the *Historia aurea* – which is not here derived from the *Polychronicon* – provides a heavily condensed summary of Guisborough's account).[121] Gray's account is closer to that of Guisborough, but paints the murder in a worse light, as a ruthless and premediated act against someone whom Bruce's own brothers could not bring themselves to kill on his behalf. As Gray was not generally given to elaborating on his sources, or to vilifying the Scots in general or Bruce in particular, it would appear that he relied on a separate source which does not now survive. For another instance, Guisborough has in common with the *Scalacronica* the detail – absent from the *Historia aurea* – that Robert de Ros' defection to the Scots in 1296 was motivated by his love for a Scottish

---

118 E.g., chapter 40, below, contains accounts of Popes Innocent V to John [XXI] derived from the *Historia aurea*, Lambeth, f. 213, and Benedict III derived from Lambeth, f. 224v.

119 Walter of Guisborough, a canon at the Augustinian Priory of Guisborough, North Yorkshire, writing probably at the beginning of the fourteenth century. His chronicle goes down to 1315. Guisborough, pp. xxiv–xxv, xxx–xxxi.

120 Lambeth, f. 224v.

121 Guisborough, 366–7; and see 222, n. 22 below. Medieval accounts of the affair are discussed by Smallwood, 'Bruces' Murder of Comyn'.

122 Below, 37.

woman (though Gray's account names her, whereas she retains her anonymity in Guisborough).[122]

Gray also made use of Scottish chronicles, although none of those that he used appears to have survived in its original form. He presumably borrowed these from the library of Edinburgh castle, which, after all, is likely to have been furnished with works of Scottish history.[123] The most obvious example is his account of the descent of the Scottish kingship (chapters 33–6), a digression inserted into his narrative of the reign of Edward I (chapters 32, 37–9). Chapter 32 ends with an account of how Edward was requested by the Scots to intervene to settle the disputed succession, following the death of Princess Margaret, the 'Maid of Norway'. The following chapter starts with the comment:

> And it should be known that according to the chronicles of Scotland, there was never anything so difficult as fixing the right lineage of their kings, which failed entirely in the time of three kings in succession, each the son of the other. And on that account, it would be desirable for this chronicle to touch on the origins and the succession of the kings who have reigned in Scotland.[124]

The following account commences with a specific reference to the *Life of St Brendan*.[125] He goes on to make references to other chronicles: 'the chronicles testify that the Picts came from Sycthia . . .'; 'as the chronicles testify, a certain son of a king of Ireland . . .'; 'the chronicles of Scotland testify that Tirg subjected all of Ireland to his lordship . . .'.[126] Indeed, his account rests on information compiled from six or seven apparently discrete sources: chapter 33 contains an account of the origin of the Scottish kingship (i); chapter 34 comprises a list of the kings of Dál Riata (ii), and an account of the origins of the Picts (iii); chapter 35 comprises a list of Pictish kings (iv) and an account of

---

123 Gransden's suggestion that Edinburgh's library was left over from the English occupation of 1296–1314 (Gransden, *Historical Writing*, ii, 93) is ruled out by Gray's own account that the castle had been demolished after its capture by the Scots (below, 121). Nor is her implication that the Scots did not read books entirely warranted; *Bruce*, ed. Duncan, 35n. Gray may also have had access to the library of Holyrood Abbey, a very wealthy institution and David II's favourite religious house (a suggestion I owe to Michael Penman).
124 Below, 17.
125 Below, 19.
126 Below, 21, 25, 27.

the defeat of the Picts by the *Scoti* (v); and chapter 36 provides an annotated list of kings from Kenneth MacAlpin down to John Balliol (vi).[127] It also provides an account of the claimants to the Scottish kingship in 1291. Gray may have translated this account wholesale from an existing Scottish compilation; or he may have compiled it himself from separate sources which he found in Scotland; or possibly he may have used an existing compilation of some of the material, and added sections from other sources himself. Certainly, items (iii) and (v) appear to have been derived from the *Polychronicon*, which Gray was familiar with, and certainly he adapted the material to fit with his own work, adding a cross-reference to an earlier part of his work, for instance.[128] Whoever put this compilation together did so with great care, displaying a concern to maintain consistency throughout its constituent parts which ensured a coherent account of the descent of the Scottish kingship. This has led modern historians to assume that Gray must have used a pre-existing compilation, on the grounds that an English layman could not, or indeed would not, aspire to produce such a coherent account.[129] However, as the *Scalacronica* amply demonstrates, Gray was entirely capable of welding different sources into a coherent whole, so he cannot be ruled out as the compiler.

Describing Robert Bruce's travails in early 1307, Gray refers to 'the chronicles of his deeds'. This suggests that Gray may have used a lost 'life' of Bruce, presumably a Scottish work, possibly the same work referred to by Jean le Bel, writing at around the same time, which he described as 'a history made by the said King Robert' (*hystoire faitte par le dit roy Robert*). Whatever his source, Gray describes episodes in Bruce's wanderings which do not appear elsewhere.[130]

Further evidence of Gray's reliance on Scottish sources is provided by his brief description of Edward Bruce's invasion of Ireland, leading to his death in battle at Faughart. In imputing regal aspirations to Edward, Gray was following the *Historia aurea*,[131] though no other English chronicle takes this line. However, the Scottish chroni-

---

127 Broun, *Irish Identity*, 84.
128 Below, 19, 214n.
129 *Ibid.*, 94.
130 Below, 57. Le Bel, i, 111; *Bruce*, ed. Duncan, 16–17; Gransden, *Historical Writing*, ii, 82, 86. It is of course possible that Gray simply copied the reference to 'the chronicles of his deeds' at second hand, from another source.
131 Below, 77, and 229, n. 20.

clers John Barbour and John of Fordun (both writing in the 1370s) –
and following him, Walter Bower (writing early in the fifteenth
century) – also attribute the Scottish invasion of Ireland to Edward
Bruce's ambition.[132] Gray goes on to relate that Bruce was slain
through overconfidence ('surquidery'), because he would not wait
for the reinforcements which were but six leagues distant. A similar
account is given by Bower, who relates, incorrectly, that 'his brother
King Robert would have come to him with a great army if he had
waited until the next day'; and Barbour, who also recorded that Scottish reinforcements were just a day's march away.[133] In this, they are
backed up by the Irish *Annals of Clonmacnoise*.[134] By contrast, no other
English account makes any mention of Scottish reinforcements, nor
do they suggest impetuosity or regal ambition on Edward's part. The
Scalacronica also comments of Edward that he 'performed there
marvellous feats of arms through great hardship . . . it would take a
great romance to recount it all'.[135] Barbour uses a similar phrase in
describing Edward Bruce's campaign in Galloway in 1308, 'And quha
wald rehers all the deid,/ Off his hey worschip and manheid/ Men
mycht a mekill romanys mak'.[136] The sentiment is hardly an excep-
tional one, but nevertheless, it is likely that Gray and Barbour were
drawing from a common (and presumably Scottish) source. The
difference in context can be explained by Gray's methods as an
abridger. The *Scalacronica* does not mention the Galloway campaign;
so having come across the phrase in his Scottish source, Gray simply
transposed it.

Finally, allowing for the fact that this part of the *Scalacronica*
survives only in summary form, Fordun's account of Gray's capture
is so similar that it is tempting to speculate that it was derived from a
version of the *Scalacronica* itself. After all, somebody in Scotland lent
Gray the various chronicles which inspired him to write; and it is not
unreasonable to assume that he should have been given a copy of
Gray's work in return, if only an early draft.

Chronicles were not the only written source that Gray relied on.
The first section of chapter 49, on the Poitiers campaign, was probably derived from a contemporary newsletter. Vocabulary such as

---

132 Barbour, XIV, lines 1–7; Fordun, 348; Bower, vi, 412–13.
133 Barbour, XVIII, lines 1–210.
134 Cited by Duncan, *Bruce*, 666.
135 Below, 77.
136 Barbour, IX, lines 495–8.

reirroit, enuailleroit and *reuygoura*, and in particular, specialist military terminology such as *eschele*, and the twice-repeated use of *Souerayne* as a synonym for God, does not occur elsewhere in the *Scalacronica*; nor does the dating by day of the month rather than by the ecclesiastical calendar.[137] The section also displays an uncharacteristic emphasis on courtly values – the prince is described as replying to Cardinal Périgord *courtoisement*, and the French king's battle is described as advancing *cheualerousement* at Poitiers. All of this suggests that Gray simply incorporated a newsletter into his text *verbatim*. If so, the text of the letter probably ends with the enumeration of the casualties and the strengths of the two armies, for the section relating to William Douglas is clearly an addition from a different source. Gray presumably learned of Douglas' involvement in the battle during his enforced sojourn at Edinburgh. He may have been following a written Scottish account, for his account of Douglas's adventure accords entirely with that of Fordun – apart from Gray's detail that Douglas had been planning a pilgrimage, which does not appear in Scottish sources.[138]

The accuracy of Gray's list of the French hostages named in the terms for the implementation of the Treaty of Brétigny[139] suggests he was working from a written copy. Such copies may have been circulated by the Crown around the county courts; but as Gray states that 'this agreement, and the conditions and the manner of the peace in the form negotiated, was agreed and confirmed by the general assent of the magnates of both the realms and was announced in parliament', copies may have been sent back to the shires and boroughs with their representatives. Northumberland's knights of the shire at this parliament were Thomas Surtees and Roger Widdrington (although Gray is unlikely to have been on good terms with either of them, for they were both amongst the many enemies of his close associate, John de Coupland). The version reproduced by Gray consistently misrepresents the name 'de Craon' as 'de Cynoun', and omits the name of the Count of Eu from the list of prisoners from the battle of Poitiers; the order of the names, and their spelling, are slightly different from the version printed in Rymer's *Fœdera*. It is, however, impossible to know whether these were errors made by Gray, or by his scribes, or were already present in the version Gray copied from.

137 See below 245, n. 2.
138 Fordun, 376–7; cf. Wyntoun, vi, 231; Bower, vii, 298–300.
139 Below, 195.

As well as written sources, the later part of the *Scalacronica* relies heavily on eyewitness testimony, particularly that of Gray's own father. Visiting Norham castle, it is easy to imagine an ageing Thomas Gray the elder whiling away the winter evenings in the great hall, sitting near the fire with a goblet of mulled wine, telling stories of his adventures fighting against the Scots; and these stories so impressed his son that he later wrote them down, as he whiled away his time as a prisoner in Edinburgh. And apart from the fact that the elder Gray ceased to be the constable of Norham in 1327, this romantic picture is probably broadly correct, for a variety of tales and anecdotes relating to the service of Thomas the elder against the Scots enlivens the *Scalacronica*'s narrative of the reigns of Edward I and of his feckless son, and these were clearly based on the elder Gray's own reminisences. There was a gap of at least eleven years between the latter's death in 1344 and his son's imprisonment in 1355; and although communication from beyond the grave was not unknown in the Gray family,[140] we can be reasonably sure that the author of the *Scalacronica* had no such means of checking his memory – which may explain some of the lapses in Gray's chronology. Furthermore, stories such as that of William Marmion, with his helm with a crest of gold, may well have improved with the telling. On the other hand, they do provide a unique insight into the *mores* and attitudes of a militarily active knight. Furthermore, Gray's father was a retainer of Henry de Beaumont, a royal favourite for much of Edward II's reign; and so Gray's father was aligned with Edward II's court. Thus the *Scalacronica* provides an alternative political viewpoint from most of the chronicles of this unhappy reign, which tend towards a decidedly pro-Lancastrian bias.[141] Nevertheless, Gray is by no means uncritical of Edward and his coterie of favourites; the Despensers, in particular, come in for considerable criticism – and it is interesting to note that the *Scalacronica* conspicuously fails to mention the association of Gray's father with the younger Despenser.[142]

The *Scalacronica*'s vivid account of Edward III's *coup* of 1330, against Roger de Mortimer and his own mother, was almost certainly

---

140 See above, xxii–xxiii.
141 See, for instance, Gray's comment on Jocelin Deyville's attack on the manor of Northallerton, below; or his unsympathetic account of Lancaster's execution, below.
142 Below, 91. For the elder Gray's links with Hugh Despenser the younger, see above, xxxii.

derived from William Montague, one of the participants. Montague's role is particularly prominent compared to other contemporary accounts, and Gray served with Montague in Flanders in 1338–9.[143] Other information must also have been supplied by personal informants. The *Scalacronica* contains a great deal of information about contemporary Scottish politics; indeed, it is one of the most important surviving sources for political events in Scotland in the mid-fourteenth century. Gray must have garnered this from his personal contacts with the Scots. Obviously, he would have been well placed to keep abreast of Scottish affairs while imprisoned in Edinburgh castle – the very fact that he was able to start writing his chronicle there demonstrates that he was not kept in close confinement. Otherwise, he would have maintained contacts with Scotland through negotiations for his ransom; through Scottish prisoners of war, such as David Graham and John de Haliburton, captured by Gray at the battle of Neville's Cross in 1346, and hostages, such as John, son and heir of John Gray, entrusted to his custody as a hostge for David II of Scotland, in October 1357;[144] and through routine business with the Scots, on occasions such as March days.[145]

Gray's account of the parliament of February 1358 (held while he was working on the *Scalacronica*) and the complaints raised there against the Papacy, was probably derived from the reports of Northumberland's knights of the shire, Sir Henry de Haverington and Richard de Horsley, to the Northumbrian county court.[146] The *Scalacronica*'s account of the capture and subsequent escape of Kestutis, Prince of Lithuania, in 1361 – unnoticed by any other English chronicler – must have been derived from one of the English men-at-arms who took part in the crusade which led to it.[147] Gray's knowledge of Spanish affairs (chapter 54), was evidently very sketchy (he does not, for instance, mention the Anglo-Castilian treaty of June 1362), and clearly dependent on the propaganda spread by the supporters of Enrique of Trastámara, the estranged bastard

143 Below, 105–7.
144 *Rot. Scot.*, i, 678; *CDS*, iii, 434.
145 Gray was appointed a warden of the Marches in Oct. 1361 and Sep. 1367; *Rot. Scot.*, i, 857, 914, 915.
146 For the role of the county court in the dissemination of information (and indeed propaganda) from Westminster, see Maddicott, 'County Community', *passim*.
147 Below, 197, 199.
148 Below, 252, n. 5.

half-brother of Pedro I of Castile.[148] However, it would appear that Gray did not regard eyewitness testimony as altogether intellectually respectable. He begins his detailed account of Bannockburn with the comment, 'and as to how this defeat happened, the chronicles relate ...'; yet his account can only have been derived, at least in part, from the reminiscences of his father.[149]

In some cases, Gray drew on his own experiences – most obviously, for his account of Edward III's expedition to France in 1359–60, on which he served himself. It would appear that he had already written the *Scalacronica* up to that date, and this account was probably composed within months of the event;[150] he may even have made notes while he was in France. Chapters 50 and 51 consist of various anecdotes about the French wars, relating events from up to twenty years previously. Given that these chapters are inserted immediately before Gray's account of the 1359–60 expedition, it may be assumed that he garnered these anecdotes while he was in France, probably from the participants themselves, and added them to the *Scalacronica* once he got back to England. Indeed, given the number of these anecdotes, he may well deliberately have set out to gather them, in a similar fashion to Jean Froissart, perhaps collecting tales told round campfires. It is particularly regrettable that the portion of MS 133 which went missing covers much of its author's adult life; for instance it contained an account of the battle of Neville's Cross (1346) from someone who actually fought there. However, the highly atmospheric description of the battle of Dupplin Moor (1332) may well rest on Gray's own experience, as he probably fought there as well.[151]

The later part of the *Scalacronica* rested on a wide range of chronicle, documentary and eyewitness sources; and Gray's access to Scottish works, and his personal contacts as a militarily active knight, provide a somewhat different perspective from the run of the monastic and clerical chroniclers of the day. And it is particularly impressive that he managed to weld these sources together to produce a coherent whole. Many monastic chroniclers simply cobbled their own works together by wholesale plagiarism, lifting large chunks of text unaltered from other chronicles, leaving a trail of irrelevant detail which they lacked the discrimination to excise. Gray,

---

149 Below, 73–7.
150 Above, xxi.
151 Below, 109–1. For Gray's possible participation in the Disinherited's expedition, above, xxxv.

however, was better able to control his diverse sources, rewriting them into a seamless work of synthesis, and omitting all that was irrelevant. He also exercised a degree of judgement, prefacing material which he considered doubtful with comments such as, 'it is said that . . . '. The *Scalacronica* thus remains uniquely valuable, not only as an insight into the political viewpoint and worldview of a fourteenth-century knight, but also of his skills as a historian and writer.

THE MANUSCRIPT

The *Scalacronica* is to be found in Corpus Christi College, Cambridge, MS 133.[152] It is bound up with the *Algorismus*, a short treatise on mathematics mostly in French verse.[153] This is written on a separate quire of three folios, ending on the *recto* of the third folio. The hand, while contemporary with that of the *Scalacronica*, is an entirely different cursive script, using a different colour of ink; clearly, it was originally a separate item. On the blank *verso* of the last folio of the *Algorismus* is a heading in a hand of *circa* the 1420s: 'Cronica Regum Anglie in gallico & incip^t in 2⁰ fo in processu libri terminer fors' ('Chronicles of the Kings of England in French beginning on the second folio in the course of the book "terminer fors" ').[154] This obviously refers to the Scalacronica, which indicates that the two items presently in MS 133 were bound together in or before the 1420s. As it now survives, the part of MS 133 containing the *Scalacronica* is made up twenty quires of twelve folios, with a total of 234 folios.[155] The discrepancy arises from the fact that the MS is now incomplete; the narrative jumps, in mid-sentence, from 1340 at f. 219v. to 1356 on f. 220. A seventeenth-century hand added the comment 'desunt folia nonnulla' at the bottom of f. 219v. This *caesura* comes in the nineteenth quire, which now has only six folios, three to either side of the break; and ff. 219 and 220 both have minor tears, near to the binding. It would appear that the missing folios had disappeared by the

---

152 The MS is described by James, *Catalogue, Corpus Christi*, i, 305–6. It should be noted that the title *Scalacronica* is the author's own, given in the text of the prologue; below, 7.

153 Wilkins, *Catalogue des manuscrits français*, 55–7; Dean and Boulton, *Anglo-Norman Literature*, no. 329.

154 The heading is repeated *verbatim* directly underneath, in an early sixteenth-century hand.

155 Note that the second quire is misplaced; f. 25 should follow f. 12 (see catch words at bottom of f. 12v.), f. 13 should follow f. 24.

mid-sixteenth century, for the chapters were numbered by a hand of approximately this date, and the numerical sequence carries on across the lacuna without interruption.[156] Despite this loss, the *Scalacronica* remains a very handsome volume. It is a large book (31x19.5cm), and the first page of the chronicle is richly and colourfully decorated, with the initial letter illuminated, using gold leaf on a red and blue background. Other illuminated initials, decorated with gold leaf drawn over eight lines of text, are to be found at intervals throughout the work, usually to mark the beginning of a king's reign, while the text is further divided into chapters by the use of blue initials, decorated with red linework, and drawn over three lines of text, and separated from the preceding chapter by a blank line. These chapters vary in length from half a column to several folios, but tend to get longer towards the end of the book.[157] The script is in a very fine mid-fourteenth-century formal book hand, with some decoration.[158] The text is written in carefully ruled double columns of forty-four lines each, with expansive margins.[159] Although the illumination is slightly heavy-handed, the text is very elegant and the overall effect is striking. It appears to be the work of a single scribe, who was obviously a highly accomplished professional, and it appears to have been copied in one stint; it cannot therefore be Gray's autograph, as he wrote his work over several years.[160] Nor is Gray likely to have been able to write in such an accomplished hand – and anyway, it is entirely likely that there never was an autograph text, as he would have dictated to a clerk rather than actually writing himself.[161]

---

156 Note also that the second quire is misplaced; f. 25 should follow f. 12 (cf. the catch words at the bottom of f. 12v.), f. 13 should follow f. 24. This may perhaps have occurred when the MS was rebound in 1952.

157 These initials and textual divisions are noted by neither Stevenson nor Maxwell.

158 *e.g.* the caricature face, added as a flourish to the 'L' at the head of the second column, f. 193v.

159 The margins were originally even more expansive, but the MS was cropped at some point after the fifteenth-century, as is revealed by the disappearence of part of many of the chapter headings added at that time; the culprit was probably Archbishop Parker, who was in the habit of cropping his MSS (my thanks to Gill Cannell for advice on this matter).

160 Above, xxi.

161 Cf. K.B. McFarlane, 'if examples of noble handwriting . . . are rare, it was because like the busy men of today the busy men of the fourteenth century preferred to dictate', *Nobility of Later Medieval England*, 239, 241 (quote at 241).

There has been some confusion concerning other possible manuscripts of the *Scalacronica*. In his 1905 catalogue of the Parker Library, M.R. James described Corpus Christi MS 133 as 'the best copy', implying that others were to be found. This was because his catalogue of the library of Jesus College, Cambridge, published some ten years previously, had identified an Anglo-Norman chronicle in Jesus College, Cambridge, MS Q.G.10 as 'the *Scala Chronica* of Sir Thomas Gray . . . in French prose, imperfect at the beginning', noting that, 'This copy goes down as far as the death of Henry III in 1272'.[162] However, while there are significant verbal correspondences with the *Scalacronica*, the very considerable differences are rather more noticeable; indeed, up until the reign of Henry I, the chronicles are entirely dissimilar. In fact, the Anglo-Norman chronicle in MS Q.G.10 is a version of the Anglo-Norman prose *Brut* chronicle, as J.C. Thiolier noticed in 1993.[163] The obvious explanation for the verbal similarities to the *Scalacronica* is that Gray simply lifted a considerable part of his text for the period 1100–1272 from a version of the prose *Brut*, more-or-less *verbatim*.[164]

This leaves Corpus Christi MS 133 as the only manuscript of the *Scalacronica*; and so the loss of several of its folios is particularly unfortunate. Even more unfortunately, the missing part covers the period 1340 to 1356, which is a large part of its author's active life. Fortunately, however, the sixteenth-century antiquarian John Leland (d. 1552) made an English abstract of the work from a complete copy,[165] and this goes some way to filling the gap. A comparison of

---

162 James, *Catalogue, Corpus Christi*, i, 306; James, *Catalogue, Jesus College*, 92–3 (no. 58).

163 Thiolier, 'La *Scalacronica*: Première Approche', 122–3. Unfortunately, Thiolier's findings do not yet seem to have reached a wide audience – perhaps because they appear in a French language essay collection published in England. And so, the Anglo-Norman Text Society's authoritative guide to Anglo-Norman manuscripts, published as late as 1999, still lists MS Q.G.10 as a manuscript of the *Scalacronica*; Dean and Boulton, *Anglo-Norman Literature*, no. 74 (even though Thiolier's article is listed under this entry). See King and Marvin, 'A Warning to the Incurious'.

164 Thus Thiolier's suggestion that Gray 'a presque recopié le *Brut d'Engleterre* pour le règne d'Henri III' rather understates the case: 'La *Scalacronica*: Première Approche', 123.

165 Leland may, of course, have used MS 133 itself before it was damaged. Indeed, if he did, given that the missing folios appear to have vanished at around the mid-sixteenth century, it is not inconceivable that Leland himself caused the damage.

this abstract with the surviving part of the *Scalacronica* reveals that it is usually accurate in so far as it goes, though there are a few major errors: for instance, Gray's account of the defeat of Edward de Balliol by Archibald Douglas, in the Vale of Annan, 1332, is actually recorded by Leland as a victory for the English.[166] Furthermore, parts of his abstract are far more condensed than others. For instance, Sir William Marmion's famous chivalric escapade at Norham in 1319 is retold almost in full, including a paraphrase of the elder Gray's speech. By contrast, the *Scalacronica*'s lengthy account of the battle of Dupplin Moor in 1332 is reduced by Leland to a brief summary, entirely losing the vividness of the original; Henry de Beaumont's pep-talk to the disheartened 'Disinherited' is rendered as 'The Lord Beaumond, seyng the ennemyes at hand, encoragid al the company', which hardly captures the spirit of his words.[167] Unfortunately, Leland gives no indication of such variations in the extent of his summarising, and where the original is lacking, it is impossible to tell just how much detail has been left out at any given point. In other places, Leland's abbreviation actually distorts the meaning of Gray's text; for example, the very last sentence of the *Scalacronica* is rendered 'Davy Bruis, king of Scottes, toke to wyfe, by force of love, one Margaret de Logy'. This completely fails to convey Gray's studied, and almost certainly derisory, allusion to the literary conventions of *fin amour*.[168] Finally, Leland also completely omits some sections; for instance, chapters 40–2, dealing with the Empire and the Papacy are excluded in their entirety. In summary, Leland's abstract can, with due caution, be used as a guide to the factual content of the missing portions of the *Scalacronica*; it will not, however, bear detailed textual analysis; nor can it be taken as a reliable guide to what the missing portions of Gray's work did *not* contain.

PROVENANCE

MS 133 has been in the library of Corpus Christi College, Cambridge, since 1575, when it was amongst the manuscripts bequeathed by Archbishop Matthew Parker; and it is possible to reconstruct the route by which it got into Parker's hands. On the *verso* of the last folio of the *Algorismus*, facing the first page of the *Scalacronica*, underneath

---

166 Below, 113; cf. *Scalacronica*, Stevenson, 295.
167 *Ibid.*, 290–1, 294; cf. below, 81–3, 109.
168 *Scalacronica*, Stevenson, 315; below, 205; King, 'Helm with a Crest', 28–9.

the heading 'Cronica Regum Anglie in gallico & incip^t in 2° fo in processu libri terminer fors', there is an erasure. The erased text is no longer legible, although it is still possible to identify it as a sixteenth-century hand; it was read by M.R. James as:

Si dieu plet	[If it please God
a moy cest livre partient	this book pertains to me
G. vst kyldare	G. viscount Kildare]

This claim to ownership is confirmed by an entry in a survey of the possessions of Gerald Fitz Gerald, Earl of Kildare (d. 1534). Included in the survey was the earl's library, under the heading, 'Bokes remayning in the lyberary of Geralde fitzGeralde erle of Kyldare the 15 day of Februarii anno Henrici 17° [1526]'. This section includes a list of 'French boks', the first item of which is 'Scalacronica: in Kyldare'.[169] Parker used a number of agents to build up his collection of manuscripts, one of whom was the bibliographer John Bale. Bale had been nominated to the see of Ossory in 1552, though he fled from Ireland after only a year, following the accession of Queen Mary. However, he certainly maintained his bibliophile interests during this time, for before his flight, he hid a collection of books, which were subsequently recovered by Parker after his death.[170] It therefore seems probable that MS 133 was acquired by Bale while he was in Ireland, and that it subsequently passed to Parker with the rest of his collection.

So how did the *Scalacronica* end up in the library of the earls of Kildare? An obvious explanation lies in the marriages that linked the Grays to the earls. The assiduous military service of the Grays, both father and son, had brought the family considerable social advancement, so much so that the chronicler's second daughter, Elizabeth, had married into the peerage, marrying Philip, Lord Darcy (d. April 1399). The Darcy family had interests and lands in Ireland, and so the couple's eldest daughter, Agnes, was married to Gerald Fitz Maurice, Earl of Kildare, by November 1397.[171] Elizabeth was certainly inter-

---

169 *Crown Surveys of Lands*, ed. Mac Niocaill, 313. Another list of the earl's books in the same survey, headed *Hec sunt nomina librorum existencium in libraria Geraldi comitis Kildarie*, includes 'The cronicles of England in Frenche'; this may well be another reference to the *Scalacronica* (*ibid.*, 355).

170 *Dictionary of National Biography*, iii, 41; xliii, 260–1.

171 Watson, 'Ormond and Kildare', 231; *CP*, iv, 62; vii, 227. I owe thanks to Richard Moll for drawing my attention to this connection. For the Grays' social climbing, see King, 'Scaling the Ladder'.

ested in books. Shortly after the death of her son, John, lord Darcy, she made her will (on 20 December 1411, at Lincoln) in which she left to Philip, John's son and heir, and her grandson, 'a book called *Bybill*, and another book called *Sang Ryalle*, and another book called *Lanselake*'.[172] More intriguingly, she also left him 'a book in French called *The Ladder of Reason*' (*unum librum de romans vocatum Leschell de Reson*); furthermore, she stipulated that should Philip fail to co-operate 'well and amicably' with her executors, this specific volume was to go to Sir Thomas Grey of Heton (the chronicler's grandson and Elizabeth's nephew). Could *Leschell de Reson* be a garbled reference to the *Scalacronica*?[173] We do not know whether, in the event, Philip co-operated with Elizabeth's executors, but he died in 1418, aged twenty, leaving two daughters; and if *Leschell de Reson* is indeed to be identified with the *Scalacronica*, it must be assumed that one way or another, it passed to his aunt Agnes, who was then still alive (she did not die until 1439), and thence to the earls of Kildare.[174]

This raises the question of whether MS 133 was the same manuscript used by Leland to make his abstract. Certainly, some of the marginalia in MS 133 is in a hand which could possibly be Leland's.[175] However, there is nothing to suggest that anyone in England had possession of MS 133 until Parker acquired it; and if he did acquire it from Bale, then this would suggest that Leland did not use this manuscript, for Bale did not go to Ireland until 1552, the year of Leland's death, by which time Leland had lost his reason. On the other hand, there is no actual evidence to link Bale to MS 133, and Parker may well have acquired it earlier, by some other means. Certainly, in the absence of any further evidence of MS 133's precise provenance, the question of Leland's possible use of it must remain open.

PREVIOUS EDITIONS

The *Scalacronica* has been noticed by historians since John Leland made his abstract in the sixteenth century.[176] As Stevenson notes in

172 *Register of Bishop Repingdon*, ed. Archer, ii, 265; *CP*, iv, 64. The books referred to are the Bible, a Grail romance and a romance of Lancelot.
173 Again, I owe thanks to Richard Moll for this suggestion.
174 Watson, 'Ormond and Kildare', 231; *CP*, iv, 65–6.
175 My thanks to James Carley for advice on this point.
176 Printed in Leland, *Britannicis*, ii, 558–66; and *Scalacronica*, Stevenson, 259–315.

his introduction, the sixteenth-century antiquarian Nicholas Wotton made brief Latin notes from the *Scalacronica*, covering the period from King Harold to Edward III, whilst one of the items in a sixteenth-century bound collection of tracts, preserved in the Parker Library, is an English translation of the prologue of the *Scalacronica*, beginning 'He y^t hath delight or wowd knowe . . .'.[177] However, no edition of the French text was published until 1836, when the Maitland Club published the text from 1066 to the end, edited by Joseph Stevenson; some seventy years later, in 1907, Herbert Maxwell published a translation of the section from 1272 to the end.[178] Stevenson's edition also includes the prologue, and an appendix of 'Extracts from the Early Portion of the *Scalacronica*' (printing four brief extracts relating to the prophecies of Merlin – and Gray's low opinion of them; King Arthur; the Scottish King *Conwak*; and Malcolm Canmore) and prints John Leland's abstract in its entirety. In addition, the sections of the *Scalacronica* which relate to Scottish history were translated (rather poorly, it has to be said), by E.J. Chinnock in 1908–10.[179] The section relating to early Scottish history, inserted by Gray in relation to the 'Great Cause' of 1291–2, was printed and translated by William Skene, in 1867;[180] and the Arthurian section has been printed by Maria Luisa Meneghetti, in a compilation work published in 1979.[181] However, the majority of the text, from the Creation till 1066, has never been edited.

It is, of course, customary for the editors of new editions of texts to

---

The section covering the portion missing from MS 133 is also printed in *Scalacronica*, Maxwell, 112–20.

177 *Scalacronica*, Stevenson, xxxv–xxxvi; BL, Harley 902, ff. 47–47v., 70v.–71v., 136v.–137v., 196v., 197v., 203–203v., 212v.–213v.; *Catalogue of the Harleian Manuscripts*, 470; Corpus Christi College, Cambridge, MS 119, item 124, ff. 367–8; James, *Catalogue, Corpus Christi*, i, 283.

178 *Scalacronica*, Stevenson; *Scalacronica*, Maxwell.

179 'The *Scalacronica*. Extracts from Sir Thomas Gray's *Scalacronica* (Ladder of Time) Relating to Scotland', *Transactions of the Dumfriesshire and Galloway Natural History and Antiquarian Society*, 2nd ser., xxi, xxii (1908–9, 1909–10). It was unfortunate for Chinnock – if not perhaps for modern scholars – that his translation appeared just after Maxwell's, and was totally eclipsed by it.

180 W.F. Skene (ed.), *Chronicles of the Picts, Chronicles of the Scots and other Early Memorials of Scottish History* (Edinburgh, 1867), 194–208. Part of this material has also been printed and analysed by Broun, *Irish Identity*, 84–95.

181 M.L. Meneghetti, *I Fatti de Bretagna, Croinache Genealogiche Anglo-Normanne dal XII al XIV secolo* (Padua, 1979). I have not been able to examine a copy of this work.

denigrate the efforts of their predecessors – if only to justify their own production of a new edition. In fact, both Stevenson's edition and Maxwell's translation have served historians very well, especially considering their age. However, only 108 copies of Stevenson's edition were printed; and inevitably, both have their faults (as no doubt does the present edition). Stevenson provides a generally very accurate transcription of the text, but his paragraphing bears absolutely no relation to the clearly marked divisions in the text of MS 133; and neither does Maxwell's. Maxwell's translation is eminently readable, and conveys the broad sense of the French very well; however, a significant amount is paraphrased rather than accurately translated. He also occasionally omits sentences or clauses; for instance, he omits any translation of the phrase, 'pensaunt qe nuls gentz vssent pris le pase sure lez soens' (correctly printed by Stevenson), unfortunately just before he draws attention to Stevenson's omission of the word 'estoient'.[182] More importantly though, both editions are unsatisfactory, by current standards, in their introductory material and annotation. Stevenson does provide an account of the careers of both Gray and his father which is comphrensive (if resolutely antiquarian in genre), and prints a variety of documents relating to them, and to the *Scalacronica* itself; his commentary on the text, however, simply peters out once the narrative of the chronicle gets past the reign of King Richard. Maxwell more or less dispenses with introductory material or commentary altogether, merely directing his readers' attention to Stevenson's introduction. Nor do either Stevenson or Maxwell make any great attempt to relate the chronicle to the lives and careers of either Gray or his father.

EDITORIAL PRINCIPLES

Expansion of abbreviations

All abbreviations and contractions have been expanded silently. As always with Anglo-Norman French, the expansion of abbreviations presents difficulties due to variations in spelling, which renders any attempt at standardisation a hazardous, and indeed rather academic, exercise. For instance, should Northumb' be expanded as Northumbre (*i.e.* 'Northumbria) following the usual expansion of this abbreviation, or as Northumbreland, or even Northumbrelaund, which is how Gray usually refers to his home county? Fortunately, the scribe

---

182 *Scalacronica*, Maxwell, 69; *Scalacronica*, Stevenson, 149.

of MS 133 was generally fairly consistent in his spelling, and expansions have followed the usual unabbreviated spelling of a word; thus g'nt is expanded as *graunt*, while g'ce is expanded as *grace*. At numerous points in the manuscript, spaces at the ends of lines have filled with a symbol not unlike a small capital 'R'. These sigils have been omitted from the transcription.

The text
The scribe's original spelling has been retained throughout (apart from his few obvious spelling errors, which have been corrected – attention is drawn to these in the footnotes). 'U's and 'v's, 'i's and 'j's, and 'i's and 'y's have not been standardised according to modern conventions, as the scribe's use of these letters is reasonably consistent, and they are clearly distinguishable; thus, *avoir* is almost invariably spelt *auoir*, while *vindrent* is usually spelt with a 'v'. Nor have accents or apostrophes been supplied. It has been thought preferable to preserve the original fourteenth-century spellings than to present a twenty-first century idea of how the text *ought* to have been spelt. On the same grounds, amendments have been kept to a minimum, reserved for very obvious scribal errors; in these cases, the original reading is indicated by a footnote. The *Scalacronica*'s French is frequently awkward and obscure, sometimes to the point where it appears to be corrupt. Whether this is due to Gray himself or to errors on the part of the copyist is not clear – though a comparison with the French text of the 'Oldest Version' of the *Brut*, which Gray used as the basis for his narrative for the period 1100–1272, shows few such linguistic anomalies, suggesting that it was not the copyist who was at fault.[183] No attempt, however, has been made to amend or correct the text. On the other hand, the scribe's capitalisation appears to be virtually random (apart from the beginning of sentences, which almost invariably take capitals). Furthermore, the scribe's capitals are not always readily distinguishable. Capitalisation has therefore been standardised according to modern convention. The MS uses a mixture of Roman and Arabic numerals; these have been reproduced in the text in the form in which they appear in the MS.

The scribe sometimes elides words; where this renders their meaning obscure, they have been separated out, *e.g.* 'a par soy' appears in the MS as 'aparsoy', below, 104; 'sen alarent' appears as

---

183 For Gray's use of the *Brut*, see King and Marvin, 'A Warning to the Incurious'.

'senalarent', below, 44. However, as noted above, apostrophes have not been introduced; thus terms such as *sen, Descoce, cest* and *lalphabet* are reproduced as they appear in the MS, rather than being modernised as *s'en, d'Escoce, c'est* and *l'alphabet*.

Note that in the MS, chapters are headed by rubricated capitals, with the beginning of the reign of each King of England marked out by illuminated capitals. These have not been indicated in the current text.

Angle brackets (<. . .>) have been used to indicate conjectural readings where the MS is stained or damaged.

Punctuation and paragraphing

The original text is punctuated copiously, if somewhat inconsistently. This punctuation has been somewhat simplified, and brought into accord with modern conventions; however, the punctuation does follow the original reasonably closely. Within each chapter, the text is divided into sections, clearly marked out by double pen strokes. These divisions have been reproduced as paragraphs.

Numbering of chapters

Although clearly marked out by rubricated initials, the chapters were not originally numbered in the surviving manuscript. However, chapter numbers were subsequently added, in a sixteenth-century hand. These appear to start at the chapter which begins with the coronation of William Rufus (f. 145v.), which is numbered '5' (in arabic numerals); and indeed, this is the fifth chapter after that dealing with the invasion by William the Conqueror in 1066, which corresponds with the beginning of the 'fourth book of these chronicles; that is, the first arrival of William the Conqueror here', as described in Gray's prologue.[184] Similarly, brief chapter headings were added to the last few chapters (from chapter 33, f. 190v.), in Anglo-Norman French in a rather untidy late-medieval hand. These chapter numbers have been reproduced, for ease of reference, as have the chapter headings.

Principles of translation

As the translation is intended to help the reader to follow the French text, it generally follows the original fairly closely, inevitably at the cost of fluency and readability. However, as Gray's sentences tend to

---

184 Below, 7.

be rather long and rambling, with somewhat tortuous strings of clauses and sub-clauses, littered with rather ambiguous prepositions, it is sometimes difficult to keep track of which subjects and objects relate to which verbs, and *vice versa*. In the interests of clarity, and to conform to modern English usage, longer sentences have been broken up into smaller units, and names sometimes substituted for pronouns. Consequently, the punctuation of the translation does not match that of the text. Similarly, the order of many of the sub-clauses has been changed, to aid comprehension. Gray's French is very clipped and compressed; it has not been possible to consistently reproduce this style, as a rather wordier style is necessary to render a readily intelligible modern English translation. Phrases such as 'le dit . . .' and 'le avant dit . . . ' have been omitted where they add nothing to the sense, to avoid an unduly anachronistic flavour. Similarly, phrases such as 'le Roy Edward' or 'le Count Robert de Flandres' have been rendered simply as 'King Edward' or 'Robert, Count of Flanders'.

Translation of names
As Gray generally uses Anglo-Norman forms for all names, irrespective of nationality, names have generally been rendered in their modern English form, where such exists; similarly, with place-names. For all his use of French, Gray had an essentially Anglo-centric world-view, and the translation aims to reflect his prejudices. Thus Dauid le freir Lewlyn Prince de Galis (*i.e.* Dafydd ap Gruffydd, below, 00) is rendered as David, rather than Dafydd. However, in some cases, where Gray uses foreign name forms, as in the case of Gillemyng de Fenygges, a Burgundian knight in English service (below, 00), a foreign form has been retained in translation. The Gaelic names in the Scottish king-lists reproduced by Gray have been left as they are, except where obvious modern English equivalents exist. Doubtless, numerous inconsistencies remain. Note that where place-names have not been identified, they have been included in the translation in italics.

Translation of military terms
Gray uses some terms with a particular military connotation. He uses the word *batail* to refer both to large-scale combats, and to divisions of an army. Medieval armies, or *osts*, were usually divided for operational and tactical purposes into three 'battles'. Following Gray's usage, the term has been translated as 'battle' for both senses. *Ost* has

been translated as 'army', in the sense of a large armed force, as opposed to the modern sense of a permanent national military institution. In his account of the English campaigns in France, Gray uses the term *glayues* (meaning polearms similar to halbards) to refer to troops; this has been translated as 'billhooks', and refers to footmen equipped with billhooks, halbards or other polearms.

Leland's Abstract

A section of John Leland's Abstract of the *Scalacronica*, covering the missing part of Gray's original text, has been printed below at the relevant point. This is intended to provide a guide to the contents of the missing folios. Leland's spelling has been retained. The missing section is discussed above, liii–liv; for Leland's abstract, see above, lv–lvi.

SCALACRONICA
1272–1363

PROLOGUE

[f. 1]

[1] Qe eit delite ou voet sauoir coment le Isle del Graunt Bretaigne, iadys Albeon, tere de geaunz ore Engleter, fust primerment enhabite, et de quel gent, et de lour naissaunce, et la processe du ligne de Rois, qe y ount este, et lour conuersacioun, solunc ceo qe cely qe cest cronicle emparla, et la m<an>er*^{a}* auoit troue en escript en diuers liuers en Latin et en romaunce, pust il conoistre en party par cest estoir suaunt la processe de eaux. Et sy ne voet pas au plain nomer soun noume, qe cest cronicle translata de ryme en prose, mais prisoner estoit, pris de guer, al hour qil comensa cest tretice. Si estoit del ordre enlumine de bons morez, as veues, as pucelis et a Saint Eglise succours.

Soun habite sa droit vesture*^{b}*
estoit autre tiel de colour;
com est ly chape du cordeler,
teynt en tout tiel maner.
Autre cote auoit afoebler,
lestat de soun ordre agarder,
qe de fieu resemble la colour,
et desus en purturature,
estoit li hardy best quartyner,
du signe teynt de la mere,
enviroun palice vn mure,
de meisme peynt la coloure.
Soit .viij. ioynt apres .xix.*^{me}* *^{c}*
si mettez .xij. apres .xiiij.*^{me}* *^{d}*
vn et .xviij. encountrez,
soun propre noun ensauerez
.vij. a .xvij. y mettez,
le primer vowel au tierce aioignez,
soun droit surnoun entrouerez,
solunc lalphabet.
Le noun propre et surenoun portoit,
qe deuaunt luy soun piere auoit.
Qe plus clerement le voet sauoir,

---

^{a} MS obsured here; maner *is a conjectural reading.*
^{b} Note that the MS text is written as continuous prose, rather than being separated into lines, as presented here.
^{c} 'me' added later [Hand A].
^{d} 'me' added later [Hand A].

PROLOGUE

[f. 1]

[1] Whoever would take delight in, or who wishes to know, how the island of Great Britain (formerly Albion, the land of giants, now England) was originally inhabited – and by what race, and of their origin, and the procession of the line of kings that there has been, and their conversion[1] – he will be able to know in part through this history, since this chronicle has enscribed these things, in the manner that has been found written down in various books in Latin and in the vernacular, following their account. And he who wrote this chronicle, translated from rhyme in prose, does not wish to reveal his name plainly, but he was a prisoner, taken in war, at the time when this treatise was begun. He was of that order which is enlightened by good customs, a support for the old, for maidens and for Holy Church.

His garment, his right attire,
Was of some such colour,
As is the cloak of a minorite friar,[2]
Dyed in just such a manner.
He had another coat he wore,
The status of his order it bore,
Which resembles the colour of fire,
And thereon, in portraiture,
Was the hardy beast, quartered
With the painted device of his mother,
The surrounding boundary, a wall,
Painted of the same colour.
Eight joined after nineteen,
If you put twelve after fourteen,
One and eighteen put together,
His personal name you will discover,
The seventh to seventeenth matched,
The first vowel to the third attached,
His correct surname you will uncover,[3]
following the alphabet.
Whoever would know this more clearly,
Shall have it from someone other than me,

dautre qe de moy lestat auoir,
sortez iettez et diuinez,
sy ymaginez qe vous poez.

[2] Et coment ly surueint corage de cest matir atreter, lestoir deuyse
qe com il fust prisoner en le opidoun mount Agneth, iadys chastel de
pucelis, ore Edynburgh, surueist il liuers de cronicles enrymaiez et en
prose, en Latin, en Fraunceis et en Engles de gestez dez auncestres, de
quoi il se meruailla et durement ly poisoit, qe il nust hu deuaunt le
hour meillour conisaunce du cours du siecle. Si deueint corious et
pensiue, com geris nauoit en le hour autre chos a fair, a treter et a
translater en plus court sentence, lez cronicles del Graunt Bretaigne,
et lez gestez dez Englessez. Et com estoit du dit bosoigne plus
pensiue, ly estoit auys vn nuyt en dormaunt, qe Sebile la sage ly
surueint et ly dist qel ly moustra voi a ceo qil estoit en pense. Et ly fust
auys qel ly amena en vn verger, ou encountre vn mure haut, sur vn
peroun, trouerent vn eschel de .v. bastouns adressez, et sur le peroun
desoutz leschel .ij. liuers au coste, et vn frer cordeler suppuoillaunt od
sa main dextre le dist eschele. Moun amy, ceo [f. 1v.] disoit la veil
Sebile, veiez cy, sen et foly; le primer liuer, la Bible, le secounde, la
Gest de Troy, queux ne greuerount a toun purpos a surueoir. Et com ly
fust auys, ele ly amena outre; si mounterent leschel, qe au boute du
primer bastoun du dist eschel au mayn dextre parmy le mure
trouerent vn bele entree, ou entrerent vn graunt cite, ou dedenz vn
manoir en vn sale, trouerent escriuaunt vn mestre bien furre. Beaux
amy, ceo dist Sebille, veez y cy Gauter erchedeken de Excestre, qe le
Brut translata de Bretoun en Latin, par ditz de Keile et de Gildas de
ditz de qi, poez auoir ensampler, com de le Bruyte, lez gestz de
Bretouns, le primer liuer de croniclis de cest isle. Puis ils sez realerent,
et remounterent le secound bastoun du dist eschel, au bout de quoi
trouerent au tiel entree com deuaunt, ou dedens vn priori com ly fust
auys, trouerent vn moigne noir, escriuaunt en vn estudy. Si disoit
Sebille, Cesti est Bede en Wermouth le reuerent doctour, qescrit le
liuer De gestis Anglorum, de quoi doiez auoir a toun purpos graunt
ensensement com de gestis Saxsouns, le secund liuer du dit cronicle.
Ils lez realerent com fust auys, et remounterent le tierce bastoun du
dit eschel, ou par tiel entree, y trouerent vn autre moigne noir et
chanu, escriuaunt en vn cloistre. Moun amy, fesoit Sebille, cesti est le
moigne de Cestre qe escript le Polecronicon, de qoi doiez prendre
graunt auisement du tierce liuer de ditz cronicles, ceo est assauoir de
la vniement qe le Roy Egbright fist de les .vij. Realmes Saxsouns, com

Throw lots and divine it,
If you imagine that you can.

[2] And as it occurred to him to examine (the history devised when he was prisoner in the citadel of Mount Agneth, formerly Maiden's Castle, now Edinburgh[1]) he looked over books of chronicles, rhymed and in prose, in Latin, in French and English, of the deeds of ancestors, at which he wondered; and it troubled him greatly that before this time, he had not had a better knowledge of the course of the world. He became curious and, as he did not have much else to do at the time, contemplated composing and translating, in a greatly shortened form, the chronicles of Great Britain, and the deeds of the English. And as he considered more about this task, he thought one night as he slept, that the wise Sybil appeared to him, and told him that she would show him the way to that which he had in mind. And he thought that she brought him to an orchard, where against a high wall, on a mounting block, they found a ladder made up of five rungs; and on the mounting block under the ladder, two valuable books, and a grey friar holding the ladder up with his right hand. 'My friend', [f. 1v.] said the aged Sybil, 'here you may see wisdom and folly; the first book [is] the Bible, the second, *The Deed of Troy*.[2] It wouldn't harm your plans to take a look at them.' And as it seemed to him, she led him further; they climbed the ladder, where at the end of the first rung on the right-hand side through the wall, they found a fine entrance, through which they entered a great city, where in a hall in a manor-house, they found a master, well dressed in furs, writing. 'My fine friend', said the Sybil, 'here you may see Walter archdeacon of Exeter,[3] who translated the *Brut* from British into Latin, from the sayings of Keile[4] and from Gildas, by whose words, you'll be able to have an exemplar, such as the *Brut*, the deeds of the Britons, the first book of the chronicles of this isle. Then they returned, and climbed back on to the second rung of the ladder, at the end of which they found an entrance, just such as before, where he dreamed that in a priory, they found a black monk, writing in a study. The Sybil said to him, 'This is Bede, the reverend doctor, in Wearmouth, who wrote the book *Of the Deeds of the English*,[5] from which you may gain much instruction for your purpose regarding the deeds of the Saxons, the second book of this chronicle. And he dreamed that they returned and climbed back on to the third rung of the ladder, where through a similar entrance, they found another white-haired black monk,

par ditz dez autours auoit touve, cest assauoir par Willam de Malmesbery, Henry de Huntyngdoun, Roger de Houdene, et Mariotus le Escot, entrepretours Englessez. Ils sez realerent com fust auys, et remounterent le quart bastoun du dist eschelle, ou au boute du dist bastoun trouerent meisme vn tiel entree, ou en vn vilette deuaunt vn fort chastel, trouerent vn chapelain escriuant sure vn lettroun. Douce amy, ceo disoit Sebille, cesti est le vikeir de Tilmouth, qe escript le Ystoria auria, de ditz de qy, tu poez auoir graunt enformacioun du quart liuer de ditz cronicles, cest du primer venu Willam le Conquerour ensa. Et beu sire, fesoit la veil Sebille, tu es ore mounte lez qatre bastouns de leschel, la droit voi as croniclis de cest isle, si bien lez voillez pursuyre. Mais le scinkisme bastoun ne poez mounter, qar il signify lez auenementz futurs, qe dez ascuns est ymagine dez aunciens ditz, com en la vie seint Edward est troue de ditz de vn saint hom, qe dist, Non solum de gente Francorum sed Scottorum, quos Anglici vilissimos reputant, etc. Et auxi par ditz du Bruyt en Engles, Þat Cadwaladre sal on Conan cal, etc., par ditz de Merlyn. Mais pusqe lez futures cheaunces ne sount pas en certain a determiner, [f. 2] fors soulement au sen deuyn, lessoms a lez deuyns lez chosis celestiens, lez hours et lez momentz, qe a cel pussaunce sount reseruez. Et si est, fesoit Sebille, le cordeler qe vous veistes suppuoillaunt leschel, Thomas de Otreburn vn Mestre de Deuinite, et del ordre de Frers Menours, qi dez cronicles de cest isle se entremist. Qe si tu pusses en cas ateindre toutes houres a les propretes de ditz bastouns du dist eschel, si cerchez lez cronicles du dist Thomas, qe bien te mousterount ta droit voy, et si bien pussez acomplir cest tretice; tu lez doys appeller, Scalacronica. Cesti qi cestz sougez auoit sounge; souenoit bien de toz lez propretez deuisez, par ensamplere de queux, comensa et pursuyst cest tretice, en lan de grace .Mile.CCC.l. et synk. Et en le noun du pier, et fitz, et saint espirit comensa lestoir de cest cronicle au comencement du siecle, a nostre primer pier Adam, et al ligne de ly, tanqe al temps Enneas, le proail Brutus, le primer roy, qe cest isle poepla, la gest de qi, et de lez successours, il voet rementoyuer, del hour qe la genealogy veigne a ly.

writing in a cloister. 'My friend', said the Sybil, 'this is the monk of Chester who wrote the *Polychronicon*,[6] from which you should draw much guidance for the third book of these chronicles; namely, concerning the union of the seven Saxon realms brought about by King Ecgberht, through the sayings of the authors he had found, namely, through William de Malmesbury, Henry de Huntingdon, Roger de Howden and Marianus Scotus, English translators'. And he dreamed that they returned and climbed back on to the fourth rung of the ladder, where at the end of the rung they again found a similar entrance, where in a village before a strong castle, they found a chaplain writing at a lectern. 'Dear friend', said the Sybil, 'this is the vicar of Tillmouth, who wrote the *Historia aurea*,[7] from whose sayings, you'll be able to gain much information for the fourth book of these chronicles; that is, from the first arrival of William the Conqueror here. And dear Sir', said the old Sybil, 'you have now climbed the four rungs of the ladder, the right way to the chronicles of this isle, if you wish to study them well. But the fifth rung you may not climb, for it signifies future events, which have been imagined by some from ancient sayings – as in the *Life of Saint Edward* [where] the sayings of a holy man are found, who said, "Not only the nation of the French but also that of the Scots, whom the English regarded as utterly vile", etc.;[8] and also from the sayings of the *Brut* in English, "That Cadwallader shall on Conan call", etc., from the sayings of Merlin.[9] But since future fortunes are not determined for certain, [f. 2] save only in the divine sense, we should leave celestial matters to the divines, and the hours and the moments to that power to which they are reserved. And', said the Sybil, 'the grey friar whom you saw supporting the ladder, he is Thomas de Otterburn, a Master of Divinity of the order of Friars Minor, who concerned himself with the chronicles of this isle.[10] And if, on occasion, you are able to devote much time to the details of the rungs of this ladder, if you examine the chronicles of this Thomas, which will show you well your right way, then you will be well able to finish this chronicle; you should call it "Scalacronica".' And he who had dreamed these dreams remembered well all the details [here] explained, by which example, he started and pursued this treatise in the year of grace 1355. And in the name of the Father, the Son and the Holy Ghost, he started this chronicle's history from the beginning of the world, from our first father Adam, and all of his line, as far as the time of Aeneas, the ultimate ancestor of Brutus, the first king, who populated this isle,[11] whose deeds, and those of his successors, he wished to remember, from the time which the genealogy reached him.

Rede fro the hande forthe a notabyll cronykyll[a]

[f. 188] lencoronement edward ... apres la conquest[b]
32. En lan de grace .Mile.CC.lxxiiij. Edward fitz Henry od sa femme
Elianor furount coronez *[f. 188v.]* et enoyntez a Westmouster de frere
Robert de Kilwardby, Erceuesqe de Cantobirs, al Assumpcioun de
nostre Dame. La graunt Rue de Chep et lez autres par ou cesti
Edward cheuaucha deuers soun encoronement furont couertz dez
tapitez et des draps de say. Lez citezeins ietterent lore et largent hors
dez fenestres a prendre qi en uoroit. Le conduyt en Chepe corust del
vn couste de vine blonk, et del autre part de vine vermaille. Le Roy
Alexander Descoce et le Duke de Bretaigne, qestoit le primer duk
apres lez countis qe y estoint, et touz dieus lour femmes, lez sores le
dit Edward, y furount, et la royne la mere. Lez queux seignours, od
tout plain dez autres countis Dengleter, furount apparez en
aparementz dore et soy, od grauntz routes dez cheualers, qy a lour
descendre, lesserent aler lour cheueaux, a prendre qy en uoroit, en
noblesce del encoronement de cesti Edward, qi al hour estoit de
.xxxvi. aunz de age. Alexander le Roy Descoce ly fist al hour homage,
se trey deuers soun pays, ou prochiegnement Margaret sa femme, la
sore Edward, morust, qauoit dieus fitz, Edward et Dauid, et vn feille
Margaret qe puis fust Royne de Norway. Lez .ij. fitz morerent de age
de .xx. aunz, viuant lour pier. Procheignement en lan suaunt cest
encoronement, Lewlin Prince de Galis enuoya outre mere pur la feile
le Count de Mounforth dauoir a femme, qe en uenaunt deuer
Snawdoun fust pris, en mere, dez mariners des Bristow, et amenez au
Roy Edward, qauoit suspessoun pur cest alliaunce de mariage, qe
Lewlin ne ly estoit bien voillaunt, et auxi pur ceo, qil ne enuenit a lour
encoronement,[c] si ly fust somoundre pur homage, qi enout despit,
moua guere. Le roy se trey en Galis, conquist le chastel Rodolan,
enchasa le dit Lewlin par force a sa grace, qi se acorda au roi pur
.l.Mile. marcz, et condicioun destre liege du roy. Sy enamena lauaunt
dit damoysel. Lan suaunt le roy ly fist somoundre par bref a soun
parlement, qi suresist, et derechef mouoit guere, mais nauoit dure,
mais autrefoitz fust acorde au roy, seur condicioun, qil ne enferroit

---

[a]   At bottom of f. 187v., in neat 15thc. hand [possibly Hand A, though much larger than
     other annotations]. A marginal hand points to the section of the text dealing with the
     death of saint Robert Grostest, f. 187v. This appears to be the first such drawing (bar
     that on f. 182v., which appears to be a 16thc. addition).
[b]   Right margin, in small, neat contemporary hand (faded).
[c]   MS: encorement.

32. In the year of grace 1274, Edward fitz Henry and his wife Eleanor were crowned [*f. 188v.*] and anointed at Westminster by brother Robert de Kilwardby, archbishop of Canterbury, on the Assumption of Our Lady [15 August].[1] The great Chepe Street and the other [streets] which Edward rode through on the way to his coronation were covered with tapestries and cloths of say. The citizens threw gold and silver out of the windows, for whoever wished to take it. The conduit on Chepe flowed with white wine on one side, and red on the other. Alexander, King of Scots, and the Duke of Brittany (the premier duke after the earls who were there), and both of their wives, Edward's sisters, were there, and the Queen-mother. These lords, with all of the other earls of England, were dressed in clothes of gold and silk, with great bands of knights; and when they dismounted, they left their horses to wander off for whoever wished to take them, from the splendour of Edward's coronation. Edward was thirty-six years of age at the time.[2] Alexander, King of Scots, did him homage at this time, and then took himself to his own country, where shortly afterwards, his wife Margaret died, who was Edward's sister. She had had two sons, [Alexander] and David, and a daughter Margaret, who was later the Queen of Norway. The two sons died at the age of twenty, while their father still lived.[3] Soon after, in the year following the coronation, Llewelyn, Prince of Wales, sent across the sea for the daughter of the Earl of Montfort,[4] to have as a wife. While coming to Snowdon, she was taken at sea by sailors from Bristol, and brought to King Edward, who suspected from this marriage alliance that Llewelyn was not well-disposed to him, and also because he had not come to his coronation, though he was summoned to make homage; outraged by this, Llewelyn made war. The king came to Wales, captured Rhuddlan castle and compelled Llewelyn by force to put himself on his mercy, binding himself to the king for 50,000 marks, and on condition of being the king's liege. And so the said young lady was brought back. The following year, the king had him summoned by writ to his parliament. He rebelled, and made war once again; but he did not persevere, and was reconciled to the king a second time, on condition that he made no offence from that time on, at his due peril.[5] David, the brother of Llewelyn, Prince of Wales, was of the king's household, and the king had given him Frodsham in heredity.[6] This David was wily, spying on the king's council; biding

del hour en auaunt nul contempt sure le peril qe apartenoit. Dauid le freir Lewlyn Prince de Galis, estoit du meynee le roy, a qi il auoit don Frodisham heritablement, qi Dauid estoit enginous, espiaunt le counsail le roy; gayta soun temps, sen alast ly Galoys, qi vnqor od soun frer recomencerent guere. Le roy se moua en graunt ost deuers Galis, qi dez barges enfist *[f. 189]* faire pounte outre vn bras de mere deuer Snaudoun, pur ceo qe lez estroitz du boys et mountaignes estoint mauues autre part a passer, lez queux lez Galoys auoint purpris. Lez gens le Roy pristrent la dit passage folement, deuaunt qe tout le array du passage fust adresse, qe furount recoillez des Galoys, qe del autre part estoient enbussez en batail, ou noyerent Roger de Clifford, Willam de Lindezey, Johan le fitz Robert, Lucas de Towny, et plusours autres pererent au presser de lour recoiller. La mere retreit Johan de Vescy, qi nouelement estoit uenuz de outre mere, passa outre en Snaudoun od Baskles et brigauns de Arragoun qil auoit amene qi le pays destruierent despitousement. Dauid le freir Lewlin se mist au fuyt, pur quoi le prince soun freir se taunt affraya, qil se mist a descoumfiture sen ala od poi de gentz, qi sodeinement encountra Johan Giffard, et Edmound de Mortimer od lour coumpaignyes, qi hors del ost le roy estoient mouez pur auenture quere, qi ly tuerent et les soenes, et sa test presentes a le roy, qe sure la Toure de Loundres fust mys.

En meisme le temps fust freir Johan de Pecchame par le pape sacre en Erceuescue de Cantobirs. Et Roger de Mortimer teint la Roundtable, se centisme dez chiualers a Kenlynworth. A quel reuel darmes de peise, vindrent lez cheualers errauntz de plusours estraunges pays. Meisme le temps comensa la roigne dez berbiz en Engleter, com cheualers venantz hors de la Terre Saint, amenoient berbiz oue gros cowes hors de Cipre, qenporterent primerment la dit roingn. Meisme le temps fust chaunge la monoy, qe furrount appellez pollardes. Procheinement apres fust Dauid le frere Lewlin pris, pres de Denbigh, et par iugement le roy penduz et treynez, ses quarters departez en diuers lieus. Le roy dona lez seignouryes de Galis as diuers seignurs Dengleter en condicioun qils demurassent, qi ceo furent, si demena iolife vie, et molt amast deduyt dez chenys et oyseaux, et coure et saultz dez cheueaux, et principalment a tuer cerfs au coure cheueaux.

En lan de grace .Mile.CC.lxxxiiij. Edward soun fitz nasqy en le chastel de Carnaueran en Galis, et meisme lan morust soun autre fitz Alfouns Wyndesor qi eynez fitz estoit du roy, e Mary sa feile deueint nonayne a Aumisbery. Le Roy Alexander Descoce prist la feile le

his time, he went back to the Welsh, who had already restarted the war under his brother.[7] The king moved a great army towards Wales, and had a bridge [f. 189] of barges made over an arm of the sea toward Snowdon, because the passes through the woods and mountains were difficult to cross by any other way, as the Welsh had seized them. The king's men rashly took this crossing, before the crossing was fully made ready, and they were thrown back by the Welsh, who were in ambush in battle formation on the other side. Roger de Clifford, William de Lindsey, John fitz Robert and Lucas de Tony drowned, and many others died in the crush of their retreat.[8] At low tide, John de Vesci, who had recently come from overseas, passed across to Snowdon with Basques and brigands of Aragon who he had brought with him, who ravaged the country pitilessly. David, the brother of Llewelyn, took to flight, and because of this, his brother the Prince was so dismayed that he left the [scene of] the defeat, setting off with just a few men. He unexpectedly encountered John Giffard and Edmund de Mortimer with their companies, who had moved away from the army of the king in search of adventure, and he was killed along with his men. His head was presented to the king, and was stuck on the Tower of London.[9]

At this time, brother John de Pecham was consecrated archbishop of Canterbury by the Pope.[10] Roger de Mortimer held a Round Table for a hundred knights at Kenilworth, and knights errant came from many foreign countries to this festival of arms of peace.[11] At the same time, sheep mange arrived in England, as knights returning from the Holy Land brought back long-tailed sheep from Cyprus, which brought in the mange for the frst time. And at this time, there was a change of currency, [the coins] being called 'pollards'. Soon after, David, the brother of Llewelyn, was captured near Denbigh and hanged and drawn by judgement of the king, and his quarters were distributed to various places.[12] The king gave the lordships of Wales to various English lords on condition that they resided on them, which they did, leading the high life, taking great pleasure in hounds and hawks, and coursing and horse-jumping, and most of all in killing stags, hunting them on horseback.

In the year of grace 1284, Edward, the king's son, was born at Caernarvon castle in Wales, and in the same year, his other son, Alphonse (the king's eldest son), died at Windsor, and Mary, his daughter, became a nun at Amesbury. King Alexander of Scotland took for his wife the daughter of the count of Flanders, after the death of the king's sister, and he did not have any offspring by her.[13] King

count de Flaundres a femme, apres la mort la sore le roy, de qei il nauoit nul engendrure. I cesti Roi Edward fist exciler lez Juys hors de soun realme, pur quoy il enprist le .xvme dez lays, et le .xme ^d de la clergie. Le Roy passa en [f. 189v.] Gascoigne, pur peiser la guere entre le Roy de Arragoun, et le Prince del More, qi tout lour debat auoint mys en soun agarde. Le Count de Cornewail remist gardein Dengleter, tancom le roy estoit par dela. Ryse ap Meraduk vn seignour de Galys mouoit guere, pur outrage qe Payn Tiptoft ly auoit fait par orgoil et despite. Qi Rise ap Meraduk, ne le voloit soeffreir pur maundement le roy, pur qoi apres fust penduz et trainez a Euerwyk, del hour qe le roy estoit venir de outre mere. En quel temps de sa absence, il troua tiel defaute en sez justices et officeris, qe lez vns fist exiler com Thomas de Weland, Rauf de Engham et Hughe del Chauncelery; Adam de Straitoun enraunsonez; lez droiturelis demurez en lour officez, com Elys de Ethingham, et Johan de Methingham.

En quel hour fust Acres perdu hors dez mains dez Cristiens. La Royn Elianor morust auxi cel ane. Le Roi Alexander Descoce venoit en vn nuyt cheuauchaunt deuers sa femme auauntdit, si chei de soun palefray pres de Kinkorne, et roumpy soun cole, a graunt encoumbreir de lez .ij. realmes; sez fitz furount mortz, et nauoit issu, fors la feile sa feile Margaret Royne de Norway. Les seignours Descoce, prelates, countis et barouns et la comune, virent mouement de graunt distaunce du chalange du realme, maunderent en Gascoyn a le Roy Edward Dengleter, qe il se vousist agreer qe soun fitz eynez Edward de Carnaueran preist a femme Margarete, la feile Margaret Royne de Norway, feile le dit Alexander, qi roumpy le cole, pur peise auoir, a quoi furount acordez lez counsaillis dez .ij. realmes en tiel gise, qe le dit Edward de Carnaueran demureroit en Escose viuaunt soun pier, et apres sa mort, qil demureroit touz iours vn ane en lun realme, et lautre ane en lautre realme; et qil leroit toutdiz sez officers et minsters del vn realme, al entree des marchis del autre realme, issint qe soun counsail enfust totdice du nacioun du realme, en quoi il demurroit pur le temps. Quel ascent au venu le roi a lostel acordez fust, et enuoiez au court de Rome pur dispensacioun. Et messagers en Norway, pur quere la dit Margaret. Qi messager fust vn clerk Descoce, Meistre Weland, qi peryst od la dit pucel en reuenaunt deuers Escoce sure lez costres de Boghane.

---

^d 'me' *added by contemporary hand, in both cases.*

Edward had the Jews exiled from his realm, on account of which he requested a fifteenth from the laity and a tenth from the clergy.[14] The king crossed to [*f. 189v.*] Gascony, to settle the war between the King of Aragon and the Prince of Morea, who had put their whole dispute to his judgement.[15] The Earl of Cornwall served as keeper of England while the king was overseas. Rhys ap Maredudd, a Welsh lord, made war, due to an insult which Payn Tiptoft had made to him out of contempt and arrogance; Rhys was unwilling to tolerate this, even at the command of the king. Therefore, he was afterwards hanged and drawn at York, at the time when the king came from over the sea. In the time of his absence, he discovered there had been such default in his justices and officials that he had some of them exiled, such as Thomas de Weyland, Ralph de Hengham and Hugh of the Chancery; Adam Stratton was fined; the conscientious ones remained in office, such as Ellis de Beckingham and John de Mettingham.[16]

At this time, Acre was lost from the hands of the Christians; also in this year, Queen Eleanor died.[17] King Alexander of Scotland came riding in the night to his wife, fell from his horse near Kinghorn and broke his neck, to the great disturbance of the two realms; his sons were dead and he had no issue, save for the daughter of his daughter, Queen Margaret of Norway.[18] The lords of Scotland, the prelates, the earls and the barons, and the community, sensing the beginnings of an eventual contest for the realm, sent word to Gascony to King Edward of England, if he would be willing to agree that his eldest son, Edward of Caernarvon, should take as his wife Margaret (the daughter of Margaret, queen of Norway, the daughter of Alexander who had broken his neck), so as to have peace. The councils of both realms agreed to this in this form, that Edward of Caernarvon should remain in Scotland while his father lived, and that after his death, he should always remain for one year in one realm, and another year in the other; and that he should always leave his officers and ministers of the one realm at the beginning of the Marches of the other, so that his council should always be of the nation of the realm in which he was staying at the time. This agreement was approved when the king came to his house, and was submitted to the court of Rome for dispensation; and envoys were sent to Norway to fetch Margaret. One of these was a Scottish clerk, Master Weland, who perished with the girl on the shores of Buchan, whilst returning to Scotland.[19]

En cest*e* mene temps, Edward Roy Dengleter qi saunz femme estoit, nauoit fitz fors vn; oyst parler de Blaunche la feile le Roi Phelip de Fraunce, si la demaunda a femme, qe fust acorde, qe le Roy Dengleter fefferoit le Roi de Fraunce de Gascoyn, de ly refeffer od sa feile en mariage, qi ceo fist. Et si ne voloit le dit Roy de Fraunce refeifer le dit Roy Engles de [*f. 190]* sa terre de Gascoyne, mais la reteint a soun ops demeyne, ne auxi ne ly noloit doner sa auaunt dit feile, mais feigna somouns sure le Roy de Engleter a uenire a soun parlement pur forfaitz qe lez Fiportz auoint fait sur mere as Normauntz, coumpassaunt encontre couenauntz a foriuger ly dit Edward de sa terre de Gascoun, per processe en sa court. Sure quoy le dit Edward se adressa de graunt aray deuers Gascoin, susrendy soun homage de Gascoigne au Roy de Fraunce, par Willam de Gaynesburgh Cordeler et Hugh de Mancestre Jacobyn, lez queux freirs, le Count de Artoys fist longement enprisoner, qi lez fist prendre, com venoint passauntz par soun pays en lour message. Le Roy Edward se adressa od graunt poair deuers Gascoyn, et fust venus a Portismouth sure soun passage qaunt nouelis ly vindrent qe Maddok et Morgan auoint leuez lez communes de Galys de guere encountre ly, qy li quiderent en le hour estre passe la mere, pur quoi le Roy lessa soun veage pur le temps, et se trey en Galis, mais aunces auoit enuoye en Gascoyne plusours barouns de sa terre, qi a lour arryuail ne auoint en Gascoyne taunt de terre, al obeisaunce le Roy lour seignour sure quoy ils purroint arriuer. Mais procheignement ceaux de Burdeux sez releuerent et enherderent oue eaux, enchacerent lez Fraunceys, qi depar le Roy Lowys de Fraunce enfuront mys. Les Engles recouereront hu pays, graunt terre al ops le roy, pur quoi toutdiz apres com fust dit, y cesty Roy Edward enclina du chief, a touz lez chiualers qen cel veage de Gascoyn estoint. Les auauntditz barouns Englesses sez coumbaterent od Charlis de Valoys oue le poair de Fraunce a Belgard, ou plusours dez Engles furount mortz et prisez, mais noun pas outriement descoumfitz, qi tout le iour tindrent les chaumps, mais dedenz la nuyt sez departerent a lour rescet, ou lez Fraunceis demurerent en la place as chaumpes tout la nuyte, pur qoi ils disoint qils auoient venqu, et pur voir dire, lez Engles auoint le greignour perde, qar la furount pris monsire Johan de Saint Johan, le pier et le fitz, monsire Rauf de Touny, et plusours autres, qi pur destresce de vilein despitouse prisoun, ne auindrent les plusours a bien. En cest mene temps le Roy auoit destruyt et

---

At this time, Edward, King of England, who was without a wife, had but one son. Hearing talk of Blanche, the daughter of King Philip of France, he asked for her for his wife.[20] It was agreed that the King of England should enfeoff the King of France with Gascony, who was to re-enfeoff him with his daughter in marriage, which was done. But the King of France was unwilling to re-enfeoff the English king with [f. 190] his land of Gascony, but retained it for his own use. Not only this, but nor did he wish to give away his daughter, but invented a summons to the king to come to his *parlement* for the misdeeds which the Cinque Ports had committed on the sea against the Normans, planning, against their agreement, to deprive Edward of his land of Gascony, by legal process in his court. Because of this, Edward assembled a great array against Gascony and renounced his homage to the King of France for Gascony, by William de Gainsborough, a Franciscan, and Hugh de Manchester, a Dominican. The Count of Artois imprisoned these friars for a long time, having taken them when they came passing through his region on their mission.[21] King Edward was going to Gascony with a great force, and had come to Portsmouth for his passage, when news came to him that Madog and Morgan had raised the commoners of Wales against him, supposing that he had crossed the sea at that time.[22] Because of this, the king abandoned his expedition for the time being, and went to Wales; but he had already sent many barons from his land to Gascony. At their arrival there, they did not have enough land in the obedience of the king, their lord, on which they could disembark. But soon, the men of Bordeaux rose up and joined with them, throwing out the French who had been sent on behalf of King Lewis of France. The English recovered the country, and much land for the king's use. Because of this, it was said that ever after, King Edward looked kindly on all those knights who were on this expedition to Gascony. The English barons fought against Charles de Valois with the might of France at Bellegarde, where many of the English were killed or captured, but they were not defeated outright. They held the field all day, but during the night they retreated to their base, while the French remained in place on the field all night, on account of which they claimed they had the victory. And to tell the truth, the English had the greater loss, for Sir John de St John, the father and the son, and Sir Ralph de Tony were captured there, and many others; and because of the privation of a base, shameful prison, the majority of them never recovered their health.[23] At the same time, the king had defeated and vanquished the Welsh rebels, and had taken Madog and Morgan,

descoumfist les Galoys rebellis, et auoit fait prendre Maddoke et
Morgan, et lez fist pendre et treyner; et se adressa a rescoure sez gentz
en Gascoyne, y enuoya soun frere Edmound, qi illoeqes morust de
bele mort, se passa meismes en Flaundres en eide du Count Robert,
qy guere *[f. 190v.]* auoit as Fraunceis. Le dit Roi Edward enuoya
meistre Johan de Glantoun, archedeken de Richemound, al Apostoil
pur pleindre de la deloialte du Roy de Fraunce, et de coumpassement
de ly toller soun heritage. Il fist par autres messagers alliaunce od le
Roi de Allemayn, et oue le Roy de Arragoun oue Lerceuesqe de
Coloyne, et od le Count de Burgoyn, od le Count de Sawoy, et od
plusours Princes de Allemayne, qi touz ly faillerent au bosoyn, mais
com cely qi ceo aparceiuoit, se peisa od le Roy de Fraunce hu mene
temps, qi ly bailla sa sore Margaret a femme, pur la iuuenesce sa feile
Blaunche, et susrendy graunt party de Gascoyn en peise fesaunt.
Taunt com le Roy Edward ieust a Gaunt, lez comunes de la vile
comencerent riot et debate as genz le roy. Lez Galoys qy y estoient
noerent outre Leschaud robberent mesouns, enfirent graunt mal. Le
Roy Edward enuoya quer le Count Robert de Flaundres, qi ly dist,
Sire Count peisez ta comune, ou ieo ferray estre dit, qe cy fust Gaunt,
pur quoy la riote fust estaunche. Endementres qe le Roy Edward
estoit a Gaunt, vindrent messagers honourables depar lez comunes
Descoce, dez prelates, countis et barouns certifiauntz qe Margaret la
feile la Royne de Norway qe feile estoit lour Roys Alexander, estoit
pery en mere envenant deuers Escoce, enpriaunt a sa seignoury, qil se
vousist entremettre pur quiete du pays, a veoir, qils vssent a roy, qi
meutz par droit le dust estre, qar ils sez doutoint de graunt debate de
diuers seignours qi enclaymerent la successioun qi pussauntz estoint
du realme, et autre part, et auxi pur diuers riotis comencez hu pays,
qar chescun grauntz siris se fist com roys en soun pays. Le roy lour
respoundy par sez lettres, qil vendroit en soun realme, et treieroit
vers la Marche et se auiseroit de lour request.

Lez cronicles de brenez [?][a]
33. Et fait asauoir qe solonc lez cronicles Descoce, nestoit vnqes tiel
difficoulte qi enserroit lour roys de droit lingue, qe outriement estoit
failly en le hour de troys roys succiement, chescun fitz dautre. Et pur
ceo voet cest cronicle toucher la originaute dez roys, et la processe de
eaux qen Escoz ount regne.

[a]   *Right margin.*

whom he had hanged and drawn.[24] He set about to rescue his men in Gascony, sending his brother Edmund, who died a good death there. He himself crossed to Flanders in aid of Count [Guy],[25] who was at war *[f. 190v.]* with the French. King Edward sent Master John de Glantoun, archdeacon of Richmond,[26] to the Pope to complain of the disloyalty of the King of France, and of his scheming to seize his inheritance. Through other envoys, he made an alliance with the King of Germany, and with the King of Aragon, with the archbishop of Cologne, and the count of Burgundy, the count of Savoy, and with many German princes – who all failed him when it came to the time of need. And so seeing them for what they were, he made peace with the King of France in the mean time, who gave him his sister Margaret as a wife (because of the youth of his daughter Blanche), and surrendered a great part of Gascony to secure the peace. While King Edward was staying at Ghent, the commoners of the town started a riot and a confrontation with the king's men. The Welsh who were there swam across the Scheldt, plundering houses and doing great harm. King Edward sought out [Guy], Count of Flanders, to whom he said, 'Sir Count, pacify your people, or I shall ensure that it is said that "Ghent *was* here" ', because of which the riot was quashed. While King Edward was in Ghent, honourable envoys came from the commoners of Scotland, the prelates and the earls and barons, informing him that Margaret the daughter of the Queen of Norway, who was the daughter of their king, Alexander, had died at sea on the way to Scotland.[27] They implored him by his lordship, for the peace of the country, that he be willing to intervene to work out who, of those who wished to be king, had the better right, because they feared great strife between the various powerful lords, from the kingdom and from other parts, who claimed the succession; and also because of various disturbances starting up in the regions, because each of the great lords had set himself up as a king in his own region. The king replied to them by letter that he would go back to his kingdom, travel to the Marches, and consider their request.

The chronicles of Brenez
33. And it should be known that according to the chronicles of Scotland, there was never anything so difficult as fixing the right lineage of their kings, which failed entirely in the time of three kings in succession, each the son of the other. And on that account, it would be desirable for this chronicle to touch on the origins and the succession of the kings who have reigned in Scotland.

En la *Vie Saint Brandane* est troue qen le pays de Attenys en Grece estoit vn noble cheualer, qi out vn fitz qy auoit a noun Gaidel, qauoit en espouse la feile Pharao le Roy de Egypt, qe out a noune Scota, de qei il auoit bele engendrure. Gaidel estoit cheualerous; se purchasa lez juuenceaux de soun pays *[f. 191]* se mist en mere en nefe, od sa femme Scota et sez enfauntz, se quist mansioun al auenture, en biaunce de le conquer, arryua en Espayne, ou sure vn haut mountain au couster de la mere Hiberynie, fist edifier vn fort chastel, et le noma Brigans. Il viuoit od lez soens de rauyn sure lez paisens du pays. Sez pescheours furount chacez vn iour par tempest parfound en la mere, qy ly reuindrent renouncier qils auoint aparsceu par uoler dez flores dez chardouns et autres enseignes, qe il y out terre pres de outre mere. Gaidel od sez fitz, qi a surnoun auoient Scoti, apres lour mere Scota, se mist en mere en trois naueaux, seglerent aual la mere trouerent vn isle graunt, mounterent a terre, trouerent le pays herbous et plesaunt de boys et reueres, mais noun pas bien poeple dez gentz; et com est ymagine et suppose, procheignement deuaunt auoit Gurguynz, le fitz Belin Roy de Bretaigne, assigne cel ile as gentz extretiz Despayne, queux il troua en Orkany com venoit de Denemarc, com auaunt est especifie. Gaidel repaira a soun chastel de Brigauns, ymaginaunt de realer al ile troue; mais ly surueint vn tresgref malady dount ly coueint murrir, si deuisoit a sez fitz qils alasent a cel ile, et y demurasent com a vn pays saunz graunt defens, leger a conquere. Eberus, le eyne fitz Gaidel et de Scota la feile Pharao, se adressa od sez freirs al auaunt dit ile, qi le seisy, et tuerent et soutzmistrent a lour obeisaunce ceaux qe ils y trouerent; et pius appellerent le ile Iberniam, apres lour freir eyne Eberus, ou apres la mere Eberiaco, qe nomez estoit ensi dez Espaynolis; mais le surenoun Scoty demura od lez autres friers, et od lour issu, bon pece en cel ile, qe entre nous est apelle Irrelande. En quel ile apres, arryua Symound Bret, le fitz pusne du Roy de Espayne, qi od ly aporta vn pere, sur quoi lez Roys Despayne soleient estre coronez, qi soun pier ly bailla en signifiaunce qil enfust roys, com cely qil plus amast de sez enfauntz. Cesty Symound deueint roy du pays de Ireland, depar vn feile extret de Scoty, qi enmyst le auaunt dit pere en le plus souerain bele lieu du pays, qe au iour de huy port le noune, li Lieu Real. Apres qoi, veint vn dez fitz de vn dez Roys de Irreland extreit de Scota, qy out a noun Fergus fitz Ferthairy, en le plus lointisme pays outre Bretaine deuer septentrioun, et de cost lez Bretouns, occupia la terre deuer Cateneys outre la laund Porry, et y endemurrerent. Et tout estoit il du nacioun de Ireland, et lez soens touz *[f. 191v.]* vnquor lez

In the *Life of St Brendan*, it is found that there was a noble knight in the country of Athens in Greece, who had a son named Gaidel, who took to wife the daughter of Pharoah, the King of Eygpt, named Scota, by whom he had fair offspring. Gaidel was chivalrous, and having sought out the young men of his region, [f. 191] he set out to sea in a ship, with his wife Scota and their children, and sought a home by chance, in the hope of conquering it. He landed in Spain, where on a high mountain on the coast of the Hibernian sea, he had a strong castle built, and named it Brigantia. He and his men lived by ravaging the peasants of the region. One day, his fishermen were swept far out to sea by a tempest; they came back to tell him that they had realised, from flying teasel-flowers and other signs, that there was land nearby across the sea. With his sons, who had the surname Scoti, after their mother Scota, Gaidel set out to sea in three ships, sailed down the sea and found a big island. They alighted on land, and found the country verdant and pleasant with woods and rivers, but not well peopled with men; and as it is presumed and supposed, [this was] shortly before Gurguynz the son of Belin, King of Britain, had assigned this island to men drawn out from Spain, who he had found in Orkney as he came from Denmark, as was related earlier.[1] Gaidel returned to his castle of Brigantia, planning to go back to the island he had found; but he was afflicted by a very serious illness of which he was bound to die, so he arranged with his sons that they should go to that island, and remain there, as [it was] a country without great defences, easily conquered. Eberus, the eldest son of Gaidel and Scota, the Pharoah's daughter, made his way with his brothers to this island, and seized it, and they killed or subjected to their obedience all those they found there. Thereafter, they called the island Hibernia, after their eldest brother Eberus, or after the Hiberic sea, which was so named by the Spaniards; but the surname Scoti remained with the other brothers and their offspring for a good while in that isle, which is called Ireland by us. Afterwards, Simon Bret, the youngest son of the King of Spain, landed on this island. He brought with him a stone, on which the kings of Spain were accustomed to be crowned, which his father had handed over to him to signify that he had been made king, as the most beloved of his children. This Simon became king of the country of Ireland, through a daughter descended from the Scoti; he put the aforesaid stone in the most sovereign and fair place of the country, which nowdays bears the name, 'the Royal Place'.[2] After this, one of the sons of one of the kings of Ireland descended from Scota, who was named Fergus son of Ferchar, went

firent nomer Scoty, et la terre Scocia apres Scota la feile Pharao Roy de
Eygpt, de qei enuindrent lez Scotois; mais lour propre[b] pays est
Ireland, lour coustom et patoys acordaunt, qi puis furount mellez od
Pices, com apres serra recordez. I cesti Fergus aporta hors de Ireland
la pere real auaunt nomez, et la fist mettre ou ore est Labbai de Scone,
sure quoy furount faitez, assise et establis les Roys Descoce touz
puscedy, tanqe Edward le primer Roy Dengleter apres la Conquest,
lenfist aporter a Loundres a Westmouster, ou ore le sege du prestre a
le haute auter.

... *Rois Escotoys*[a]

[b] **34.** Et fait asauoir <qe>[c] Fergus fitz Ferthair de Ireland, extrait de
Scota, estoit le primer qy se disoit Roy Descoce. Si regna .iij. aunz
outre Dunbretaine en Ynchegalle. Dungal fitz Fergus regna .v. aunz;
Congal fitz Dungal, .xxij. aunz; Constan fiz Doengard, xxij. aunz;
Edhan fitz Godfray, .xxxiiij. aunz; Conel fitz Congelle, .xiiij. aunz;
Eokebrid, .xvi. aunz; Kynather fitz Conel, .iii. moys, Ferthaire fit
Ewyne, .xvi. aunz; Fercarfod, .xxi. aunz; Dopnaldebrec Eokebrid .xiiij.
aunz; Maldun fitz Dopnaldebrech, .xvi. aunz; Eorhetinen Danel fitz
Donengard, fitz Donald Bret, .iiij. aunz; Armelech fitz Findan, .i. ane;
Congan fitz Findan, .xvi. auns; Moredath fitz Armkelec, .iiij. ans., en le
temps de qy, estoit le primer batail entre lez Bretouns et les Pices qi
eiderent les Escosez; Selnach fitz Cogan, .xxiiij. aunz; Ergheche fitz
Achfin, .xxx. aunz; Donald fitz Sealnech, .vii. aunz; Alpyn fitz
Beghach, .iiij. aunz. Cesty fust tue en Goloway, com il le auoit
destruyt, de vn soul hom qi ly gayta en vn espesse boys enpendaunt
al entree dun ge de vn ryuere, com cheuaucheoit entre sez gentz. Cely
estoit le darain de Escotoys qi al hour regna, procheynement deuaunt
lez Pices. La sum dez aunz du regne dez Escotois auaunt lez Pices,
.ccc. et .v. aunz et iij. moys. Lez cronicles tesmoignent qe lez Pices
vindrent de Syke, et entrerent Albanye, qor est Escoce,

---

[b]   MS: prpre.

---

[a]   *Left margin.*
[b]   *Marginal hand, pointing to* Et fait asauoir.
[c]   *Supplied; the MS is indecipherable at this point.*

to the most remote country beyond Britain to the north, and beside the Britons, occupied the land towards Caithness beyond the land of Porry,[3] and settled there. And he was wholly of the Irish nation, and all his men [f. 191v.] were still named Scoti, and the land Scotia, after Scota the daughter of Pharoah, King of Eygpt, and from them came the Scots; but their true country is Ireland, with the according customs and speech. Subsequently, they were merged with the Picts, as will be related later. Fergus brought the afore-named royal stone there from Ireland, and had it put where Scone Abbey is now; on this stone, the kings of Scotland were made, seated and inaugurated ever afterwards, until Edward the first after the Conquest, King of England, had it brought to London to Westminster, where it is now the priest's seat at the high altar.

... Scottish Kings

34. And it should be known that Fergus son of Ferthair of Ireland, descended from Scota, was the first who called himself King of Scotland. He reigned for three years, beyond Dumbarton in Inchgall. Dungal son of Fergus reigned five years; Congal son of Dungal, twenty-two years; Constan son of Doengard, twenty-two years; Edhan son of Godfray, thirty-four years; Conel son of Congelle, fourteen years; Eokebrid, sixteen years; Kynather son of Conel, three months; Ferthaire son of Ewyne, sixteen years; Fercarfod, twenty-one years; Dopnaldebrec Eokebrid, fourteen years; Maldun son of Dopnaldebrech; sixteen years; Eorhetinen Danel son of Donengard, son of Donald Bret, three years; Armelech son of Findan, one year; Congan son of Findan, sixteen years; Moredath son of Armkelec, three years; in his time, there was the first battle between the Britons and the Picts, who supported the Scots; Selnach son of Cogan, twenty-four years; Ergheche son of Aclifin, thirty years; Donald son of Sealnech, seven years; Alpin son of Beghach, three years; he was killed in Galloway, when he was ravaging it, by a single man who lay in wait for him in a thick wood, overhanging the approach to a ford in a river, as he rode among his men. He was the last of the Scots who ruled at that time, just before the Picts. The sum of the years of the reign of the Scots, before the Picts, is 305 years and three months. The chronicles testify that the Picts came from Sycthia, and entered Albany, that is now Scotland, straightaway after the death of Alpin. And they came into Britain, that is now England, in the time of Vespasian the Roman, and in the time of Maurius, son of Arviragus, King of Britain. The Picts were a martial nation, bred for war and ever

procheinement apres la mort cesti Alpin. Et entrerent Bretaigne, qor est Engleter, en le temps Vaspasian le Romayn, et en le temps Maurius fitz Aruiragoun Roy de Bretaigne. Si estoint lez Pices vn nacioun baillous, norriz et charniz troutditz en gere, qi sez acompaignerent oue Roderik, al auenture pur terre conquere. Qi Rodrik fust tue de Maurius le Roy de Bretain en batail, pres de Cardoill. Plusours de sez Pices fuerent au boys, reenuoyerent au [f. 192] Roy Maurius requeraunt sa merci, qi lour graunta sa peise, lez assigna pur lour homage vn pays outre Albany, qe de gentz Irroys estoit en parti comense a habiter, qi Escocez sez appellerent. Lez queux Pices qi coumbatauntz estoient, surmounterent lez Escocez Irroys, lez tindrent en subieccioun.[d] Lez queux Pices ne auoint my moillers, et par cause qe lez Bretouns ne voloint my marier od eaux, sez qistrent femmes hors de Ireland, sure condicioun qe lour issu parlascent Irrays, quel patois demurt a iour de huy, hu haute pays entre lez vns qest dit Escotoys.

... *Roys pices* ... *[as fine?]*[a]

35. Cruthene Kenek, deboner, fust le primer qi se fist nomer Roy du Monarc du regne dez Picis, qi regna .L. auns; Gede, .CL. aunz; Taren, .C. aunz; Dinortechest, .xx. aunz; Dugil, .xl. auns; Gamaldebold, .ix. aunz; Verpeiropnet, .xxx. aunz; Fiachna le blank, .xxx. aunz; Calnatuhel, .vi. aunz; Denornach Lecdales, .i. ane; Stradach Fingel, .ij. aunz; Garnard le riche, .L.x. aunz; Talarg le fitz Kecter, .xxv. aunz; Drust fitz Irb, .C. aunz, et ly conquist .C. batails; Talarg fitz Amil, ij. aunz; Nectane Celtaniech, .x. aunz; Drust Gortinoch, .xxx. aunz; Galan, .xv. aunz; Drust fitz Gigurnus, .L. aunz; Drust fitz Hidrofigus, .viij. aunz; autrefoitz le primer Drust, .iiij. auns; Garnarde fitz Gigurnus, .vi. ans; Kyburcan soun freir, .vi. auns; Talarg fitz Mendeleghe, .xi. ans; Drust fitz Menech, .i. ane; Talagach, .iiij. aunz; Drust fiz Methor, .xxx. aunz. Saint Columbe et Paladius conuerterent cesti a la foy Cristien. Et fait asauoir, qe cest nacioun nestoit vnqes conuerty fors vn foitz, qe tanqe en sa ount perseuere; et pur ceo ne vssent lours prestres point des paulers a lour aubes, ou lez prestres Engles ount dieus, pur ceo qe dieus foitz ount este conuerty. Garnald fitz Dompnach, .xxx. aunz. Cesti edifia leglis de Abirnithin .cc. aunz et .xxv. aunz, et .xi. moys, deuaunt qe leglis de Dulkedin fust edifie du

[d] MS: subiec-ieccioun.

[a] *Left margin. Rest illegible.*

bold in war, who banded together with Roderik, on the chance of conquering land. This Roderik was killed in battle by Maurius the King of Britain, near Carlisle. Many of his Picts fled to the woods, and they sent to [f. 192] King Maurius seeking his mercy; he granted them his peace, and assigned them a country beyond Albany, for their homage, which the Irishmen, who called themselves Scots, had partly started to inhabit. These Picts, who were fighters, overwhelmed the Scottish Irish, and held them in subjection. These Picts did not have any wifes, and because the Britons were not at all willing to marry with them, they sought women from Ireland, on the condition that their offspring should talk Irish. This tongue survives to this day in the highlands, amongst those who are called Scots.

... the kings of the Picts ... [to their end?]
35. Cruthene Kenek, the mild, was the first who called himself king of the monarchy of the realm of the Picts, who reigned for fifty years;[1] Gede, 150 years; Taren, 100 years;[2] Dinortechest, twenty years; Dugil, forty years; Gamaldebold, nine years; Verpeiropnet, thirty years; Fiachna the white, thirty years; Calnatuhel, six years; Denornach Lecdales, one year; Stradach Fingel, two years; Garnard the rich, sixty years; Talarg the son of Kecter, twenty-five years; Drust son of Irb, 100 years, and he won 100 battles; Talarg son of Amil, two years; Nectane Celtaniech, ten years; Drust Gortinoch, thirty years; Galan, fifteen years; Drust son of Gigurnus, fifty years; Drust son of Hidrofigus, eight years; the first Drust once again, four years; Garnarde son of Gigurnus, six years; Kyburcan his brother, six years; Talarg son of Mendeleghe, eleven years; Drust son of Menech, one year; Talagach, four years; Drust son of Methor, thirty years. Saints Columba and Palladius converted him to the Christian faith. And it should be known that this nation was converted no more than once, and they have persevered in [the faith] ever since; and because of this their priests do not wear any apparels on their albs, while the English priests have two, because of having been converted two times. Garnald son of Dompnach, thirty years. He built the church of Abernethy 225 years and eleven months before the church of Dunkeld was built by King Costentin, King of the Picts.[3] Kenech son of Sugthen, twenty-four years; Nectan son of Fode, eight years; Bride son of

Roy Costentin, Roy des Picis. Kenech fitz Sugthen, .xxiiij. aunz;
Nectan fitz Fode, .viij. aunz; Bride fitz Fathe, .v. aunz; Drust soun
freir, .vi. aunz; Drust fitz Hole, .xx. aunz. En soun temps fust Saint
Edmonane. Tharan fitz Amfodech, .iiij. aunz; Brude fitz Dergert,
.xxxi. ane. En quel temps ueint Saint Seruanus en Fiffe. Iactan frer
Brude, .xviij. aunz; Garnarde fitz Feradhegh, .xxiiij. aunz; Denegul
fitz Fergusagin, .xvi. aunz; Nectan fitz Fergaleg, .ix. moys; Fergus fitz
Frude, vn moys; Alpin fitz Eferadheche, .vi. moys, a vn foitz, qi fust
enchace, mais puis regna .xxx. aunz; Brude [f. 192v.] fitz Tenegus, .ij.
aunz; Alpin fitz Tenagus, .ij. auns; Drust fitz Telargbin, vn ane;
Talargan fitz Drustane, .iiij. aunz; Talargan fitz Tenagus, .v. aunz;
Costantin fitz Fergusa, .xl. aunz. Cesti fist edifier Dunkeldyn.
Hungus fitz Fergusa, .x. aunz. Cesty edifia Kelrimonech, ore saint
Andrew, quel temps venit saint Fegulus od sez disciple al eglis de
Saint Andrew. Duf Tolorg, .iiij. aunz; Egganus fitz Hungus, .iij. aunz;
Feradagus fitz Badoghe, .iij. ans; Brud fitz Feradhach, .i. moys;
Kenech fitz Feradhach, .i. ane; Brude fitz Fochel, .ij. auns; Drust fitz
Feradhach, .iij. ans. Cesti fust le darain Roy dez Picys, si fust tue a
Scone par treisoun. Qe com les cronicles tesmoignent, vn fitz dun roy
de Ireland, qi out a noune Redda, arryua en Galeway, et aukes per
pruesce, et affinite du sank Yrois de quoy lez Pices furount mellez,
occupia cel pays et auxi Ergeille, et autres dez Iles, le issu de qy, qi sez
nomerent Scoty, coumpasserent toutdice encountre lez Picys, issi qen
le temps cesti Drust fitz Feradhach, lez Escocez ietterent couyne, et a
vn counsail general, estoient priuement armez, et dedenz la mesoun
du counsaill, tuerent ly auauntdit roy et lez grautz seignours dez
Picys touz, qi ne pensoient si bien noune, si enuoierent apres autres qi
lour plust, et com ils venoient, toutdice lez tuerent, tanqe ils auoint
fait ceo qils desiroint, et de cel hour en auaunt, failly le Regne dez
Picys, qauoit durre .Mile.C.lxxxvij. aunz, et recomence le Regne
Descoce, quel Regne comensa deuaunt lez Pices, .CCCC.xliij. aunz
deuaunt le Incarnacioun.

De Kenet Alpin ... roys apres ... Pices.[a]

36. Les Picys destruytz a la maner, Kynet fitz Alpin regna sure lez
Escoce, et fust le primer Roys Escotoys apres lez Picys. Il soutzmist a
sa seignoury la terre tout a Twede, enfist enchacer lez Engles et
Bretouns qe y enhabiterent, fist nomer la terre Escoce. Il estably lez

---

[a]   *Rest indecipherable. Left margin.*

Fathe, five years; Drust, his brother, six years; Drust son of Hole, twenty years. St Adomnan lived in his time. Tharan son of Amfodech, four years; Brude son of Dergert, thirty-one years. St Servanus came to Fife at this time. Iactan, brother of Brude, eighteen years; Garnarde son of Feradhegh, twenty-four years; Denegul son of Fergusagin, sixteen years; Nectan son of Fergaleg, nine months; Fergus son of Frude, one month; Alpin son of Eferadheche, six months, at one time; he was driven out, but afterwards reigned for thirty years; Brude [f. 192v.] son of Tenegus, two years; Alpin son of Tenagus, two years; Drust son of Telargbin, one year; Talargan son of Drustane, four years; Talargan son of Tenagus, five years; Costantin son of Fergusa, forty years. It was he who had Dunkeld built. Hungus son of Fergusa, ten years; it was he who built Kilrymont, now St Andrews, at which time St Regulus came with his disciple to the church of St Andrews. Duf Tolorg, four years; Egganus son of Hungus, three years; Feradagus son of Badoghe, three years; Brud son of Feradhach, one month; Kenneth son of Feradhach, one year; Brude son of Fochel, two years; Drust son of Feradhach, three years. He was the last King of the Picts, he was killed at Scone by treason. As the chronicles testify, a certain son of a King of Ireland, who was named Redda, landed in Galloway and, to some extent through prowess, and through the affinity of Irish blood, with which the Picts were mingled, he occupied the country and Argyll as well, and others of the Isles. His offspring, who called themselves Scoti, were always scheming against the Picts; and so in Drust son of Feradhach's time, the Scots arranged a plot. They came to a general council secretly armed, and in the council room, they killed the aforesaid king and all the Picts' great lords, who had not suspected that all was not well. Then they sent for any others it pleased them, and when they came, they killed them all, until they had done what they wanted. And from that time, the kingdom of the Picts failed, having lasted 1187 years, and the kingdom of Scotland began again, which kingdom had begun before the Picts, 463 years before the incarnation.

Concerning Kenneth Alpin [and the] kings after [the] Picts.
36. With the Picts destroyed in this way, Kenneth son of Alpin ruled over the Scots, and was the first King of Scots after the Picts. He subjected all the land to the Tweed to his lordship, he had the English and Britons who lived there driven out, and had the land named Scotland. He established the laws that still endure in Scotland. And this was in the time soon after Ecgberht had united the Seven Realms

loys qe vnqor en Escoce durent; et ceo estoit en le temps tost apres qe Egbright auoit vny les .vij. Realmes dez Saxsouns en Bretaigne, qe taunt auoint a faire lez roys Engles en lour terre demeyn, a establir lour conquest, qils ne sez entremistrent rien deuers Albany, si longement, tanqe lez Escotz auoint pris tiel reaul saunz empediment, qe asseitz le tenoient estable et droiturel. Kynet fitz Alpin regna .xvi. aunz, et morust a Fertenyoth, et fust enterrez en le Isle de Yona, pres de Hert, Loern, et Fergus, trois frers qy amenerent lez Escotz en Archady sure lez Picys. Donald fitz Alpin regna .iiij. aunz; [f. 193] Costantin fitz Kynache, .xvi. aunz, qestoit tue dez Norways en batail; Athe mak Kinath, .i. ane, qi fust tue de Tirg fiz Dungald; Tirg mac Dungald, .xij. auns. Lez croniclis Descoce tesmonent, qe cesti Tirg soutzmist a sa seignoury tout Ireland et graunt party Dengleter. Cesti dona primerment fraunchiz as eglis Descoce, qauaunt le hour esoint en seruitude dez lays as vsages de Picys. Donald mak Dunstan, ij. aunz. Edmound, freir Athelstan, dona a cesti Donald Roy Descoce tout Combirland, pur quoi lez Escoces ount fait clayme, tanqe al Reir Croiz de Stayn more; mais cel donne ad este souent conquys puscedy et relesse en maint peise fesaunt. Costantin mac Edha .xl. aunz regna, qi guerpy soun realme, se rendy en religioun, et fust Abbe de Saint Andrew .v. aunz, et illoeqe fust enterrez. Malcolme mac Donald .xxi. ane regna, qi fust tue par treisoun dez Norways, et ceo fust en le temps le primer Edward, pier Athelstan. Indel mac Costantin regna .x. aunz, et fust tue dez Norwais. Duf mac Maucloun, .iiij. aunz et .vi. moys, qi fust mourdri a Forays, et musse desoutz le pount de Kinlos, et tancom il ieust la, le solail ne se aparust. Si fust troue et a porte al Ile de Yona, ou touz sez auncestres de Kinek mac Alpin furount enterrez, fors cely qi Abbe estoit de Saint Andrew. Culen mac Indolf .iiij. aunz regna et .vi. moys. Il fust tue de Amthar fitz Donald, pur sa feile qe fust tue en Lownes. Kinec fitz Malcol, .xxiiij. aunz et .ij. moys; et fust tue de ses homs, par treisoun de Fumel la feile Cunithar, Zayn de Angus, fitz de qi Kinak auoit deuaunt fait tuer. Costantin mac Culen, .i. ane et .vi. moys; et fust tue de Kynnech fitz Malcolm. Grige mac Kynech mac Douf, .viij. aunz; et fust tue de Malcolme fitz Kynech. Cesti Malcolme regna .xxx. aunz noblement et fust uicturous. Dunkan mac Kryn de Dunkeldy et de Betowe fitz[b] Malcolme mac Kynech, .vi. aunz; et fust tue de Macbeth mac Sinley, qi regna .xvi. aunz; et fust tuez de Malcolm[c] mac Dunkan. Lulach le fole regna .i.

---

[b] r.: *feile.*
[c] *MS:* Chalcolm.

of the Saxons in Britain; and so the English kings had so much to do
in their own lands to establish their conquests, that they did not
concern themselves with Albany at all, for so long, while the Scots
were taking this regal authority without impediment, that [the Scots]
held it long enough for it to be well-established by right. Kenneth son
of Alpin reigned sixteen years, and died at Forteviot. He was buried
on the Isle of Iona, near to Hert, Loern, and Fergus, three brothers
who led the Scots into Archady against the Picts. Donald son of Alpin
reigned four years; [f. 193] Constantine son of Kenneth, sixteen years,
who was killed by the Norsemen in battle; Athe mac Kenneth, one
year, who was killed by Tirg son of Dungald; Tirg macDungald,
twelve years. The cronicles of Scotland testify that Tirg subjected all
of Ireland to his lordship and a great part of England. It was he who
first gave freedom to the Scottish church, which had been in servitude to laymen before that time, following the custom of the Picts.[1]
Donald macDunstan, two years. Edmund, the brother of Athelstan,
gave all of Cumberland to Donald King of Scotland, which the Scots
had laid claim to, as far as the Rere Cross on Stainmore; but this gift
has often been conquered since then, and handed back many times to
make peace. Constantine macEdha reigned forty years. He abandoned his realm, and gave himself up to religion; he was Abbot of St
Andrews five years, and was buried there. Malcolm macDonald
reigned twenty-one years; he was treacherously killed by the
Norsemen, and this was in the time of the first Edward, father of
Athelstan. Indel macConstantine reigned ten years, and was killed by
Norsemen. Duf macMalcolm, four years and six months; he was
murdered at Forres, and hidden beneath the bridge at Kinloss, and as
long as he lay there, the sun would not show itself. He was found and
carried to the Isle of Iona, where all of his ancestors from Kenneth
macAlpin were buried, except for the one who was Abbot of St
Andrews. Culen macIndolf reigned four years and six months. He
was killed by Amthar son of Donald, because of his daughter who
was killed in Lothian. Kenneth son of Malcolm, twenty-four years
and two months; and he was killed by his men, through the treachery
of Fumel the daughter of Cunithar, whose son, the Thane of Angus,
Kenneth had previously had killed. Costantine macCulen, one year
and six months; and he was killed by Kenneth son of Malcolm. Grige
mac Kenneth macDuf, eight years; and he was killed by Malcolm son
of Kenneth. This Malcolm ruled nobly for thirty years and was victo-
rious. Duncan macCrinan of Dunkeld and of Bethoc the [daughter] of
Malcolm macKenneth, six years;[2] and he was killed by Macbeth

mois; et fust tue en Strabolgy. Toucz[d] ceaux roys furount enterrez en
Lile de Yona. Malcolm Kenmour mac Duncan regna .xxxvij. aunz et
.vi. moys; et fust tue a Alnewyk, et enterrez a Tynmothe. Cesti estoit
le marry Saint Margaret de Dunfermelin. Donald soun freir mac
Dunkan regna primerment .vi. moys, qi fust enchacez de Dunkan fitz
Maucloun, qi regna .vi. moys, qi fust tue de Malpedre mac Loern, [f.
193v.] Count del Meiernys; et gist en Lile de Yona. Donald mac
Dunkan regna autrefoitz .iij. aunz, qi fust enuoegle et mort par Edgar
fitz Maucloun; et fust enterre a Dunkeldin, et puis translatez en le Isle
de Yona. Edgar regna .ix. aunz et .iiij. moys; et gist a Dunfermelyn.
Alexander soun freir, et fitz Maucloun, regna .xvij. aunz et .iij. moys
et demy; et gist a Dunfermlyn. Dauid soun freir regna .xxxix. aunz et
.iij. moys; et morust a Cardoil, et gist a Dunfermelin. Maucloun le
fitz Henry Count del Garuyaghe, de Huntingdoun, et de
Northumbreland, qi fust le fitz Dauid le roy, regna .xij. aunz, et .vi.
moys, et .xx. iours, qi morust auaunt le pier a Jedworthe, et gist a
Dunfermelin. Willam soun freir, et fitz meisme cely Henry, Count de
Northumbreland, du donne le Roy Esteuen, regna .L. aunz; et morust
a Streuelyn, et gist a Abirbrothok, qe meismes edifia. Alexander soun
fitz regna .xxxvij. aunz, qi morust a Kenbray en Orkany, et gist a
Melros. Alexander, le fitz Alexander, qi de .viij. aunz de age comensa
a regner, regna .xxxvij. aunz, qi roumpy le cole a Kinkorn, sours de
quoy enueint graunt mal.

La soume dez aunz entre Kenech fitz Alpin, et cesti Alexander
sount .CCCC.xxx. aunz, vn moys, et .vi. iours. Et si est la sum dez
aunz de touz lez Roys Picys et Escotes, .Mille.D.CCCC.lxxvi. aunz et
.ix. moys, et viij. iours, tanqe lencorounement Johan de Baillolf. Et fait
asauoir, qe y ny out nul gere entre ceaux .ij. realmes qe soit a countier
.lxxx. auns, deuant qe par Johan de Baillolf fust comense. Mais pur
ceo qe y ny out point de issu de lez .ij. Roys Alexanders, couenoit
retourner al issu de Dauid, Count de Huntingdoun, freir Willam, le
Roy Descoce, fitz le Roy Dauid. Qy Dauid, Count de Huntingdoun,
auoit vn fitz Johan, qy morust saunz engendrure, et trois feilles. La
primer fust Margaret, qe Alayn seignur de Galeway auoit en espouse.
La secund fust Isabelle, qe Peris de Bruys auoit en espouse. La tierce,
Ade, qe Johan de Hastinges auoit a feme. De la primer, Margaret, ne
vesqy nul issu, fors vn feile, qe out a noun Dorworgul, qe fust marie a
Johan de Baillolf. De Isabelle, la secound feille le Count Dauid de
Huntindoune, marye a Peris de Bruis, nasqy Robert de Bruis le eyne.

---

[d]   MS: *voutz, corrected to* Toutz *by main scribe's hand.*

macFinlay, who reigned for sixteen years; and he was killed by Malcolm macDuncan. Lulach the fool reigned for one month; and he was killed in Strathbogie. All these kings were buried on the Isle of Iona. Malcolm Canmore macDuncan reigned thirty-seven years and six months; and he was killed at Alnwick, and buried at Tynemouth.³ He was the husband of Saint Margaret of Dunfermline. Donald macDuncan, his brother, reigned for six months at first; he was driven out by Duncan son of Malcolm, who reigned six months; and he was killed by Malpedre macLoern, [f. 193v.] Earl of Meiernys; and he lies buried on the Isle of Iona. Donald macDuncan ruled once again for three years; he was blinded and killed by Edgar son of Malcolm; and he was buried at Dunkeld, and later moved to the Isle of Iona. Edgar reigned nine years and four months; and he lies buried at Dunfermline. Alexander his brother, the son of Malcolm, reigned seventeen years and three-and-a-half months; and he lies buried at Dunfermline. David, his brother, reigned thirty-nine years and three months; and he died at Carlisle, and lies buried at Dunfermline. Malcolm, the son of Henry, Earl of Garioch, Huntingdon and Northumberland, who was the son of King David, reigned twelve years, six months and twenty days; he died before his father, at Jedburgh, and lies buried at Dunfermline.⁴ William, his brother, and the son of the same Henry, Earl of Northumberland, by the gift of King Stephen, reigned fifty years; and he died at Stirling, and lies buried at Arbroath, which was built by him. Alexander, his son, reigned thirty-seven years; he died at Kerrera in Orkney, and lies buried at Melrose.⁵ Alexander the son of Alexander, who began to reign at the age of eight, reigned thirty-seven years; he broke his neck at Kinghorn, from which great misfortune arose.⁶

The sum of the years between Kenneth son of Alpin and Alexander is 430 years, one month and six days. The sum of the years of all the kings of Picts and Scots is 1976 years and nine months and eight days, up until the coronation of John de Balliol. And it should be known that there was no war worth counting between these two realms for eighty years before the one that was started by John Balliol.⁷ But because the two King Alexanders had no issue, it was necessary to go back to the issue of David, Earl of Huntingdon, the brother of William, King of Scotland, son of King David. David, Earl of Huntingdon, had a son John, who died without offspring, and three daughters. The first was Margaret, who Alan, lord of Galloway, took in marriage. The second was Isabella, who [Robert] de Bruce took in marriage. The third, Ada, [Henry] de Hastings took to wife.

De la tierce, Ade, feile le dit Count Dauid, marye a Johan de Hastinges, nasqy Johan de Hastinges. [f. 194] Pur quoi sourdi graunt debat qi enserroit Roys, chescun voroit qe soun amy le vst este; pur quoi par comune ascent, lez prelatez, countis et barouns oue la comune, enuoierent au Roy Edward Dengleter a la maner auaunt dit.

Enuiroun cel hour, chey le pount de Berewik outre lew de Twede de graunt cretyne de eaw, pur ceo qe lez archis estoient trop lassez, quel pount nen dura fors .ix. aunz apres ceo qil fust parfourny. Tost apres cel hour, Willam de Vescy dona lonour de Alnewyk a Antoyn de Bek, Euesqe de Durresme, qi pur chaudez paroles de Johan, fitz bastard le dit Willam, le vendy a Henry de Percy.

De Joh' de <Bailof> Roy de ...[a]

37. Del houre qe le Roy Edward Dengleter le primer apres la Conquest auoit parfourny ceo qil auoit a fair en Flaundres a la maner auauntdit, il repaira en Engleter, sen trey sure la Marche Descoce, ou a Norham il fist faire somouns de parlement, ou lez grauntz touz Descoce y enuyndrent, requiraunt le dit roy qil uousist ferre trier qi serroit lour roys de droit com souerayne seignour, qy rien se nousist entremetter, tanqe ils ly auoint susrendu touz forteresces Descoce, com a lour souerayne, qy ceo firent, et il enmist sez ministres et officers, quel souerainete reconustrerent touz lez grauntz Descoce, par ouert declaracioun, et touz y ceaux qi droit enclaimerent hu realme Descoce, sez mistrent de tout en sez iugementz. A quoi ils mistrent touz lours seals, en affermaunce de chos purparle. Cest parlement de Norham fust apres la Pasche, lan de grace .Mile.CC.xcj., de quel lieu ils auoint iour, tanqe le vtas de saint Johan en vne ane, qe qi clamoit droit en Escoce, uenist a Berewik au dit iour et aueroit droit iugement. Le Roy Edward se trey deuers le sue, ou en le mene temps il enuoia a touz lez uniuersetes de la Cristianete par sez honourables messagers pur ent sauoir lez opiniouns et lez discreciouns de cest matier, de touz les sages del lay Ciuille et Canoun. Le dit Roy Edward reuenit au dit iour, et au iour nome, ou touz lez grauntz de lez dieus Realmes furount assemblez par somouns, ou veindrent a chalanger plusours

---

[a]   *Rest indecipherable. Left Margin.*

No issue survived from the first, Margaret, except for a daughter named Dervorguilla, who was married to John de Balliol. From Isabella, Earl David of Huntingdon's second daughter, married to Peter de Bruce, was born Robert de Bruce the elder. From Earl David's third daughter, Ada, married to John de Hastings, was born John de Hastings.[8] *[f. 194]* Because of this, a great argument arose over who should be the king, everyone wishing that his friend should have been it; and because of this, by common assent, the prelates, earls and barons, and the community, sent to King Edward of England in the manner related before.

Around this time, the bridge over the river Tweed at Berwick collapsed during a great flood, because the arches were too weak; this bridge lasted for just nine years after it was finished.[9] Soon after this time, William de Vesci granted the honour of Alnwick to Antony Bek, Bishop of Durham; and because of some heated words with John, William's bastard son, he sold it to Henry de Percy.[10]

Concerning John de Balliol King of ...

37. As soon as King Edward of England, the first after the Conquest, had finished that which he had had to do in Flanders, in the manner abovesaid, he returned to England and took himself to the March of Scotland, where at Norham, he had parliament summoned.[1] The magnates of all Scotland came there, requesting the king as sovereign lord that he be willing to have the case tried, as to who should be their king by right. He was wholly unwilling to interfere, until they had surrendered all the fortresses of Scotland to him, as to their sovereign; this they did, and he put in his ministers and officers. All the magnates of Scotland recognized this sovereignty by open declaration, and all those there who claimed the realm of Scotland by right, relied entirely on his judgement. They all set their seals to this, in confirmation of what had been agreed. This parliament at Norham was after Easter, the year of grace 1291; from there they adjourned until the octave of St John [2 July] in one year, so that whoever claimed right in Scotland, should come to Berwick on that day and accept right judgement.[2] King Edward took himself to the South, where in the mean time he sent to all the universities in Christendom, by honourable envoys, so as to know the opinions and the adjudications on this matter of all the experts of Civil and Canon Law. King Edward returned on that day; and on the day named, when all the magnates of the two realms were assembled by summons, many came there to challenge for the right of the realm of Scotland on

le droit du Realme Descoce par diuers causes, cest assauoir, Florens, Count de Holand, Johan de Baillof, Robert de Bruys, Johan de Hastinges, Johan de Comyn, Patrik, Count de la Marche, Johan de Vescy, Nichol de Sowlis, Willam de Ros et Patrik Galightly; toucz cestis y enmistrent clayme par diuers chalange par peticioun *[f. 194v.]* deuaunt le dit Roy Edward. Si estoit ordeine depar le dit roy, qe .xx. persouns de plus suffisauntz Dengleter, et autres .xx. persouns Descoce meutz suffisauntz, et auisez par comun eleccioun, dussent trier lour chalange, qi furount elieus, nomez, triez et iurez, et auoint iour de eaux auiser, tanqe la saint Michel procheigne ensuaunt. Le Roi Edward se retourna en Engleter, qi reuenit a la Saint Michel a Berewik, ou en leglis de la Trinite fust iuge le droit du successioun du realme Descoce, soulement al issu de .iij. feils le Count Dauid de Huntyngdoun, qi freir estoit le Roy Willam, lez autres foriugez. Mais graunt difficulte y estoit au mainz del issu de lez .ij. primers feilles le dit Count Dauid, cest asauoir entre Johan de Baillof, qestoit fitz la feille Margaret, eyne feile le dit Count; et Robert de Bruis le eyne, qestoit fitz Isabel, la secound feile li dit Dauid, Count de Huntingdoun, entre queux estoit graunt plee. Le droit Johan de Hastings oste de tout, issu de la feile pusne. Gilbert de Clare, Count de Gloucestre, maintenoit grauntement la querel Robert de Bruys, pur ceo qe sa sore auoit espose; le count de Garain, et Antoin, Leuesqe de Doresme, la party Johan de Baillof. Lez pleidours et auoketz disoint pur Robert de Bruys, qil estoit le plus procheine eyre mal, qi fitz estoit de Isabele, feile le dit Count Dauid de Huntindoun, vn degre plus pres le dit count, qe Johan de Baillof nestoit, qi estoit le fitz Derworgule, feil Margaret, la feile le dit Count de Huntingdoun, espous Alayn de Galeway, pur quoi com le plus prochein heir demaundoit il droit real. Lez countours Johan de Baillof disoient qe pusqe sa mere ne pooit regner, qe il demaundoit le droit succiement de soun auncestre linielement, com droit heir descendaunt, et solonc la loy lour iuge, a qoi ils estoint acordez, obligez, et entreassurez. Si estoit awardez par lez .xl. persouns de touz .ij. lez realmes sure lour serement, le droit a remeindre a Johan de Baillof, com al issu del eyne feile le count Dauid de Huntingdoun. Au sentence de quel verdit, le Roy Edward Dengleter iugea le droit du realme a Johan de Baillof, ou en presentz e dit Roy Edward, toucz les grauntz Descoce atournerent au dit Johan de Baillof par serement et homage, fors Robert de Bruys le eyne, qi enmist clayme, qi en audience du Roy Edward disoit qil ne ly ferroit ia homage, qi susrendist sa terre qil out en Escoce, le vale de Anand, a soun fitz Robert le secound, et fitz la feile le count de

various grounds, that is to say, Florence, Count of Holland; John de Balliol; Robert de Bruce; John de Hastings; John de Comyn; Patrick, Earl of March; [William] de Vesci; Nicholas de Soules; William de Ros and Patrick Golightly. All of these there put in a claim by various challenges by petition [f. 194v.] before King Edward.[3] It was arranged on behalf of the king that twenty persons of great standing from England, and another twenty of good standing from Scotland, decided by common election, should sit to determine their claims; these men were elected, nominated, examined and sworn-in, and they were given the day for their judgement, on Michaelmas [29 September] next following.[4] King Edward took himself back to England. He returned to Berwick at Michaelmas, where, in the Church of the Trinity, the right to the succession to the realm of Scotland was judged, solely on the issue of the three daughters of Earl David of Huntingdon (who was King William's brother), the other [claimants] having being ruled out.[5] But there was great difficulty at the hands of the issue of Earl David's first two daughters, that is, between John de Balliol, who was the son of the daughter of Margaret, the eldest daughter of the earl; and Robert de Bruce the elder, who was the son of Isabella, the second daughter of David, Earl of Huntingdon; and there was a great dispute between them. The right of John de Hastings, the offspring of the youngest daughter, was rejected entirely. Gilbert de Clare, Earl of Gloucester, wholeheartedly supported Robert de Bruce's cause, because he had married his sister; the Earl of Warenne and Anthony, Bishop of Durham, [supported] John de Balliol's party.[6] The pleaders and advocates for Robert de Bruce claimed that he was the nearest heir male, as he was the son of Isabella, daughter of Earl David of Huntingdon, one degree closer to the earl than was John de Balliol, who was the son of Dervorguilla, daughter of Margaret, the daughter of the Earl of Huntingdon, wife of Alan of Galloway;[7] and therefore he demanded the royal rights as the nearest heir. John de Balliol's pleaders claimed that since his mother could not reign, he demanded the right in succession to his lineal ancestor, as the heir right descended, and according to the law they judged, to which they were agreed, bound and affirmed. It was ruled, on their oath, by the forty persons from both of the two realms that the right remained to John de Balliol, as he was from the issue of the eldest daughter of David de Huntingdon. Following the ruling of this verdict, King Edward of England adjudged the rights to the realm to John de Balliol; at this, in the presence of King Edward, all the magnates of Scotland attorned to John de Balliol by oath and

Gloucestre, qi Robert ne voloit plus faire atournement [f. 195] au dit
Johan de Baillof, qe son pier non fesoit. Si disoit a soun fitz Robert le
tierce, qi estoit fitz la feile et heire le Count de Carrik, qi puis fust Roy
Descoce, preigne tu nostre terre Descoce, si encoueignez, qar iames
ne serroms sez homs. Qi Robert le tierce, qi al hour estoit joen
bacheler du chaumbre le Roy Edward, enfist homage au dit Johan de
Baillof, qi Johan fust corone au gise du pays a Scone, le iour de saint
Andrew, lan de grace .Mile.CC.xcij. Qi Johan de Baillof auoit .iij.
sores, la primer Margaret, la dame de Gillisland, la second fust dame
de Counsy, la tierce auoit Johan de Comyn a marry, pier cely qi Robert
Bruis tua a Donfres. Et si nauoit le dit Johan de Baillof fors vn fitz qi
out a noun Edward.

... Joh' de Bailof ... homage [a]
38. Cesti Johan de Baillof, Roy Descoce, au Nowel prochien apres
soun encorounement, veint au Noef Chastel sur Tyne, si enfist
homage real au Roy Edward le primer apres la Conquest, pur le
realme Descoce; si estoit reseisy de touz lez fermetes Descoce, qe
furount seysez en la main le Roy Dengleter. Procheignement apres
estoit comense vn appele dun gentil hom Descoce a la court le Roy
Dengleter, de ceo qil ne pooit auoir droit, com ly sembloit, en la court
le Roy Descoce, de vn de ses veisins; pur qoi le Roy Johan Descoce
fust somouns par bref le Roy Dengleter a fair droit au dit hom, pur
qoi le counsail Descoce estoit tot troeble.
    Meisme le temps sourdy la guere derechief, entre le Roy Dengleter
et le Roi de Fraunce, par comencement dez Baiounais et Fyportes
mariners a Saint Mahu, encountre le nauy de Normendy; pur quoi le
counsail Decoce ordenerent .iiij. euesqes et .iiij. countis, et .iiij.
barounis a reauler la terre Descoce, per counsail dez queux, fust
coumpasse a rebeller encountre le Roy Dengleter. Si enuoierent
messagers au Roy de Fraunce, Johan de Sowlis et autres, qi od ly
firent allyaunce encountre le Roy Dengleter. Qi Roy Dengleter nestoit
pas de tout assurez de lez Escocez, maunda li Euesqe Auntoin de
Doresme pur tretir od eaux, a quel tretice a Jeddeworth par melle, pur
combatre dez petitz chenetis, fust tue vn dez cosyns le dit Euesqe de

[a]   *Left margin.*

homage, except for Robert de Bruce the elder, who maintained his claim, and in King Edward's hearing, said that he would never do him homage. He surrendered his Scottish lands, Annandale, to his son, Robert the second, son of the daughter of the Earl of Gloucester; and this Robert no more wished to make his attornment [f. 195] to John de Balliol than did his father, so he said to his son, Robert the third, who was the son of the daughter and heir of the Earl of Carrick, and who was afterwards King of Scotland, 'You take our Scottish lands, if you'll agree, for we will never be his men'. Robert the third, who at this time was a young bachelor of King Edward's chamber, did homage to John de Balliol.[8] John was crowned in the fashion of that country at Scone, St Andrew's day [30 November],[9] the year of grace 1292. John Balliol had three sisters: the first Margaret, lady of Gilsland, the second was lady of Coucy, the third had John de Comyn as husband, the father of he who Robert Bruce killed at Dumfries.[10] And John de Balliol had just one son, who bore the name Edward.[11]

38. At the first Christmas after his coronation, John de Balliol, King of Scotland, came to Newcastle upon Tyne and did royal homage to King Edward the First after the Conquest, for the realm of Scotland;[1] and he was put back in possession of all the Scottish fortresses which had been taken into the hands of the King of England. Soon after this, an appeal was initiated by a Scottish nobleman at the King of England's court, because it seemed to him that he could not get justice in the King of Scotland's court, concerning one of his neighbours.[2] Because of this, King John of Scotland was summoned by writ of the King of England to do justice to this man, and because of this the Scottish council quickly became worried.

At this same time, war broke out again between the King of England and the King of France, started by sailors from Bayonne and the Cinque Ports at [Cape] Saint-Mathieu, against the navy of Normandy. Because of this, the Scottish council decreed that four bishops, four earls and four barons should rule the land of Scotland, by whose advice, it was decided to rebel against the King of England. They sent envoys, John de Soules and others, to the King of France, who made an alliance with him against the King of England.[3] The King of England was not at all sure about the Scots, and ordered Bishop Antony of Durham to negotiate with them. At these negotiations, at Jedburgh, one of the Bishop of Durham's cousins was killed, in a brawl over a lapdog fight, someone who bore the surname Buscy.

Doresme, vn qi out le sournoun Buscy. Qi Euesqe de Doresme demaunda de lez Escocez depar le Roy Dengleter, ostages de quatre chasteaux, Berewik, Roxburgh, Edinburgh et Striuelyn, qil poet estre assurez de eaux, duraunt la guere de Fraunce. Sur quoi, il presenta lez brefs le roy de somouns de lour Roi Johan, de personelement aparir a [f. 195v.] Noefchastel sur Tyne au parlement le Roy Dengleter au my qarresme; au quel lieu au dit temps, ny enuenit le Roy Descoce, ne nully pur luy. Pur quoi le Roy Edward de Engleter se adressa vers Escoce od graunt ost, teint la fest de Pasche a Werk, de quel chastel, Robert de Ros, qi enfust siris, sen fuy del obeisaunce le dit Roi Dengleter dedens le tierce iour deuaunt la venu le roy, et lessa le chastel voide, et sen trey a Senewar, vn petit chastel qil auoit en Escoce, tout pur paramours, qil ama Cristiane de Moubray, qe apres ne ly deigna auoir. Quel temps .vij. Countis Descoce, de Boghan, de Menteth, de Stratheren, de Leynaux, de Ros, de Athetle, et de Marre, od Johan Comyn, et plusours autres barouns, entrerent Engleter en ost, ne esparnirent nuly, arderent la surburbe de Cardoil, et la assistrent. Le Roy Edward, qi ceo auoit oy, se trey deuaunt Berewik; et le primer iour qe il enueint, com le roy seoit a manger en sa tent, vn nief de sez vitaillers, pur mesconisaunce de sez maryners, secchist sur terre decoste par deuers la vile, qe al hour nestoit pas murez, mais enuyroune de haut fosse. Lez comuns de la vile encurrerent a la neif, enmystret fiew, decouperent lez homs. Huyn sourdy en lost le roy, chescuns as armes. Ferrerent cheueaux dez esperouns, lez sauuages iuuens gentz mounterent lez fosses tout a cheual, et par ou lez gentz de la vile auoint fait vn centre au longur de la fosse, si entrerent testousement od eaux a cheual qi en pooist plus tost enuenire, ou furrount dedenz mortz graunt noumbre dez comuns de Fyffe et de Foritherik, qen garnysoun de la vile estoient. Meisme la nuyt conquist le dit Roy Edward la vile od le chastel tout, ou il fist sa demure, et ou ly ueint vn Frer Meneour, gardein dez Freirs de Roxburgh, depar le Roy Johan de Escoce, qi ly emporta lettres de susrendre del homage le Roy Descoce, par lettres pupplis du roy et de la comune Descoce, quelis lettres le Roy Dengleter accepta, et lez fist registreir noturement. Mesime le hour, lez auantditz Countis Descoce reentrerent Engleter et arderent la Priory de Hexham, et enfirent hu pays graunt mal. Le Count de la Marche, Patrik od le noire barbe, qi soul estoit demurez de touz lez seignours Descoce al obeisaunce le Roy Dengleter, qi od le roy estoit au pris de Berewyk, uenoit nouncier au roy, qe sa femme auoit ens pris en soun chastel de Dunbarre lez enemys Descoce, sez parentz, qauoint enbote sez ministres, et tenoint

On behalf of the King of England, the Bishop of Durham demanded four castles from the Scots as securities, Berwick, Roxburgh, Edinburgh and Stirling, so that he could be sure of them during the war with France.[4] After this, he presented the king's writs of summons to their King John, to appear in person at [f. 195v.] Newcastle on Tyne at the King of England's parliament at mid-Lent; [but] the King of Scotland did not turn up at this place and time, nor anyone for him. Because of this, King Edward of England made his way towards Scotland with a great army, and held the feast of Easter at Wark.[5] Robert de Ros, who was lord of this castle, fled from the King of England's allegiance, on the third day before the king's arrival, left the castle empty, and took himself to Sanquhar, a small castle he had in Scotland, all for the sake of love, for he loved Christine de Mowbray – who would not deign to have him afterwards.[6] At this time, seven Scottish earls, Buchan, Menteith, Strathearn, Lennox, Ross, Atholl and Mar, with John Comyn, and many other barons, entered England in force; sparing nobody, they burned the suburbs of Carlisle and besieged it.[7] Having heard about this, King Edward took himself to Berwick; and on the first day that he got there, as the king sat down to eat in his tent, one of his supply ships, due to an error by its sailors, ran aground on the side towards the town, which at that time was not walled, but surrounded by a deep ditch. The commoners of the town ran to the ship, put it to the flames, and cut down the men. An outcry broke out in the king's army, 'Everyone to arms', and staying on horseback spurring on their horses, the wild young men mounted the ditches and just where the men of the town had formed up in a group along the length of the ditch, they broke in impulsively with those on horseback who were able to get in the quickest. A great number of the commoners of Fife and Fothrif in the town garrison were killed within there. That same night, King Edward conquered all of the town and castle, and took up residence there.[8] A Friar Minor, warden of the Friars of Roxburgh, came to him there on behalf of King John of Scotland, bringing him letters renouncing the homage of the King of Scotland, by public letters of the king and the community of Scotland. The King of England accepted these letters, and had them notorially registered.[9] At the same time, the previously mentioned Scottish earls re-entered England and burned the Priory of Hexham, and did great harm to the country.[10] The Earl of March, Patrick with the black beard, who alone of all the lords of Scotland remained in the obedience of the King of England, and who was with the king at the taking of Berwick, came to tell the king that his wife had received Scottish

le chastel encountre ly. Si prioit au roy eide, qe meisme *[f. 196]* la nuyt
uoroit aler. Le roy ly bailla les Countis de Garain et de Warwik, od
graunt estuffe par mere et terre, qe deuaunt solail leuaunt lendemain
auoit assys le chastel de Dunbarre. Lez seignours Descoce qestoint
assemblez oyerent de lassege, trenuyterent laundroit, enueindrent
matin a Spout, ou entre le dit lieu et Dunbarre, sez combaterent od lez
ditz Engles de lassege, ou furount descoumfitz lez Escocez, la primer
batail de cel guer, ou en le chastel furount pris lez countis de Menteth,
Athedle et de Ros, et .vi. barouns, Johan Comyn le iouen, Willam de
Saint Clere, Richard Syward le eyne, Johan de Ynchemartin,
Alexandre de Murref, Edmound Comyn de Kilbride, oue .xxix.
chiualeris, .lxxx. esquiers, les queux furount enuoiez en prisoun en
diuers lieus Dengleter. Le Roy Descoce, Johan de Baillof, maunda au
roy pur peise; se mist en sa grace, se rendi au roy od soun fitz
Edward, qi il ly profry en ostage sure soun bon port, qi touz dieus
furont prises et enuoyez a Loundres et defenduz, qils ne passasent
.xx. lieus entour la cite. Le Roy Edward Dengleter enprist lez
chasteaux touz Descoce, et cheuaucha la terre parmy, tanqe il enuenit
al Stokforthe, et enmist sez ministres; et en soun repairir, il enfist
enporteir del Abbay de Scone, la pier sur quoi lez Roys Descoce
solaint estre surmys a lour nouel regnement, et la enfist aporter a
Loundres a Westmouster, et la ordeina le sege du prestre al haut
autier. Le Roy Edward Dengleter fist somoundre soun parlement a
Berewik, ou de toutz les grauntz Descoce, il prist homage, sur quoi il
auoit lour sealis pendauntz en perpetuel memoir;*b* et de illoeqes
repaira en Engleter, ou al Abbay de Newmouster, il bailla la garde
Descoce au Count de Garayn et vn seal du gouernaille de y cel, si ly
disoit en bourdaunt, Bon bosoigne fait, qy de merde se deliuer. Le roy
ordeigna Hugh de Cressingham soun chaumbrelayn de Escoce, et
Willam de Ormesby justice; si lour comaunda qe toutez gentz outre
.xv. auns Descoce feissent homage, et qe lour nouns fussent escriptz.
Lez clerks*c* pristrent de chescun vn dener, de qoy ils deuindrent richis
gentz. Le roy ordeina qe touz lez seignours Descoce demurascent
outre Trent, tanqe sa guer durrast de Fraunce. Quel ane de grace
.Mile.CC.xcvij., il prist de chescun sak de layn Dengleter et Descoce
vn demy mark destirlings, ou deuant ne donerent fors .iiij. d., pur
quoi estoit apelle, la mal tol. Le roy se adressa en Gascoine.

---

b   *MS:* meroir.
c   *MS:* clers.

enemies, her kinsmen, into his castle of Dunbar.[11] They had ousted his officials, and held the castle against him. He asked the king for help, [f. 196] wanting to go the same night. The king gave him the Earls of Warenne and Warwick, along with great supplies by sea and land, so that the castle of Dunbar was besieged before sunrise on the next day. The assembled Scottish lords heard about the siege, and marched there through the night, arriving at Spott in the morning, where between there and Dunbar, they fought with the English at the siege. Here, the Scots were defeated, in the first battle of this war.[12] The Earls of Menteith, Atholl and Ross were taken in the castle, and six barons, John Comyn the younger, William de Sinclair, Richard Siward the elder, John de Inchmartin, Alexander de Murray and Edmund Comyn of Kilbride, along with twenty-nine knights and eighty squires, who were sent to prison in various places in England.[13] The King of Scotland, John de Balliol, sent to the king [asking] for peace, and put himself in his grace, surrendering himself to the king with his son, Edward, who he offered him as a hostage for his good conduct. Both of them were taken and sent to London, and were forbidden from going beyond twenty miles from around the city. King Edward of England seized all the castles of Scotland, and rode through the land, until he came to Stokforthe, and appointed his ministers. On his return, he had the stone, on which the kings of Scotland were customarily installed at the beginning of their reign, taken away from Scone Abbey, and carried to London to Westminster, and set it up as the priest's seat at the high altar.[14] King Edward of England had his parliament summoned at Berwick, where he took the homage of all the magnates of Scotland, and had their seals appended in permanent record concerning this.[15] From there, he returned to England, where at Newminster Abbey, he gave the custody of Scotland to Earl Warenne, and a governmental seal for the place, saying to him jokingly 'He does good business, who rids himself of shit'.[16] The king appointed Hugh de Cressingham his chamberlain of Scotland, and William de Ormsby his justice; he commanded them that all Scottish men over the age of fifteen should do homage, and that their names should be written down. The clerks took a penny from each one, from which they became rich men. The king ordered that all Scottish lords should remain beyond the Trent, while his war with France lasted. In this year of grace 1297, he took half a mark sterling from each sack of wool in England and Scotland, where before they had paid no more than four pennies, because of which, it was called 'the evil toll'. The king took himself to Gascony.[17]

En quel temps, hu moys de Maii, Willam Walays estoit choise de la
[f. 196v.] comune Descoce destre cheuetain a mouoir gere as Engles, qi
au comencement tua William de Hesilrig a Lanark, qestoit viscount
de Clidisdale depar le Roy Dengleter. Le dit Willam Walais trenuta
sure le dit viscount et luy supprist, ou Thomas de Gray,*d* qen la
coumpaignie du dist viscount estoit, illoeqes fust lesse despoille pur
mort a la melle, com lez Engles sez defenderent. Le dit Thomas ieust
tout la nuyt despoille entre .ij. mesouns ardauntz, qe les Escotez
auoint enz mys le fieu, chalour dez queux tenit sa vie, ou en laube du
iour il estoit conu, et enporte par Willam de Loundy, et ly fist garrir. Et
le prochein yuer, ly dit Willam Walays ardy tout Northumbreland. Le
Count de Garayn qi la gard Descoce auoit depar le Roi de Engleter,
estoit deuers le Sue; se dressa deuers Escoce, ou al pount de Striuelin,
il fust descoumfist de Willam Walais, qi pres estoit en batail, qy lessoit
passer le dit pount a tauntz dez Engles com ly plesoit, qi a soun point
les surecurroit, fist roumper le pount, ou furount plusours dez Engles
mortz, Hugh de Cressingham le tresorer le roy. Et fust dit les Escocez
ly firent depeller, et de soun pele en despite, lour firent layniers. Le
Count de Gareine sen fuy a Berewic. Willam Walais, a qi lez Escocez
enherderent, sodeignement apres cest descoumfiture, suyst le dit
Count de Garain od graunt ost; si enueint decoste Berewik a Hotoun
More en bataile, qi quidoit lez Engles estre araiez pur combatre od
luy, pur quoy il nen ueint plus pres de Berewyk, mais se retourna, et
se herbisa en le park de Duns. Le dit Count de Garain sen departy de
Berewik, lessa la dit vile gast, au procher qe Willam Walays fist, et sen
ala au fitz le roy, qestoit Prince de Galis, pur ceo qe le roy estoit en
Gascoyn, pur quelis nouelis le dit roy sen trey en Engleter. Leuesqe de
Glasgou et Willam, seignur de Douglas, sez vindrent excuser, au
primer venu le dit Count de Garain en Escoce, qils nestoient
conscentaunt au riote de Willam Walays; tout estoint ils deuaunt
enherdauntz, pur quoi le dit count lez fist mettre en prisoun, leuesqe
en le chastelle de Roxburgh, Willam de Douglas en le chastelle de
Berewik, ou de meschef il morust. Willam Walays, qi aparceust le
departir le dit Count de Garain, enuoya Henry de Haliburtoun
cheualer, pur seiser Berewyk, et ordeina autres de graunt aray de
asseger Robert de Hastings en le chastel de Roxburgh. Robert le fitz
Roger, *[f. 197]* qi al hour estoit sires de Wercworth, od Johan le fitz
Marmaduk, od autres barouns du counteez de Northumbreland et de

---

d The name is underlined in red pencil, very clumsily, by a later hand.

At this time, in the month of May, William Wallace was chosen by the [f. 196v.] community of Scotland to be leader, to bring the war to the English. First of all, he killed William de Heselrigg, the King of England's sheriff of Clydesdale, at Lanark.[18] William Wallace marched through the night against the sheriff and surprised him; Thomas de Gray, who was in the sheriff's company, was stripped and left for dead in the melée there, as the English defended themselves. Thomas lay for all the night, stripped, between two burning houses, which the Scots had put to the flame, the heat of which kept him alive. At daybreak, he was found there and carried away by William de Loundy, and was made well.[19] In the following winter, William Wallace burned all Northumberland. The Earl of Warenne, who had the keeping of Scotland for the King of England, was in the South; he took himself to Scotland, where at Stirling Bridge, he was defeated by William Wallace, who was nearby in battle [array].[20] He let as many of the English cross the bridge as he pleased, and overran them at the moment of his [choosing], breaking the bridge. Here, many of the English were killed, [including] Hugh de Cressingham, the king's treasurer. And it was said the Scots had him skinned, and had thongs made from his skin, out of spite. The Earl of Warenne fled to Berwick.[21] Straight after this defeat, William Wallace, who the Scots were following, pursued the Earl of Warenne with a great army. He arrived beside Berwick in battle [array], at Hutton Moor;[22] and he thought that the English were arrayed to fight with him, because of which he did not go any nearer to Berwick, but turned back, and camped in the park at Duns. At William Wallace's approach, the Earl of Warenne left Berwick, leaving the town ruined, and went off to the king's son, the Prince of Wales, because the king was in Gascony; and because of this news, the king came to England.[23] On the Earl of Warenne's first arrival in Scotland, the Bishop of Glasgow and William, lord of Douglas, had come to make excuses for themselves, that they did not consent to William Wallace's rising; both had been his adherents previously, and therefore the earl had them put in prison, the bishop in Roxburgh castle, William de Douglas in Berwick castle, where he died from hardship.[24] Having observed the Earl of Warenne's departure, William Wallace sent Henry de Haliburton, knight, to capture Berwick, and ordered others to besiege Robert de Hastings in Roxburgh castle, with a great force. Robert fitz Roger, [f. 197] who was the lord of Warkworth at the time, and John fitz Marmaduke,[25] with other barons of the counties of Northumberland and Carlisle, rapidly assembled themselves and marched through the

Cardoil, sez assemblerent sodeignement et trenuyterent a Roxburgh, qe si priuement surcurrerent lez Escocez, qe deuaunt qils auoint aparceiuaunce, lez Engles qe suruenuz estoint, auoint tuez lez enginours com auoint en mains lez clikes de lez engines a treir pur getter au chastel; pur quoi estoint mys a descoumfiture, plusours morz. Henry de Haliburtoun od autres qe y estoient en Berewyk, qi de cest descoumfiture oyerent, sez departirent sodeignement, lesserent la dit vile voide. Lez ditz seignours Engles resceyuerent la dit vile de Berewik, et la tindrent tanqe la venu le roy, qy repairez estoit de Gascoyne, enueint deuers Escoce de graunt aray. Entra par Roxburhe, se trey a Tempillistoun, et a Lithcow, et puis deuers Streuelyn, ou encheminaunt, Willam Walays, qi tout le poair Descoce auoit assemble, se adressa a combatre od le dit Roy Dengleter, ou desa le*e* Fawkirk ils sez entre combaterent le iour de la Magdelein, en lan de grace .Mile.CC.lxxx. et .xv.*f* ou les Escotez furount descoumfistz; pur quoi fust dit graunt temps puscedy, qe Willam Walays lour auoit amene au karole dauncent sils uolount. Waulter le freir le Seneschal Descoce, qi descenduz estoit a pee entre lez comuns, fust mort od plus de .x.Mile. dez comuns. Willam Walays, qy a cheual estoit, sen fuy od lez autres seignours Descoce qi y estoient. A quel batail Auntoyn de Beke, Euesqe de Doresme, estoit od le Roy Edward Dengleter, si estuffe dez retenauntz, qe en sa batail estoint .xxxij. baners, se tiercisme dez Countis, le Count de Warwyk, le Count de Oxsenford, et le Count Dangus. En quel hour fust destruyt la vile de Saint Andrew. Le roy remist ses officeris en Escocez, se trey en Engleter, serchaunt les corps saintz en pelerinage, enmerciaunt Dieu de sa victoir, com acoustomez estoit apres tielis affairs.

La delyueraunce Jo…[a]
39. En lan suaunt, lan de grace .Mile.CC.Lxxx.xix., vindrent legatis de la court de Rome, le iour de la traunslacioun saint Thomas, au Roi Edward a Cantorbirs, en priaunt et en monestant le roy, qil lessast Johan de Baillof, iadiz Roy Descoce, en la garde du Saint Pier, depus

---

e   sic
f   r. .Mile.CC.lxxx. et .xviij.

a   Right margin.

night to Roxburgh. They came up to the Scots so stealthily that the English were on them before they had seen them, killing the engineers as they had hold of the latches of the siege-engines [ready] to draw-back to shoot at the castle; and in this way, they were routed, with many dead. Having heard about this defeat, Henry de Haliburton and the others who were there in Berwick, left without delay, leaving the town empty.[26] These English lords took possession of the town of Berwick, and held it until the arrival of the king, who having returned from Gascony, came up to Scotland with a great force. Having entered by Roxburgh, he took himself to Temple Liston, and to Linlithgow, and then towards Stirling; on the way there, William Wallace, who had assembled all the forces of Scotland, made ready to fight with the King of England. There, beside Falkirk, they fought with each other on Mary Magdelen's day [22 July], in the year of grace [1298], where the Scots were defeated; and for this reason it was said for a long time afterwards, that William Wallace had brought them to the jig, and they could have danced if they wished.[27] Walter, the brother of the Steward of Scotland, who had dismounted on foot with the commoners, was killed along with 10,000 of the commoners. William Wallace, who was on horseback, fled along with the other Scottish lords who were there. Antony Bek, Bishop of Durham, was with King Edward of England at the battle, so well provided with retainers, that there were thirty-two banners in his battle, and a trio of earls, the Earl of Warwick, the Earl of Oxford and the Earl of Angus.[28] At this time, the town of St Andrew was destroyed. The king reappointed his officers in Scotland, took himself to England, and sought out the relics of saints in pilgrimage, thanking God for his victory, as he was accustomed to do after such affairs.

The Release of Jo<hn>…

39. In the year following, the year of grace 1299, on the translation of St Thomas [7 July], legates from the Court of Rome came to King Edward at Canterbury, praying and exhorting him that he should leave John de Balliol, formerly King of Scotland, in the keeping of the Holy Father, since he had submitted to his grace. The king granted this, provided that he should not enter Scotland. This was guaranteed, and he released John, who took himself to his lands at Bailleul, his inheritance [f. 197v.] in Picardy, and remained there for all his life.[1] In the year following, letters came to King Edward of England from Pope Boniface, at the procurement and information of the Scots,

qe il estoit rendu au grace de ly. Le roy le graunta, issi qil ne entrast
Escoce. Quoi fust assure, et ly dit Johan deliuers, qi se trey en la terre
de Baillof, soun heritage *[f. 197v.]* en Picardy, qy y endemurrast tout
sa vie. Lan suaunt, vindrent lettres du Pape Boneface par procurement et informacioun de ceaux Descoce, par toutes lez euidentz qils
sauoint deuisere, au Roy Edward Dengleter, purportauntz qe la terre
Descoce estoit tenuz de la Court de Rome, et qe il auoit fait introisoun
en desheritaunce de leglis Romayne, enpriaunt et enamonestaunt a
oster la mayne. Le roy fist somoundre parlement general a Nichol, ou
fust declarez par toutis loys emperialis, ciuilis, canouns et regalis, et
par le vsage de lyel de Bretaigne, en tot temps puis le hour Brutus, qe
la souerainete Descoce apartenoit au regaute Dengleter, quoi fust
nouncie au pape. Le dit Roy Edward se trey en Escoce, assist le
chastel de Carlauerok, et le prist. Apres quel assege, Willam Walays
fust pris par Johan de Mentethe pres de Glaskow, et amenez au Roy
Dengleter, qy ly fist treiner et pendre, a Loundres. Le dit roi fist
enclose[b] la vile de Berewic de mure de pier; se trey en Engleter, lessa
Johan de Segraf gardeyn Descoce. Les Escocez recomencerent a
rebeller encountre le Roy Edward Dengleter, et establirent Johan de
Comyn lour gardein et cheuetaine de lour querel. En quel temps
auindrent grauntz pointz de guere entre lez Marchies, et nomiement
en Teuydale hors du chastel de Roxburhe, entre Ingram de
Houmframuyle, Robert de Kethe, Escotoys, et Robert de Hastang,
Engleis, gardein du dist chastel. Johan de Segraf, le gardein Descoce
depar le Roy Edward Dengleter, mouoit en ost en Escoce, od plusours
grauntz dez Marchies Engleis, et od le Count Patrik de la Marche,
qenherdaunt estoit au Roy Engles, sen veint a Rosselyn, se herbisa en
la maner, sa batail entour ly. Soun auauntgarde fust herbise vn lieu
loinz en vn vilet. Johan Comyn od sez enherdauntz trenuyterent sure
le dit Johan de Segraf, et ly descoumfirent sur la nuit; et soun
auauntgard, qe herbisez estoit de ly vn lieu loinz, aparsceurent sa
descoumfiture, sez vindrent au matin en counray de batail, au
meisme le lieu ou a saire lesserent lour cheuetain, pensaunt a faire
lour deuoir, ou furount outriez et descoumfitz par force Descotois. Et
Rauf le Coffreir illoeqes mort, pur quelis nouelis, meisme lan suaunt,
le Roy Edward se trey en Escoce, qi au primer entree, se herbisa a
Driburgh. Hugh de Audeley od .Lx. homs darmys, qi esiement ne
purroient *[f. 198]* my estre herbisez de lee le roy, sen alerent a Melros,
senherbiserent en labbay. Johan Comyn, adonqes gardein de Escoce,

---

[b]   *MS:* enclore.

devised from all the evidence which they knew of, purporting that the land of Scotland[2] was held of the court of Rome, and that he had invaded it to the disinheritance of the Roman Church, praying and admonishing him to remove his hand.[3] The king summoned a general parliament at Lincoln, where it was declared that by all the laws, imperial, civil, canon and royal, and by the custom of the Isle of Britain at all times since the era of Brutus, the sovereignty of Scotland pertained to the kingship of England; and this was announced to the pope.[4] King Edward took himself to Scotland, besieged Caerlaverock castle, and took it. After this siege, William Wallace was taken by John de Menteith near to Glasgow, and brought to the King of England, who had him drawn and hanged at London.[5] The king had Berwick enclosed with a wall of stone, and took himself to England, leaving John de Segrave as keeper of Scotland.[6] The Scots again began to rebel against King Edward of England, and established John de Comyn as their Guardian and the leader of their cause. At this time, great encounters of war occurred between the Marchers, and particularly in Teviotdale outside Roxburgh castle, between Ingram de Umfraville and Robert de Keith, Scots, and Robert de Hastang, Englishman, keeper of this castle.[7] John de Segrave, keeper of Scotland for King Edward of England, moved into Scotland with an army, with many magnates from the English Marches, and with Earl Patrick of March, who was an adherent of the English king.[8] He came to Roslin, and quartered himself in the manor, with his own battle around him.[9] His vanguard was quartered a league further away, in a village. John Comyn with his adherents marched through the night against John de Segrave, and defeated him in the night-time. His vanguard, which was quartered a league further away from him, realised he had been defeated, and in the morning, they came in battle formation to the same place where they had left leader in the evening, intending to do their duty, but they were overrun and defeated by the Scottish force.[10] Ralph the Cofferer died there.[11] Because of this news, in the year following, King Edward went to Scotland;[12] and on his first arrival, he quartered at Dryburgh. Hugh de Audley and sixty men-at-arms, who could not [f. 198] conveniently be quartered in the king's vicinity, took themselves to Melrose, quartering themselves in the Abbey. John Comyn, then guardian of Scotland, was in the Ettrick Forest with a great band of men-at-arms. Seeing Hugh's encampment at Melrose in that manner, he marched through the night against him, and had the gates broken; and while the English within the abbey were arraying and mounting

estoit entre la forest de Ettrik od graunt rout de genz darmis; aparceynoit lerbigage du dit Hugh a Melros a la maner, trenuyta sure luy, fist roumper lez portes, et endementiers lez ditz Engles dedenz labbay estoient araiez et mountez lour cheueaux en my la court, firent gettere ouertz lez portez. Lez Escoces entrerent a cheuaul, graunt noumbre, enporterent a tere lez Engles, qi poy furount, les pristrent et tuerent toucz. Thomas Gray^c cheualer del hour qil estoit abatu, enprist la mesoun outre la port, qy la teint en espoir de rescouse, tanqe la mesoun comensa ardoir sure sa test, qi od autres fust pris. Le Roy Edward se trey auaunt, teint la fest de Nowel a Lynlithcow, pius cheuaucha par tout la terre Descoce, sen trey a Dunfermelin, ou Johan Comyn, qi aparceynoit qil ne pooit countre ester le poair le Roy Dengleter, se mist au grace le roy sure condicioun qil reaueroit od touz sez enherdauntz lour droitz possessiouns, qi redeuindrent sez gentez lieges; sure quoi, nouelis instrumentz publiement furround notez. Johan de Soulis ne voloit lez condiciounes, voida Escoce, sen ala en Fraunce ou il morust. Willam Olifart vn iouen bacheler Descoce fist garnir le chastel de Striuelyn, ne deigna conscentir as condiciouns Johan de Comyn, mais se clamoit a tenir du Lioun. Le dit Roy Edward, qi le atournement auoit a poy de touz ceaux Descoce, et possessioun de lez fermetez, se muyst deuaunt le chastel de Stryuelyn et lassist, et lassailla par diuers engynes, et le prist par force, et par assege de .xix. semains. A quel assege, Thomas de Gray,^{d} cheualer, fust feru dun garot dun espringal parmy la test desoutz lez oillis, treboucha a terre com mort, desoutz lez barreirs du chastelle, com auoit rescous soun meister Henry de Beaumound, qi pris estoit as ditz barreirs de vn tenail enmys par engine, et aunces a poy outre lez barreirs, qaunt le dit Thomas ly arasa hors del meschief. Le dit Thomas^e estoit emporte, et le aray attourne de ly auoir enterrez, sure quel point, il comensa a mouoir et regardir, et garry apres. Le roy enuoia le chastelain, Willam Olyfart, a Loundres en prisoun; si fesoit iouster lez cheualers de soun ost deuaunt lour departir, au remuer de lassege. Il enmist sez officeris par tout Escoce, sen treyt en Engleter, et lessa Eymer de Valoyns Count de Penbrok, gardein Descoce, a qi il dona lez forestes de [f. 198v.] Selkirk et de Etryk, ou a Selkirk le dit Eymer fist afermer vn piele, enbota graunt garnisoun.

En qel hour fust le Count de Flaundres pris a Betoyn, et retenu en

---

^{c} MS: Thomas Gray *finely underlined, in black ink.*
^{d} MS: Thomas de Gray *underlined in red pencil, by a later hand.*
^{e} MS: Le dit Thomas *underlined in red pencil.*

their horses in the middle of the courtyard, the gates were thrown open. The Scots entered on horseback in great numbers, forcing the English (of whom there were few) to the ground, taking or killing them all. At the time he was struck down, Thomas Gray, knight, had seized the house outside the gate; he held it in the hope of rescue, until the house began to burn down over his head, and he was taken along with the others.[13] King Edward moved forward, and held the feast of Christmas at Linlithgow. Afterwards, he rode through the land of Scotland, and took himself to Dunfermline, where John Comyn, realising that he could not stand against the power of the King of England, put himself at the king's mercy, on condition that he and all his adherents should have back their rightful possessions. They became his liege men again, and new legal documents concerning this were publicly noted.[14] John de Soules would not agree to the conditions, left Scotland and went off to France, where he died.[15] William Oliphant, a young bachelor of Scotland, garrisoned Stirling castle, not deigning to consent to John de Comyn's conditions, but claiming that he held of the Lion.[16] King Edward, who had the submission of nearly all of the Scots, and possession of the strongholds, came up to Stirling castle and besieged it, attacking it with various siege-engines; and he took it by force, by a nineteen week siege.[17] At this siege, Thomas de Gray, knight, was hit by a bolt from a springald through the head beneath the eyes; he was thrown to the ground as though dead, underneath the castle barricades, just as he had rescued his master Henry de Beaumont, who had been caught at the barricades by a hook [thrown] from an enemy engine and was already almost across the barricades, when Thomas snatched him out of trouble. Thomas was carried away, and a troop was got ready to bury him – at which point, he started to move and to look about, and afterwards he recovered. The king sent the castellan, William Oliphant, to prison in London. He arranged for the knights of his army to joust before their departure, at the end of the siege. He sent his officials through all of Scotland, and went back to England, leaving Aymer de Valence, Earl of Pembroke, as keeper of Scotland, to whom he gave the forests of [f. 198v.] Selkirk and Ettrick. At Selkirk, Aymer fortified a peel, and put in a large garrison.

At this time, the Count of Flanders was taken at Béthune, and kept in the King of France's prison. Because of this, the commoners of Flanders rose up in war against the French, and on St John's day in mid summer [24 June], they fought with the forces of France at Coutrai.[18] Here, the Count of Artois along with many other French

prisoun du Roy de Fraunce, pur quoi lez comunes de Flaundres sez
mouoint en guere as Fraunceys, ou le iour de saint Johan en my este,
ils coumbaterent od le poair de Fraunce a Courteray, ou le Count
Dartoys oue plusours autres countis et barouns Fraunces furrount
mortez par orgoil et lour suquydery, qe lez Flemens surcurrerent a
cheual en lours fossez, pur corouce de qoi, le Roy de Fraunce od tout
soun poair assist Lisle. Les Flemens enuoierent au Roi Edward
Dengleter en requeraunt succours, qi roi estoit enueillez et malaious
et soun tresor espendu en sez gueris Descoce, en quoi sez gentz
furount enlacez, issint qe bonement ne se pooit meller, qe volountiers
se entremist de lour eider, se queist engyn, fist forger vn lettre depar
lez Eskeuinis de Gaunte, directe a ly meismes, qe parlerent ensy:

A lour tresdoute seignour Roy Dengleter, sez pouers seruauntz
de Gaunt, toutes honours et seruices. Pur ceo qe nous quidoms
qil agreeroit a la noblesce de vous, de sauoir ioyous nouellis du
bien estre nostre seignour le Count de Flaundres, uostre alye si
vous plest, pleise a la hautesce de vous a entendre qe nous
auoms purchase pur le nostre asseitz largement, couyne de
gentz priuez et pussauntz dedenz lost le Roy de Fraunce, qi
nous ount en couenaunt par surete suffisaunt a prendre le roy
dedenz cez .xv. iours hors de sa tent, et de nous ly enuoyer a
certain lieu limite a faire eschaunge od nostre dit seignour. Si
pleise a la tresexcellent seignourie de vous a tenir cest chos en
ferre, et eider et maintener, sustener et gouerner voz simples
enherdauntz, sils enbosoignent de succours, lez bosoignes
acompliz susditz, qe grautement ferrount en encressement de
uostre estat, qe bonement ne pocount failler, lez queux nous
esperoms escheuez, qe sils ne soint faitez vn iour, ne purra
failler vn autre, taunt sumos en certain.

Le Roy Edward prist cest lettre, et vn iour com il sen leua du lite la
royne sa femme, qe sore estoit le Roy de Fraunce, qe al hour estoit en
Kent, se feigna a sercher sa bours apres lettres; si lessat cest lettre
gesire sure le lite sa femme, sen ala en vn chapel a oyer messe. La
royne aparsu la lettre, qe la prist, et la luyst, et la remist. Le roy en my
la messe reueint hastaunt en la chaumbre la royne, demaundaunt
irrousement et sodeignement, si nul trouoit vn lettre, sen alast au lite,
troua la lettre, si ly hasta de la prendre, [*f. 199*] qi ioyousement la
happa, et sodeignement reala saunz plus dire. La royne qe auoit lieu
la lettre, aparceu le countenaunce le roy, auoit graunt doute et dolour,
qe soun freir serroit ensy trahi dez vileins, fist faire en le hour priues
lettres au Roy de Fraunce soun freir de tout la sentence du dit lettre

counts and barons were killed through their pride and arrogance, charging on horseback against the Flemings in their ditches. Enraged by this, the King of France besieged Lille with all his forces. The Flemings sent to King Edward of England asking for assistance, but the king was old and ill, and his treasure was spent on his Scottish wars, in which his men were entangled. However, although he could not embroil himself properly, he wanted to intervene to help them, [and so] he came up with a scheme, and had a letter forged from the échevins of Ghent, addressed to himself, which was worded thus:

> To our most dread lord the King of England, his poor servants of Ghent, all honours and services. Because we believe that it will be pleasing to your honour to know glad tidings of the well-being of our lord the Count of Flanders, your ally if you please, may it please your highness to know that we have purchased for us, plentily enough, the support of secret and powerful men within the King of France's army, who are bound to us, on sufficient security, to take the king outside his tent within these fifteen days, and to send him to us to a certain specifed place to make an exchange with our said lord. If it pleases your most excellent lordship to keep this plan in motion, and to aid and maintain, sustain and govern your humble adherents, if they should be in need of help, [when] the aforesaid business is accomplished, which will work greatly to the increase of your estate, and which cannot readily fail; and we hope to achieve these things, for if not done one day, they cannot fail on another, so much are we certain.

King Edward took this letter, and one day as he got up from his wife the Queen's bed, who was the sister of the King of France, and who was in Kent at this time, he pretended to search his pouch for letters. He left this letter lying on his wife's bed, and went to a chapel to hear mass. The queen noticed the letter, took it and read it, and put it back. In the middle of mass, the king hurriedly returned to the queen's chamber, and angrily and abruptly demanded whether anyone had found a letter. He went to the bed, found the letter, and grabbing it hurriedly, [f. 199] happily took possession of it, and abruptly left without saying more. Noticing the king's expression, the queen, who had read the letter, greatly feared and sorrowed that her brother would be betrayed in this way by villeins; within the hour, she had secret letters written to the King of France, her brother, embellished with the full sense of the letter, so that he might watch out for himself. These letters were hastened, and as soon as the King of France was

engarnisaunt, qil se agardast. Cestes lettres furount hastez, et del
hour qe le Roy de Fraunce auoit aparceu la maner dez lettres sa sore,
il se delogea de lassege meisme la nuyte, et ensi eida engyn qe moult
vaut maint foitz, qaunt force y faut; ceocy aueint apres la saint
Michel. Et meisme leste apres, le Roy de Fraunce assembla ost,
reentra Flaundres, et meisme le iour de saint Johan, en vn ane
prochein de la batail de Courtray, furount lez Flemyns descoumfitz a
Mouns en Paiwir; et lour cheuetain mort Willam de Juleris, qi freir
estoit du Count de Julieris. Apres qoi fust le Count Robert deliuers de
prisoun, en maner qe lez trois viles de Flaundres sure la marche de
Fraunce demurasent au Roy de Fraunce, Doway, Lile, et Betoyne.

En cest mein temps Robert de Bruis Count de Carrik, qi fort se
tenoit de gentz de sanguinite, et de alliaunce, esperaunt toutditz
accioun de soun droit, du chalange du successioun du realme
Descoce, en lan de grace .Mile.CCC.vj. 4.kalendes de Februare,
enuoya sez .ij. freires Thomas et Neil, de Loghmaban a Dalscuentoun
a Johan Comyn, enpriaunt, qil ly vousist encountreir a Dromfres au
freirs menours qils purroint entreparler, si auoint couyne od sez .ij.
auaunt ditz freirs, qen chemynaunt ils tuasent le dit Johan Comyne.
Lez queux furount si amiablement resceus du dit Johan Comyn, qils
ne sez purroint assenter de ly fair nul mal, mes sez acorderent qe lour
freir enfeist soun meillour. Le dit Johan Comyne, qi nul mal pensoit,
se mist od lez dieus freirs le dit Robert de Bruys a Dromfres a parler
od ly; se veint au freirs ou troua le dit Robert, qi ly uenoit a
lencountre, sy lui amena al haute auter. Lez .ij. freirs le dit Robert ly
disoient en secre, Sire, fesoint ils, il nous fist si bele acoil, et od si
larges dounes, et taunt se assura de nous par si ouert countenaunce,
qen nul maner ly purrioms maufaire. Voir, fesoit il, bien estez lectous.
Lessez moy conuenir. Il prist le dit Johan Comyn, sez apporterent *f* al
autere. Sire, ceo disoit le dit Robert de Bruis au dit Johan Comyne,
cest terre Descoce est de tout soutz, mys en seruitude dez Engles par
perresce du cheuetain, qe soun droit et la fraunchise du realme ad
lesse perdre. Choisez de .ij. voys lun; ou preignez moun heritage, et
me [f. 199v.] eidez a estre roys; ou baillez moi le toun, si te eideray a
ceo estre, pusqe tu es de soun sank qi lad perdu, ou ieo qe le espoir
par successioun de mez auncestres qy droit claimerent a auoir, qe par
lez voz estoient destourbez, qar ore est temps, en veillesce de cesty
Roy Engles. Certis, ceo disoit ly dit Johan Comyne, ieo ne fauseray
iames a mon seignour Engles de ceo qe ieo ly su atourne, de serement

---

f   MS: appoerent.

aware of the content of his sister's letters, he decamped from the siege that same night; and thus trickery helped, which on many occasions avails more, when force fails. This took place after Michaelmas [29 September].[19] And that next summer, the King of France assembled an army, went back into Flanders, and on the same St John's day, one year after the battle of Courtrai, the Flemings were defeated at Mons-en-Pévèle; and their leader, William of Juliers, the brother of the Count of Juliers, was killed.[20] After this, Count [Guy][21] was released from prison, on condition that the three Flemish towns on the French march, Douai, Lille and Béthune, should remain with the King of France.

In the mean time, Robert de Bruce, Earl of Carrick, maintained a force of men of his blood and of his allegiance, hoping always for the establishment of his right to his claim to the succession to the realm of Scotland; and on 29 January, in the year of grace 1306,[22] he sent his two brothers, Thomas and Neil, from Lochmaben to John Comyn at Dalswinton, asking that he be willing to meet him at Dumfries at [the church of] the Friars Minor, so that they could talk, having plotted with his two brothers that they should kill John Comyn on the way. They were received so amiably by John Comyn, that they could not bring themselves to do him any harm, but agreed with each other that their brother could do his best. John Comyn, who did not suspect any harm, went with Robert Bruce's two brothers to Dumfries to speak with him. He came to the friars [church] where he found Robert, who came to meet him and led him to the high altar. Robert's two brothers spoke to him in secret, 'Sir', they said, 'he gave us so fine a welcome, and with such large gifts, and we were so assured by his open manner, that in no way could we do him wrong'. 'Well', he said, 'you're a right pair of milksops! Leave me to do what's necessary'. He took John Comyn, leading them to the altar. 'Sir', and so spoke Robert de Bruce to John Comyn, 'this land of Scotland is wholly subjected, put in servitude to the English through the negligence of its leader, who allowed his rights and the freedom of the realm to be lost. Choose one of two ways: either take my inheritance, and help me [f. 199v.] to be king; or grant me yours, if I will help you to be the same, since you are of his blood who has lost [the realm], while I hope for it in succession to my forebears who claimed the right to have it, and who were obstructed by yours.[23] For now is the time, in the dotage of this English king.' 'Certainly', spoke John Comyn, 'I will never be false to my English lord in a matter in which I could be accused of treason, because I have submitted to him, by oath and homage'. 'No',

et homage, en chos qe me purra estre surmys tresoun. Non, fesoit ly it Robert de Bruys, ieo auoy en vous autre espoir, par promes de toi et toens, si mas descouery au roy par tes lettres, pur quoi, viuaunt toy, ne pusse escheuer moun voloir, tu aueras toun guerdoun; si ly fery du cutel, autres lui decouperent en my leglis deuaunt le auter. Vn chiualer soun vncle qi present estoit, fery le dit Robert de Bruys dun espey hu pice, mais armez estoit qe ne ly greua, qy vncle fust illoeqes tue. Le dit Robert se fist coroner en Roys Descoce a Scone, en la fest del Annunciacioun nostre Dame, de la Countesse de Boghan, pur absence du count soun fitz, qi adonqes demura en Engleter a soun maner de Vituik, ioust Laycestre, a qy loffice del encorounement dez Roys Descoce apertenoit heritablement, abscent le Count de Fiffe qi al hour estoit en garde le roi en Engleter. La dit Countesse fust meisme cel ane pris dez Engleis, et amenez a Berewik, et par comaundment le Roy Edward Dengleter mys en vn mesounceaux de fust, en vn tour de le chastelle de Berewyk, lez parrays escheqerez, qe touz la porroint agarder pur meruail. Le Roy Edward Dengleter qi aparceust la riote, qe Robert de Bruis fesoit en Escoce od sez enherdauntz, y enuoya Eymer de Valoins, Count de Penbrok, od autres barouns Dengleter, et od plusours Descoce extraitz du sank Johan Comyne, qi touz sez adresserent encountre le dit Robert de Bruys. Le dit Count de Penbrok se mist a la vile de saint Johan, y endemurra vn pece. Robert de Bruis auoit assemblee tout le poair de Escoce, de se enherdauntz, et dez sauuages iones gentez, legers a mouoir countre Engles; enueint deuaunt la vile de saint Johan en dieus grauntz bataillis, proferaunt batail au dit count et as Engles, qi y endemura deuaunt la dit vile, de matin tanqe apres haut noune. Le dit Count de Penbrok se teint tot coy tanqe a lour departir, qe par counsail dez seignours Descoz dez bienvoillauntz Johan Comyn, qi as Engles furount enherdauntz, et od ly en la dit vile, lez sires de Moubray, de Abirnethin, de Brighen, et [f. 200] de Gordoun, od plusours autres, sen issit en .ij. bataillis, lour enemys Descoce estoient denouez, auoint enuoye lours herbisours de lour herbiger a Methfen; relierent com purroint, sen vindrent combatre tout a cheual od la dist issu, mais furrount descoumfitz lez Escocz, ou fust arene le dit Robert de Bruys, et lesse eschaper par Johan de Haliburtoun, del hour qil aparceust qil estoit, qy nauoit point de cote armur, mais vn chemys blaunk. Thomas Randolf, neueu le dist Robert de Bruys, qi apres fust Count de Morref, fust pris a meisme cest batail de Methfen, et au prier Adam de Gordoun fust deliuers et demora Engles, tanqe autrefoitz fust repris de lez Escocez. Robert de Bruys, les plusours dez soens mortz et pris a cest bataille de

said Robert de Bruce, 'I had other hopes of you, by the promise of you and yours, but you have revealed me to the king by your letters, so that I cannot achieve my aims while you live; you shall have your deserts'. He struck him with a knife, and the others cut him down in the middle of the church in front of the altar. A knight, [Comyn's] uncle, who was present, struck Robert de Bruce with a sword in the chest, but he was wearing armour and so was not injured, and the uncle was killed there.[24] Robert had himself crowned as King of Scotland at Scone, on the feast of the annunciation of Our Lady [25 March], by the Countess of Buchan, in the absence of the earl, her son, who was then staying in England at his manor of Whitwick, near Leicester, and to whom the office of coronation of the kings of Scotland belonged in heredity. The Earl of Fife was absent because at the time he was in the keeping of the King in England.[25] The countess was taken by the English in that same year, and brought to Berwick; and at King Edward of England's command, she was put in a wooden hut, in one of the towers of Berwick castle, with criss-crossed walls, so that all could watch her for spectacle.[26] Seeing the disorder that Robert de Bruce was causing in Scotland with his adherents, King Edward of England sent there Aymer de Valence, Earl of Pembroke,[27] along with other English barons, and with many Scots who were of John Comyn's blood, who had all turned against Robert de Bruce. The Earl of Pembroke went to the town of Perth, and remained there for a while. Robert de Bruce had assembled all of the forces of Scotland, from his adherents, and from the wild young men who were easily moved against the English. They came up to the town of Perth in two great battles, offering battle to the earl and the English, remaining there before the town from morning until after high noon. The Earl of Pembroke stayed calm until their departure. By the advice of the Scottish lords amongst John Comyn's well-wishers, who were adherents of the English, and who were with him in the town (the lords Mowbray, Abernethy, Brechin and [f. 200] Gordon, with many others),[28] he made a sortie in two battles, their Scottish enemies having moved out, sending their foragers to set up their camp at Methven. [The Scots] rallied as well as they could, and all those on horseback came to fight against the sortie, but the Scots were defeated.[29] Here Robert de Bruce was arrested, but was allowed to escape by John de Haliburton, as soon as he realised who he was, for [Bruce] did not have any coat armour, but just a white shirt.[30] Thomas Randolph, Robert Bruce's nephew, who was later Earl of Moray, was taken at this same battle of Methven, and he was released

Methfen, fust enchacez en Kentire par lez Engles, qi assistrent le chastelle hu dit pays quidauntz qe ly dit Robert y vst este, qi ne ly trouerent point au pris du dit chastelle, mais y trouerent sa femme, la feile le Count de Hulster, et Neil soun freir; et procheignement fust le Count de Athelis pris, qi de dit chastel fust fuys. Le dit Neil freir le dit Robert de Bruys, od Alain Duruard et plusours autres, furount penduz et treynez par iugement a Berewyk. Et la femme le dit Robert enuoyez en garde en Engleter. Le Count de Athelis pur ceo qe cosyn estoit le Roy Dengleter, fitz Maude de Doure sa aunte, fust enuoyez a Loundres, et pur ceo qe du sank estoit le roy, fust penduz sure plus hautis fourches qe autres, de .xxx. pees. Meisme lan, le roy fist soun fitz Edward Prince de Galis cheuaucher a Westmouster od graunt noumbre dez autres juuenceaux nobilis de soun realme, et ly enuoya de graunt aray en Escoce, od touz ceux noueaux cheualers. Thomas Count de Lancastre et Houmfray de Bouhun, Count de Herforde, qi passerent lez mountez Descoce, assistrent le chastel de Kyndromy en Marre, et le gaigna. En quel chastel, fu troue Cristofre de Setoun od sa femme, la sore Robert de Bruys, qi com Engles renoye fust, enuoie a Dunfres, et illoeqes penduz, trainez et decollez, ou deuaunt auoit fait tuer vn cheualer viscount du pays, mys depar le Roy Dengleter. Lez euesqes de Glascow et de Saint Andrew et labbe de Scone furont pris meisme la seisoun, et enuoyez en Engleter en gard.

Peris de Gauirstoun fust accuse au roy de diuers crimes et vices, pur quoi nen fust dignes a estre pres le fitz le roy, pur quoi il fust excilez et foriurrez. En lan de grace .Mile.CCC.vj., le Roy Edward estoit venuz a Dunfermelin, soun fitz Edward Prince de [f. 200v.] Galis estoit reuenuz du outre lez mountz, y endemora od graunt ost a la vile de saint Johan. Et endementers Robert de Bruys estoit reentrez hors dez Iles, se auoit acoilly vn rout en lez estroitez de Athelis, enuoya messagers pur auoir tretice od le dit fitz le roy, qi auoit conduyt a venir tretre, qi enueint a le pount de la vile de saint Johan, si entra en tretice a taster sil empoait nul grace auoir. Quel parlaunce fust lendemain nouncie au roi a Dunfermelin. Il estoit a poy enrage qaunt il oy de le tretice, qi demaundoit, qi en fust si hardy de attainere tretice od noz traitours saunz scieu de nous, qi ne voloit oyer parler. Le Roy et soun fitz sez treierent sure Marches Dengleter. Eymer de Valoins fust demurre lieutenaunt le roy en Escoce. Robert de Bruys recomensa graunt couyn, enuoya sez .ij. frers Thomas et Alexander deuers Niddisdalle et le Vale de Anande pur attreier lez queres des gentz, ou furount suppris dez Engles et pris et amenez par comaundement le roy a Cardoil, illoeqes penduz, traynez et decollez.

at the request of Adam de Gordon and remained English, until he was recaptured by the Scots on another occasion.[31] With most of his men killed or taken at the battle of Methven, Robert de Bruce was pursued to Kintyre by the English, who besieged the castle in that region, thinking that Robert might be there. They found no sign of him when they took the castle, but they found his wife there, the daughter of the Earl of Ulster, and Neil his brother; and soon afterwards, the Earl of Atholl was taken, who had fled from the castle.[32] Neil, Robert de Bruce's brother, along with Alan Durward and several others, was hanged and drawn under sentence at Berwick. And Robert's wife was sent to England under guard. Because he was a cousin of the King of England, the son of his aunt Maud of Dover, the Earl of Atholl was sent to London, and because he was of the king's blood, he was hanged from a gallows thirty feet higher than the others.[33] In the same year, the king knighted his son Edward, Prince of Wales, at Westminster with a great number of other noble youths of his realm, and sent him to Scotland with a great force, with all these new knights.[34] Thomas, Earl of Lancaster, and Humphrey de Bohun, Earl of Hereford, crossed the Scottish mountains, besieged Kildrummy castle in Mar, and won it.[35] Christopher Seton was found in this castle, with his wife, Robert de Bruce's sister.[36] As an English renegade, he was sent to Dumfries and hung, drawn and beheaded there, where he had previously had a knight killed, [who was] the sheriff of the region appointed by the King of England.[37] The Bishops of Glasgow and St Andrews and the abbot of Scone were taken in the same season, and sent to England under guard.

Piers Gaveston was accused by the king of various crimes and vices, because of which he was not fit to be near the king's son; because of this, he was condemned and exiled.[38] In the year of grace 1306, King Edward came to Dunfermline, and his son Edward, Prince of [f. 200v.] Wales, returned from across the mountains, and remained there with a great army at Perth.[39] Meanwhile, Robert de Bruce had come back from beyond the Isles, and had gathered together a band in the glens of Atholl. He sent messengers to have negotiations with the king's son, with a safe-conduct to come to negotiate. They came to the bridge at Perth, and entered into negotiations to find out whether he might not be able to have [the king's] grace. These talks were made known to the the king at Dunfermline on the next day. He was almost demented when he heard about the negotiation, demanding, 'who has made so bold as to manage to negotiate with our traitors without our knowing?', and would not hear talk of it. The king and his son

Robert de Bruys se auoit [g] assemble sez enherdauntz en Carryk.
Eymer de Valoins qi ceo auoit oy, se trey deuers ly, ou a Loudoun le
dit Robert encountra oue le dit Eymer de Valoins, et ly descoumfist, et
ly enchasa au chastel de Are; et dedenz le tierce iour, le dit Robert de
Bruys descounfist Rauf de Monhermer, qi fust dit Count de
Gloucestre, par cause qe Johan la feile le roi et Countesse de
Gloucestre, ly auoit pris par amours a marry. Si ly enchasa au chastel
de Are, et illoeqes ly assist tanqe lost Dengleter ly rescourent, qi
enboterent le dit Robert de Bruys a tiel meschef qil ala a pee par lez
mountez et de ile en ile, et a la foitz a tiel meschief, qe auscun foitz ne
auoit nuly od ly, qar com tesmoignent lez croniclis de sez gestis; il
enueint en cel houre a vn passage tout soul de .ij. illis, et com il estoit
en le batew od .ij. mariners, ils ly demaunderent nouelis, si rien auoit
oy parler ou Robert de Bruys estoit deuenus. Nenyl, fesoit il. Certis,
fesoint ils, nous vodroms qe nous ly tenissims en le hour, si murreroit
de noz mains. Et pur quoi, fesoit il. Pur ceo qe il enmourdit Johan
Comyn nostre seignour. Ils ly mistrent a terre, ou ils ly auoint en
couenaunt, qi lour dit, Beaux seignours, vous auez sueide qe vous
tenicez Robert de Bruis. Veiez moy cy, qe vous plerra, et si ne fust qe
vous mauez fet curtosy, qe mauez mys outre cest estroit passage,
vous encoumparez uostre voloir. Si sen ala soun chemyn, qi a tiel
[*f. 201*] meschief estoit enchace. Ly auaunt dit Roy Edward Dengleter
auoit en cest meine temps grauntement demore maladiz a Lanercost,
qy de illoeqes remua de chaungier leire, et pur attendre soun ost qil
auoit somouns a reentreir Escoce; si enuieint a Burh sure le Sabloun,
et illoeqes morust en le moys de Juyl, en lan de grace .Mile.CCC.vij.,
et de illoeqes enporte et enterre sollempnement a Westmouster delee
sez auncestres, apres qe il auoit regne .xxxiiij. auns .vij. moys, et .xi.
iours; et en lan de soun age, lxviij. auns, et .xx. iours. I cesti Roy
Edward nauoit de sa primer femme la feile le Roy de Casteil, fors vn
fitz qi vesqy. De la secound espous la sore le Roy de Fraunce, auoit il
.ij. fitz, Thomas et Eadmound. A Thomas dona il la counte de
Northfolc, et de Southfolk, oue la Marshalsy Dengleter, quel countee
od loffice apartenoit de heritage a Roger Bigod, qi nauoit point
dengendrur, qi fist le roy soun heir, en party pur doute qe le roy ne ly
surmeist mal port, qentre ly et autres comencerent vn foitz a Nicol
couyn encountre ly. A Edmound[h] soun fitz pusne deuisa il en soun
testament, quatre mille marche de terre, et pur estre acomply de

---

[g]   MS: se auoit *repeated.*
[h]   MS: Emound.

went to the English Marches. Aymer de Valence was left as the king's lieutenant in Scotland.[40] Robert de Bruce resumed his great scheming, sending his two brothers Thomas and Alexander to Nithsdale and Annandale to win over the hearts of men. Here, they were surprised by the English, taken, and brought by the king's command to Carlisle; there they were hung, drawn and beheaded.[41] Robert de Bruce had assembled his adherents in Carrick. Having heard about this, Aymer de Valence marched towards him; and at Loudon Hill, Robert fought with Aymer de Valence and defeated him, and pursued him to Ayr castle.[42] And within three days, Robert de Bruce had defeated Ralph de Monthermer, who was called Earl of Gloucester, because Joan, the king's daughter and Countess of Gloucester, had taken him as husband, for love.[43] [Robert] pursued him to Ayr castle, and besieged him there until an English army rescued him. This put Robert de Bruce in such trouble that he went through the mountains on foot, and from island to island, and sometimes in such trouble, that on some occasions he had no one with him, as the chronicles of his deeds testify.[44] At this time, he went on a crossing between two islands all alone; and when he was in the boat with two sailors, they asked him for news, and whether he had heard nothing said of what had become of Robert de Bruce. 'No', said he. 'For sure', said they, 'we wish that we could get hold of him right now, so he might die at our hands.' 'Why?', said he. 'Because he murdered John Comyn, our lord.' They took him to land, where they had arranged with him; and he said to them, 'My good lords, you wished that you had hold of Robert de Bruce. You see me here, if you please, and were it not that you had done me courtesy, taking me over this narrow crossing, you might have had your desire.' He went down his road, [f. 20l] having escaped from great danger. In the mean time, King Edward of England remained at Lanercost for a long while, in poor health, moving from there for a change of air, and to meet his army which he had summoned to go back into Scotland. He came to Burgh by Sands, and there he died in the month of July, in the year of grace 1307, and he was born from there and buried solemnly at Westminster beside his ancestors, after he had reigned for thirty-four years, seven months and eleven days, and in his sixty-eighth year, and twenty days.[45] This King Edward had but one son who lived by his first wife, the daughter of the King of Castile. By his second wife, the sister of the King of France, he had two sons, Thomas and Edmund.[46] To Thomas he gave the earldom of Norfolk, and Suffolk, with the Marshalsey of England. The earldom with the office pertained by

Edward soun fitz et heire, sur sa benisoun. Qi heir puis dona au dit Edmound la counte de Kent, od party de la terre a ly deuyse, mais tout ne ly estoit my parfourny deuaunt le temps le tierce Edward. Cesty Edward le primer apres la Conquest auoit plusours feilles; vn estoit espose au Count de Glowcestre, vn autre au Duk de Braban, la tierce au Count de Baris, la quart au Count de Holand, apres mort de qi, el fust autrefoitz espose au Count de Herforde; la quint fust nonayne a Aumesbery.

du pape Innocens[a]

40. Innocens le .5. fust pape apres Gregoir le 10 .5. moys. Cesti estoit apelle Petrus de Tarent, il fust de lordre de Prechours, et Meistre en Diuinite. Apres qi Innocens, fust Adrian le .5., pape .2. mois. Il auoit este enuoie du Pape Clement en Engleter, pur peiser debat entre le roy et lez barouns. Apres qi Adrian, Johan le .5. fust pape .9. auns. Il estoit primes nome Petrus, qi asseitz plus saint estoit deuaunt, qe apres qaunt il auoit soun[b] estat. Il auaunsa uolountiers lez grauntz clerks, il esperoit long vie, mais sodeignement treboucha de vn chaumbre qil auoit edifie a Vetourbe, et morust. Apres qi Johan le .ij.,[c] Johan le .3. fust pape .3. auns. Apres qi Johan, Nicholas fust pape, qi ordena Robert de Kilwardby en cardenal,[d] et freir Johan de [f. 201v.] Pecham del ordre dez Menurs et Meistre de Diuinite, en Erceuesqe de Cantorbires. Apres qi Nicholas le .3. Honorius le .4. fust pape .7. auns. Cesti chaungea labit de Freirs Carmes, qe deuaunt estoit pale. Apres qi Honorius le .4., Nicholas le .4. fust pape .6. aunz. Il estoit de lordre de Freirs Menours. Il declara lordre dez Freirs Menours, en temps de qy aueint vn tiel tempest la veil saint Margaret en Engleter de foudre yuernail, qe defist lez blez, de quoi enueint graunt cherete, qe apoi durra la vie Edward le primer apres la Conquest. En quel temps lez taxsis des eglis furount chaungez a plus haut valu.

[a] *Right margin.*
[b] *MS:* sou.
[c] *sic.*
[d] *MS:* Robert de Kilwardby en Cardenal *underlined in red pencil.*

hereditary right to Roger Bigod, who did not have any offspring; he had made the king his heir, partly for fear that the king might suspect him of ill-will, because he and some others had once started between them a plot against him at Lincoln.[47] To Edmund his youngest son, he left four thousand marks worth of land in his will, and this was to be carried out by Edward his son and heir, on his blessing. This heir afterward gave Edmund the earldom of Kent, with part of the land left to him, but [the bequest] was not completely fulfilled until the time of the third Edward.[48] This Edward the first after the Conquest had several daughters; one was married to the Earl of Gloucester, another to the Duke of Brabant, the third to the Count of Bar, the fourth to the Count of Holland, after whose death, she was married again, to the Earl of Hereford. The fifth was a nun at Amesbury.[49]

40. Innocent V was pope after Gregory X for five months; he was called Peter of Tarentaise, he was of the order of preachers, and a Master of Divinity.[1] After Innocent, Adrian V was Pope for two months.[2] He had been an envoy of Pope Clement [IV] to England, to settle the dispute between the king and the barons. After Adrian, John [XXI] was pope for nine years.[3] He was first named Peter, and proved to be more holy before he held his office than after. He willingly promoted great scholars. He hoped for a long life, but fell suddenly out of chamber which he had built at Viterbo, and died. After John II, John III was pope for three years.[4] After John, Nicholas [III] was pope, who ordained Robert de Kilwardby a cardinal, and brother John de [f. 201v.] Pecham of the order of Minors (and a Master of Divinity), as Archbishop of Canterbury. After Nicholas III, Honorius IV was Pope for seven years.[5] It was he who changed the habit of the Carmelite Friars, which had formerly been pale. After Honorius IV, Nicholas IV was pope for six years;[6] he was of the order of Friars Minor, which order he reformed. In his time, in England, on the eve of St Margaret [15 November],[7] there was such a winter thunderstorm that the corn was destroyed, which brought about great scarcity, a shortage which lasted for the life of Edward the first after the Conquest. At this time, church taxes were raised to a higher rate.

… apres Nicoli ᵃ

41. Celestin le .5. fust pape .3. aunz apres Nichol. Cesty Celestin estoit
vn pouer eremyt en desert, pres de Rome qi innocent estoit de maner,
noun pas lettre, ne sage, ne aparaunt. Vn cardinal qi desiroit la
gouernail du court, ou a estre pape, qi se doutoit qe la Colege ne ly
choiseroint, feigna cause, et fist entendre a sez autres freirs cardenalis
apres la mort le dit Pape Nichol, en lour eleccioun du papee, qun
voice ly estoit venu en auision par trois foitz, qils choiseroint en papeᵇ
le dit simple ermyt, de qi il auoit premesse, qil ne ferroit rien saunz li.
Les autres quiderent qe ceo vst est lexpiracioun de dieu, ly choiserent
en pape, qi rien ne sauoit gouerner soun estat, de qy la court fust tout
troeble et ly meismes ensanle. Le auaunt dit cardinal, qe apres auoit a
noun Boneface, ly lessa foleier, qi rien ne se entremist de soun bon
gouernment, tanqe il estoit taunt foruoie, qe bonment ne pooit estre
amende, et adonqes ly counsailla et pressa de resigner soun estat a ly,
et il prendroit garde, qil viueroit honourablement. A qoy il se
conscentist. La College sez concenterent pur sa foly, enmistrent
lautre, et ly apellerent Boneface, qe del hour qe il auoit pris soun estat,
ne prist rien garde de Celestin, mais ly lessa repairer a soun primer
estat, a soun pouer hermitage. Qy Celestin del hour qil aparceust qil
estoit engine, prophetiza de Boneface soun successour, qi ly disoit, Tu
y enuenistes com vn gopille, tu regneras com vn lioun, si murreras
com vn chien, qoi y enaueint, qar ly dit Boneface, regna
orgoillousement, defist cardinalis de greignour ligne de Rome,
extreitis de Columpna, grauntment trauersa le Roy de Fraunce, pur
quoi coueinerent ensemble pristrent le dit pape, ly amenerent hors de
Rome, sa face *[f. 20]* tourne au cue de soun cheuall a vn chastel pres,
ou il murust de feyme. Apres qi Boneface, Benet le .3. de lordre dez
Prechours fust pape vn an, de qi fust parle de vn gullyurdas en Latin,
A re nomen habe, benedic, benefac, benedicte. Aut rem peruerte,
maledic, malefac, maledicte.

Auntoin de Beke Euesqe de Duresm fust estably Patriarch de Jerusalem, mais vnqes nen veint en le patriarche, mes durement fust
noble en soun pays. Clement le .5. fust pape apres Benet .12. auns. Il
deueint durement riche de tresors, purchasa grauntz terres, fist
edifier fortis chasteaux. Il amena la court de Rome. En soun temps
furont lez Templers defaites. Il fist defaire ascuns dez decretalis, qe
meismes auoit estably, lez queux Johan soun successour renouela.

ᵃ *Left margin.*
ᵇ MS: en pape *repeated.*

… after Nicholas

41. Celestine V was Pope for three years after Nicholas.[1] Celestine was a poor hermit in the wilderness, near Rome, who was innocent in manner, unlettered, neither wise, nor eminent. A cardinal who desired the governance of the *curia*, or to be pope, but who feared that the College would not elect him, invented a reason; and after the death of Nicholas, at the election to the Papacy, he gave his brothers, the other cardinals, to understand that a voice had come to him in a vision on three occasions, saying that they should chose as Pope this simple hermit, from whom he had a promise that he would do nothing without them. The others supposed that this might be God's inspiration, and chose the hermit to be pope; but he knew nothing about governing his office, due to which the *curia* was put to great trouble and he himself as well. The cardinal, who afterwards took the name Boniface, left him to his folly, and would do nothing to intervene for the sake of good government, until he had gone so wrong that he was not well able to put things right; then he advised and pressed him to resign his office to him, and took care that he should live honourably. To this, he [Celestine] consented. In their folly, the College consented, appointed the other, and called him Boniface;[2] and as soon as he had got hold of his office, he took no care of Celestine, but left him to go back to his former estate, at his poor hermitage. As soon as Celestine saw that he had been tricked, he prophesized to Boniface, his successor, saying, 'You entered as a fox, you will reign as a lion, but you will die as a dog'; and this came about, for Boniface reigned arrogantly, deposing cardinals from the senior lineage of Rome, descended from Colonna, and seriously crossing the King of France. Therefore, joining together, they took the pope and dragged him away from Rome, with his face *[f. 202]* turned to his horse's tail, to a nearby castle, where he died of hunger. After Boniface, Benedict [XI] of the order of Preachers was pope for a year, of whom it was said by a certain satirist, in Latin: 'He has the name, say-well, do-well, be blessed; but it's been perverted to say-ill, do-ill, be cursed.'[3]

Anthony de Bek, Bishop of Durham, was appointed Patriarch of Jerusalem, but he never went to the patriarchy, as he was a great noble in his own region.[4] Clement V was pope after Benedict, for twelve years.[5] He became very wealthy with treasure, purchased great estates, and had strong castles built; he took the *curia* away from Rome. In his time, the Templars were abolished. He had some decretals annulled, the same ones which he had had decreed, and

Cesti Johan le .21. fust pape apres Clement, plus de .xx. aunz, qi
graunt clerk estoit en Grec, Ebreu et Latin. Il fist coiller grauntz
tresoris ensemble. Il mainteint grauntz gueres en Lombardy. Il auansa
uolountiers lez grauntz clers. Il dampna lez pluralites, il reserua lez
primers fruytes, apres la mort dez prelatis, a sa chaumbre. Il fist les
matynes de la croice. Il vesquist tout le temps le secound Roy Edward
apres la Conquest, et apres en le temps soun fitz le tierce Edward.

[a]42. Av fine du regne Edward le primer apres la Conquest, et au
commencement du regne de soun fitz, Edward le Secound, Henry
Count de Lussemburhe fust Roy de Allemain, et Emperour, qi
vaillaunt et noblis estoit, resceust honourablement sez dignetes de
sez troys corouns. Il dona le Realme de Bahayn a soun fitz Johan od la
feile le Roy, qi Johan conquist le dit realme, et prist la cite de Prag de
assaute sure ceaux qi claimerent droit par autre successioun masle. Le
dit Emperour Henry sentremist cheualerousement en Tuskane, et en
Lumbardy, a reconquer lez droitez del Empir, pur quoi com il gesoit
deuaunt Brise, il estoit enpusoune en resceit du corps Dieu, par soun
confessour vn Jacobin, qy a lowes estoit par lez Gelfes, qi durement
estoint espountez de sa pruesce. Sez phisiciens qi bien aparsceurent
la maner, ly voroint auoir deliuers, mais ne voloit oster soun
creatoure, mais disoit, qe pur poour a murrir, ne departeroit od le
corps Dieu. Apres mort de qy, estoit graunt debat pur la eleccioun del
Empire. Le Duk de Ostrik auoit voice dascuns dez elisouriz, Lowys
Duk de Bayuer[b] auoit autresy eleccioun du [f. 202v.] remenaunt dez
elisours, pur quel debate, lez auauntditz seignurs sez entre-
combaterent od lour poair en Swawe, le Bayuer auoit la victoir, par
eide du Johan Roy de Bahayne. Le dit Bayuer emprist lestat del
Emperour, resceust sez trois corouns, mais le pape et la court de
Rome li estoint en contrair, pur quoi a soun encoronement a Rome
par ascent dez Senatours, et de ceaux de la College, qen demurascent
en le hour entour Leglis saint Perre et saint Poel, enchoiserent vn
nouel pape vn cordeler, qi out a noune Nichol, aleggerent cause, pur
ceo la court fust a Auynioun, ou dust estre a Rome par auncien
constitucioun canonise. Cesti Nichol ne perseueryst my longement

---

[a] At bottom of page, under the first column, in contemporary hand: … henry de
Lussenburgh' et de seu' …
[b] MS: Bayner. The MS consistently refers to Bayner, when Bayuer would clearly be
more appropriate; whether the error is Gray's or his scribe's is impossible to determine.

which John, his successor, renewed. John [XXII] was pope after Clement, for more than twenty years,[6] and was a great scholar of Greek, Hebrew and Latin. He collected together great treasures; he fought great wars in Lombardy; he willingly promoted great scholars;[7] he condemned pluralities, and reserved to his chamber the first fruits after the death of prelates; he established the matins of the Cross. He lived throughout the time of the second King Edward after the Conquest, and after in the time of his son, the third Edward.

42. At the end of the reign of Edward the First after the Conquest, and at the beginning of the reign of his son, Edward the Second, Henry, Count of Luxemburg, was King of Germany and Emperor;[1] he was brave and noble, and bore the dignity of his three crowns honourably. He gave the kingdom of Bohemia to his son, John, along with the daughter of the king. John conquered the kingdom and took the city of Prague by assault, from those who claimed the right by another male line. The Emperor Henry chivalrously intervened in Tuscany and in Lombardy, to recover the rights of the Empire. Because of this, when he was before Brescia, he was poisoned while receiving the sacrament, by his confessor, a Dominican hired by the Guelfs, who were greatly frightened by his prowess. His doctors, who realised what had happened, wanted to save him; but he did not wish to throw up his Creator, and said that for fear of death, he would not be parted with the sacrament.[2] After his death, there was great controversy over the election to the Empire. The Duke of Austria had the votes of some of the electors, and likewise, Lewis, Duke of Bavaria, had the support of the [f. 202v.] remainder of the electors; and because of this dispute, the lords fought with all their might in Swabia. The Bavarian had the victory, through the help of John, King of Bohemia.[3] The Bavarian took up the estate of emperor and received his three crowns, but the Pope and the court of Rome were against him; because of this, at his coronation at Rome, by assent of the Senators, and of those of the College who were at that time around the Church of SS Peter and Paul, they chose a new Pope, a Franciscan by the name of Nicholas, citing cause that the court was at Avignon, whilst by ancient canonical constitution it should have been at Rome. This Nicholas did not persist for long in his office, but in the hour that the Emperor returned to Bavaria, he threw himself on the mercy of Pope John, who at that time dwelt in Avignon.[4] Because of this, the court of Avignon never again accepted the Bavarian as emperor, who lived under sentence for the rest of his days. He lived a good long time, but

en soun estat, mais del hour qe le auaunt dit Empour estoit repairez
en Bayuer, se mist en la grace du Pape Johan, qen le hour demurra en
Auynioun, pur quoy la court de Rome, ne accepta ia mes, le dit
Bayuer pur Empour, qi touz iours mes vesquist en sentence. Il vesqy
bon pece, mais poi fist qe soit acounteir darmis. Il fust durement
artillious de sa mayn, il dona a soun fitz eyne le Markys de
Brandesburgh com droit est de la Empire, qe tieux seignourages soint
al disposicioun del Empour, qaunt heir y faut masle. Il dona a meisme
ce ly de Brandesburgh la Duche de Carentane oue la counte de Tyrol,
oue la feile et heir du duk. Il dona a soun pusne fitz, qil auoit
engendre del eyne feile Willam Count de Henaw, lez Countez de
Seland, Holand et de Henaw. Vn autre de sez fitz le Romer de meisme
sa espouse, fesoit esposer la feil le Roy de Crakow et soun heir. Il
vesqyst bien longement, en le temps le tierce Roy Edward Dengleter
apres la Conquest, com apres serra recordez.

^a 43. Apres la mort le primer Edward apres la Conquest, regna le
secound Edward soun fitz en graunt tribulacioun et aduersite, qi ny
estoit pas oeurous, ne amez dez grauntz de soun realme; ia le mainz,
il estoit large, et amyable trop outre mesure as ceau qil amoit, et
moult coumpaignable a sez priuez. Et si fust de soun corps, vn dez
plus fortz hom de soun realme. Il prist a femme Isabelle la feile le Roy
Phelip de Fraunce ly beaux, qi la esposat a Amyas, et la amena en
Engleter, ou furount coronez a Loundres od graunt solempnete. Le
Roy od sa dit femme Isabelle, autrefoitz passa en Fraunce a Parys pur
treter de [*f. 203*] lez bosoignes de Gascoyne, ou le dit Roy Edward a
Saint Germayn en Prees, festia le dit roy de Fraunce, de quel fest
estoit en le hour graunt renome. En quel hour fust counte au dit Roy
Phelip de Fraunce qe lez femmes de sez fitz sez auoint malment
porte, dount il auoit trois, et vn feile meisme cest Isabelle Royne
Dengleter, Phelip, Lowys et Charlis, de sa espouse la feille le Roy de
Nawar, del heritage de qei, il estoit Roy de Nawar. La mere de quel
espous, Edmound le freir le primer Edward Dengleter apres la
Conquest auoit espose, de qei il engendra Thomas et Henry, puis
countis de Lancastre; cest assauoir, qe lez ditiz dames auoint par
amours faitz auoutry od cheualeris de sa court, qoi grauntement ly
gisoit au quer, pur qoi apres departir du dit Roy Dengleter, le dit Roy

did few deeds of arms which ought to be recorded. He was very skilful with his hands. He gave to his eldest son the Mark of Brandenburg, which is a right of the Empire, that in default of a male heir, such lordships should be at the disposal of the Emperor. At the same he gave him Brandenburg, he gave him the Duchy of Carinthia with the County of Tyrol, with the daughter and heir of the Duke. He gave to his younger son, whom he had by the eldest daughter of William, Count of Hainault, the counties of Zeeland, Holand and Hainault. Another of his sons by the same wife, [Ludwig] the Roman, was married to the daughter and heir of the King of Crakow.[5] He lived long, to the time of the third King Edward of England after the Conquest, as will be recorded later.[6]

43. After the death of the first Edward after the Conquest, the second Edward, his son, reigned in great tribulation and adversity. He was not hard-working, and nor was he loved by the magnates of his realm; on the other hand, he was generous, and genial well beyond measure to those whom he loved, and very affable to his close companions. And physically, he was one of the strongest men in the realm.[1] He took to wife Isabella, the daughter of King Philip the Fair of France, whom he married at Amiens, and brought to England, where they were crowned at London in great solemnity. With Isabella his wife, the king once again crossed to France to Paris, to discuss [f. 203] the business of Gascony, where King Edward feasted the King of France at St Germain-des-Prés, a feast which was greatly renowned at the time. At this time, King Philip of France was told that the wives of his sons had been behaving wickedly.[2] He had three [sons], Philip, Lewis and Charles, and a daughter, who was Isabella, Queen of England, by his wife, the daughter of the King of Navarre, by whose inheritance he was [himself] King of Navarre. His wife's mother had married Edmund, the brother of Edward the first of England after the Conquest, by whom he fathered Thomas and Henry, subsequently earls of Lancaster.[3] To wit, [Philip was informed] that the ladies had wantonly committed adultery with knights of his court, which bore heavily on his heart; therefore, after the departure of the King of England, the King of France enquired of Philip de Aunay, a venerable knight of his council, what he should do with those who had slept with the wives of the sons of the king, the princes of France. 'Sir', said

de Fraunce demaundoit de Phelip Dawnay, vn auncien cheualer de soun counsail, quoi serroit a faire de ceaux qauoint parieu lez femmes dez fitz le Roy et realis de Fraunce. Sire, ceo disoit ly prodhom, ils sount dignes a estre escorchez toutz vifes. Tu as done le iugement, ceo disoit ly roys, ces sount voz fitz lez dieus qi porterount le coup, com iuge auez. Lun fust dampne en le hour, lautre eschapa en Engleter, qi fust pris a Euerwyk, et reenuoye au dit Roy de Fraunce, de quoi le dit Roy Dengleter de murmure dez comunes enportoit blame, depuisqe le dit chiualer estoit venuz pur succours en soun realme. Le dit chiualer fust escorche tout vyue. Lez .ij. dames furount mys a vileyn mort. La tierce fust enuyrone dun haut mure saunz manger ou boire, ou morust. Il estoit dit de parol du comune qe cest esclaundre fust descouert au Roy de Fraunce par sa feille Isabelle Royne Dengleter, quoy estoit suppose de plousours qe nestoit pas uerite. Pur quel crualte, dez comunes fust arrette et notifie, qe le pier ne lez fitz ne auoint dure. Le pier murrust procheignement. Sez trois fitz auaunt nomez, estoint Roys de Fraunce, chescun apres autre court sesoun. Le eyne de eaux qi Roy estoit de Nawar viuaunt le pier, nauoit engendrur fors vn feile, qe puis fust marie au Count de Euerus, qi apres de heritage sa dit femme, deueint Roy de Nawar. Ly autre freir secound auoit de sa espous, la feile le Count de Artoys, trois feilles, qe puis departerent leritage de Artoys. Le Duk de Burgoin auoit vn, le Count de Flaundres vn autre. La tierce, puis prist paramours le sire de Faucony. Charlis le tierce freir et darein roys, morust saunz engendrur, pur quoi le droit del heritage de Fraunce de droit, deueroit descendre a Edward [f. 203v.] Dengleter, fitz Isabelle, sore dez ditz trois freirs et roys com al plus prochein heire masle, qar en le houre, les feiles de lez dieus auaunt ditz freirs et roys nauoint point dengendrur masle au discesse le dit Charlis, le darein roy de .iij. freirs lour vncle, pur quoi, le dit Edward fitz Isabel Dengleter estoit le plus prochein mal [mes]*b* tout ne mist il point de chalange com apres serra recorde, au mort soun dit vncle Charlis, pur defaut de bon counsail, com estoit iones et entagles dautres bosoignes; tanqe vn autre collateralle le fitz del vncle le auaunt dit Charlis estoit corone pur roys, par eide de sez aliez, principaument de Robert de Artoys, a qy apres estoit le greinour enemy, pusqe nul autre en droit sesoun, ne enmistrent a droit chalange, tanqe bon pece puscedy, com apres serra recorde, qe bien est et doit estre notable chos, et memorial par tout.

b Supplied.

this worthy man, 'they deserve to be flayed wholly alive'. 'You have given judgement', said the king; 'it is your two sons who will suffer this blow, as you have judged'. One was condemned straightaway, the other escaped to England, and was captured at York, and sent back to the King of France; and the mutterings of the commoners held the King of England to blame for this, since the knight had come to his realm for help. The knight was flayed alive. The two ladies were put to a shameful death; the third was enclosed by a high wall with nothing to eat or drink, where she died.[4] Common gossip had it that this scandal was revealed to the King of France by his daughter, Isabella, Queen of England, though many considered this was not true.[5] Because of this cruelty, it was held by the commoners and noised about, that neither the father nor his sons would last long. The father died soon after; his three sons were kings of France one after another, in a short time. The eldest of them, who was King of Navarre whilst his father lived, had no offspring except for one daughter.[6] She was later married to the Count of Evreux, who afterwards became King of Navarre through his wife's inheritance. The second brother had three daughters by his wife, the daughter of the Count of Artois, who subsequently shared the inheritance of Artois. The Duke of Burgundy had one, the Count of Flanders another; later, the third took the lord of Faucogney as a lover.[7] Charles, the third brother and last king, died without offspring,[8] on which account, the right to the inheritance of France was rightfully bound to descend to Edward [f. 203v.] of England, the son of Isabella, the sister of these three brothers and kings, as the nearest heir male; for at this time – at the death of Charles (the last king of the three brothers, and their uncle) – the daughters of the said two brothers and kings did not have any male offspring. Therefore, Edward the son of Isabella of England was the nearest male, [but], as will be related later,[9] he did not make any claim at all at the death of his uncle Charles, in the absence of good counsel, for he was young and tied up with other business. So another collateral, the son of Charles' uncle, was crowned as king, by the help of his allies (particularly of Robert de Artois, to whom he was afterwards the greatest enemy[10]), since no one else put in a rightful claim at the right time, until a good while afterwards, as will be related later; and this is something which is well worth noting, as a reminder for all.

Thomas de Gray estoit en le hour gardein du Chastel de Coupir de Fif,^{c} depar le Roy Dengleter, et com uenoit hors Dengleter del encorounement le Roy, vers le dit chastelle, Waulter de Bickirtoun chiualer Descoce qenherdaunt estoit a Robert de Bruys, auoit espie la reuenu du dit Thomas, estoit enbusse od plus de .iiii.^{c} homs, par ou le dit Thomas couenoit passer, quoy fust nouncie au dit Thomas, geris plus dun dimy lieu pres del enbussement. Il nauoit od ly fors .xxvi. homs darmes. Il aparceust qil ne pooit saunz meschief eschaper, qi par asscent dez soens, emprist le chemyn deuers lenbussement, fist bailler vn estandard a sez garsouns lez fist comaunder qils venisent en rout par dereir eaux, et qe ils ne fuassent trop tost. Lez enemys mounterent a cheual, vindrent en batail, pensauntz qe ils ne lour purrount eschaper. Le dit Thomas od lez soens, qe tres bien estoient mountez, ferry destreir dez esperouns alast assembler en my la route dez enemys parmy eaux, portoit en soun aler plusours a terre de hurt du cheual, et de sa launce, si tourna la rein, reuient en meisme la gise et reenala, et autrefoitz reueint parmy le plus graunt route, quy taunt enbaudist lez soens, qe toucz ly suerent a la gyse, qy tauntz auoint abatuz des enemys, lour cheueaux corauntz en routes, eaux meismes releuez de terre, aparceurent les garsouns le dit Thomas uenauntz en aray, sez comencerent fuer en vn sek marras tourberis, qe y out pres, pur qoy touz comencerent a fuer a le marras, lesseront lour cheueax pur poi touz. Le dit Thomas od lez soens ne lour purroit aprocher a cheual, pur quoi [f. 204] fist chacer ensemble lour cheueals en rout deuaunt ly au dit chastel, ou a nuyt auoint .ix.$^{xx.}$ cheueaux selez, en botyne. Autrefoitz Alexander Frisel, qenerdaunt estoit a Robert de Bruys, od cent homs darmes, estoit enbussez vn demy lieu pres le dit chastelle, vn iour de Marche, la vile plein dez veisines, et auoit enuoiez autres de sez gentz de lautre part le chastel a ryffler vn vilet, le dit Thomas oy la hue, mounta vn beau destreir deuaunt qe lez soens purroint estre adressez, sen alast veoir qe ceo fust. Lez enemys du dit enbussement, ferrerent cheueaux dez esperouns deuaunt lez portez du dit chastel, quy bien ly sauoint issu, pur quoy ils ceo firent. Ly dit Thomas qi ceo aparceust, reueint le petit pas parmy la vile de Coupir, en la bout de quoy estut le chastel, par ou ly couenoit a cheual entreir, ou la ru auoint purpris tout outre; il fery cheueaux dez esperouns com veint pres de eaux, lez primers qi sez aauncerent a

---

^{c} *MS:* et de Fif.

Thomas de Gray was at this time keeper of the castle of Cupar, in Fife, for the King of England. When he was coming towards the castle from England from the king's coronation,[11] Walter de Bickerton, a Scottish knight who was an adherent of Robert de Bruce,[12] having spotted Thomas returning, laid an ambush with 400 men-at-arms, where Thomas had planned to pass. This was made known to Thomas scarely more than half a league from the ambush. He had with him only twenty-six men-at-arms, but seeing that he would not be able to escape without trouble, he took the road towards the ambush with the assent of his men, having given a banner to his grooms and ordered them to come behind them in a company, and that they should not flee too readily. The enemy mounted on horseback and came on in battle [array], thinking that [the English] could not escape them. Thomas, along with his men, who were very well mounted, spurred on his warhorse and charged through the midst of the enemy company, knocking many down to the ground as he passed, by the thrust of his horse, and with his lance. He turned his rein, came back in the same manner and charged again, coming back another time straight through the biggest company, which so emboldened his men that they all followed him in the same manner, and knocked down many of the enemy, whose horses ran around in groups. Picking themselves up from the ground, and seeing Thomas' grooms coming up in array, these men began to flee into a dried-up peat-marsh which was nearby; because of this, all [the Scots] began to flee to the marsh, nearly all of them abandoning their horses. Thomas and his men were unable to get to them on horseback, so [f. 204] he had their horses driven together in a herd before them to the castle, where by that night, they had 180 saddled horses in booty. Another time, on a market-day with the town full of local people, Alexander Fraser,[13] who was an adherent of Robert de Bruce, lay in ambush only half a mile from the castle with a hundred men-at-arms, having sent some of his other men to the other side of the castle to plunder a village. Thomas heard the outcry, mounted a fine warhorse before his men had been able to get ready, and went out to see what it was. Well aware that he was coming out, which was why they had arranged this, the enemies in the ambush spurred their horses on in front of the gates of the castle. Seeing this, Thomas went back a little way through the town of Cupar, at the end of which stood the castle, which he intended to enter on horseback, right where [the Scots] had completely occupied the street. He spurred his horse on as he came near to them, and felled the first of them who came forward before

deuaunt, il abaty de eaux lez vns de sa launce, autres de hurt du chiual, se passa parmy eaux toucz, descendy deuaunt la port, enschasa soun cheual, se trei meismes dedenz lez barreirs, ou troua lez soens issuz.

[43a]*ᵃ* Cesti Roy Edward le secound apres la Conquest ietta graunt affeccioun viuaunt soun pier a Peris de Gauirstoun, vn ioen hom nee de Gascoyn, de quoi le pier prist malencoly, qil se douta qil amenast soun fitz desordeinement, qy luy fist exiler de soun realme, et fist meisme soun fitz y cesty Edward, et soun neuew, le Count Thomas de Lancastre, et autres grauntz du realme iureir le exillement du dit Peris, saunz recouncillement pur touz iours, qe procheynement apres la mort le pier, le fitz fist reapeller le dit Peris sodeinement, et ly fist prendre a femme la feil sa sore, vn dez feiles de Gloucestre, et luy fist Count de Cornewail, qy deueint tresnoblis, largis et gentil de maner, mais orgoillous et souzqidrous en party, de quoi lez vns dez grauntz du realme enpristrent graunt despit, qy coumpasserount sa destruccioun, com il fust en Escoce a la guer le roy qauoit fait a fermer la vile de Dundee, qi trop apertement se auoit porte illoeqes, au plesauns dez gentilis homs du pays, qe ly couenoit retourner au roy pur debate dez barouns, qen soun reuenir, ly suppristrent a Scarthburgh, mes sure condicioun fust rendu a Eymer de Valoyns, de luy auoir amenez au Roy, des gentz de qy il estoit repris ioust Oxsenforth, qy luy amenerent au Count de Lancastre, qi ly fist decoller pres de Warwyk, pur quoy sourdist mortiel heyn du Roy, *[f. 204v.]* qe toucz iours mes dura entre eaux. Adam Banastre, vn bacheler de la counte de Lancastre, mouoit ryote countre le dit count par couyne le roy, mais il ne pooit endureir, mais fust pris et decollez par comaundement du dit count, apres grauntz iournes qil auoit hu sure sez gentz. Durant cest debat entre le roy et le dit count, reuigura Robert de Bruys en Escoce, qi ia estoit leuez viuaunt le roi le pier, qi clamoit accion du realme Descoce, qi conquist tauntz dez pays en Escoce, qestoient a deuaunt conquys et soutzmys al obeisaunce du roy Dengleter, et moult par caus de mauues gouernail dez ministres le roy, qi trop asprement lez gouernoient pur singuler profit. Lez chastellis de Roxburgh et de Edynburgh emblez et abatuse, lez queux chastelis estoint en gard dez aliens; Roxburgh, en la gard Gillemyng

---

ᵃ Note that this rubricated letter was not numbered by the later annotator who added chapter numbers. Nor is there any sign of an added 'chapter heading'.

him, some with his lance, others by thrust of his horse. He passed straight through them all, dismounted in front of the gate, drove his horse in, and went inside the barricades himself, where he found his men making a sortie.

[43a] Whilst his father was still alive, this King Edward the second after the Conquest had lavished great affection on Piers Gaveston, a young man born in Gascony. His father was saddened by this, for he feared that [Piers] would influence his son excessively, and had him exiled from his realm. Likewise, he made his son Edward, and his nephew, Thomas Earl of Lancaster, and other magnates of the realm, swear to Piers' exile for all of his days, without recall. Soon after the death of his father, the son had Piers recalled without notice, gave him as wife his sister's daughter, one of Gloucester's girls, and made him Earl of Cornwall.[1] [Piers] became noble, generous and refined in manner, but somewhat arrogant and overbearing; because of this, some of the great men of the realm took great offence, and plotted his downfall when he was in Scotland for the king's war. He had the town of Dundee at farm, and bore himself too arrogantly there for the liking of the noblemen of the country, so that he felt compelled to return to the king because of the dispute with the barons. On his return, they captured him at Scarborough, but on the condition that he was handed over to Aymer de Valence who was to have brought him to the king. He was taken back from [Valence's] men near Oxford, and was brought before the Earl of Lancaster, who had him beheaded near Warwick; this aroused the king's mortal hatred, [f. 204v.] which endured between them for all their days.[2] Adam Banaster, a bachelor of the county of Lancaster, led a rising against the earl by the connivance of the king, but he was unable to hold out, and was seized and beheaded by command of the earl, after having great fighting there against his men.[3] During this strife between the king and the earl, Robert de Bruce recovered his strength in Scotland; he had already risen whilst the king's father was living, and had laid claim to the realm of Scotland. He conquered many of the Scottish lands which had previously been conquered and subjected to the obedience of the King of England, mostly because of the bad government of the king's ministers, who governed too harshly, for their personal profit. The castles of Roxburgh and Edinburgh were taken and razed, which castles were in the guard of foreigners; Roxburgh was in the guard of Guillemin de Fiennes, a knight and Burgundian, from whom James de Douglas seized the castle on the night of Shrove

de Fenygges cheualer et Burglioun, sure qi James de Douglas embla le dist chastel, la nuyt de quarrem pernaunt. Le dit Gilmyng fust mort dun sete, com teint la graunt tour. *b*Peris Lebaud, cheualer, vn Gascoyne, fust viscount de Edenburgh, sure qi lez gentz Thomas Randolf Count de Murref, com le dit chastel estoit assis, le emblerent a le plus haut du Roche, de quoi il ne se dotoit. Le dit Peris deueint Escotoys, a la foy Robert de Bruys qi puis apres ly surmist tresoun, ly fist pendre et treyner, com fust dit, pur ceo qil se doutoit de ly, pur ceo qe trop estoit apert, pensaunt toutdice qil estoit llour point de ly greuer.

Ly dit Roy Edward couenoit treier celys partyes, ou al rescous du chastel de Stryuelin, il fust descomfist, et graunt noumbre de sez gentz mortz, le Count de Gloucestre et autres tresnoblis gentez; et le Count de Herford pris a Botheuille, com tanqe la estoit retreit, ou du chastelain fust traye, qi puis fust deliuers pur la femme Robert de Bruys et pur Leuesque de Seint Andrew. Et coment cel descoumfiture enaueint, lez croniclis deuisent qe apres ceo qe le Count de Athelis auoit emble la vile de saint Johan sure Willam Olifart capitayn depar le Roy Dengleter, al vse Robert de Bruys, com cely qenherdaunt estoit a ly al hour, mais tost ly guerpy, qi Robert se trey en ost deuaunt le chastel de Striuelyn, ou Phelip de Moubray cheualre quauoit le chastel de Striuelyn a garder depar le Roy Dengleter auoit pris condicioun od le dit Robert de Bruys du rendre du dit chastel com lauoit assys, qe sil ne fust rescouse; issi qe lost Dengleter venist a trois lieus pres le dit chastel, dedenz .viij. iours apres le *[f. 205]* saint Johan en este adonqes procheine auenir, qil ly renderoit le dit chastel. Le dit Roi Edward Dengleter y enueint pur la dit cause, ou le dit chastelein Phelip ly encountra trois lieus du chastel ly Dymange la veil de saint Johan, qi ly disoit, qe y nenbosoignoit my qil uenist plus pres qil se tenoit rescous, si luy counta coment lez enemys auoint fowez lez estroitz chemyns du boys. Lez ioenes gentz ne aresterent my, tindrent lour chemyns. Lauaunt garde, dount le count de Gloucestre estoit gouernour, entrerent la voi dedenz le Park, ou tost furount recoillez par lez Escocez quauoint purpris la voy, ou fu tue Peris de Mountforth cheualer, dez mains Robert de Bruis dun hache, com fust dit. Endementiers qe le dit auaunt garde sez adresserent cel chemyn, Robert seignour de Clifford, et Henry de Beaumound od .iiij. centz homs de armis enuironerent le boys del autre couste deuers le chastel, demurrerent as beaux chaumps. Thomas Randolf count de Murref,

---

b   *marginal hand, pointing to* 'Peris Lebaud'.

Tuesday [20 February, 1314]. Guillemin was killed by an arrow, as he held the great tower.[4] Piers Libaud, knight, a Gascon, was sheriff of Edinburgh; when Thomas Randolph, Earl of Moray, besieged the castle, his men took it at the highest part of the Rock, which Piers had not been concerned about.[5] Piers became Scottish, in the allegiance of Robert de Bruce, who afterwards suspected him of treason and had him hanged and drawn. It was said that he doubted him because he was too open; he believed that he had always been English at heart, and was waiting for his best chance to harm him.[6]

King Edward agreed to go these parts, where, at the relief of Stirling castle, he was defeated, and a great number of his men were killed, [including] the Earl of Gloucester and other great noblemen; and the Earl of Hereford was captured at Bothwell (which was as far as he had retreated), where he was betrayed by the constable. He was exchanged afterwards, for the wife of Robert de Bruce and the bishop of St Andrews.[7] And as to how this defeat happened, the chronicles[8] relate that after the Earl of Atholl had taken the town of Perth from William Oliphant, the King of England's captain,[9] for the benefit of Robert Bruce (as he was an adherent of him at the time, though he soon deserted him[10]), Robert drew up an army before Stirling castle, where Philip de Mowbray, knight, who had the ward of the castle for the King of England, had made terms with Robert Bruce to surrender the castle when it was besieged, if he was not relieved; unless the English army came nearer than three leagues from the castle, within eight days of [f. 205] St John's day in the summer next to come [ie., by 1 July], he would surrender the castle.[11] King Edward of England came there for this reason, where the constable, Philip, met him three leagues from the castle on Sunday, St John's eve [23 June]. He said to the king that he need not trouble himself to come any nearer, as he considered himself relieved, and then he related how the enemy had dug up the narrow paths through the wood. The young men would not stop, but held their course. The vanguard, of which the Earl of Gloucester was the commander, took to the road in the park, where they were soon repulsed by the Scots who had occupied the road. Here Peter de Montfort, knight, was killed at the hands of Robert Bruce, with an axe, so it was said.[12] While the vanguard took this road, Robert, Lord Clifford, and Henry de Beaumont, with three hundred men-at-arms, went round the wood on the other side, towards the castle, keeping to open fields. Thomas Randolph, Earl of Moray, Robert Bruce's nephew and the leader of the Scottish vanguard, having heard that his uncle had thrown back the English

neuew Robert de Bruys, qi dustre estoit del auaunt garde Descoce, auoit oy qe soun vncle auoit rebote le auauntgard dez Engles al autre part du boys, pensa qil vousist auoir sa part, issist du boys od sa batail, enpristrent le beau chaumpe deuers lez dieus seignours auaunt nomez. Monsire Henry de Beaumound disoit as soens, Retreyoms nous vn poy, lessez lez uenir, donez lez chaumps. Thomas Gray cheualer ly disoit, Sire, ieo me dout qe tant lez dorrez en le hour, pur quoi tout auerount trop tost. Voir, fesoit le dit Henry, Si tu eiez poour, fuez; Sire, fesoit ly dit Thomas, pur poour ne fueray ieo huy, si fery cheual dez esperouns entre ly et Willam Dayncourt cheualer, assemblerent en my lieu dez enemys. Willam fust mort, Thomas fust pris, soun cheual tue dez launces, ly meismes tyre od eaux a pee, qi sen alerent descoumfirer le auaunt dit route de .ij. seignours outriement. Lez vns dez queux fuerent au chastel, autres al ost le roy, qy ia auoint gerpy la voy du boys, estoint venuz en vn plain deuers leau de Forth, outre Bannokburn, vn mauueis parfound ruscelle marras, ou le dit ost dez Engles detrusserent, demurrerent tout nuyt, durement auoint perdu countenaunce, et estoint de trop mal couyne pur la iournee passe. Lez Escocez hu boys penserent qe asseitz auoint ils bien fait quant a la iourne, estoient tout en point de auoir deloge, et dauoir dedenz la nuyt, trey dedenz lez Leuenaux, plus fort pays, quant Alexander de Setoun cheualer qi a la foy Dengleter estoit, et uenuz illoeqes ouesque le roy, sen departist [f. 205v.] priuement hors del ost engles sen ala a Robert de Bruys hu boys, qi ly disoit, Sire, ore est temps si iamais mes empensez a entremetter a Escote reconquer, lez Engles ount perdu lour quers et sount descoumfitz, ne attendent rien, fors vn sodein apert assaut. Si ly counta lour couyn, qi ly disoit sure sa test et sure pain destre penduz et traynez, qe sil lez uoloit surrecour le matin, il lez descoumfiroit legerment saunz perde. Par excitement de qy, ils empristrent a combatre, et au matin au solail leuaunt, isserent le boys en trois bataillis a pee, tindrent reddement lour chemyn deuers lost dez Engles, qi tout la nuyt auoint este armez, lour cheueaux freinez, qi mounterent a cheual od graunt affray qi nestoint my acoustomez pur descendre a coumbatre a pee, ou lez ditz Escotez auoient pris ensaumpler a lez Flemenges, qi deuaunt auoint a Courtray descoumfist a pe le poair de France. Lez auaunt ditz Escocez uindrent de tot aleyn en schiltrome, assemblerent sur lez bataillis des engles, qi entassez estoint, qi rien remuerent deuers eaux, tanqe lours cheueaux estoient enbuaillez dez launces. Lez gentz dereir dez Engles recoillerent hu fosse de Bannokburne, chescun cheoit sur autre. Lez batails dez Engles, desaroutez par bouter dez

vanguard on the other side of the wood, decided that he wanted his share [of the action]; he came out of the wood with his battle and took the open field in front of the two aforementioned lords. Sir Henry de Beaumont said to his men, 'Let us pull back a little, let them come, give them the field'. Thomas Gray, knight, said to him, 'Sir, I doubt that we should give them so much ground now, for they'll have the lot all too easily'. 'Right', said Henry, 'if you're afraid, then flee'; 'Sir', said Thomas, 'I shall not flee for fear today', and spurring his horse with William Deyncourt, knight,[13] they charged into the midst of the enemy. William was killed, Thomas was captured, his horse killed by spears, and he himself was taken with [the Scots] on foot, as they went on to defeat the forces of the two lords outright.[14] Some of these fled to the castle, others to the king's army, which had already left the woodland road and had come to a plain near the river Forth, beyond the Bannockburn, a foul, deep, marshy stream, where the English army unpacked and remained all the night, having seriously lost face, and in a very poor state from the past day's fighting. The Scots in the wood reckoned that they had done well enough during the day's fighting, and were on the point of decamping, and moving into the Lennox, a more defensible country, when Alexander de Seton, knight,[15] who was of the English allegiance, and had come there with the king, [f. 205v.] secretly left the English army and came to Robert Bruce in the wood. He said to him, 'Sir, now is the time if ever you thought to try your hand at reconquering Scotland; the English have lost heart and are defeated, they expect nothing but a sudden, open assault'. He described their situation to him, saying by his own head and on pain of being hanged and drawn, that if [Robert] wished to attack them in the morning, he would defeat them easily without loss.[16] With his encouragement, they decided to fight, and in the morning at sunrise, they came out of the woods on foot in three battles, and steadily held their course towards the English army, which had been armed for all of the night, their horses bridled. [The English] mounted on horseback in great consternation, for they were not at all used to dismounting to fight on foot, while the Scots had taken the example of the Flemings, who had previously defeated on foot the forces of France, at Coutrai. The Scots came quickly, lined in *schiltroms*, and attacked the English battles, which were crushed together so that they could not move against them, whilst their horses were being disembowelled by spears. The men in the English rear fell back on the Bannockburn ditch, falling one over another. The English battles, disarrayed by the blows of spear points to their

pointez dez launces sur lez cheueaux, comencerent a fuyre. Ceaux qestoint assignez au freyn le roy, aparceurent le meschief, treierent le roy auaunt par la reyn hors de chaumpe deuers le chastel, maugre qil enhust, qi enuyte sen departist. Qe com lez cheualers Descoce qestoient a pee penderent od lour mains sur la couertour du destreir le roy, de ly auoir arestu, il ferist dereir ly si reddement od vn massu qe y nestoit nul qil consceust, qil ne ly abatist a terre. Com ceaux qauoint sa reyne ly tyrerent toutdiz auaunt, Gilis de Argenten vn de eaux, vn cheualer renome, qi nouelement estoit uenuz de outre mere de gueres Lemperour Henry de Lussemburgh, disoit au roy, Sire, vostre reyne me fust baillez, ore estez a sauuete; veez cy vostre chastel, ou vostre corps purra estre sauuve. Jeo nay pas este acoustome a fuyre, ne plus auaunt ne voil ieo faire; a Dieux vous comaunde. Si fery cheual dez esperouns, si reenala a sembler, ou fust mort. Le destrier le roy fust enbuaille, qe plus auaunt ne poaist. Il fust remounte sur vn courseir qi tout enuyroun le boys de Torre fust amene, et par les playnes de Lownesse; ceaux qi sen alerent od ly furount sauuez, touz lez autres auoient mescheif. Le roy eschapa a graunt payn de illoeqes, se trey deuers Dunbarre, ou le Count *[f. 206]* Patrik de la Marche ly resceut honourablement, et ly bailla son chastel, et voidy meismes la place, et touz lez soens, pur ceo qe nul ne vst doute ne suspessoun qil feist a soun seignour rien fors soun deuoir, qar il estoit al hour soun homager. De illoeqes sen departy le roy par mere a Berewyk, et puis^c deuers le sew. Edward de Bruys freir au Robert le Roy Descoce desiraunt a estre Roy, passa en Ireland od graunt poair hors Descoce, en espoir de le auoir conquys, qi demura illoeqes .ij. aunz et dimy, qi fist illoeqes meruailles darmys par grauntz meschiefs, et de vitailis et dez autres auenementz et grauntz pays conquist, qi serroit vne graunt romaunce a rementyuer tout. Il se clama Roy de Roys de Ireland. Il fust descoumfist et mort a Dundalg, par lez Engles du pays, qy pur surquidery ne voroit attendre soun poair, qe procheynement estoint arryuez, et pres de ly a .vi. lieus. En meisme le temps, le Roy Dengleter enuoya le Count de Aroundel cheuetayn sur la Marche Descoce, qi fust rebukez a Lintelly en la forest de Jedeworth, par James de Douglas, et mort Thomas de Richemond. Ly dit Count se retrey deuers le sew, saunz plus faire. Le dit James descoumfist autrefoitz la garrisoun de Berewike, a Scaithmor, ou furrount mors toutes playnes de Gascoins. Il auoit vn autrefoitz par couyne dez faus traitres des Marchies, vn

---

^c MS: pi*us*.

horses, began to flee. Seeing this misfortune, those who had been assigned to the king's reins pulled him away from the field by his rein, towards the castle, against his will, for it pained him to leave. When the Scottish knights, who were on foot, grabbed the caparison of the king's warhorse with their hands to bring him to a halt, he struck behind him with a mace, so forcefully that there were none that he hit, whom he did not beat to the ground.[17] As those who had his rein drew him further forward, one of them, Giles de Argentine, a renowned knight who had recently come from overseas from the wars of the Emperor Henry of Luxemburg, said to the king, 'Sir, your rein was committed to me, now you are in safety; see, here is your castle, where you will be safe. I am not accustomed to fleeing, and I don't wish to go any further; I commend you to God.' He put his spurs to his horse, and went back to fight, where he was killed.[18] The king's warhorse was wounded in the belly, and could not go any further. He was remounted on a riding horse, which was led all the way round the Torwood, and to the plains of Lothian; those who came away with him were saved, all the others came to grief. The king escaped from there with great difficulty, and took himself to Dunbar, where [f. 206] Patrick, Earl of March, received him honourably and handed over his castle, leaving the place himself along with all his men, so that there should be neither doubt nor suspicion that he had done anything to his king save his duty, since at the time he was his liegeman. From there, the king left by sea for Berwick, and then for the south.[19] Aspiring to be a king, Edward de Bruce, brother of Robert, King of Scotland, crossed to Ireland with a great force from Scotland, in the hope of conquering it.[20] He remained there two and a half years, and performed there marvellous feats of arms through great hardship, and captured supplies and other materials and much land; it would take a great romance to recount it all.[21] He proclaimed himself King of kings of Ireland. He was defeated and killed at Dundalk by the English of the land, as through arrogance, he did not want to wait for his forces, which had recently arrived, and were just six leagues from him.[22] At the same time, the King of England appointed the Earl of Arundel as commander on the Scottish March. He was defeated at Lintalee in Jedburgh forest by James de Douglas, and Thomas de Richmond was killed.[23] The earl withdrew to the south, without doing anything more. On another occasion, the same James defeated the garrison of Berwick at Scaithmoor, where a great many Gascons were killed. At another time, by the connivance of false traitors of the Marches, there was a defeat at Berwick[24] on the

descoumfiture a Bewyk*ᵈ* sure lez Marchies, ou fust mort Robert de Neuylle. Qy Robert auoit tue procheignement deuaunt, Richard le fitz Marmaduk, qi cosyn estoit Robert de Bruys, sure le veutz pount de Doresme, pur coroucesours entre eaux par enuy qi le plus graunt meistre, pur quoi pur gree conquer du roy a sa peise auoir de cest forfait, comensa il de trauailler en la guere le roy, ou morust. Meisme la sesoun le dit James de Douglas par eide du Cont Patrik de la Marche, embla Berewyk hors dez mayns dez engles par couyne de tresoun de vn de la vile Perys de Spalding; le chastel se tenoit .xi. semains apres, et adonqes le rendy a lez escoces pur defaut des rescous, com nestoit pas vitaille. Roger de Horsley le chastelein perdy illoeqes le vn oyl dun sete. Eymer de Valoins Count de Penbrok, enchemynaunt deuers la court de Rome, fust pris par Johan de la Moiller vne Burglioun, et amenez en Lempire et raunsone, pur .xx.Mile. lyuers dargent, pur ceo qe le dit Johan disoit qe il auoit seruy le Roy Dengleter, et qe le Roy ly deuoit sez gages.

Y cesty James de Douglas auoit tres graunt couyne en Northumbre. [f. 206v.] Robert de Bruys fist abatre toutez lez chasteaux descoce, hors pris Dunbretaigne. Cesty Robert de Bruys fist prendre Willam de Sowles et ly fist murrer en le chastel de Dunbretaigne a sa penaunz en prisoun, suremettaunt a ly qil auoit enbrace couyne od autres grauntz Descoce a ly defair, a qi ils estoint attournez soutzgiz, quoi le dit Willam reioy, pur quel reconisauns. Dauid de Breghen, Johan Logy, Gilbert Malherb, furount penduz et treinez a la vile de seint Johan, et le corps Roger de Moubray foriugez qaporte estoit mort sure vn litter al parlement de Scone deuaunt lez iuges. Quel couyne fust descouert par Muryogh de Menteth, qy puis illoeqes fust count, qi longement auoit demore en Engleter a la foy le roy, qi pur descouerer cel couyne sen ala a lostel, et deueint Count de Menteth par reles sa nece, feile de soun freir eyne, la quel autrefoitz apres sa mort estoit countays. Le Roy Dengleter ne se entremist geris plus rien deuers Escoce, tanqe il auoit perdu par peresce, tanqe*ᵉ* soun pier auoit conquys, et auxi tot plain dez forteresses dedens sez Marchis Dengleter, et auxi tout plain de Northumbreland leuez encountre ly. Gilbert de Middiltoun qy en le Euesche de Doresme robba .ij. cardinalis, qi vindrent pur sacreir leuesqe, et prist Leuesqe*ᶠ*

ᵈ Probably a scribal error for Be'wyk, the abbreviation habitually used for Berewyk, i.e. Berwick on Tweed. See 230, n. 24, below.
ᵉ MS: qanqe.
ᶠ MS: Leueqe.

Marches, where Robert de Neville was killed. Shortly before, Robert had killed Richard fitz Marmaduke, cousin of Robert de Bruce, on the old bridge at Durham, due to rancour between them from envy over who should be the greatest lord; therefore, to regain the king's grace and to have his pardon for this offence, he began to serve in the king's war, where he perished.[25] In the same season, James de Douglas, with the help of Earl Patrick of the March, seized Berwick from the hands of the English by the treasonous connivance of one of the townsmen, Piers de Spalding; the castle held out for eleven weeks afterwards, and then surrendered to the Scots for want of relief, as it was not provisioned. Roger de Horsley, the constable, lost an eye there from an arrow.[26] Aymer de Valence, Earl of Pembroke, was on his way to the *curia* at Rome when he was captured by Jean de Lamouilly, a Burgundian, and taken off to the Empire and ransomed for £20,000 of silver, because Jean said that he had served the King of England and that the king owed him his wages.[27]

James de Douglas had a great deal of support in Northumberland.[28] [f. 206v.] Robert de Bruce had all the castles of Scotland demolished, except for Dumbarton. He had William de Soules seized, and had him incarcerated in Dumbarton castle, in prison as his punishment, accusing him of having formed a conspiracy to bring him down, with other Scottish magnates who had submitted themselves to him as subjects, by recognisances, at which William had rejoiced. David de Brechin, John Logie and Gilbert Malherbe were hanged and drawn at the town of Perth, and the body of Roger de Mowbray was condemned, having being brought, dead, on a litter before the judges at the parliament of Scone.[29] This plot was revealed by Murdoch of Menteith, who was subsequently the earl there, who had remained in England for a long while in the allegiance of the king; he came to the [Scottish] court to reveal this plot, and became Earl of Menteith by quittance of his niece, the daughter of his elder brother, who was countess for some time after his death. The King of England hardly troubled himself any more about Scotland, since through apathy, he had lost as much as his father had gained, and also all the fortresses in his English Marches; and furthermore, the whole of Northumberland rose against him. Gilbert de Middleton robbed two cardinals in the bishopric of Durham, who had come to consecrate the bishop, and captured the bishop of Durham, Lewis de Beaumont, and his brother Henry de Beaumont, because the king had had Adam de Swinburne, who was his cousin, arrested for speaking too plainly about the state

de Doresme Lowys de Beaumound, et soun freir Henry de Beaumound, par caus qe le roy auoit fait arester Adam de Swynburne, a qy il estoit cosyn, qi ly auoit parle trop rudement de lestat dez Marchies. Y cesti Gilbert par enherdaunce dez autres dez Marchies, cheuaucheoit de guere en Cleueland, et fist autres grauntz destrucciouns, qauoit apoi tout Northumbreland de sa couyne, hors pris lez chasteaux de Baumburgh, Alnewyk, et Norham, ou lez .ij. primers nomez furrount en tretice oue les enemys, lun par ostages, lautre par affinite, quant le dit Gilbert fust pris en le chastelle de Mitteford par couyne de sez gens propres, par Willam de Feltoun, Thomas de Hetoun, et Robert de Hornclif, et penduz et trenez a Loundres. Od tout ceo cy, lez Escotez furount deuenuz si prus qils soutzmistrent lez Marchez Dengleter, et abaterount lez chastelis de Werk et de Herbotle, qe a pain ne osat nul engles lez attendre, qe tout Northumbre auoint ils souzmys par mauueys couin dez faus gentz du pays, qe geris trouerount ils a faire nul part en ceaux Marches fors a Norham, ou vn cheualer Thomas de Gray, oue sez charneaux amys furount en garnisoun, qe trop prolinqest matier serroit a rementiuer lez punyes et lez faitz de armys et lez meschefes de defaut [f. 207] dez vitailis et dez assegis qe ly auindrent lez .xi. auns qil demurra en tiel mauueise mesoeuerous temps as Engles. Et ia le meinz ascuns de sez iournes en le dit chastel enuoet lestoir deuiser. Voir fust qe apres qe la vile de Berewike fust traye hors dez maynes dez Engles, lez Escocez estoint tant adesus et si surqiderous, qe a pain rien ne acounterent lez Engles, lez queux ne sez entremistrent de la guer, mais le lesserent perire.

   8En quele hour a vn graunt fest dez seignurs et dames en le Counte de Nichol, vn Damoisel faye aportoit vn healme de guere, od vn tymbre de vn eel endorez, a Willam Marmyoun cheualer od vn lettre de comaundement de sa dame, qil alast en la plus perillous place de la Graunt Bretaigne, et qil feist cel healme estre conuz. Il y estoit awardez illoeqes dez chiualers, qil alast a Norham pur le plus perillous auenturous lieu du pais. Le dit Willam sen ala a Norham ou dedenz le quart iour de sa venu, monsire Alexander de Moubray, freir monsire Phelip de Moubrai adonqes gardein de Berewik, veint deuaunt le chastelle de Norham od la plus apart cheualery de la Marche Descoce, od plus de .viij.ˣˣ homs darmis, arresterent deuaunt le chastelle a hour de noune. Huyne comensa hu chastel com seoint a manger. Thomas de Gray le chastelain sen ala od sa garnysoun

---

8   *left margin:* no'., *in same hand as main text.*

of the Marches.[30] This Gilbert, with the adherence of others of the Marches, raided in war into Cleveland, and committed other great depredations, and had almost all of Northumberland on his side, except just the castles of Bamburgh, Alnwick and Norham – of which the first two named were in negotiation with the enemy, the one for hostages, the other for affinity – when Gilbert was captured at Mitford castle through the connivance of his own men, by William de Felton, Thomas de Heton and Robert de Horncliffe, and was hanged and drawn at London.[31] Because of all of this, the Scots became so bold that they overran the English Marches, and razed the castles of Wark and Harbottle,[32] so that scarcely any of the English dared to bother them; they had overrun all of Northumberland through the wicked connivance of false men of the region, so they could not find much to do in any part of the Marches except at Norham, where a knight, Thomas de Gray, was in the garrison, with his close friends;[33] and it would be too lengthy a matter to relate the combats and the feats of arms, and the hardships from the lack [f. 207] of supplies, and the sieges, which befell him in the eleven years he remained there in such dreadful bad times for the English.[34] And surely it would tax anyone to work out the history at that castle. The truth was that after the town of Berwick was treacherously taken from the hands of the English, the Scots were so ascendent and so arrogant, that they reckoned the English of no account; and the latter did not bother themselves with the war, but allowed it to die out.

At this time, at a great feast of lords and ladies in the county of Lincoln, a faithful lady-in-waiting brought a war helm, with a crest of a gilded wing, to William Marmion, knight, with a letter from his lady, commanding that he go to the most perilous place in Great Britain, and that he make the helm famous. It was decided there by the knights that he should go to Norham, as the most perilous, adventurous place in the country.[35] William went off to Norham, where during the fourth day after his arrival, Sir Alexander de Mowbray, brother of Sir Philip de Mowbray, then warden of Berwick, came before the castle of Norham with the greater part of the chivalry of the Scottish March, more than eight score men-at-arms, and stood before the castle at the hour of noon. The alarm started in the castle just as they sat down to eat. Thomas de Gray the constable went up to the walls with his garrison, and saw the enemy stood nearby in battle order; looking behind him, he saw the knight, William Marmion, coming on foot, all gleaming with gold and silver, so equipped that it was a marvel, with the helm on his head. Knowing well the reason for

deuaunt sez barreirs, vist lez enemys arestuz pres en batail, regarda dereir ly, vist uenir a pee le dit cheualere Willam Marmyoun, tout relusaunt dor et dargent, si aparaille qe a meruail, le healme a test. Le dit Thomas auoit bien entendu la maner de sa venu, si ly dist en haute, Sire cheualer, vous y estez venuz cheualer erraunt, pur faire cel healme estre conuz, et si est meutz seaunt chos, qe cheualry en soit fait a cheual, qe a pee, ou couenablement ceo purra faire; mountez uostre cheual, veez la voz enemys, si ferrez cheual dez esperouns, va assemblere en mylieu dez eaux, si renay ieo Dieux, si ieo ne rescouroi toun corps viue ou mort, ou ieo murreray. Le cheualer mounta vn bel destreir, fery cheual dez esperouns, assembla en mylieu dez enemys, qi ly frapperent, ly naufrerent hu visage, ly tirerent a terre hors de la seil. En quel point, le dit Thomas veint od tout sa garnisoun, lour launcez enbessez ferrerent lez cheueaux hu buaillis, qengetterent lour meystres, recoillerent lez enemys mountez, susleuerent le cheualer abatuz, ly remounterent meisme soun cheual, enchacerent lez enemys. A quel primer auenuz, furount lessetz mortz, pris .l. cheueaux de pris. Lez femmes du chastelle enamenerent lez cheueaux a lours homs, qi mounterent, firent la chace, abaterent cea<ux>^h qils purroint ateindre. Thomas [f. 207v.] de Gray fist tuer en le Yarforde, Cryn, vn Flemyng, vn amyrail de la mere, vn robbeour, qi graunt meistre estoit od Robert de Bruys; lez autres eschapez, furount enchacez as Noneyns de Berewik. Autrefoitz, Adam de Gordoun, vn baroun Descoce se auoit assemble plus de .viij.^{xx} homs darmis, veint deuaunt le dit chastelle de Norham, en pense dauoire soutzpris lez bestes qe pasturerent hors du dit chastel. Joefnes gentz de la garnisoun courrerent testousement au plus loinz boute de la vile, qe al hour fust gast decheu, qi comencerent le eskirmouche. Lez enemys Descoce lez enuyronerent. Lez ditz gentz del issu sez tindrent dedenz veutz mures, sez defenderent apertement. Au quel poynt, Thomas de Gray, le dit chastelain od sa garnisoun, issist du chastel; aparceust lez soens en tiel daunger dez enemys, si disoit a soun soutz conestable, Jeo te bail cest chastelle, qoy qe aueigne a moy le gardez al ops le roy, qe verraiement ieo beueray de meisme le hanope, qe mes gentz illoeqes beyuent, si sen alast lez grauntz alures, qi dez comunes et autres, il ne auoit my plus de .lx. en toutis gentz. Lez enemys ly aparceurent venaunt en la maner, gerperent lez eskirmoucheours en lez veutz mures, sez treierent as beaux chaumps. Lez gentz qe enuyronez estoint hu fossez, virent lour cheuetain venir a la gise,

^h Stain on MS.

his arrival at Norham, Thomas spoke to him from on high, 'Sir knight, you have come here as a knight errant, to make that helm famous, and it's more fitting that chivalric deeds should be done on horseback than on foot, whenever this can suitably be done. Mount your horse. See, there are your enemies, put spurs to your horse and do battle in their midst; I'll renounce God if I don't rescue your body, dead or alive, or die trying!' The knight mounted a fine warhorse, put spurs to his horse, and gave battle in the midst of the enemy, who struck him, wounding him in the face, and pulled him from his saddle to the ground. At which point, Thomas came with all his garrison, and with their lances lowered, they stabbed the horses in the guts, so that they threw off their masters, beat back the mounted enemies, picked up the felled knight, remounted him on his horse, and pursued the enemy. From this first encounter, some [Scots] were left dead, and fifty valuable horses were captured. The women of the castle brought horses to their men, who mounted and gave chase, cutting down those they could catch. At the Yair ford, Thomas [f. 207v.] de Gray killed Cryn, a Fleming, a sea captain and a reiver, who was a prominent commander with Robert de Bruce;[36] the others who escaped, they chased to the Nunnery at Berwick. On another occasion, Adam de Gordon, a Scottish baron, having assembled more than eight score men-at-arms, came before the castle of Norham, thinking to catch the beasts which were being pastured outside the castle. The young men of the garrison rushed headily to the furthest end of the town, which at the time had fallen into ruin, and began to skirmish. The Scottish enemy surrounded them. The men of the foray kept themselves within the old walls, defending themselves boldly. At this point, Thomas de Gray, the constable, came out from the castle with his garrison; having seen his followers in such danger from the enemy, he said to his under-constable, 'I'm giving you charge of the castle, which fell to me to guard for the king's benefit, for indeed I'll drink from the same cup from which my men are drinking out there', and went out at great speed, though he had scarcely more than sixty men in all, common soldiers and others. Seeing him coming in this manner, the enemy left the skirmishers in the old walls, and took to the open fields. Seeing their leader coming in this way, the men who had been surrounded amongst the ditches leapt out of these ditches and charged across the fields at the enemy, who were forced to turn round, spurring their horses back against them. With this, Thomas came up with his followers, and you would have seen horses being knocked down, and men on foot killing the horses as they lay on the

launcerent outre lez fossez, currerent as chaumps sur lez ditz enemys, qe de force lour couenoit retourner, si fererent cheueaux dez esperouns areir sur eaux. Od quoy, enveint le dit Thomas od lez soens ou veissez lez cheueaux treboucher, lez gentz a pee tuerent lez cheueaux com gesoint a terre; relierent sur le dit Thomas, currerent sur lez enemys, lez enchacerent hors dez champes outre leau de Twede, pristrent et tuerent plusours; plusours cheueaux giserent mortz, qe sils vssent hu cheueaux, a pain ny vst eschape nul.

Le dit Thomas de Gray estoit .ij. foitz assege hu dit chastel, vn foitz apoy vn ane, lautrefoitz .vij. moys. Lez enemys assermerent forterescez deuaunt ly, vn a Vpsedelingtoun, vn autre a leglis de Norham. Il fu vitaille dieus foitz, par les seignours de Percy et de Neuil en graunt rescous du dit chastel, queux deuindrent sagis noblis et richis, qi graunt eide firent as Marches. Le auaunt bail du dit chastelle fust vn foitz tray, la veille de la Katerine, en soun temps, dun dez soens, qi tua le porens, lessa ens lez enemys embussez deuaunt la port, en vn mesoun. Le deuzisme garde od la dounioun se teint. Lez enemys ny estoint fors trois iours, le guerperent et le arderent apres ceo, qils auoient [f. 208] failly du myner, com ils sez douterent de la sureuenu le dit Thomas, qi adonqes reueint du sue, ou auoit en le hour este. Maintz beaux faitz darmys auindrent au dit Thomas, qen cestes ne sount pas recorde.

Entour quel hour, Gosselyn Daiuel fist enforcer le maner de Allertoun, le tenoit com de guere; y ly out tiel ryot, par cause qe lez barouns ne obeyerent pas a droit le roy, qe chescun fesoit qe ly plust.

En quel houre, Johan le Irroys rauist la Dame de Clifforde. Lez maufesurs estoint appellez Schaualdours. Lez barouns vindrent en cel hour a vn parlement a Loundres, lour gentz vestuz de sute, oue cotis esquartele, ou comensa le mortiel heyne entre eaux et le roy.

En quel temps apparust lestoil comete, et auxi estoit vn cher ane dez blez, et tiel defaut de viaunde, qe la mere mangea le fitz, et par qoy, lez poueres murrerount touz apoy. Le roy auauntdit demurraunt deuers le Sew, ou il se delita tout en niefes od marineres, et trop en autres desordenez labours, viles a soun estat, qi geris ne sentremist dautre honour ou profite, par qoi il perdy bienuoillaunce de sez gentz.

En meisme celle temps veint vn hom, disaunt soy estre de droit roy, com cely qi fust oste du biere, et cesti Edward adonqes roy remys. I cely fust pendu a Northamton, reioyaunt qe le deable en semblaunce dun chate li auoit fait ceo dire. Qy roy fust acorde par mediacioun dez graunz du realme, oue Thomas Count de Lancastre,

ground; they rallied round Thomas, charged against the enemy, and drove them back from the fields across the Tweed, capturing and killing many; many horses lay dead, and if they themselves had been on horses, hardly any would have escaped.

Thomas de Gray was twice besieged in the castle, once for almost a year, the other time for seven months. The enemy put up fortresses near him, one at Uppsettlington [Borders], the other at Norham church. He was re-supplied twice, to the great relief of the castle, by Lords Percy and Neville, who became wise, noble and powerful, and who were a great help to the Marches. Once during [Gray's] time, the outer bailey of the castle was betrayed, on St Katherine's Eve [24 November], by one of his men who killed the porter, and let in the enemy, [who were] hiding in ambush in front of the gate, in a house. The second ward held out, along with the great tower, and the enemy did not stay for more than three days, after which they burned it and abandoned it, having [f. 208] failed to undermine it, as they feared the arrival of the said Thomas, who was then returning from the south, where he had been at the time. There were many fair feats of arms which befell Thomas, which are not recorded here.

At this time, Jocelin Deyville attacked the manor of Northallerton, and held it as if by right of war;[37] disorder such as this occurred because the barons would not obey the king's law, and each did what he pleased.

At this time, Jack le Irish ravished Lady Clifford; the evildoers were called 'Schavaldours'.[38] At this point, the barons came to a parliament at London with their men dressed in livery, with quartered coats;[39] a mortal hatred arose here between them and the king.

At this time, the comet star appeared; and it was also an expensive year for corn, and there was such a shortage of food that mothers ate their sons, and because of this, nearly all of the poor perished. The king remained in the South, where he entertained himself wholly with ships and sailors, and with many other unsuitable labours shameful to his estate, hardly concerning himself with anything of either honour or profit; and because of this, he lost the good will of his men. At this same time there came a man, claiming that by right he should be king, as he had been snatched from the cradle, and that this Edward was therefore wrongfully king. This man was hanged at Northampton, pleading that the devil, in the form of a cat, had made him say it.[40] Through the mediation of the magnates of the realm, the king was reconciled with Thomas Earl of Lancaster concerning the quarrel over the death of Piers de Gaveston; this goodwill between

pur debate du mort Peris de Gauirstoun, qe bon pece auoit dure entre
eaux, et apres tost renouely. Cesti Roy Edward estoit vn foitz deuaunt
Berewik od tout soun poair real et auoit assise la vile, qe
procheignement deuaunt estoit perdu de ly, par treisoun de Peris de
Spalding, com il la auoit baily en maynz dez burges de la vile, pur
esparnier lez grauntz freses qil auoit deuaunt mys.

Meisme le hour, lez Escotez entrerent par Cardoille et
cheuaucheront parfounde en Engleter, ou a Mitoun, comuns des
burges, et de gentez de Seint Eglis sez relierent, qestoient illoeqes
descoumfitz, com gentz mesconisauntz de guere, hors de array,
encountre gentz darmis encharniez, pur quel cause, le roy se delogea
de soun assege, en purpos dauoir hu afere oue sez enemys dedenz
soun realme, lez queux tindrent lez gastes pays deuer Escoce, del
hour qils sauoint lassege roumpu, la caus de lour veage. Le roy lessa
sez Marchies en graunt tribulacioun saunz rescous, et se retrey deuers
le Sewe, ou de nouel lez grauntz de soun realme rebellerent encontre
ly, le dit Count Thomas de Langcastre et autres, qi assistrent [f. 208v.]
sez chasteaux de Tykhille. Le chastel de Knaresburgh fust soutzpris
par Johan de Lilleburn qi puis se rendy sure condicioun au roy. La
royne assist le chastel de Ledys, a qei il estoit renduz, qe lez barons ne
le voroint rescoure pur reuerence de la Royne Isabel. Lez ditz barouns
uindrent en ost, baneris desploiez encountre le roy au pount de
Burtoun sur Trent, ou ils furount descoumfitz, qy ses treierent deuers
Escoce, com fust dit, pur auoir hu rescous et suppuail, ou au pounte
de Burghbrig, Andreu de Herkeley et autres chiualeris et esquyers du
North, qestoient deuers le Roy, aparceurent qe lez barouns vindrent a
la maner, si pristrent lun boute del auaunt dit pount, lour chemyn par
ou lour couenoit passer, ou lez countis et barons furount descoumfitz,
mortz et prisis. Le Count de Herford tuez, le Count de Lancastre pris,
et lez plusours des barouns, et amenez au roy, ou a Euerwyk furount
penduz lez sires de Moubray et de Clifforde, en cotis esquartelez com
lour gentz estoint vestuz a Loundres. Le Count Thomas de Lancastre
estoit decollez a Pountfret en vengeaunce de Peris de Gauirstoun, et
dez autres vilenies qil auoit souent et coustumablement fait au roy, et
en meisme la place ou il auoit vn foiz hue, et fait huer sure le roy com
il cheminoit deuers Euerwik. Andrew du Herkeley fu fait Count de
Cardoil, qi geris ne dura, qi par orgoil voroit auoir chace le Roy
dauoir hu peisee oue lez Escotez, en autre maner qil nestoit charge,
com disoit le counsail le roy. Quel Andrew fust tray dez plus grauntz
de soun counsail a Cardoil, et illoeqes treynez et penduz. Andrew de
Herkeley se auoit maint foitz bien porte sur lez Escocez a la foitz a

them lasted for a while, but afterwards, [their quarrel] was quickly resumed. On one occasion, King Edward was before Berwick with all his royal army, and was besieging the town; it had been lost to him shortly before, by the treason of Piers de Spalding, when he had put it in the hands of the burgesses of the town, to save himself the huge expenses which he had previously incurred.

At the same time, the Scots invaded through Carlisle and raided deeply into England, where, at Myton-on-Swale [N. Yorks], the common men of the towns and the men of the Holy Church had rallied, and were defeated there, as men untrained in war, in disarray, against emboldened men-at-arms.[41] Because of this, the king decamped from his siege, in order to have it out with his enemies there inside his realm; and they took to the devastated lands towards Scotland as soon as they heard that the siege was broken, [which had been] the purpose of their expedition. The king left his Marches in great tribulation without relief, and went back to the South, where the magnates of his realm had rebelled against him anew, the Earl of Lancaster and others besieging his castle of Tickhill.[42] [f. 208v.] The castle of Knaresborough was captured by John de Lilleburn, who later surrendered it to the king on terms.[43] The queen besieged Leeds castle, which was surrendered to her, for the barons were reluctant to relieve it out of respect for queen Isabella. These barons came in force against the king with banners displayed to the bridge at Burton upon Trent, where they were defeated. They were pulling back towards Scotland, so it was said, so as to get relief and support there, when at the bridge at Boroughbridge, Andrew de Harclay and other knights and esquires of the North who were for the king, seeing that the barons were coming in this manner, seized one end of the bridge, the route by which they had to pass; here the earls and barons were defeated, killed and captured. The Earl of Hereford was killed; the Earl of Lancaster and many of the barons were captured and brought to the king.[44] The lords Mowbray and Clifford were hanged at York in quartered coats, just as their men had worn in London.[45] Earl Thomas of Lancaster was beheaded at Pontefract in revenge for Piers de Gaveston, and for other villainies which he had frequently and habitually committed against the king, and at the same place where he had once jeered and raised an outcry against the king as he [the king] was going to York.[46] Andrew de Harclay was made Earl of Carlisle. He did not last long, for in his arrogance he wished to force the king to accept a peace with the Scots, in a manner in which he had not been ordered; or so said the king's council. Andrew was brought before the

bon chef, et ascun foitz a meschief, en mayntz beaux faites darmes, ou fust pris de eaux et durement raunsonez. Le roy apres la mort le Count de Lancastre, le procheyn este, se dressa od tres graunt ost deuers Escoce, ou il auoit de chescun vile Dengleter vn hom arme a pee, hors pris sez cheualeris et esquiers. Quelis comunes combaterent au Noefchastelle, od les comunes de la vile, ou tuerent Johan de Penreth cheualer, et autres esquiers, qi seruauntz estoient au Conestable et au Mareschalle, sure le pount de la dit vile, qi voroint auoir attache lez meffesours, pur auoir estaunche la riot, tant estoint lez comunes en lour aler orgoillous. Le dit roi se trey deuers Edynburgh, ou a Lethe y auoit taunt de malady et de famyne entre lez comunes en cel graunt ost, qe de force lour couenoit retourner pur meschief de vitail, qe del hour qe lez hoblours le roy [f. 209] furount descoumfitz a Melros en foraier par James de Douglas, nuls ne bogast hors del ost pur quere vitail; de fure taunt estoint lez Engles rebukes et mescharnys de guere, qe deuaunt lour venu al Noefchastel, estoit vn tiel morin en lost pur defaut de vitail qe de necessite lour couenoit departir. Le roy se retrey od lez grauntz de soun realme deuers Euerwyk, qaunt Robert de Brus auoit fait assembler tout le poair Descoce, dez Iles et dez autres pays hautz, qi touz iours pursuy le roy, qestoit aparsu de sa venu, si se trey en Blakhowmore oue le poair qil pooit sodeignement assembler, qi pristrent vn forteresce dun mountaigne pres de Bilaund, ou lez gentz le roy furount descoumfitz, et pris le Count de Richemound, et le sire de Sully vn baroun de Fraunce, et tout plain dez autres qe apain eschapa le roy de Ryuauls, ou il estoit meismes, pensaunt qe nuls gentz vssent pris le pase sure lez soens; mais lez Escocez estoient si encharnys, et si enparnauntz lez chefetains, et lez Engles si rebukez, qe y ny auoit entre eaux, mais com du leuer deuaunt leuereres. Lez Escoces cheuacherocount outre le Walde, et deuaunt Euerwyk, et firent damage a lour pleser, saunz countre ester de nully, tanqe bel lour fust de retourner. De cel hour en auaunt prist le roy trewys oue lez Escoces pur .xiij. aunz, qi se tenoit tout coy, en pese, qi rien ne se entremist de honour ne pruesce, mais soulement par counsail Hugh le Despenser a deuenir riche, qi reteint deuers ly, qanqe il pooit happer dez terres, dez auaunt ditz barouns forfaites. Lez communes de soun realme furont en soun temps riches et maintenuz en reudes loys, mes lez grauntz ly auoint countre quere pur crualte et desordene vie qil menoit, et par cause du dit Hugh, qi al hour il amoit et creoit tout. Et ia le mainz, le dit Hugh fust mys par lour counsail a vn parlement Deuerwik entour le roy, encountre uolounte le roi adonqes, et autres de sez priuez qil amoit, remuez par

greater men of his council at Carlisle, and was drawn and hanged there. Andrew de Harclay had born himself well against the Scots on many occasions, at times to good effect, sometimes to ill, in many splendid feats of arms, until he was captured by them and put to a heavy ransom.[47] After the death of the Earl of Lancaster, in the next summer, the king set out with a very great army towards Scotland; he had with him an armed foot-man from every town in England, aside from the knights and squires.[48] At Newcastle, these commoners fought with the commoners of the town, where they killed John de Penrith, knight, on the town's bridge, along some other squires who were servants of the Constable and the Marshal, who had wanted to have the malefactors arrested so as to put an end to the riot, so impudent were the commoners in their doings.[49] The king went on towards Edinburgh, where at Leith there was such sickness and famine amongst the commoners of this great army that he was forced to turn back for lack of supplies, for at this time the king's hobelars[50] [f. 209] were defeated by James de Douglas, whilst foraging at Melrose, and no one would budge from the army to search for food; the English defeats and mishaps of war were of such cost, that there was such a loss of life in the army for lack of provisions before its arrival at Newcastle that it was obliged to disperse from necessity.[51] The king retreated with the magnates of his realm towards York, where Robert de Bruce had assembled all the forces of Scotland, the Isles and the other highlands, and pursued the king without cease, who, having seen him coming, went to Blackhowmoor with all the forces he was able to immediately gather; they held a stronghold on a mountain near to Old Byland, where the king's men were defeated,[52] and the Earl of Richmond was taken, and the Lord of Sully, a French baron,[53] and very many others, so that the king barely escaped from Rievaulx, where he had been meanwhile, thinking that no one would be able to take the pass from his men; but the Scots were so emboldened, and their leaders so audacious, and the English so cowed, that they were just like a hare before greyhounds.[a] The Scots raided across the Wolds, and as far as York, and caused devastation at their pleasure, without anyone to stand against them, until it suited them to turn back. From this time on, the king made a truce with the Scots for thirteen years,[54] keeping himself wholly quiet, in peace, concerning himself with nothing of honour or prowess, but only with getting rich, on the advice of Hugh le Despenser, keeping for himself what-

---

[a]   Lit.: 'that it was not between them, but as a hare before greyhounds'.

eaux, qi puis par lour counsail ly firent baneir du realme, ou en soun
exile, il robba sure mere dieus tarrites plains dauoir de pois, qoy
cousta le realme Dengleter grauntement apres. Le roy ly fist
recounsiller procheignement saunz gre de eaux, apres qi, il fist tout,
qi tout ly discounsailloit a cheualry, delitaunt soy en auarice, et en
delitz du corps desheritaunt sez gentz, qe auoint rebellez encountre
ly, et a deuenir meismes riche dez grauntz possessiouns de terres. Et
en le meisme temps surdist guere en Gascoyne du Roy de Fraunce,
entour quoy, le roy Dengleter despendy graunt tresor, com pur terre
et nacioun [*f. 209v.*] qil plus amoit. Sy enuoya soun freir le Count de
Kent et autres grauntz qi geris ne esploiterent, mais perderent graunt
terre, com en temps mesœurous as Engles, qe tout le temps auoit dure
de cest roy. Le roy dona la Duche de Gyane a soun fitz eyne, Count de
Cestre, mais lez barouns de la Duche ne voroint atourner a ly, ne a
nully viuaunt, fors a la coroune Dengleter. Il enuoya soun dit fitz a
Parys oue sa mere la Royne Isabel, la sore le Roy de Fraunce, pur faire
soun homage a soun vncle, et pur estauncher la guer de Gascoigne.
Qe qaunt ils uindrent en Fraunce, la mere et le fitz, ils ne voroint
repairer en Engleter, mais enbracerent autre couyne, encountre lour
seignour, marry, et pier, qi par enherdaunz dez gentz banyes hors
Dengleter, le seignour de Mortymer et autres, et par ascent du Count
de Kent, le freir le Roy, qi repairast de Gascoyne a Parys pur cest
couyne, qi lessa la gerre soun freir, et par tretice de alyaunce entre le
Count Henaunde, et la royne, du mariage soun fitz, et de Phelip, feile
du dit count, qi puis sa prist. La dit royne od ses enherdauntz sa trey
en Seland, qe si ele vst demurre .viij. iours en le Realme de Fraunce
plus longment qel ne fist, ele vst este reenuoye od toz lez autres
enbraceours de cel couyne, au Roy Dengleter, taunt auoit Hugh de[i]
Despenser enbrace le counsail de Fraunce par soun auoir, qe par
colour qe el estoit venuz en message son seignour au gre le Roy de
Fraunce et sure soun conduyt, et la dit busoigne guerpy, la cause de sa
venu, et autres riotis enbracez dedenz le conduyt, le roy soun freir la
vst reenuoye a soun marry, de quoi el fust garny, pur quoy sa trey en
la seignourye le Count de Henawd, qi count enuoya soun freir, Johan
de Henaude, oue tout plain des gentz darmes od eaux, qe arryuerent
a Herwelle au furre de guere, saunz damage resceyuoir du graunt
nauy le roi ordeyne encountre eaux, prest arayez a Yarmouth. Ils

---

[i]   sic.

ever he was able to grab of the lands forfeited by the aforesaid barons. In his time, the commons of his realm were wealthy, maintained by tough laws, but the magnates were opposed to him due to his cruelty and the dissolute life which he led, and because of Hugh, whom at the time he loved and trusted completely. Nevertheless, Hugh was brought by their counsel before a parliament at York at that time in the presence of the king, against the king's will; other beloved intimates of his were removed by them, and then they had Hugh banished from the realm by their counsel.[55] Whilst in exile, he robbed two merchant ships full of merchandise at sea, which cost the realm of England dearly afterwards.[56] The king was soon reconciled with him, without [the magnates'] agreement, after which he gave himself completely to that which completely debarred him from chivalry, delighting himself in avarice and in the delights of the flesh, disinheriting his men who had rebelled against him, and at the same time getting rich from their great landholdings. And at the same time, war broke out in Gascony with the King of France, on which the King of England expended a great fortune, as though for the land [f. 209v.] and nation which he loved most. He sent his brother, the Earl of Kent,[57] and other magnates, who did not achieve much, but lost much land, as these were bad times for the English, which lasted for the whole time of this king. The king gave the Duchy of Guienne to his eldest son, the Earl of Chester,[58] but the barons of the Duchy were unwilling to submit to him, nor to anyone living, except the crown of England. He sent his son to Paris with his mother, Queen Isabella, the sister of the King of France, to make his homage to his uncle and to put an end to the Gascon war. When the mother and the son had got to France, they were unwilling to return to England, but planned another conspiracy against their lord, husband and father, with the adherence of men banished from England, Lord Mortimer and others, and with the support of the Earl of Kent, the king's brother, who came from Gascony to Paris for this conspiracy, abandoning his brother's war; and by a treaty of alliance between the Count of Hainault and the Queen, for the marriage of her son to Philippa, the count's daughter, which took place later.[59] The Queen went to Zeeland with her adherents, for if she had remained for eight days longer in the realm of France than she did, she would have been sent back to the King of England, along with all the other plotters in this conspiracy; Hugh le Despenser had so fixed the French council by means of his wealth, that – on the pretext that she had come as an envoy from her lord for a settlement with the King of France, and on

gaignerent Engleter, saunz coup fereir, qe touz lez seignours et comunes leuerent od eaux, encountre le roy, qi lors a lour arryuail estoit a Loundres, qi se trey deuers Galis, ou Hugh le Despenser quidoit rescouse et suppuaile qe touz ly faillerent. A Schipstow le roy gerpy sa menie et se mist sodeignement en leaw de Wye, qi par mere se uoroit auoir departy oue Hugh le Despenser en estrange tere, pur ceo qe lez soens ly guerperent, mais vent et marray ly estoint si contrair, qe .xv. iours entiers, il ne pooit bouger hors de Seuerne pur tempest. En le mene temps, *[f. 210]* veint la royne et soun fitz et Roger de Mortimer, adonqes gouuernour de cel counsail, quel Roger estoit adeuaunt del acorde le Count Thomas de Lancastre et dez barouns, mais il lour gerpy, qi se mist en la grace le roy, le primer mescoumfort de lour meschief. Il fust mys par counsail Hugh le Despenser en la Tour de Londres, tanqe graunt pece apres il eschapa de prisoun, qi se trey en Fraunce, vn dez plus graunt embraceour de cest veage. Ils vindrent od lez estrangers, et od touz lez grauntz seignours Dengleter a Bristow, ou fust pris Hugh le Despenser le pier, Count de Wyncestre, et treinez et penduz illoeqes. Donald Count de Marre estoit en le houre od le Roy Dengleter et nurry oue ly, qi auoit la garde du chastel de Bristow du baille le Roy, qi le rendy a la royne, se trey en soun pays en Escoce. Tretouz le mene le roy vindrent de Scheppistow et Bristow a la royne et a soun fitz, tenaunt lostel le roy. Gentz darmis del acorde la royne, sez adresserent par nief, la tempest failly, a courrer sure le roy, qy vncor ieust en nief deuaunt eaux en Seuerne. Le Roy aparceyuaunt toutes cestes aduersetez, qi ly suruindrent, se mist a terre en Glaumorgane, ou il fist couenaund ou vn Galay du pays, en qy Hugh le Despenser se assioit pur graunt garisoun, a musser le dit Hugh, qi ne estoit pas trop cheualerous, depusqe ils auoint failly .ij. foitz ou trois le passage de la mere. Ly quel Galays rendy fausement le dit Hugh a la royne, qi a Gloucestre fust penduz et treynez. Le Count de Arundelle fust decolle en la Marche de Galis en cest temps, qestoit du counsail le roy. Le roy qi rien se douta de soun corps, enuoi a *j* la royne sa femme, qil se voroit amendre de ceo, qil se auoit mesporte deuers ly, et deuers touz lez soens par bon ordinaunce, et qil serroit troue en vn certeyn lieu, pensaunt qe ele vendroit a ly, com espouse dust a soun marry. Mais ly aloist qere le Count Henry de Langcastre, qi ly amena a Kennylworth a dire, com prisoner. La royne

---

j   MS: a *repeated.*

his safe-conduct, and that the business which had caused her to come was finished, as well as other contentions covered under the safe-conduct – her brother the king would have sent her back to her husband. She was warned of this, and therefore took herself into the lordship of the Count of Hainault;[60] and the count sent his brother, John de Hainault, and a great many men-at-arms with him, who landed at Orwell in manner of war, without taking any loss from the large fleet ordered against them by the king, arrayed ready at Yarmouth. They gained England without striking a blow, for all the lords and commons rose with them, against the king, who at the time of their landing was at London; he took himself towards Wales, where Hugh le Despenser expected help and support, which completely failed him.[61] At Chepstow, the king abandoned his house-hold and abruptly took to the river Wye, because he hoped to leave with Hugh le Despenser by sea for a foreign land, because of which his followers abandoned him; but the wind and the tide were so against him, that for fifteen days running, he was unable to budge from the Severn for the storm. In the meantime, [f. 210] the queen and her son and Roger de Mortimer, then governor of her council, arrived. Roger had previously been in alliance with Earl Thomas of Lancaster and with the barons, but he had deserted them and put himself at the king's mercy, the prime misfortune amongst their toubles. He was put in the Tower of London on the advice of Hugh le Despenser, until he escaped from prison a long time after, and took himself to France, and was one of the greatest supporters of this expe-dition. They came to Bristol with the foreigners,[62] and with all the great lords of England, where Hugh le Despenser the father, Earl of Winchester, was taken, and drawn and hanged there. Donald, Earl of Mar, was with the King of England at the time, having been fostered with him; he had the keeping of Bristol castle by the king's grant, which he surrendered to the queen, and took himself off to his lands in Scotland.[63] All the king's following came to Chepstow and Bristol to the queen and her son, [who] held the king's household. Men-at-arms of the queen's allegiance embarked aboard ship, as the storm died down, to chase after the king, who still lay in a ship before them on the Severn. Seeing all these tribulations which had occurred to him, the king made landfall in Glamorgan, where he made an arrangement with a Welshman of the region, in whom Hugh le Despenser trusted for great reward, to hide Hugh (who was not overly chivalrous), since they had failed two or three times to make the passage by sea. This Welshman deceitfully surrendered Hugh to

fist somoundre vn parlement a Loundres, ou par assent dez prelates,
countis, barouns et comunes et cytezeins de Loundres, queux
Loundrais, a le arryuail la royne, en my lieu de Chepe, decollerent le
tresoreir le roy, Leuesqe de Excestre. Le roy fust depose par lour
comune assent, et si renderent sus lour homagis par escript desoutz
lours sealles par Leuesqe de Hertforth, qi fist cel message a
Kennylworth au roy depose, qi ly nouncia despitousement lez articles, qe lez comunes, sez soutzgis, ly surmistrent cause [f. 210v.] de sa
deposicioun, com cely qi ly heoit de quere pur singuler duresce qe le
roy auoit fait. Il prist tout cest affaire en pacience, qi dona a soun fitz
la beneisoun de Dieu, et la soen, qi prioit a Dieu, qe il ly feist
prodhom, et lui donast meilliour grace et gree du poeple, qil nauoit
hu. Il fust remue de Kennilworth a Bercelay, ou il morust; la maner
coment ne fust pas scieu, mais Dieux le sciet. Il fust enterre a
Gloucestre, et regna .xix. aunz. Il fust sagis, douce et amyable en
parole, mais mesoeurous en fait. Il estoit artilious, en quoi il se delita
de sa main propre. Il fust compaignable trop as sez priues, as
estrangis soleyn, et trop amast vn soul persoun singulerement. Soun
fitz fust coronez a cest auaundit parlement, uiuaunt soun pier, par
comune ascent, qi prist lez homages dez grauntz, et les obeisauns de
toutz lez comunes, qi ioyous estoint de nouelle gouernail, pur le
mesoeure du pier, et pur lour chaungeable costome, com par
condicioun de vn coillet de diuers naciouns. Pur ceo uolount ascuns
genz dire, qe la diuersete dez corages dez Engles est la caus qe moue
lez chaungementz du siecle entre eaux, qe plus est muable en la
Graunt Bretaigne, qen autres pays, qar en temps de chescun roy puis[k]
Vortiger, ount aliens este grauntement auauncez illoeqes de toutz
naciouns, qi diuers ount condiciouns, par quoy lour estayt[l]
desacorder en voloir, chescun enuoroit estre sires, pur ceo qe lez
seignurages illoeqes ne suount pas nature, mes fortune, pur ceo
desirent ils le mouement, qe chescun qiude le sort le soen. Tout soit
ceo dit, qe eau curraunt est la plus fort chos qe soit, vncor est ele
suefe, mole de nature, mais pur ceo qe touz lez parcelis del eau
butount lour part en lour cours owelement, pur ceo perce el la dure
pere. Tout ensi est il dun nacioun, qe dun corage mettount la mayn a
maintener lestat lour siris, qi ne desirent fors le bien estre du comune,

[k] MS: pi*us*.
[l] MS: estuyt.

the queen, and he was hanged and drawn at Gloucester. The Earl of Arundel, who was of the king's council, was beheaded in the March of Wales at this time. The king, who was not afraid for his own head, sent a message to the queen, his wife, that he wished to make amends, for the wrongs he had done to her, and to all his men, by good governance; and that she could find him at a certain place, thinking that she would come to him, as a wife should to her husband. But Earl Henry of Lancaster went to search for him, and took him to Kenilworth as a prisoner, so to speak. The queen had a parliament summoned at London, where by the assent of the prelates, earls, barons and commons and citizens of London, these Londoners, on the arrival of the queen, beheaded the king's treasurer, the bishop of Exeter, in the middle of Chepe.[64] The king was deposed by their common assent, and they renounced their homage by a deed under their seals, via the Bishop of Hereford, who took this message to Kenilworth to the deposed king. He contemptuously announced to him the articles by which the commons, his subjects, informed him of the reason [f. 210v.] for his deposition, as he hated him heartily for the particular adversity which the king had caused him. [The king] accepted this whole affair with patience, giving to his son God's blessing, along with his own, praying to God that he should make [his son] a worthy man, and grant him better grace and favour from the people, which he had not had. He was removed from Kenilworth to Berkeley, where he died; it what manner is not known, though God knows it.[65] He was buried at Gloucester, and reigned for nineteen years. He was wise, charming and affable in conversation, but malevolent in deed. He was clever at whatever he fancied to turn his hand to. He was overly friendly with his intimates, reserved with strangers, and he loved too much a certain person in particular.[66] His son was crowned at the aforesaid parliament by common assent, while his father was still alive, and took the homage of the magnates, and the fealty of all the commoners, who were very happy with the new government, because of his father's wrong-doing, and because of their capricious nature, from their condition as a [people] gathered together from diverse nations. Therefore some men like to argue that the diversity of temperments in the English is the cause that provokes amongst them upheavals of society, which is more unstable in Great Britain than in other countries, for foreigners of all nations have been greatly advanced there in the time of every king since Vortiger.[67] These were of diverse condition, and so their estate was disunited in its aims, each one wanting to be a lord, because lordships there came

ne^m tirent autre acorde singulerement. Entre tiel gent est moult rerement vieu chaungement du siecle, au mainz muement de lestat lour siris, le greindre deshonour a le poeple. Cesty Edward le secound apres la Conquest, auoit .ij. fitz et .ij. feilles. Le primer fitz Edward, fust estably roy, viuaunt soun pier. Lautre fitz auoit a noun Johan, si fust Count de Cornwail, et morust a la vile de saynt Johan, si nauoit engendrure. La primer feile Isabel, fust puis marye au Count de Geller, qi puis fust Duk. La secound feile Johan, fust puis marye a Dauid fitz Robert de Bruis Roy Descoce.

[*f. 211*] ^a **44.** Cesti Edward le tierce apres la Conquest nestoit fors de .xiiij. aunz a soun encoronement en la fest de la Chaundelour, qi de tout estoit gouerne et soun realme, par sa mere, et par Roger de Mortimer, al hour Count de la Marche. Le primer ane de soun regne, lez Escocez firent graunt destruccioun par diuers foitz en sa tere. Lez Countis de Lancastre et de Kent, oue lez seignurs de Wake, Ros, Moubray et Beaumount et autres grauntz barouns, od mile homs darmes, furount enuoyez al Noef Chastelle sure Tyne pur enforcer la Marche, ou James de Douglas veint par deuaunt eaux a .iiij. lieus pres ardaunt et destruyaunt le pays au plain vieu de eaux toucz, qe nuls de eaux ne voroit isser taunt estoint ils mescharnys et noun empernauntz de guere. Tost apres cel hour, furent assemblee tout la cheuelery Dengleter, et tout plain dez alienes, lez queux estrangers sez combaterent a Euerwyk oue comunes dez countes, qi furent illoeqes graunt party mortz, qi par yueroyne curerent sure les estraungers, qi pres de eaux estoient loges en les suburbes de la dit vile. Cel melle estaunche par ascent du counsail pur ceo qils estoint estrangeris et venuz en lour eyde; si mouerent touz deuers lez enemys Descoce qi ia estoint derechief entres la terre Dengleter. Le dit

---

^m   MS: ne *repeated.*

^a   Edouardus Tertius, *added above the illuminated 'C' in very late 16thc. hand.*

not from nature, but fortune; therefore they long for change, each supposing that the lot will fall to him. It is always said that running water is the strongest thing that can be, for although it is gentle and soft by nature, because all of the particles of water take their part pushing equally in the flow, therefore it pierces hard stone. It is just so with a nation that with one mind, turns its hand to maintaining the estate of its lords, who do not desire anything save the good of the community, nor individually strive for any other aim. Amongst such a people an upheaval of society is seen very rarely, at least regarding changes in the estate of their lords, which is the greatest dishonour to the people. This Edward the second after the Conquest had two sons and two daughters. The first son, Edward, was made king whilst his father still lived. The other son was named John; he was Earl of Cornwall and died at the town of Perth, and had no off-spring. The first daughter, [Eleanor], was married to the Count of Guelders, who was subsequently the Duke. The second daughter, Joan, was later married to David, son of Robert de Bruce, the King of Scotland.[68]

[f. 211] **44.** This Edward, the third after the Conquest, was no more than fourteen years old at his coronation on the feast of Candlemas [2 February],[1] and in all things he was governed, along with his realm, by his mother, and by Roger de Mortimer, [who was] by that time the Earl of March. In the first year of his reign, the Scots caused great devastation in his land on several occasions. The earls of Lancaster and Kent, with lords Wake, Ros, Mowbray and Beaumont and other great barons, with a thousand men-at-arms, were summoned to Newcastle on Tyne to reinforce the March.[2] Here, James de Douglas came before them, four leagues away, burning and devastating the country in plain view of them all; none of them were willing to make a move, so much were they disheartened and unenterprising in war. Soon after this time, all of the chivalry of England was assembled, and a large number of foreigners, and at York, these strangers fought with the commoners from the counties, a large part of whom were killed there; they had attacked the strangers, who were lodged near them in the suburbs of the town, due to drunkeness.[3] This brawl was brought to an end by order of the council, because the foreigners had come to help them; they all set off towards the Scottish enemy who had already entered the land of England once again. The young king with his great army took the road towards Stanhope, where he was told that his Scottish enemies were quartered; as he was on the way there, the scouts from his

jouen roy od soun graunt ost teint le chemyn deuers Stanhop, ou ly
fust dit qe sez enemys Descoce estoient logez, ou encheminaunt les
descouerours de soun auaunt garde ly venoient nouncier, qe lez
enemys sez alerent descoumfitz et fuauntz; et si nestoit pas ensy, ne
ne^b firent rien, mais delogerent et lour choiserent meilliour place pur
attrendre de combatre. Lez gouernours del ost le dit roy, quyderent qe
lez descouerours auoint dit verite, lesserent le chemyn deuers
Stanhop, sez hasterent par counsail dez ascuns dez Marchies, dauoir
forclos lez enemys, pensaunt qils auoint tenu lour chemyn deuers
lour pais en fuaunt, cheuaucherent tout le iour de este, bien .xxvi.
lieus od tout cel graunt ost, parmy Anandredalle et Tyndalle, sez
herbigerent a Haydenbrig, demurerent illoeqes .viij. iours, ne auoint
nuls nouelis dez enemys. Fust crie en lost, qe qy porteroit au roy
certain dez ditz enemys, aueroint cent lyuere de terre. Thomas de
Rokeby aportoit lez nouelis, qils estoient tout coy a Stanhop ou lez
auoint lesse, qy enioy le dit gerdoun et deueint cheualer. Le roy se
delogea, se trey areir deuer eaux od tout soun graunt ost. En le mene
temps Archebald de Douglas oue lez forreiours dez enemys, auoint
curru apoi tot [*f. 211v.*] leuesche de Doresme, enchacerent a lour ost
grauntz prays, encountrerent a Derlington vn graunt route dez
comunes deuers lost dez Engles, les tuerent apoy toutz. Cest graunt
ost dez Engles trouerent lours ditz enemys prestes ioust Stanhop en
trois bataillis en beaux chaumps, et si nestoint qe poy dez gentez,
trois cheuetains soulement, lez Countis de Murref, de Marre et James
de Douglas. Le roy se logea deuaunt eaux sure leaw de Were troys
iours, et la quart nuyte sez delogerent lez Escotez, et remuerent vn
petite lieu de illoeqes, dedenz le park de Stanhop, qi illoeqes
attenderent .vi. iours, deuaunt cest graunt ost dez Engles, Allemauns,
et Hanueris, qi rien ne firent de armys, fors lez Escocez oue Jamys de
Douglas, fererent vn nuyt dedenz lost al vn bout dez loeges, qi
tuerent dez comunes des countes graunt party, et departerent saunz
damage. La tierz nuyt apres cestez punyeres, sez delogerent lez
Escocez, et sen alerent en lour pays, qi graunt damage auoint fait en
Engleter, si encounterent meisme le iour de lour departire od Patrik
Count del Marche et od Johan le Seneschal, qi se disoit Count
Dangous, od .v. mil homs dez gentez Descoce, qi venoint en rescous
de eaux, qi lez auoint oy dire assegez, qe sils vssent hu vitaillis com
fust dit, ils vssent retournez, taunt estoint encharnys guerriours. Le

---

^b *Sic.*

vanguard came to inform him that the enemy were running, defeated and put to flight; but it was not so, for they were doing nothing but decamping and chosing themselves a better place to wait to fight. The commanders of the king's army, presuming that the scouts had spoken truly, left the road to Stanhope, spurred on by the advice of some of the Marchers, in order to cut off the enemy, thinking that they had taken the road to their own country in flight. They rode all of the summer's day, a good twenty-six miles[4] with all of this great army, across [Allendale][5] and Tynedale, and quartered themselves at Haydon Bridge, remaining there for eight days, having no news of the enemy. It was proclaimed in the army that whoever brought reliable [news] about the enemy to the king, should have a hundred pounds of land. Thomas de Rokeby brought the news that they were still quiet at Stanhope, where they had been left; he enjoyed his reward and became a knight.[6] The king struck camp, and took himself back towards them, with all of his great army. In the mean time, Archibald de Douglas, with the enemy's foragers, had run through almost the whole [f. 211v.] of the bishopric of Durham, bringing great plunder to their army. At Darlington, they encountered a large band of commoners [marching] towards the English host, and killed nearly all of them. The great English army found their enemies just near Stanhope, in three battles in open fields; and they had but few men, with only three leaders, the earls of Moray, Mar and James de Douglas. The king camped before them on the river Wear for three days, and on the fourth night, the Scots decamped and moved back a short league from there, within Stanhope park. They waited there for six days before this great army of English, Germans and Hainaulters, which accomplished nothing by way of feats of arms, save the Scots under James de Douglas, who attacked the army one night at one end of the camp, killed a great part of the commoners from the counties, and departed without loss. The third night after these fights, the Scots broke camp, and took themselves back to their country, having caused great damage in England. On the same day as their departure, they met with Patrick, Earl of March, and John the Steward, who called himself Earl of Angus, with 5000 Scotsmen, who had come to relieve them, having heard it said that they were besieged.[7] If they had had supplies, so it was said, they would have turned back, such bold warriors were they. The king, an innocent, wept.[8] He broke camp and turned back towards York, concerning himself no more with this war whilst his mother's rule lasted, and that of Roger Mortimer, Earl of March;

roy vn innocent plora dez oils, qi se delogea et se retrey deuers Euerwyk, qi plus ne se entremist de cel guerre, dorant la gouernail qil auoit de sa mere, et del auaunt dit Roger de Mortimer, Count de la Marche, qar ou Robert de Bruys adonqes Roy Descoce auoit assys le chastel de Norham, ou Robert de Maners estoit conestable adonqes, qi issist od soun garnisoun, descoumfist vn iour le gayt dez enemys Descotais deuaunt la port du chastel, ou vn baners Descoce Willam Mouhaud fust tue; le cheuetain du gait [pur]*c* cretyn del eau ne voloit suffrire qils fussent rescous, qe nul en la vile ne lour aprochasent. Le Count de Murref, od James de Douglas, auoint assege adonqes le seignour de Percy en Alnewyk, ou estoient grauntz ioustes de guere par couenaunt taille, queux seignours ne tindrent pas lassege, mais treyerent a Robert lour roys, au sege de Norham. En quel hour, le sire de Percy od lez Marchies firent vn cheuauche en le costere de Teuydal, ne demurrerent my .x. lieues de voy, et vncor fust ceo nouncie a James de Douglas, qi sodeignement de Norham se mist od soens entre le dit seignour de Percy et soun chastelle de Alnewyk, qi luy [*f. 212*] fist treir deuers le Noefchastel de nuyt, taunt estoient lez Engles mescharnis en le hour de guer. Le counsail auauntdit du dit Roy Dengleter enuoierent qu dit Robert de Bruis a Norham, Willam de Denoum vn hom de ley, pur pese et taillerent vn mariage du fitz le dit Robert Dauid, et de Johan la sore le Roy Dengleter, qi pius se prist a Berewyk. Au parlement de Euerwik ou cesti roi Edward Dengleter prist a femme Phelip la feile le Count Willam de Henaud, fust peise cest guere Descoce, et renduz les reliqes et lez endentures del obeisaunz dez seignours Descoce, lour sealis pendauntz, qe hom appelloit 'Ragman', qe le Roy Edward le primer apres la Conquest auoit conquys en tiel tail, qe le Roy Dengleter quitclameroit soun droit Descoce, et pur le mariage sa sore .xl.Mile. marcz dargent, et qe touz ses enherdauntz perdeissent lour heritage en Escoce, hors pris lez seignours de Wak, Percy, Beawmound et la Sowche, qi de lour condiciouns rien nestoit tenu, de quoy pius enaueint graunt mal. De tot cest tail nestoit acordaunt le roy, mais pur soun ioen age, la Royne et le Mortimer le firent tout, vn dez causis de lour deffesauns apres.

A meisme cesti parlement vindrent nouelis de la mort le Roy de Fraunce, Charlis, le vncle de cesti Roy Edward Dengleter depar sa mere qi trespassa saunz heyre de soun corps; et pur ceo le droit du realme de Fraunce solonc descret de ascuns, descendy a cesti Edward Dengleter soun neuew, fitz de sa sore, com a plus procheyne heire

c Supplied.

whereupon Robert Bruce, then King of Scotland, had the castle of Norham besieged, where Robert de Manners was then constable.[9] [Manners] made a sortie with his garrison, [and] defeated the Scottish enemy's guard in front of the castle gate one day, where a Scottish banneret, William Mowat was killed; the leader of the guard would not allow them to be rescued, because of a flood, as none in the town could get near them.[10] The Earl of Moray, with James de Douglas, then besieged lord Percy at Alnwick, where there were grand jousts of war by formal agreement; these lords did not maintain the siege, but went to Robert their king at the siege of Norham.[11] At this time, lord Percy and the Marchers made a *chevauchée* on the edge of Teviotdale, remaining no more than ten leagues away; nevertheless this was reported to James de Douglas, who immediately [set out] from Norham placing himself with his men between lord Percy and his castle of Alnwick, which [f. 212] forced [Percy] to head for Newcastle, by night, so disheartened were the English at this time of the war. The King of England's council sent William de Denum, a man of law,[12] to Robert de Bruce at Norham for peace talks and they arranged a marriage for Robert's son, David, and Joan, the sister of the King of England, which took place later at Berwick. At parliament at York,[13] where King Edward of England took to wife Philippa the daughter of Count William of Hainault, the Scottish war was settled; and the relics were restored, and the indentures of obeissance of the Scottish lords with their seals appended, which men called 'Ragman', which King Edward the first after the Conquest had exacted in this form. The King of England conceded his rights over Scotland; and 40,000 marks of silver for the marriage of his sister;[14] and that all his adherents should lose their inheritance in Scotland, except for lords de Wake, Percy, Beaumont and la Zouche. Nothing was settled about their situation, and great evil arose from this later. This agreement was wholly unacceptable to the king, but because of his young age, the queen and Mortimer arranged it all, [which was] one of the causes of their downfall afterwards.

News came to this same parliament of the death of the King of France, Charles, the uncle of King Edward of England on his mother's side, who passed away without heir of his body.[15] Therefore, according to the learned opinion of some, the right to the realm of France descended to Edward of England, his nephew, the son of his sister, as the nearest heir male; but due to the king's young age, and the malign, slothful and negligent counsel by which he was governed in all things, no claim at all was put forward at that time for

masle; mais pur le ioen age de le Roy, et le mauueis, parsouse,
necligent counsail, par qoy il estoit de tout gouernez, ne estoit point
en le hour a droit chalange mys du coroun de Fraunce, tanqe le fitz
del vncle de le auncestre fust corone, Phelip de Valoys, pur ceo qe il
estoit nee du realme, et tauntz auoit dez amys et dez alyes qe saunz
regard auoir au droit de nuly, par affinite, ly pristrent au roy, de quoi
pius ensourdist graunt guer. Le dit Phelip descoumfist lez Flemyngs
a Casselis en le primer ane de soun regne. Puis cel hour bon pece ne
fust rien parle de cest chalange du droit de coroune de Fraunce du
Roy Dengleter. La Royne Isabelle et le Mortimer gouernerent tout
Engleter, en la maner, qil despluyt as plusours grauntz du realme, qi
senherderent ensemble le Count de Lancastre et autres de cel couyn,
qi comencerent a mouer riote en purpos dauoir oste cel gouernement,
mais ceaux del acorde la royne sez auoint faitez si fortis dez alies et
des enherdaunz, qe lez autres nestoient de poair a riot<re>^d eaux,
com lour fust auys; si peiserent cest debat par tretice en maner qils sez
mettroint [*f. 212v.*] en la grace le roy, qe tout ne rebellerent ils my
encountre ly, vncor fesoint ils le roi partie, com ceaux qi ly auoint tout
en gouernail. Cest obeisaunz fust fait a Bedforde ou toutz furent
rescieus a la grace le roy, hors pris lez seignours de Wak et de
Beaumound et Thomas Rosselin qi voiderent le realme, et
embracerent lour amys de pardela, pur auoir ariue en Engleter, mais
deuaunt le temps de lour empris, le siecle estoit chaunge. En meisme
le temps de cest riot dez barouns, vindrent cheualers et esquiers en
eide del acorde le roy hors de Northumbreland a Rothewel ou ils
auoint vn graunt puynez au fure de guere od lez paysens enuyroun,
qi furount illoeqes mortz et descoumfitz par cestes auaunt ditz
Marchies. Apres cel hour graunt pece y auoit graunt reuel dez ioustes
et tournays. La royne oue le counsaille du Count de la Marche auoit
tout en gouernail. Vn de sez priues fist entendre a le Count de Kent le
vncle le roy, qe soun freir le roy, le pier viuoit, et qe si il luy voroit
eider, qe il ly purroit remettre en soun estat, qy estoit leez de la vie
soun frere si ly disoit, qe a murreir il ly eideroit; et fust gette cest
compassement,^e pur assaier la volounte du dit Count. Tout qanqe il ly
auoit dist, lautre ala nouncier a la royne. A vn parlement a Wyncestre,
le dit count fust attache et areynez de cest bosogne. Il graunta
deuaunt le coroner del ostel le roy, qil voroit auoir eide soun freir, sil

---

^d MS: *The 're' of 'riotre' has been partially erased, and there is a short lacuna after*
    riotre; er is supplied in right margin.
^e MS: compassemet.

the right to the crown of France. And so the son of the predecessor's uncle, Philip de Valois, was crowned, because he was born within the realm, and had so many friends and allies that they accepted him as king by affinity, without regard for the rights of anyone; and because of this, a great war ensued later. Philip defeated the Flemings at Cassel in the first year of his reign.[16] After this time, nothing was said for a good while about this claim of the King of England's to the right to the crown of France. Queen Isabella and Mortimer ruled all of England in this manner, which was displeasing to many magnates of the realm, who gathered themselves around the Earl of Lancaster and others of that party, and began to raise rebellion in order to get rid of this government; but those of the Queen's allegiance had made themselves so strong with allies and adherents, that the others did not have the power to threaten them, as they were advised. They settled this dispute by treaty in a manner by which they put themselves *[f. 212v.]* in the king's grace, for they had not rebelled against him at all; indeed they formed the king's party, for it was they who had him wholly under their rule. This obeissance was made at Bedford, where they were all received into the king's grace, except for lords Wake and Beaumont and Thomas Roscelyn who quit the realm, and conspired with their friends overseas to invade England; but the regime was overthrown before the time for their enterprise.[17] At the same time as this rising of the barons, knights and squires came from Northumberland to Rothwell, to aid the king's faction, where they had a great fight, like a war, with the peasants of the area, who were killed and defeated there by these Marchers.[18] After this time there was a grand festival of jousts and tournaments for a long while. The queen had everything under her rule, with the advice of the Earl of March. One of her intimates convinced the Earl of Kent, the king's uncle, that his brother the king, the father [*i.e.* Edward II], was alive; and that if he were willing to help him, he would be able to restore him to his estate. He was overjoyed that his brother lived and told him that he would aid [his brother] to the death; and this plot was set up to check the earl's intentions. Everything whatsoever [the earl] said to him, the other went and told to the queen. At a parliament at Winchester, the earl was attached and arraigned over this affair.[19] Before the coroner of the king's household, he admitted that he had wanted to help his brother, if he lived, to have him restored to his estate at his pleasure. They advised him that this was treason, as the restoration of the father would be the destruction of the son, to whom he was submitted as to his liege lord; they had him beheaded imme-

vst vesqu, de luy auoir mys en soun estat a soun gree. Ils ly
suremistrent qe ceo estoit treisoun, qar refesaunz du pier vst este
defesauncz du fitz, a qi il estoit atournez com a soun seignour liege;
pur qoi en reuerence de soun haut sank ils ly pardonerent le haut
iugement, si ly firent decoller al hour. Le roy comensa de crestre de
corps et de sen, qy desplesoit la gouernail de la royne sa mere, et heoit
le Count de la Marche, apres qi, la royne fist tout. Le roy enbrasa
couyne oue lez ioenes gentz entour luy a remuer cest gouernail, et a
destruyer le dit count. Si priuiement ne ietterent ils my cest chos, qils
nestoint descouerez. Qe a Notingham a vn counsail, le roy et touz
ceaux de cest couyne furont aresonez de cest purpos seauntz toutz en
counsail, qi toutz le dedissoient qils nensauoit rien, com chescun fust
aresone a par soy, hors pris Willam de Mountagow qi se adressoit en
soun esteaunt, disaunt, qe qy ly suremettroit si bien non, ou autre
couyne qe soun deuoir, qil ly ferroit haut respons, et se passa par tiels
parolis, nul ne ly repoundy fors en general. Le counsail failly, le
[f. 213] dit Willam disoit au roy, qe meutz serroit a mangier de le
chien, qe chien de eaux, si ly counsailloit a parler au conestable du
chastel en ly chargeaunt par serement et legeaunce de celer le
counsail, et qil lessoit vn posterne ouert deuers le park meisme la
nuyt, et qe sil ne le fesoit, qil ly ferroit pendre, a <quel>*f* hour qil
venoit a desuys. Le dit Willam coueyna oue ses coumpaignouns
dencountreir dedenz la nuyt en la park, a vn certain bussoun, qe
vindrent touz, mais ils faillerent de lour tristre, hors pris le dit Willam
de Mountagow, et Johan de Neuyl, oue .xxiiij. homs qi tyndrent bien
lour signal. Ils sez douterent qe lour compaignouns lour failleroint, et
ils ne oserent fair noys pur lez gaytes du chastel, si disoint qils
assaieroint le auenture meismes, pusqe la chos estoit sy auaunt alez,
com ceaux qi estoint apertz et empernauntz. Ils sen alerent et
trouerent le posterne ouert com le roi auoit comaunde. Ils entrerent le
chastel et mounterent lez degrees du deuzisme bayl saunz
encountreir de nuly, qar il estoit bien anuyte, et lez comunes de gentz
voidez le chastel a lour osteaux. La royne, le Mortimer et lour priuez
enherdaunz furent en counsail pur ordener encontre cest couyne, qe
lour estoit descouerez. Ils entrerent la sale, ou la royne estoit en la
chambre, en counsail. Le vsseir fist noys a lour entree; Hugh de
Turpintoun qi fust seneschal del ostel le roy, qestoit de couyne la
royne, launcea hors du counsail, et lez encountra en my la sale,

diately, because they had pardoned him the highest penalty, out of respect for his high blood line.[20] The king began to grow in body and mind, despising the rule of the queen his mother, and hating the Earl of March, for the queen did everything in accordance with him.[21] The king hatched a plot with the young men attending him to remove this government, and to destroy the earl; but they did not plan this affair so secretly that they were not found out. So at a council at Nottingham, the king and all of those in this conspiracy were interrogated about this plan, in full session of the council. When each was interrogated separately, they all denied that they knew anything, except for William Montague, who addressed them in person, saying that if anyone were to suggest that [he had been engaged in] anything improper, or in any other business than his duty, he would make a forceful response; and having defended himself with such words, no one replied to him except in general terms. The council having come to an end, [f. 213] William said to the king that it was better to eat the dog, than the dog [eat] them. He advised him to speak to the constable of the castle,[22] commanding him by his oath and allegiance to keep the plan secret, and that he should leave a postern-gate to the park open that same night; and that if he did not do this, then he would be hanged, in the very hour that [the king] got the upper hand. William arranged with his companions to meet during the night in the park, at a certain bush. All of them came, but they missed their rendevous, except for William de Montague, and John de Neville, with twenty-four men who got their signal properly. They were afraid that their companions had failed them, and they did not dare to make a noise because of the castle's watchmen; so they decided that they should attempt the adventure by themselves, as the bold and daring men that they were, since the affair had gone so far ahead. They set off and found the postern open as the king had ordered. They entered the castle and climbed the steps of the second bailey without meeting anyone, because it was well into the night, and the common people had left the castle for their homes.[23] The queen, Mortimer and their closest adherents were holding a council to plan against this conspiracy which had been revealed to them. [The conspirators] entered the hall where the queen was in her chamber, in council. The doorkeeper made an outcry at their entry; Hugh de Turpington, the steward of the king's household, who was of the queen's party, dashed out of the council, and met them just inside the hall. Saying, 'Traitors for nought!',[24] he was about to strike the first [of them] with a knife when John de Neville stabbed him to death,

disaunt, Treiturs pur nient, qi quidoit auoir ferru le primer dun cotele, qaunt Johan de Neuyl ly ferist parmy le corps mort, et vn esquier, qi fesoit debat; si passerent outre en la chaumbre et pristrent le Mortymer, et ceaux qils voroint auoir, qe deuaunt la iournaunt, nuls nestoint remys en la vile fors ceaux du couyn le roi, qi se auoit arme a lour entre hu chastel. Il fust ordener pur sa mere, et prist le Mortimer oue ly a Laycestre, ou il pensoit dauoir fait murrir; mes il prist autre counsail, qi fist somoundre vn parlement a Loundres, ou le Mortimer fust treynez et penduz, par cause del assent du mort le roy, le pier; et pur la mort de le Count de Kent; et pur la desherisoun du droit Descoce; et pur la destruccioun du tresor le roy, qe ly estoit remys de soun pier; et dez autres articles qe hom ly surmyst. Lez seignurs qi furent bannez, furount recounsaillez. De cel hour en auaunt graunt pece, fust ly roy counsaillez de Willam de Mountagow, qi touz iours ly mouoit a bien et honour, et damer lez armes, et si demenerent iolyfe ioen vie, en attendaunt greignour sesoun de greignour affair. Le [f. 213v.] Roy Philip de Fraunce chasoit de apres dauoir le attournement de le roy, pur la Duche de Gyene. Le counsail le roy regardaunt le nounage de ly, le temps et le noun poair de tresor, ly firent priuement passer la mere et faire soun homage a Amyas, de quoi ils porterent pius blame; et pur quoy lez Fraunces disoint, qe le atournement du roy conferma lestat soun seignour al hour qaunt a soy. Mais le nounage de ly donoit le escusement. I cesti roy demenast galiard vie dez ioustes et tournays, et a festoier lez dames, tanqe lez seignours qestoint desheritez pur ly et pur sez auncestres en Escoce, ly firent supplicacioun, qil lour voroit restorere lour heritage, qils auoint pur ly perduz, ou lez lesser couenyr. Le roy maunda tout cest supplicatioun au Count de Murref, adonqes gardeyn Descoce, pur le nounage le Roy Dauid, mort le pier le Roy Robert, qi mort estoit de lepre, vn poy deuaunt. Qy count au roy respoundy honourablement par sez lettres, requeraunt, qil lour lessoit couenyr, et le pellot aler.

... age Edward de ...[a]

45. Cest message entendu, lez seignours desheritez en Escoce, le Seignour de Beaumounde, lez Countis de Athelle et Dangus, Richard[b] Talbot, Henri de Fereirs, Johan de Moubray, et tout plain dez

[a]   *Left margin in small contemporary hand.*
[b]   *MS:* Richar.

through the middle of the body, and an esquire, who joined in the brawl. They went through to the chamber and seized Mortimer, and those they wanted to hold, so that before the dawning of the day, none were left in the town except for those of the king's party, who had armed themselves at [the conspirators'] entry to the castle. [The king] made arrangements for his mother, and took Mortimer with him to Leicester, where he had intended to have him put to death; but he took other counsel, and had a parliament summoned at London, where Mortimer was drawn and hanged, because of his consent for the death of the king, the father [*i.e.* Edward II]; and for the death of the Earl of Kent; and for the disinheritance of [the king's] Scottish rights; and for the dissipation of the king's treasure, which he had been left by his father; and for other articles of which he was accused. The lords who had been banished were recalled. At this time and for a long while after, the king was advised by William de Montague, who always encouraged him to virtue and honour, and to a love of arms, and they led a jolly young life, awaiting a greater season for greater affairs. [*f. 213v.*] King Philip of France was pursuing the king's attornment, for the Duchy of Guienne. Considering his minority, the season and the lack of money, the king's council had him secretly cross the sea and do his homage at Amiens, for which they later took the blame; and because of this, the French said that the king's attornment confirmed their lord's status over him at this time. However, his minority gave him an excuse. So this king led a merry life of jousts and tournaments, and feasting the ladies until the lords who had been disinherited in Scotland for the sake of him and his ancestors, petitioned him that he should be willing to recover their inheritance, which they had lost on his account, or leave them to try. The king sent the whole petition to the Earl of Moray, then guardian of Scotland, during the minority of King David (King Robert the father being dead, having died of leprosy a little before). The earl replied honourably to the king by letter, requesting that he leave them to try, and let the ball roll.[25]

45. Having understood this message, the lords [who had been] disinherited in Scotland, lord Beaumont, the earls of Atholl and Angus, Richard Talbot, Henry de Ferrers, John de Mowbray and many others, attached themselves to Edward de Balliol, through the plotting of Lord Beaumont. [Edward was the] son of John de Balliol, formerly King of Scotland by the election of the whole of the two

autres par enbracement le Sire de Beaumounde, sez enherderent a
Edward de Baillof fitz Johan de Baillof, iadiz Roy Descoce par^c
eleccioun de touz dieus lez realmes, qestoit tenuz hors de Escoce plus
de .xxx. aunz, qy eschipperent a Rauenshere, et arryuerent a
Kyncorn, poy dez gentz a regard, qe nestoint pas passe .iiij. cent homs
de armys. Le primer iour de lour aryuail, ils coumbaterent od le
Count de Fyf, et ly descoumfirent, ou fust^d tuez Alexander de Setoun
le fitz. Ils tindrent lour chemyn a Dunfermelyn, ou ils trouerent et
pristrent tauntz dez bastouns ferrez, nouelement faitez, qe le Count
Thomas de Murref auoit fet faire, qi procheignement estoit mort
dedenz lez .viij. iours de lour arryuail. Ils tindrent lour chemyn
deuers la uile de saint Johan, ou al eau de Erne ils trouerent vn graunt
ost des enemys deuaunt eaux, qar lez seignours Descoce estoint
assemblez a lour aryuail, pur lour choiser vn gardeyn, qy choiserent
le Count de Marre, qy auoit fait assembler cest graunt ost, et pris le
graunt tertre sure le gee del eau de Erne deuaunt cestez gentz aryuez,
qestoint en la valey dautre part leau, qi ne resemblerent qun petit
chos a regard dez autres. Cestez gentz del ost le Count de Marre
disoint, qe lez autres estoient regettez com vn leuer. Si getterent qe
lendemayn ils enuoyerent vn graunt poair enuiroun de eaux, pur lez
assailler *[f. 214]* de toutes coustes, qe touz iours lour encresoit lour
poair. Cestes seignours desheritez estoint si espountez du graunt
multitude dez enemys, qils comencerent a raunponer le seignour de
Beaumound en point de coursus, surmettaunt qil les auoit treye, et qil
lour auoit fet entendaunt qils aueroint graunt couyne en Escoce.
Certes seignours, fesoit il, noun y le, mes puisqe lez chosis sount si
auaunt alez, pur Dieux eidoms nous nous^e meismes, qe nuls ne sceit
qoi Dieux ad ordene pur nous, et pensoms de nostre graunt droit a
moustreir qe nous sumes extraitez dez bons cheualeris, et du graunt
honour et profite qe Dieu nous ad deistene et du graunt hount qe
nous auendroit si en cest graunt bosoigne nous ne moustroms
apertice. Issi qe par les bons motes de prodhom, et le espirement de
Dieu, ils sez acorderent, qen la nuyt ils passeroint le gee, et
enuyrouneroint lez enemys, et mounteroint le tertre desus eaux, et
prendroint lour auenture dedenz la nuyt. Ils passerent leau, ou Roger
de Swenarton fust noez. Lez enemys par le resoun de lour passage si
aualerent a pee, qi deuaunt qe ils purroint au gee ateindre, lez autres

^{c} MS: p.
^{d} MS: fut.
^{e} Sic.

realms, who had been kept out of Scotland for more than thirty years. They embarked at Ravenser and landed at Kinghorn [Fife], with few enough men, for they did not exceed 400 men-at-arms.[1] On the first day of their arrival, they fought with the Earl of Fife, and defeated him; and Alexander de Seton the son was killed.[2] They made their way to Dunfermline, where they found and seized many newly made iron-shod staffs, which Earl Thomas of Moray had had made (he was dead soon after, within eight days of their arrival).[3] They made their way towards the town of Perth, where at the river Earn, they found a great enemy army before them, for when they invaded, the lords of Scotland had been assembled to choose themselves a guardian. They chose the Earl of Mar,[4] who had had this great army assembled, and had seized the large hill above the ford of the river Earn before the [Disinherited] men had arrived; they were in the valley on the other side of the river, looking nothing if not paltry in comparison to the others. The men of the Earl of Mar's army were saying that the others would be thrown back like hares. They arranged that on the morrow they would send a large force to surround them, so as to attack them [f. 214] from all sides, as their strength was increasing all the time. The disinherited lords were so terrified by the great multitude of enemys, that they started to deride Lord Beaumont regarding the expedition, accusing him of betraying them, and of leading them to believe that they would have a lot of support in Scotland.[5] 'Indeed, my lords', said he, 'it is not so, but since things have gone so far, by God, we'd better look after ourselves, for no one can know what God has ordained for us. We should think of our great duty to prove that we are descended from good knights, and of the great honour and profit that God has destined for us, and the great shame which will befall us if we do not boldly prove ourselves in this great affair.'[6] Thus, due to the fine words of this worthy man, and the inspiration of God, they agreed that in the night, they would cross the ford, go around the enemy and climb the hill above them, and take their chance during the night. They crossed the river, where Roger de Swinnerton was drowned.[7] Because they were crossing, the enemy came running down on foot, but before they could reach the ford, the others had crossed; they went around the hill and fell suddenly on the enemy's grooms and horses, whom they defeated, believing them to be the main force of their enemy's army. They pursued them here and there, so that at daybreak, there were not forty of them gathered together. But, by the light of the flames from a house that had been set on fire, they drew together like partridges; and as the day began to get light,

furount passez, qi enuirounerent le tertre et cheierent sodeignement
sure lez garsouns et cheueaux de lour enemys, qi les descomfirent,
pensaunt qils vssent este le poar del ost lours enemys, et lez
enchacerent sa et la, qen la iournaunt, ne estoint ensemble .xl. de
eaux, mais par clarete dun fu dun mesoun qe prist a ardoir, ils
relierent com perdricis, et com le iour comensoit a esclareir, ils
aparsceurent lez enemys en dieus grauntz batails, qi venoint a pee
pres de eaux, qi tout la nuyt auoint este ensemble, qe a pain sez
purroint boter en aray, qaunt lez enemys vindrent assembleir. Lour
auaunt sen aresty vn poy, au scentir dez pointz dez launces et setis
qaunt lour areirgard assembla si desarayment, qen en lour hastif *f*
assembleir, ils porterent a terre tout playn de lour auauntgard, entre
eaux et lez enemys, qi venoient si asprement sur eux, qe lez autres sez
recoillerent chescun sure autre, qe en vn petite hour, vous veissez
crestre vn mount dez corps dez homs com cestes gentz aryues lez
enuyrounoint, si furent en cest maner par miracle de Dieux
descoumfitz, et mortz le Count de Marre, Alexander Frisel, Robert de
Bruys fitz bastard le Roy Robert, et touz plain dez barouns, cheualers
et esquiers, qe toucz plains estoient estuffez de alayn com chescun
iesoit soutz autre, et mortz a la maner deuisa saunz coup darme nul.
Cest iourne acoumply, ils tindrent lour chemyn [*f. 214v.*] a la vile de
saint Johan, ou ils trouerent bien estoffez de touz estoffers, si
enfermerent la vile en reparaillaunt lez veutz fossez, qe chescun
reparailla sa gard de bretage. Dedenz lez .viij. iours de la batail,
vindrent deuaunt eaux vn tiel multitude dez gentz de touz lez pays
Descoce, qe a meruail. Ils iurent deuaunt eaux .viij. iours, qi pur
defaut de vitail, ils delogerent chescun en soun pays. Cest assege
leue, les seignours arriuez firent coroner Edward de Baillof pur Roy a
Scone, et departerent de la vile de seint Johan parmy Coil et
Conyngham, deuers Galeway, ou ceaux pardesa leau de Cree,
leuerent oue eaux. De illoeqes ils pristrent lour chemyn par
Craufordmore deuers Roxborugh, ou pres de Jeddeworde, Archebald
de Douglas estoit enbussez, qestoit descouert, et descoumfit, et
Robert de Lowedre le fitz, pris, et autres. Le Roy Edward de Baillof
fust herbise a Kelsow et soun ost en Roxburh qe meisme le iour pur
dout de cretyn de eau, remua soun herbigage en Roxburgh. Andreu
de Murref, adonqes gardein Descoce depar le Roy Dauid de Bruys,
auoit espie lerbigage du dit Roy Edward de Baillof a Kelsow, et

---

f   MS: hostif. *The 'o' is marked in a 15thc. hand, and an 'a' added in the central margin.*

they noticed the enemy in two great battles, coming up to them on foot, who had been together for all of the night. They were scarcely able to form themselves in array, when the enemy came up to attack. [The Scottish] vanguard was brought to a halt momentarily, at the feel of the spear-points and arrows, when their rearguard attacked in such dissarry that in their haste to attack, they knocked to the ground the whole of their vanguard, between them and their enemies [*i.e.* the English], who came up against them so forcefully that they fell back one over another.[8] In a short time, you would have seen a mound of men's bodies piling up as the invaders surrounded them. So in this manner, by a miracle of God, they were defeated, and the Earl of Mar, Alexander Fraser, and Robert de Bruce the bastard son of King Robert were killed, and very many barons, knights and esquires, of whom nearly all were suffocated as each lay under another, and died in the manner described without any weapon's blow.[9] The battle done, they made their way [*f. 214v.*] to the town of Perth, which they found well stocked with all kinds of goods. They fortified the town and repaired the old ditches, each man repairing his section of the palisade.[a] Within eight days of the battle, such a multitude of men from all the regions of Scotland came before them, that it was a marvel. They stayed before them for eight days; then, for want of supplies, they decamped, each to his own country. With the siege raised, the invading lords had Edward de Balliol crowned as king at Scone,[10] and left the town of Perth, [heading] through Kyle and Cunningham, towards Galloway, where the men across the river Cree rose in their support. From there they made their way by Crawfordmuir towards Roxburgh, where near Jedburgh, Archibald de Douglas was lying in ambush. He was discovered and defeated, and Robert de Lauder the son was taken, and others. King Edward de Balliol was lodged at Kelso and his army in Roxburgh; that same day, he moved his lodging to Roxburgh, for fear of a flood on the river. Andrew de Moray, then guardian of Scotland for King David de Bruce, had spied out King Edward de Balliol's lodging at Kelso, and noticed the rising of the river Tweed. He was nearby with a great force, and without warning, he made for the end of the bridge at Roxburgh and had began to break the bridge up, hoping to take King Edward by surprise, when the alarm was raised amongst the army in the town, and all [stood] to arms, on horse and on foot. They seized the bridge

---

[a]   *Lit.*: 'his watch of the palisade'.

aparceust le crestre del eau de Twede; sy estoit pres oue graunt poair, si se mist sodeignement au boute du pount de Roxburh et comensa a roumper le dit pount, en pensaunt dauoir suppris le dit Roy Edward, qaunt huyn comensa en la dit vile en lost, et touz a armys a cheual et a pee, si pristrent le pount sure lez enemys, et cheueaux noyerent outre leaw, et descomfiterent cestez genz, ou fust pris le cheuetain, Andreu de Murref. Prochienement apres, auoit le Roy Dengleter soun parlement a Euerwik, ou lez plus grauntz del ost Edward de Baillof sez alerent. A quel parlement, messagers del acorde Dauid de Bruys vindrent, fesaunt supplicacioun au Roy, qil eydast lour seignour, com alye dust faire, depuisqe il auoit sa sore a femme saunz tretice de autre condicioun. Fust auys a counsail le Roy, qil nestoit pas tenuz a ceo faire encountre sez gentz propres, qestoient desheritez par caus de ly, et de lez auncestres, qi graciousement auoint comensez a reconquer lour heritage. En cest mene temps du parlement auaunt dit, le Roy Edward de Baillof Descoce se delogea de Roxburgh, et se trey deuers le West Marche a Anand, ou en vn aube de iour, Archebald de Douglas oue vn poair dez [enemys][g] trenuyta sure ly et ly descoumfist, qe a graunt payn eschapa meismes a Cardoil, et graunt plente de sez gentz mortz, et toucz les soens [f. 215] enchacez hors Descoce, a recomencer de nouel tout lour conquest. Al hour comencea Edward de Baillof a treter oue le Roi Dengleter, a quel Roy estoit auys et a soun counsail, qe il estoit fraunk a faire soun profite depuisqe en la pese fesaunt a Robert de Bruys, estoit hors pris et especifie qe la aliaunce de Fraunce se tendroit od lez Escocez, et qe le Roy Dengleter ne fust loyez as eaux de nul enherdaunce, de pusqe par counsail le count Thomas de Murref, lez Escocez ne voloint lesser la alyaunce de Fraunce, enemys apparauntz a le Roy Dengleter, ne autre condicioun especifie, fors qe le Roy Dengleter quitclameroit le droit qe il auoit en Escoce, qe estoit eschue au coroune Dengleter en le temps soun ayel, par forfaiture Johan de Baillof, adonqes Roy Descoce, qi disclamoit a tenir de ly, depuisqe il meismes ly auoit atourne par soun homage de le haut seignourie Descoce, et par condicioun taille a soun clisement deueint soun hom, quant debat estoit du dit Realme, entre le dit Johan de Baillof, et Robert de Bruys, le ayel cesti Robert, qi se clama Roy Descoce, et Johan de Hastings, le quel Johan de Baillof rendy soun homage par dieus Jacobyns oue vn

---

[g] MS: Engles, *all but the first two letters are partially erased.* enimys *has been added in the right margin in the 15thc. hand;* escoces *in the central margin, in a late 16thc. hand.*

from the enemy, and the horsemen swam across the river and defeated these men, and the leader, Andrew de Moray, was captured.[11] Soon after, the King of England held his parliament at York, to which the greatest magnates of Edward de Balliol's army came.[12] Messengers of David de Bruce's allegiance came to this parliament imploring the king that he should aid their lord, as an ally ought to do, since [David] had married his sister without the agreement of any conditions. It was advised by the king's council that he was not bound to act against his own men, who had been disinherited for the sake of him and his ancestors, and who had freely started to reconquer their inheritance. In the meantime, during this parliament, King Edward de Balliol of Scotland had left Roxburgh and was going towards the West March at Annan, where one day at dawn, Archibald de Douglas marched against him with a force of enemies and defeated him. He himself escaped with great difficulty to Carlisle, a great many of his men were killed and all his followers [f. 215] were chased out of Scotland, to begin all of their conquest again from the start. At this time, Edward de Balliol began to negotiate with the King of England, who, along with his council, was advised that he was free to follow his own interests, since in the peace made with Robert de Bruce, it had been specifically excepted that the French alliance with the Scots could be maintained, and that the King of England was not bound to them by any commitment; and since, by the advice of Earl Thomas de Moray, the Scots were not willing to abandon the alliance with France, an open enemy of the King of England. Nor was there any other specific condition, save that the King of England should quitclaim his rights in Scotland, which had escheated to the English crown in his [i.e. Edward III's] grandfather's time, by the forfeiture of John de Balliol, then King of Scotland, who had denied that he held of him [i.e. Edward I], even though he himself had submitted to him for the overlordship of Scotland by his homage, and had became his man by formal agreement at his inauguration,[b] when there was a debate over that realm between the said John de Balliol and Robert de Bruce, the grandfather of that Robert who claimed to be King of Scotland, and John de Hastings;[13] this John de Balliol had renounced his homage by two Dominican friars with a burnished sword, disclaiming that he held anything of him.[14]

---

[b] 'Clisement' *is not a common Anglo-Norman word; its meaning has been guessed from the context.*

espey fourby, en desclaymaunt a rien tenir de ly; pur quoy fust auys au dit roi qe par nouel mocioun, nouel guer. I cesti Edward de Baillof dona au Roy Dengleter, la vile de Berewik oue .v. Countees, lez viscountes de Berewic, de Roxburgh, Dedinburghe, Peblis et Dunfres, et qe il ly ferroit homage pur le remenaunt Descoce, et qe le Roy ly suppuelleroit, maintendroit, et ly remetteroit en soun estat.

Lassege de Berew...[a]

46. Le Roy desirant lez armys et honours, et soun counsail enparnauntz, et coueitaunz lez gueres, qy tost sez acorderent a cest condicioun, et le plus tost pur desire a reconquer lour pris sure eaux, par queux ils le auoint perduz. Dez plus priues du counsail le roy mouerent oue Edward de Baillof, qi en le secound semayn de qarresme assistrent la vile de Berewyk par mere et terre; et procheynement deuaunt la Pentecost, le Roy Dengleter y veint meismes, et assaillerent la vile, mais ne la pristrent point, mais reaparaillerent meutz lour horduz pur reassailler la dit vile. En le mene temps, ceaux dedenz la vile parlerent de condiciouns, qe sils ne vssent rescous deuaunt vn certain iour, qe ils renderoint la vile, et sur ceo bailerent[b] hostages; deuaunt quel temps limitez, tout le poair Descoce, vn si graunt multitude dez gentz qe a meruail, passerent leaw de Twede en vn aube de iour a le Yarforde, et sez moustrerent deuaunt Berewik del autre [coste del][c] Twede deuers Engleter, au plain vieu du roy, et de soun [f. 215v.] ost, et bouterent gentz et vitaillis dedenz la vile, et demurrerent la, tout le iour et la nuyt. Et lendemain a haut hour, delogerent et mouerent parmy la terre le Roy en Northumbreland, ardauntz et destruyauntz le pays au plain vieu del ost as Engles. Cestes gentz departys a la maner, le counsail le roy al assege demaunderent la vile solonc lez condiciouns, le terme passe de lour rescous. Ceaux dedenz disoint qils estoint rescous, et dez gentz et des vitails, si moustrerent nouelis gardeins de la vile et cheualers eynz butes de lour ost, dount Willam de Keth estoit vn, od autres. Fust auys au dit counsail, qe ils auoint perduz lour ostages, si firent pendre le fitz Alexander de Setoun, gardeyn de la vile. Cest ostage mort a la maner, lez autres dedenz la vile le, pur tendresce de lour enfauntz qestoient ostages, renouelerent condicioun par assent

---

[a]   *In right margin, in small contemporary hand.*
[b]   MS: ballerent.
[c]   *Supplied.*

Because of this, the king was advised that from a new cause, a new war. Edward de Balliol granted the town of Berwick to the King of England, with five counties (the sheriffdoms of Berwick, Roxburgh, Edinburgh, Peebles and Dumfries), and did him homage for the remainder of Scotland; and for this, the king was to support him, maintain him and restore him to his estate.

The Siege of Berw[ick]
46. The king desired arms and honours, and his council was bold, and longed for war, and so they readily agreed to this condition, and the more readily for the desire to regain their esteem from those by whom they had lost it. Some of the more intimate of the king's council went with Edward de Balliol, who in the second week of Lent besieged the town of Berwick by sea and by land; and just before Pentecost [23 May], the King of England came there himself, and they attacked the town, but did not take it; but they prepared their hoard-ings better, so as to attack the town again. In the meantime, those within the town treated for terms, that if they had not been relieved before a certain day, they would surrender the town, and gave hostages for this. Before this time limit, all the forces of Scotland, such a great multitude of men that it was a marvel, crossed the river Tweed one day at dawn at the Yair ford, and mustered before Berwick on the other [bank of the] Tweed towards England, in full view of the king and his *[f. 215v.]* army. They put men and supplies into the town, and remained there all day and night. And on the following day when the sun was high, they upped camp and advanced through the king's land in Northumberland, burning and destroying the country in full view of the English army. These men having departed in this manner, the king's council at the siege demanded the town according to the terms, as the time limit for its relief had passed. Those within said that they had been relieved, with men and supplies; they presented new keepers of the town and knights newly sent from their army, of whom William de Keith was one, among others. It was the council's opinion that they had forfeited their hostages, so they had the son of Alexander de Seton, keeper of the town, hanged.[1] With this hostage dead in this manner, the others within the town, out of concern for their children who were hostages, renewed the terms with the consent of the newly-sent knights, who were of the opinion that their Scottish force surpassed the army of the King of England. They accepted these new terms, that within fifteen days, they would put 200 men-at-arms into the town by force, by dry land between the

dez cheualers einz boutes, as queux estoit auys qe lour poair Descoce surmountoit le ost le Roy Dengleter; si pristrent tiel nouel condicion qe deuaunt lez .xv. iours, ils butroient .ij. centz homs darmis par force par sek tere dedenz la vile entre lost dez Engles et la haut mere, ou qe ils sez combaterount au playn. Willam de Keth, Willam de Prendregest, et Alexander Gray cheualers, qestoient einz boutez dedenz la vile, auoient conduyt a passer parmy lost deuers lour gentz Descoce, od cest condicioun, qe furent amenez par conduyt parmy Northumbre, qi lour ost Descoce trouerent a Wittoun Undrewod, et lez reamenerent a Berewik a parfourner lour rescous, ou ils vindrent combatre et ou ils furent descoumfitz. Archebald de Douglas al hour gardein Descoce depar le Roy Dauid de Brus fust la mort. Lez Countis de Ross, de Murref, de Meneteth, de Leuenaux, et de Sothirland furent la mortz. Le seignour de Douglas fitz James de Douglas (qi morust en le frounter de Gernate sure lez Sarazins, qauoit enpris cest saint veage od le quere Robert de Bruys lour roys, qe le auoit deuise en soun moriaund) et touz plain dez barouns, dez cheualers et dez comunes, furent illoeqes vn tresgraunt noumbre mortz. La vile se rendy sur condiciouns taille. Le count de la Marche, qauoit le chastel de Berewik a garder, deueint Engles, qi nauoit my graunt gree de nul coste, qi en le mene temps fist affermer par suffraunce le Roy, soun chastelle de Dunbar, qe puis fist graunt mal. Cest batail finy, le Roi Dengleter se trey deuers le Sew, ou il hauntoist curiousement lez faites darmes de pese. Edward de Baillof Roy de Escoce se trey a la vile de seint Johan, ou il auoit soun parlement a Scone, et le atournement de plousours Descoce. Tretout Escoce estoit en soutzieccion [f. 216] du Roy Dengleter et de luy, hors pris le chastel de Dunbretain, de ou le Roy Dauid de Bruys, qestoit enfes adonqes, fust remue en Fraunce au Chastel Galiard, ou il demura grant pece et sa femme la sore le roi tanqe il fust parcruz qil se pooit ariuer. Le secound ane apres la batail de Berewyk, Edward de Baillof reueint a Noefchastel sure Tyne et fist soun homage au Roy Dengleter pur la terre Descoce solonc lez condiciouns auaunt parlez, et puis se retrey areir en Escoce, pur ceo qe lez vns de la tere estoint releuez encountre luy oue le Count de Murref, vn enfaunt parcru. Le dit Edward estoit a Streuelyn oue soun poair, ou comensa vn poi de corouce par enuye entre ascuns de soun counsail, qi sodeignement sez departerent de ly, a lours rescettis, pur quoi le dit Edward se retrey en Engleter. Henry de Beaumound adonqes Count de Boghan, depar le heritage sa femme, se trei a Dungarg, vn chastel qil auoit de nouel enferme en Boghane. Le Count de Athelis se retrey en soun pays, lez autres a lour

English army and the high tide [line], or that they would fight them in the open.[2] William de Keith, William de Prendergast and Alexander Gray, knights, who were newly-sent into the town, had safe-conduct to pass through the army towards the Scotsmen with these terms. They were taken through Northumbria under safe-conduct, found the Scottish army at Witton Underwood, and led them back to Berwick to accomplish their relief; here they came to battle and here they were defeated. Archibald de Douglas, at that time guardian of Scotland for King David de Bruce, was killed there. The earls of Ross, Moray, Menteith, Lennox and Sutherland were killed there. The Lord of Douglas, son of James de Douglas (who died on the frontier of Grenada against the Saracens, having undertaken this pilgrimage with the heart of Robert de Bruce their king, who had had this arranged as he was dying), and nearly all the barons, knights and commoners died there, in very great numbers.[3] The town surrendered under the agreed terms. The Earl of March, who had custody of Berwick castle, became English, having no great respect for either side; in the mean time he had his castle of Dunbar strengthened, with the king's permission, from which great trouble subsequently arose.[4] With the battle over, the King of England took himself to the South, where he diligently practiced the feats of arms of peace.[5] Edward de Balliol, King of Scots, went to the town of Perth, where he held his parliament at Scone, and received the attornment of many Scots. All of Scotland was subjected [f. 216] to the King of England and him, except for the castle of Dumbarton; from there, King David Bruce (who was then still a child) was taken away to France to Chateau Gaillard, where he remained for a long time with his wife, the sister of the king [i.e. Edward III], until he was full-grown and able to return.[6] The second year after the battle of Berwick, Edward de Balliol returned to Newcastle upon Tyne and made his homage to the King of England for the land of Scotland according to the conditions agreed before;[7] afterwards, he withdrew back to Scotland because certain men of that land had risen against him with the Earl of Moray, a grown-up minor.[8] Edward was at Stirling with his forces, where a petty squabble broke out from envy between some of his council, who abruptly left him for their homes; because of this, Edward withdrew to England. Henry de Beaumont, then Earl of Buchan by his wife's inheritance, took himself to Dundarg, a castle which he had fortified from new in Buchan. The Earl of Atholl took himself back to his own country, the others to their homes.[9] Richard Talbot was beyond the mountains, on the lands inherited by his wife, the

rescettes. Richard Tallebot estoit pardela lez mountes, en lez terres del heritage sa femme, la feile Johan de Comyn, qauoit lez nouelis de cest departisoun, se trey deuers Engleter, ou en Lownes, il fust pris, et Johan de Striuelin, dez gentz qestoint a la foy Edward de Baillof qi fauserent lour foy, pur couaitise du pris de eaux; Henry de Beaumound fust assege en Dungarg, ou il rendy le chastel sure condicioun a departire hors du pays. Le Count de Athelis se atourna a la foy Dauid de Bruys, et guerpy la foy Edward de Baillof, qe de force ly couenoit ceo faite, ou murreir, et touz playn dez cheualers Engles en sa compaigny, qi en autre maner ne lez pooint sauuer. A cel hour nestoit remys dedenz Escoce, nul de les enherdauntz le Roy Dengleter qi fussent acounteir, fors le Count de la Marche, qi veint au maundement le Roy Dengleter a ly a Noefchastel sur Tyne, qi en soun realer a lostelle, estoit gayte dez maufesours de Northumbre, pur coueitys de argent, qe le Roy ly auoit done a soun departire, et en point dauoir este mourdry. Il fist moustreir soun compleint au Roy Dengleter, qi ia estoit venuz a Roxburgh, ou il fist enfermer le chastel en yuer, qestoit emblez et abatuz en le temps soun pier. Le counsail adonqes entour le Roy, ne ly voroint fair auoir tiels amendez de les ditz meffesours, com resoun voroit demaunder, com ly fust auys, en ensaumple de tieux mesprisiouns. Si rendy sus soun homage a le Roy par lettre, com il veint pres de Dunbarre, dun cheuauche qil auoit de Roxburgh [f. 216v.] fait en Lownes, entres mauueys temps de yuer, fesaunt en lez ditz lettres suggestioun, qe plus ne se pooit assureir. Meisme le temps fust Edward de Bowne, cosyn le roy, noez en leaw de Anand, com il vousist auoir rescouz vn vadlete du cretyn del eau, qe ly enbrassa par lez espaulis, qi ly trey hors de la sele desoutz ly; le cheualer pery, le vadlet fu sauue. Le dit chastel de Roxburgh afferme, le dit Roy de Engleter se trey deuers Loundres qi se dressa countre le prochein este; si repaira en Escoce oue tresgraunt poair. Il enuoya od Edward de Baillof, lez Countis de Garayn, Daroundelle, de Oxsinford et de Angous, lez Sires de Percy, de Neuil, de Berkelay et de Latimer, od vn graunt ost, qentrerent par Berwic; ly meismes entre par Cardoille oue tout la sureplus de sa cheualery, qi auoit od luy le Count Gelleris, qi pius fust Markys, et apres Duk, oue graunt coumpaigny dez Allemauns. Lez .ij. ostes vindrent pres ensemble sure leau de Clide, le Roi Dengleter en vn lieu, Edward de Baillof oue soun ost a Glascow, ou il auoit vn graunt chaud melle en lost pur vn esquyer qi portoit le surenoun[d] de Gournay, qi lez Marchies tuerent

---

[d]   MS: *suronoun*.

daughter of John Comyn; having had news of this division, he took himself towards England, but he was captured in Lothian, along with John de Stirling, by men who were in Edward de Balliol's allegiance, who broke their faith from greed for their [ransom-] price.[10] Henry de Beaumont was besieged in Dundarg; he surrendered the castle on condition that he depart from the country.[11] The Earl of Atholl submitted himself to the allegiance of David Bruce, and abandoned the allegiance of Edward Balliol; he agreed to do this under duress, else he would have been killed, as well as the many English knights in his company, who were unable to save themselves in any other manner. By this time there were no adherents of the King of England back in Scotland who were of any account, except for the Earl of March, who, at the king's command, came to him at Newcastle on Tyne. On his way back to his lodging, he was waylaid by Northumbrian criminals, out of greed for the silver which the king had given at his departure, and was almost murdered.[12] He had his complaint explained to the King of England, who had gone to Roxburgh by then; here, during the winter, [the king] had the castle fortified, which had been seized and razed in his father's time. The council, [which was] in attendence on the king at the time, was unwilling to make him such amends for these criminals as reason might, in his opinion, demand as a deterrent for such crimes. He renounced his homage to the king by letter, when [the king] came near Dunbar on a chevauchee which he led from Roxburgh [f. 216v.] into Lothian, at the worst time of winter; and in these letters, he suggested that he could no longer feel secure.[13] At the same time, Edward de Bohun, a cousin of the king, was drowned in the river Anann, when he attempted to rescue a valet from flood water; [the valet] grabbed him by the shoulders, and dragged him from the saddle beneath him; the knight perished, the valet was saved.[14] Having strengthened Roxburgh castle, the King of England took himself towards London and made himself ready for the coming summer; and he returned to Scotland with a great force. He sent with Edward Balliol, the earls of Warenne, Arundel, Oxford and Angus,[15] and lords Percy, Neville, Berkeley and Latimer, with a large army, which entered [Scotland] by Berwick. He himself entered by Carlisle with all the rest of his knights; he had with him the Count of Juliers, who was subsequently Margrave, and Duke after that, with a great company of Germans. The two armies came nearly together on the river Clyde, the King of England at one place, [and] Edward de Balliol with his army at Glasgow, where there was a great,

par caus qe suremist fust qe vn qi portoit cel surnon fust assentaunt a
la mort le roy le pier. Lez .ij. ostes encountrerent a la vile de saint
Johan, ou en lour chemynaund laundroitz, estoit gaynez par assaut le
chastel de Combrenald. A la dit vile de seint Johan reuindrent a la
pese le roy, le Count de Athelis, Godfrai de Rosse, et Alexander de
Moubray oue autres, et si fust comence illoeqes tretice du Seneschal
Descoce. A meisme le hour tancom le roy ieust a la vile de saint Johan,
veint le Count de Nemure a Berewik et autres cheualeris Dengleter, qi
nestoint pas prestis al entre le roy; si enpristrent folement a pursuir le^e
roy, dauoir ale a ly par tere a la vile de saint Johan, ou a Edinburgh ils
furent suppris du Count de Murref, qe de force lour couenoit prendre
la Roche du chastel abatuz, ou ils ses defenderent vn nuyt, et
lendemain, tanqe ils hurent condicioun, qi le dit Count de Nemure
periureroit destre arme del hour en auaunt encountre la querel Dauid
de Brus, et qe lez Engles illoeqes fussent touz prisoners pur vn some
de argent. Le dit Count de Nemure reueint a Berewyk, de ou il veint
par mere en la coumpaignye la Royne Dengleter au roy, a la vile de
seint Johan. Meisme le hour fust pris le Count de Murref a vn punyes
sure Marchis de Willam de Presfen.

Meisme la seysoun, fust murdri le Count de Hulster de sez gentz
propres^f en Ireland; le quel Count fust fitz et heire a vn dez feilles de
Gloucestre, et pres cosyn le Roi [f. 217] Dengleter, feille et heyre a qi,
Lionel fitz au roy, cesti Edward le tierce apres la Conquest, auoit
espose puscedy. Le Roi Dengleter se delogea de la vile de saint Johan,
et se trey a Edynburgh, ou il fist enfermer le chastel, ou veint a la pese
Robert le Seneschal Descoce qi fust fitz la feile Robert de Bruys, et
apoy touz lez comunes. Le roy y fist mettre hu chastel graunt
garnisoun, et repaira en Engleter. Le yuer apres, fust tue le Count de
Athelis, qi estoit remys depar le roy, gardein de pardela la mere
Descocz qi se combaty oue Andreu de Murref, et oue le Count de la
Marche, et oue Willam de Douglas et oue gentz reliez du couin Dauid
de Bruys, et fust auxi tuez Thomas Rosselyn a vn autre punyez
meisme la sesoun com il arryua hors de mere pres de Dunotre, mais
lez soens auoint la victoir. Le prochein este apres, le Roy Dengleter, qy
auoit enuoye a la vile seint Johan en eide de Edward de Baillof dez
plus grauntz de soun Realme, soun frer, Johan Count de Cornewail,

---

^e   MS: le *repeated erroneously.*
^f   MS: ppres.

hard-fought mêlée within the army, over a squire who bore the surname of Gurney; the Marchers killed him because it was claimed that one who bore that surname had been an accessory to the death of the king's father.[16] The two armies met at the town of Perth, and on their way there, the castle of Cumbernauld was taken by assault. At the town of Perth, the Earl of Atholl, Godfrey de Ross and Alexander de Mowbray, amongst others, came back to the king's peace, and negotiations with the Steward of Scotland were started there. At the same time, while the king was at the town of Perth, the Count of Namur came to Berwick along with other English knights, who had not been ready at the king's arrival; foolishly, they endeavoured to catch up with the king, going to him by land, to the town of Perth. At Edinburgh, they were surprised by the Earl of Moray, so they were forced to take to the Rock, in the demolished castle; here they defended themselves for one night, and the day following, until they obtained terms, that the Count of Namur should forswear to take up arms against the cause of David Bruce from that time on, and that the English there should all become prisoners for a sum of money. The Count of Namur returned to Berwick, from where he came to the king at Perth by sea, in the company of the Queen of England.[17] At the same time, the Earl of Moray was taken in a skirmish on the Marches, by William de Presfen.[18]

In the same season, the Earl of Ulster was murdered by his own men, in Ireland.[19] The earl was the son and heir of one of the daughters of [the Earl of] Gloucester, and a close cousin of the King of England; [f. 217] his daughter and heiress was subsequently married to Lionel, the son of the king (that is, Edward the third after the Conquest).[20] The King of England decamped from the town of Perth and took himself to Edinburgh, where he had the castle strengthened; here, Robert, the Steward of Scotland, who was the son of Robert Bruce's daughter, came to his peace, and almost all the commoners. The king had a large garrison put into the castle, and retired to England. The winter following, the Earl of Atholl was killed; he had been appointed keeper beyond the Scottish sea [i.e. the Forth] on behalf of the king, and had fought with Andrew de Moray, and with the Earl of March, and with William Douglas and with rebellious men of David Bruce's party.[21] Also killed was Thomas Roscelyn, at another skirmish in the same season when he landed from the sea near to Dunnottar; however, his men had the victory.[22] The following summer, the King of England – who had sent the greatest magnates of his realm to the town of Perth in support of Edward de Balliol,

qy morust illoeqes de bele mort, auoit oy dire, qe lez Escocez estoint assemblez pur combatre oue sez gentz, ioust la vile de saint Johan, si veint sodeinement sure la Marche Descoz oue geris plus de .l. homs de armys, qi prist lez Marchies qestoint remys a lostel pur garder le pays, et sy enprist testousement a aler a la vile de saint Johan, qy nauoit oue ly outre .v.^{xx} homs darmys; si veint si sodeinement a la dit vile, qe touz sez meruaillerent de sa venu, et qi ly osast counsailler a ceo faire a la maner. De illoeqes il cheuauchea outre les mountes, ou il rescouy la Countais de Athelis, qestoit assege en Loghindorm, ou il y auoit en soun ost pur vn temps graunt defaut de vitail, mais tost furent coumfortez par foraier de Robert de Ogle et autres Marchis; si repaira a Striuelin, ou il fist enfermer le chastel. Et de illoeqes se trey a Botheuille, ou en yuer il fist enfermer le chastel autresy, et y fist mettre bon garnysoun. Le seignour de Berclay condusoiet lez vitaileris de Edynburgh a Botheuille, ou vn nuyt il descomfist Willam de Douglas, qy gisoit en agait de ly. Le roi perdy procheignement touz les chastelis et viles qil auoit fet enfermer en Escoce, par defaut de bon reaule du pursuyt de sa conquest. Le dit roy repaira a Loundres a soun parlement, ou soun fitz eyne, Count de Cestre, fust fait Duk de Cornewail, Henry de Langcastre fust fait Count de Derby, Willam de Bowne de Northamtoun, Willam de Mountagow de Salisbirs, Hugh de Audeley de Gloucestre, Robert de Vfforthe de Southfolk, Willam de Clyntoun de Huntyngdoun. As queux countis et autres ses bons gentz, le roy departy sy [f. 217v.] largement de sez possessiouns, qe a pain reteint il rien deuers ly de terres apurtenaunz a sa coroune, mais ly couenoit viure de sureuenous et subsides a graunt charge de poeple. Il auoit bon pece le disme de Saint Eglis, la quindezisme dener dez layes, et de chescun sak de layn .xlvij.s. .viij.d. Cest subside ly fust graunte du comune pur vn temps, mais plus dura qe le temps limyte. Il auoit .ij. auns la neofisme garbe de soun realme. A meisme cest parlement estoit auys au counsaille le roy, par auysement du clergie, qe plus longment ne serroit a sureser de soun droit, ne du clayme du coroune de Fraunce; si enfust enpris la guere au plain, et susrendu le homage au Roy de Fraunce Phelip de Valoys, qi deteint le droit le roy, et defialis auxi enuoyez. Messagers enfurent tramys en Allemain depar le Roy Dengleter, pur faire alyaunce del Emperour le Bayuer, qauoit lautre sore espose du Count de Henau, et retenu dez seignours illoeqes, qe costa tresgraundisme tresor saunz profite; et furent messageris Henry de Borewase, Euesqe de Nichol, lez Countis de Salisbirs et de Huntyngdoun, qi reuindrent au parlement de Loundres od respounz de lour message.

[with] his brother John, Earl of Cornwall (who died a fine death there[23]) – having heard it said that the Scots had assembled to fight with his men, near Perth, came unexpectedly to the Scottish March with barely more than fifty men-at-arms;[24] he took the Marchers who had been sent back home to guard the country, and set out in head-strong fashion to go to the town of Perth, having with him no more than five score men-at-arms. He came to the town so suddenly, that all were amazed at his arrival, and that he should have dared to consider doing it in this manner. From there, he rode over the mountains, where he rescued the Countess of Atholl,[25] who was besieged in Lochindorb. Here, there was a serious shortage of supplies in his army for a time, but they were soon relieved by the raiding of Robert de Ogle and other Marchers; and so he went back to Stirling, where he had the castle strengthened.[26] And from there he took himself to Bothwell where, during the winter, he had that castle strengthened as well, and had a strong garrison stationed there.[27] Lord Berkeley guided the victuallers from Edinburgh to Bothwell, where one night he defeated William de Douglas, who had been lying in ambush for him. The king soon lost all the castles and towns in Scotland which he had had strengthened, through a lack of good goverment in his pursuit of conquest. The king went back to London to his parliament, where his eldest son, the Earl of Chester, was made Duke of Cornwall, Henry of Lancaster was made Earl of Derby, William de Bohun [Earl] of Northampton, William de Montague [Earl] of Salisbury, Hugh de Audley [Earl] of Gloucester, Robert de Ufford [Earl] of Suffolk and William de Clinton [Earl] of Huntingdon. So generously did the king distribute his estates [f. 217v.] to these earls and to his other favourites, that he scarcely retained for himself any of the lands pertaining to his crown, and was obliged to live off windfalls and subsidies at great cost to people.[28] He had a good part of the Holy Church's tithe, the fifteenth penny from the laity, and 47s 8d from each sack of wool. He was granted this subsidy by the commons for a certain time, but it continued beyond the time limit; and he had the ninth sheaf from his realm for two years.[29] At this same parliament, it was decided by the king's council, on the advice of the clergy, that he should no longer neglect his rights, nor [his] claim to the crown of France; and so they decided on open war, renounced the homage to the King of France, Philip de Valois, who had witheld the king's rights, and sent their defiance as well. Envoys from the King of England were sent to Germany, to make an alliance with the Emperor, the Bavarian, who had married the other daughter of the Count of

Tost apres en cel hour, Andrew de Murref gardein Descoce depar
le Roy Dauid, qy tost se lessa morir apres, fist graunt destruccioun en
la counte de Cardoille, qe sen ala de illoeqes, et assist le chastel de
Edinburgh, adonqes en mayn dez Engles. Lez Marchies sez
adresserent al rescous; oy de lour venu, lez Escocez sez delogerent et
lour vindrent a lencountre a Clerkintoun, et lez Engles a Krethtoun,
ou entre eaux a Krethtounden, y auoit vn graunt punyes; gentz mortz
dampartz mais plus perderent lez Engles. Les Escocez sez delogerent
de illoeqes, fesaunt countenaunce de treier en Engleter, et sez
herbiserent a Galuschelle; lez Engles sez logerent deuaunt eaux outre
leaw de Twede, ou ils demurrerent .ij. iours, et la tierce nuyt, lez
Escocez sez delogerent et sen alerent lour chemyne.

Procheinement apres, le Count de Salisbirs, qestoit vn dez plus
priuez du counsail le roy al hour, estoit auys qe lour enbracement de
lour alyaunce dez Allemaunz nestoit pas resemblaunt a treir a profitable issu, et qe le roy ne serroit pas de poair a soeffrer lez costages dez
condiciouns qils ly demaunderent; en apersceyuaunt lour couaityse,
soun charge moustre a le parlement enchois au roy, se trey deuers
Escoce, pur soy excuser de cest counsail, qi sen ala od lez Countis de
Aroundel et de Gloucestre, lez sires de Percy et de Neuille a lassege
de Dunbarre, ou le Roy Dengleter lour aprocha a le Whitekirk, pur
prendre lour purpos [f. 218] de sez affaires; pur queux, il ne pust al
hour a lassege demurrer. Ils ieseroint a cel assege tot le Quarresme et
tanqe la Pentecost, tanqe Leuesqe de Nichol, et le Count de
Northamtoun et autres qauoint contenuz lez treticez dez alyaunz des
Allemauns, estoint reuenuz a Loundres, qauoint escheue vn bele
auenture darmys en lour passage de cest message, qi descoumfirent
lez Flemens en Lile de Ragent, ou fust pris Gy de Flaundres, par gentz
Wauter de Mauny. Dez queux messagers a lour reuenir ascuns
disoient, com fust dit, as ceaux qi estoint entour le roy adonqes, qe qy
endestourbast le passage le roy en acomplicement de lour tretice, qils
serrount vnqor tenuz traiters, et qe il ne amenoit oue ly, fors Giliot de
la Chaumbre; qil serroit asseitz fort de sez alyez depardela pur
conquer soun heritage de Fraunz. Cestes nouelis oyes a Dunbarre,
oue lez seignours illoeqes qestoint sure le point du rendre du chastel,
sez delogerent oue trewis, qy noserent plus demurrer pur blame qe
hom lour suremettroit, qils destourbassent le passage le roy, de
puisqe les chosis estoint si auaunt alez.

Hainault, and [they] retained lords there, which cost a huge amount
of treasure to no profit; and the envoys were Henry de Burghersh,
Bishop of Lincoln, and the Earls of Salisbury and Huntingdon, who
came back to the parliament at London with the response to their
message.

Soon after this time, the guardian of Scotland under King David,
Andrew de Moray (who happened to die soon after[30]), caused great
devastation in the county of Carlisle; and coming from there, he
besieged the castle of Edinburgh, then in English hands. The
Marchers came to the rescue; hearing of their coming, the Scots
decamped and came up against them to Clerkington, with the
English at Crighton, where between them there was a great battle at
Crighton Dean. Men were killed on both sides, but the English lost
more. The Scots decamped from there, seeming as though they were
going into England, and setting up camp at Galashiels. The English
camped near them across the river Tweed, where they remained for
two days; and on the third night, the Scots decamped and went on
their way.[31]

Soon afterwards, the Earl of Salisbury, who was one of the most
intimate of the king's council at that time, realized that their support
for their German alliance did not seem to be drawing to a profitable
conclusion, and that the king would not have the resources to bear
the costs of the terms they had demanded from him. Having realised
their avarice, he put his complaint before parliament rather than the
king and took himself to Scotland, so as to disassociate himself from
this counsel; he left with the earls of Arundel and Gloucester, and the
lords Percy and Neville, for the siege of Dunbar.[32] There, the king
approached them at Whitekirk, to find out their intentions [f. 218]
about his affairs; because of this, [Salisbury] could not stay at the
siege at that time.[33] They remained at this siege for all of Lent and
until Pentecost [31 May], while the bishop of Lincoln and the Earl of
Northampton and others, who had undertaken the negotiations for
the alliance with the Germans, had returned to London; they accomplished a fine venture of arms on their way [back] from this mission,
defeating the Flemings at the Isle of Cadzand, where Guy of Flanders
was captured by Walter de Mauny's men.[34] When these envoys
returned, there were some, it was said, who were saying to those then
around the king, that any who hindered the king's expedition in
fulfillment of their treaty, should be regarded as traitors forthwith,
and that he should not take [anyone] with him except for Giliot of the
Chamber; for with his allies over there, he would be strong enough to

47. Le roy, par counsail de ceaux qy auoint cest alyaunce au fin enbrace, passa la mere, et aryua a Andewerp, ou il gisoit .xv. moys, saunz rien faire de guere, fors a iouster et a demener iolif vie, ou nasqy Lyonel le fitz le roy.

En quel temps, lez Marchies dez Engles, qi furent lessez pur garder la Marche dereir lez gardeyns et cheuetains, qi furent cheuauche en ost en Escoce, furent descoumfitz a Presfen. Robert de Maners pris, et touz playn mortez et prisoners, qy pur noun couenablis irous parolis, alerent hors de aray, enuyousement assembler, en lieu noun couenable.

Le roy dedenz lez .ij. primers moys de soun aryuail, se trey al Emperour Lowys a Couelens, ou il teint coustoir plener, ou fust pronouncie en playn coustoir le droit le Roy Dengleter de coroune de Fraunce et accepte en cel court; qe tout auoint ils .ij. sores espose, vnqor le roy nauoit illoeqes autre eide, fors com de gentz qe ia ne servount en san le de argent, qi disoient, qe pur le soen, ils ly seruiroint volountiers, mais ceo estoit pur vn tiel demesure some, qe impossible serroit a luy a chef venir.

Meisme la seisoun qe cesti Roy Edward estoit en Brabane, lez Fraunces aryuerent hors dez galeys a Hamtoun, et la vile pristrent de assaut, et la destruyerent, qi ne furent pas graunt demore. Lez galeys de Fraunce pristrent meisme la sesoun de ioust Middilburgh .iiij. dez greignours nefes Dengleter, *[f. 218v.]* qe gisaunt estoint illoeqes, pur egarder la plesanz le roy, si rien vousist de eaux, qen le hour gisoit a Andewerp.

Le Roy Dengleter auoit commissioun com Vikair General del Empire, et qe toz ceaux del Empire ly fussent obeisaunz. Le roy repaira a Andewerp, pensaunt eide de sez alyes, tretaunt toz iours oue eaux, qe rien ne ly vailli tanqe pur meschief de long attend, talent ly surueint qe plus longment ne voroit attendre. Si enuoya a le Duk de Brabham soun cosyn germain, et au Duk de Gellire, qauoit sa sore espose, et au Markeis de Jolers soun freir en ley, et as autres sez alyes qauoint pris de soun, qe a vn certain iour il serroit sure Marches de Fraunce, ou il prendoit sez auentures; si lour fist somouns com vikair lemperour a estre prestez au dit iour, ou lez vns dez alyes le roi

conquer his inheritance of France. When this news was heard at
Dunbar, the lords there, who had been on the point of [receiving] the
castle's surrender, broke camp and [made] truce; they did not dare to
remain any longer, for men might have held them to blame for
hindering the king's expedition, since things were so far gone.[35]

47. On the advice of those who had supported this alliance to the end,
the king crossed the sea and landed at Antwerp, where he remained
for fifteen months, without doing anything warlike, except for
jousting and leading a high life; Lionel, the king's son, was born here.

At this time, the English Marchers were defeated at Pressen,
having been left to guard the March to the rear of the wardens and
leaders, who were raiding in force in Scotland. Robert de Manners
was taken, and there were many dead and prisoners; because of some
ill-chosen angry words, they had become disarrayed and attacked
ill-temperedly, at an ill-chosen location.[1]

Within the first two months from his landing, the king took
himself to the Emperor Lewis at Coblenz, where he held a plenary
council, where the King of England's right to the crown of France was
proclaimed in open council, and acknowleged at this court; yet the
king did not get any help there, for all that they had married two
sisters, except from men who would not serve except for silver,
saying that for their part they would serve him willingly, but it was
for such an excessive sum that it would be impossible for him to bring
it off. [2]

In the same season that King Edward was in Brabant, the French
landed at Southampton in galleys, and took the town by assault and
destroyed it, not staying there for long. In the same season, the French
galleys took four of the largest English ships near Middelburg.
[f. 218v.] These were lying there, waiting on the king's pleasure, in
case he wanted anything from them (he was at Antwerp at the time).[3]

The King of England received a commission as Vicar General of
the Empire, that all the people of the Empire should be obedient to
him.[4] The king returned to Antwerp, expecting help from his allies
and negotiating with them continuously, which availed him nothing
but the trouble of a long wait, [until] he was overcome with the
feeling that he could not bear to wait any longer. He sent to the Duke
of Brabant, his first cousin, and to the Duke of Guelders, who had
married his sister, and to the Margrave of Juliers his brother-in-law,
and to others of his allies who had taken his money, that on a certain
day he would be on the marches of France, where he would take his

vindroient, qi ne sez purroint detenir pur hount, quy cheuaucherent
oue ly en Fraunce, deuaunt Saint Quyntyn et en Trerage, ou en quel
veage, lez Englez oue lez Allemaunz assaillerent la vile de
Honycourt, mais ils ne la pristrent my. A quel assaute, Thomas de
Ponyngis fust mort, et autres bons gentz Engles. Le Roy Phelip de
Fraunce veint a Berenfos sodeinement aprocher le dit Roy Dengleter
de vn lieu pres, saunz scieu del ost le roy. Le dit roy ly attendy
lendemayn en beaux chaumps apoy tot le iour, qencountre le vespre
se trey a Auaynes, pur ceo qe lost nestoit pas vitaille, ou ils
demurrerent lendemain tot le iour. Le Roy Phelip de Fraunce ne
pursuist plus auaunt. En la vespre surdist de cest Auainis vn tiel
chaud melle en lost le Roy Dengleter, entre lez archers Engles, et
ascunz dez Allemaunz, qe tout la nuyte, lez gentz de armys dez
Engles estoint armez en batail. Lez vns dez Allemaunz cheierent
desus vne pane de lost dez Engles, en vn vilet dehors lost, qi tuerent
touz plain dez comunes dez Engles, et robberent cheueaux et
harnoys, et sez departerent chescun soun chemyn. Le roy se trey en
Brabann a Andewerp ou le counsail de Flaundres treterent oue ly, et
sez atournerent a ly, par lour homages et serementz, com a lour
souerain seignour Roy de Fraunce, qi par lour counsail, il prist le
noune et lez armes du Roy de Fraunce, a Gaunt, ou nasqy Johan fitz le
roy, Count de Richemound. Il se trey en Engleter pur soi meutz
arayer, ou en soun passer de la mere, estoit en graunt perille de
tempest; si lessast les Countis de Salisbirs et de Southfolk gardeins de
Flaundres, qi pur lour noun auisement de vn fole cheuauche, furent
suppris deuaunt Lile, et prisoneris, et menez au Chastelet de Parys.
Le Count de Warwik fust fait gardein de Flaundres [f. 219] depar le
Roy Engleis. Les autres countis prises, le Roy de Fraunce assist le
chastelle de Tunis en Cambresy, qe les Engles auoint suppris, ou le
Duk de Braban et les comunes de Flaundres, et le Count de Henaw,
qauoit defye le Roy de Fraunce nouelement, pur outrage qil ly auoit
fait faire, alerent a rescous, ou ils pristrent hors du chastel lez Engles
qi auoint done lour ostagez qi lez perderent, si arderent le chastel au
vieu le Roy de Fraunce. En cest mene temps qe cestez gentz furent as
champs entour cest rescous, le Roy Edward Dengleter estoit sure
soun passage a Erwelle od soun ost deuers sez alies, qauoit fait
eschipper sez cheueaux, quant nouelis ly vindrent qe le amerail de
Normendy od tout la nauy le Roy de Fraunce Phelip, estoint deuaunt
Lescluse pur asseger Flaundres par mere, qe nuls vitails ne
marchaundys lour venisseint par eaw, et pur auoir destourbe le
passage le roy. Cestez nouelis entenduz, il fust remettre sez cheueaux

chance;[5] he summoned them, as vicar of the emperor, to be ready on that day. Certain of the king's allies came there, unable to hold themselves back for shame; they rode with him in France, up to Saint Quentin and in Thiérache. On this expedition, the English attacked the town of Honnecourt, with the Germans, but they did not take it.[6] Thomas de Poynings was killed in the assault, along with other good English men. King Philip of France came suddenly to Buirenfosse, approaching within a league of the King of England, without the king's army knowing. On the next morning, the king waited for him in open fields for nearly all of the day; and towards evening he went to Avesnes, because the army did not have supplies of food, where they remained for all of the next day. King Philip of France did not pursue any further. In the evening, a very heated melée erupted at Avesnes in the King of England's army, between the English archers and some of the Germans, and so the English men-at-arms were armed and arrayed for all the night. Some of the Germans fell upon a part of the English army, in a village away from the army; they killed nearly all the English commoners, and robbed horses and harness, and split up, each by his own road. The king went into Brabant to Antwerp where the council of Flanders negotiated with him, and submitted to him, by their homage and oaths, as to their sovereign lord the King of France; by their counsel, he took the name and the arms of the King of France, at Ghent, where the king's son, John, Earl of Richmond, was born.[7] He went to England to prepare himself better, and on his sea crossing, he was in great peril from a storm.[8] He left the Earls of Salisbury and Suffolk as keepers of Flanders; through their own ill-judgement, they were surprised on a foolhardy chevauchée before Lille, and taken prisoner, and led off to the Châtelet at Paris.[9] The Earl of Warwick was made keeper of Flanders [f. 219] for the King of England. With the other earls captured, the King of France besieged the castle of Thun-l'Evêque in the Cambrésis, which the English had taken. The Duke of Brabant and the Flemish commoners, and the Count of Hainault (who had recently defied the King of France from outrage at what [the king] had had done), came to the rescue; they brought the English (who had given hostages, who they forfeited) out of the castle, and burned it down in full view of the King of France.[10] In the mean time, while these men were in the field engaged in this rescue, King Edward of England was at Orwell with his army, on his way towards his allies; he had had his horses boarded on ship, when news came to him that the admiral of Normandy was before Sluys with all of King Philip of France's navy,

a terre, et mounta od sez gentz del ost sur mere, qy la veil de saint
Johan en este veint deuaunt Lesclus en la mere; et lendemain le iour
saint Johan, sen ala combatre od cest graunt nauy de Fraunce, qi par
grace de Dieux lez descomfist, ou furount lez nefs touz conquys, et le
amerail mort, Hugh Keret, et tiel multitude dez Fraunceis, qe a
meruail outre mesure. Le aryua a Lesclus, ou ly vindrent lez
seignours de Braban, de Gelir, de Juleris, et de Henaw, et le counsail
de lez bons viles de Flaundres, ou par lour counsail, le roy se trey a
Gaunte, de ou, dedens lez .viij. iours, il remua de illoeqes deuaunt
Tournay, qi lassist. Il departist lost de Flaundres en dieus, ceaux de
Gaunte prist il od ly a Tournay, ceaux de Bruge et de Ypre, enuoia il a
Robert de Artoys, qestoit al hour de sa enherdaunce, qi pur tort qe
Phelip de Valoys, qi se clamoit Roy de Fraunce, li auoit fait du Counte
de Artoys, qil clamoit de heritage, qi Robert auoit sa sore en espouse,
qi se atourna au dit Roy Dengleter, com au droit Roi de Fraunce. Le
roy enuoya sez lettres au Phelip de Valoys et ly profery chois, ou de
batail arest, poair countre poair en lieu couenable, et iour assigne; ou
de cent cheualers encountre cent sur bons assuraunz; ou personal
darrein de lour .ij. corps. Le counsail de Fraunce disoint qils ne auoint
conysaunce a qy les ditez lettres alerent, depuis qe eles firent
mensioun de Phelip de Valoys, et ils ly tyndrent Roy de Fraunce,
feignaunt excusacioun du respouns du terminacioun du point
especifie. Ly dit Robert sen alast deuaunt Saint Thomer od *[f. 219v.]*
touz plain dez Engles, et od cestes auaunt ditz gentz de Flaundres, ou
le Count de Ermynak et le Duk de Burgoyn estoint dedenz, qi sen
isserent en dieus bataillis; Robert de Artoys od lez Engles et ceaux de
Brige, sen alerent descoumfire la batail au Duk de Burgoin, et apoy
vssent entrez la dit vile ouesqes eaux, si pres lez chaceroint. Le Count
de Ermynak od sa route sen ala descoumfire la reirgarde le dit Robert,
ceaux de Ypre, qi lez enchasa durement loynz. Au repairer Robert de
Artoys en la vespre le Count de Ermynak se repaira deuers Saint
Thomer et encountrerent ensemble, mais ceo estoit dedens la nuyt, qe
chescun se garda de autre, saunz plus faire. Au repairer le dit Robert
as sez loeges, ils trouerent lour autre batail de Ypre descoumfitz et
fuys, pur quel chos, ils sez delogerent touz meisme la nuyt, qe
lendemain sen alerent a Tournay au Roy Dengleter, qauoit assys la
vile, ou estoient dedenz lez Countis de Ew, conestable de Fraunce, et
le Count de Foys, od .Mile.D. homs darmis de estraungers. Le roy
auoit iue a cel assege .xi. semains quant le Roy Phelip de Fraunce
veint od soun graunt ost vn lieu pres de Tournay, ou comencerent
tretice, qe lez alies le roy ly chacerent a cest tretice, pur ceo qils ne

to blockade Flanders by sea, so that no supplies or merchandise could come to them by water; and so as to obstruct the king's crossing. Hearing this news, [Edward] had his horses put back on land, and put out to sea with his men from the army. And on the eve of St John in the summer, he came up to Sluys by sea; and on the morrow, St John's day [24 June], he went to fight with this great French navy, which by God's grace he defeated. All the ships were captured, and the admiral, Hugh Quiéret, was killed, and such a multitude of Frenchmen that it was a marvel beyond measure.[11] He landed at Sluys, where the lords of Brabant, Guelders, Juliers and Hainault came to him, and the council of the good towns of Flanders; and by their counsel, the king took himself to Ghent, from where, within eight days, he moved away towards Tournai, which he besieged.[12] He divided the army of Flanders in two; the men of Ghent he took with him to Tournai, the men of Bruges and Ypres, he sent to Robert of Artois, who was in his allegiance at the time. This was because of the wrong that Philip de Valois (who called himself King of France), had done [Robert] over the county of Artois, which he claimed as his inheritance, though Robert was married to his sister; so he gave his allegiance to the King of England, as to the rightful King of France.[13] The king sent letters to Philip of Valois and offered him the choice of a set-piece battle, force against force in a suitable place and on an appointed day; or of 100 knights against 100 on firm assurances; or of personal combat with their two bodies.[14] The council of France said that they did not recognise who these letters had been sent to, since they made mention of Philip de Valois, and they held him to be the King of France, feigning excuse for providing an answer on the specific point.[15] The said Robert came up to Saint-Omer with [f. 219v.] a great number of Englishmen, and with the men of Flanders; the Count of Armagnac and the Duke of Burgundy were within, and they sortied out in two battles. Robert de Artois with the English and the men of Bruges, went on to defeat the Duke of Burgundy's battle, and almost managed to get into the town along with them, so closely did they chase them. The Count of Armagnac and his band went on to defeat Robert's rearguard, the men of Ypres, and pursued them relentlessly for a long way. As Robert de Artois returned in the evening, the Count of Armagnac was returning towards Saint-Omer and they met together, but it was in the night, and so each guarded themselves against the other, and did nothing more. When Robert returned to his lodgings, he discovered that their other battle, from Ypres, had been defeated and had fled; for this reason, they broke

voroint plus demurreir, si sez departerent od vn trew de vn ane. Lez prisouners de toutis costes delyueres pur le temps, lez Countis de Salisbirs et de Southfolk dez Engles, ly sires de Mountmaracy, et autres dez Fraunceis qi furent prisis ioust Tournay. La sentence od lez grauntz obligatoirs as queux lez Flemenges estoient lyes en la court de Rome au pape en le temps le Roy Philip de Fraunce ly beaux sure payn, qils ne leueround iames encountre la coroune de Fraunce, lour estoint relessez au suyte de cesti Phelip de Valoys, qi al hour se disoit Roy de Fraunce, par condiciouns taillez au pris de trewys, deuaunt Tournay, pur touz iours.

a **48.** En quel temps du sege de Tournay, Benet estoit Pape prochein apres Johan, qestoit nome deuaunt, 'le Cardenal Blaunk', et estoit del ordre de Sisteux. Il estoit durement de bon conscience. Il restreynoit plus lordre de Sisteux par sez constituciouns, qil nestoit deuaunt soun temps. Il sentremist durement de la pese par mediacioun dez cardinaux, entre cesti Roy Edward le tierce apres la conquest, et le Roy de Fraunce Phelip de Valoys, mais ne poait a chief venir, si ne estoit enherdaunt as nuls dez parties.

En le mene temps de cest assege a Tournay, lez Countes de la Marche et de Sothirland Descoce vindrent prendre pray dedenz lez Mar...*b*

a   MS: de pape benet apres johan, *in 15thc. hand, right margin.*
b   MS: desunt folia nonnulla *added at bottom of the folio, in a 17thc. italic hand.*

camp all the same night, and on the morrow they went off to Tournai
to the King of England, who was besieging the town.[16] Within it were
the Count of Eu, constable of France, and the Count of Foix, with 1500
foreign men-at-arms. The king had played about at this siege for
eleven weeks when King Philip of France came up with his great
army one league from Tournai, where he began negotiations. The
king's allies compelled him to [attend] these negotiatons, because
they did not wish to stay any longer, and so they dispersed, with a
truce for one year. The prisoners on all sides were freed for the time
being, the Earls of Salisbury and Suffolk for the English, and lord
Montmorency, and others of the French who were taken near Tournai.
In the time of King Philip the Fair of France, the Flemings had been
bound to a judgement under great obligations to the Pope under
penalty in the court of Rome, that they should never rise up against
the French crown; they were released [from this] at the suit of Philip
of Valois, who at the time called himself King of France, under the
conditions agreed at the taking of the truce, before Tournai, for all
time.[17]

48. At the time of the siege of Tournai, Benedict was Pope (following
after John), who had previously been called 'the White Cardinal', and
who was of the Cistercian order.[1] He was of very good conscience.
Through his constitutions, he brought the order of Citeaux under
control, which it had not been before his time. He concerned himself
greatly with peace between King Edward the third after the Conquest
and the King of France, Philip of Valois, through the mediation of the
cardinals, but he was unable to bring this off, as he was not an
adherent of any of the parties.

   In the meantime, during the siege of Tournai, the Scottish Earls of
March and Sutherland came to take plunder in the Marches ...[2]

LELAND'S ABSTRACT, 1340-56[1]

[Place-names have been identified in italics in square brackets where they are not immediately obvious.]

Whil the King was at the sege of Turnay *[Tournai]*: the erles of Marche and Sothirland made a Rode yn to England: and were discomfitid by Thomas Gray there.[2]

Robert Maners and John Coplande[3] with the garnison of Roxburg then yn the Englisch mennes handes but after won by covyne of the Scottes on ester day at the very hour of the resurrextion. But al they that were capitayne of this covyne dyed after an il death.[4] Alexander Ramsey capitayne of this deade dyed for hunger put in prison for very envy that Wylliam Duglas bare hym.

King Edwarde repayrid into England and was in yeopardy of drouning at the Tamys *[Thames]* mouth: and at his arrival caussid his treasorers to be arrestid by cause he was so il furnishid of mony: the which was the greate cause of leving of his sege at Turnay.[5]

The wynter after the sege of Turnay King Edward went to Melros and rode thorough part of the forest of Etrik in a very il season and cam to Melros agayne: wher Henry erle of Darby sunne and heyre to Henry counte of Lancastre justid with Wylliam Duglas by covenaunt yn the Kinges syte.

The King Edward taking a trews departid from Melros half in a melancoly with them that movid hym to that yornay.

The counte of Derby went to Berwik and there were justes of werre by covenaunt with yn the toune of many knightes and esquiers: and there were killid ii. Englisch knighttes.

This season David Bailliol cam out of Fraunce and yn the wynter after about Candelmas made a roode in to the Englisch marches and brent much corne and houses: And yn somer after he made a rode yn to Northumbreland on to Tyne.

The same yere debate Rose in Britayne *[Brittany]* by the death of John duke there betwixt the counte Montforte brother by half bloode to duke John and Charles de Bloys that had to wife the doughter to the counte of Penthuvir *[Penthièvre]* brother to duke John by father and mother.

Counte Montfort escapid out of prison in Fraunce and cam to King Edward as King of Fraunce and Edwarde mayntenid his quarel and sent Water Mauney yn to Britayne.

And after sent the counte of Northampton into Britayne as his lieutenant with Robert of Artoys that dyed ther on fayr death.

Bohun comes Avoniae Mediterraneae[a]

The counte of Northampton faught with the barons of Britayne and great pour of Fraunce at Morlays and discomfitid them wher Geffray de Charny was taken.[6]

King Edwarde cam yn to Bretayne and assailid the toune of Vannes wher ii. cardinales cam to make treuse betwene the Kinges and the toune was delyverid to them: but King Eduarde wan it afterwarde.

King Edward with great peril of tempest and ther he gave his eldest sunne the principalite of Wales.

The countes of Saresbyri and Southfok that had beene prisoners yn Fraunce and were deliverid for the counte of Murref in Scotland and 3000 poundes sterlinges with many other knightes of England took there yourney into Spayne to the fronter of Granate to the sege of Algesirs a great toune of the Saracenes apon the straites of Marok that the good King Alphonsus had besegid and after wan it by famyne.[7]

King Edwarde made agreat fest at Wyndesore [Windsor] at Christemes wher he renewid the round table and the name of Arture and ordenid the order of the garter making Sainct George the patrone therof.

King Edward sent an army yn to Flaunders by the meane of James Arteville capitayn of the communes of Flaunders: the which when they saw the army at Scluse they of Gaunte cutte of Artevilles hed.

King Edward sent the counte of Derby the erle of Lancasters sunne with many gentil men yn to Gascoyne wher he discomfitid his ennemyes at Albaroche [Auberoche, 21 October 1345]. Ther the erls of Lisle and Valentinoys wer taken: and ther they did many great feates of armes beside.

The first erle of Stafford of the Staffordes[b]

The baron of Staford that after was erle and many other Englisch menne were besegid yn Agiloune [Aiguillon] yn Gascoyne by John duke of Normandy eldest sunne to Philip King of Fraunce: but he left the sege be cummyng of King Eduarde yn to Normandy.

King Edward sent the countes of Northampton and Oxford with counte Montfort in to Britayn that claymid to be duke there: and that shortely after dyed there of fayr death.

The aforesayd counte assegid the toune of Kemperkaretyne [Quimper] and at the laste toke it by assaute

[a] *Left margin.*
[b] *Left margin.*

Charles de Bloys cam with great pour to rescue the toune: and theaforsaid erle cam foreward to fight with them: but yn deade they fought not to gither.[8]

The counte of Northampton rode thorough the cuntery and wan the toun of Rochedirien [*La Roche-Derrien*] by assaut and so returnid yn to England with yeopardy of tempest.

Thomas Dagworth sent warden ynto Brytainne anone after this fought with Charles de Bloyse and put hym to flyte.

A nother tyme he layd wayte for Charlys de Bloys wher he had assegid Rochedirien and toke hym and sent hym prisoner yn to England. And at this tyme were many of the barons of Britayn slayne. Abowt this season King Edwarde landid at Oges [*La Hougue*] in Normandy and wan the towne of Cane [*Caen*] by force: wher the counte of Owe [Ew][c] the conestable of Fraunce: and Tankerville the chambreleyn wer taken and sent yn to Englande.

King Edward went up yn length [*Lent*] yn Normandy apon the ryver of Sene wher al the bridges wer broken and made the bridg of Pontoyse wher many French men wer slayn.

Then went King Edwarde thorough Beauvoisin and Pykardy to the water of Sowme: wher a great sorte of Frenchmen wylling to stop the passage were slayn.

Philip Valoyse[9] cam with his great hoste to have stoppid King Edward at the passage of Soun but he was over or he cam.

King Edward passing the forest of Crescy was sodenly beset with Phylip Valoys great hoste: But yet he chase a plott of ground equal to fight yn and wann a great victory of hym: wher were taken John King of Boheme [*Bohemia*] the duke of Loreyne [*Lorraine*]: the counte Alaunsun [*Alençon*] the brother of Philip Valoys that caullid hym self King of France: the counte of Flaunders and many other countes.[10]

King Edwarde went thens to Calays wher he lay a hole yere at the sege.

King Davy of Scotland yn the meane while wan agayne part by strenght, parte by treason, part by famyne al the holdes that King Eduard had yn Scotland saving the only toun of Berwik. And the tyme of the ii. firste monithes of the assege of Calays he enterid ons in somer in to the parties of Cairluelshir [*Carlisleshire – i.e. Cumberland*]: And a nother by Sulwath and after assaylid the pile of Lidel and wan it by assaute and then cut of the hedde of Water Selby capitayne there

---

that afore had beene of the covyn of Gilbetert Midleton that kept Mitford castel and Horton pile agayne King Eduarde.[11]

Davy King of Scottes went forth in to the bisshoprik and there did much hurte: wher the archbisshop of York: the counte of Angous the lorde Percy: the lorde Neville and lord Moubray with other marchers wan the batelle and John Coplande toke hym prisoner.[12] The countes of Murref *[Moray]* and Strathern wer killid: and also Morice Murref *[Moray]*, with many barons banerettes and knightes wer killid. The counte of March and the seneschal of Scotland fled. The counte of Marche was taken and the counte of Menteth that shortely after was hangid and drawen at London. Wylliam Duglas that had greatly holp the quarel of King David was restorid to his castel of the Heremitage apon conditions that he never after should bere wepen agayn King Edwarde and alway be ready to take his part. This Duglas was sone after slayn of the lord Wylliam Duglas yn the forest of Selkirk.

Many lordes, knightes and esquires of Scotland taken yn batayle with theyr King David wer sodenly ransomid the which after they cam yn to Scotland made great riottes agayn.

After this batayle cam to the King of Englands peace the countes of Berwik, Roxburg: Peblys *[Peebles]* and Dunfres: with the forestes of Selkirk, and Etrik: the valleis of Anand, Nide, Esk, Euwide, Muffet, Tevyot, with the forest of Jedworth. The castelles also of Roxburg and Heremitage wher delyverid in to the Englisch mennes handes.

King Edward lay stille afore Calays: and there the counte of Flanders practisid with hym to have his doughter Isabelle.

King Philip of Fraunce to the borders of Calays to remeve the sege: but he prevailid not.

Calays beyng over cum with famyne, the capitayne and burgeses of the toune cam with halters about theyr nekkes submitting them self to King Edwarde: the which put a right strong garnison yn the toune and so cam yn to Englande.

Then cam to King Edward messagers from Rome to treate for peace for viii. yeres folouing. About this tyme the electors of the empire sent to King Edward offering hym theyr voyces to be emperor Lowys of Bavar beyng deade. But he for his other great afferes refusid it:[d] and then was electid Charles King of Boeme *[Bohemia]* sun to King John that was killid at the batail of Cressy.

This Charles electid emperor fled at the batail of Cressy.

---

[d] *Left margin:* Edwarde ye 3. refusid to be emperorour [sic].

Henry duke de Lancastre chalengid at the coronation of Charles[e] themperor at Rome a greate part of Province *[Provence]*: the which by deathe of his auncetors was faullen to hym by reason of his fathers mother quene of Navar.

King Edward had prepared to armyes one at Sandewiche: and a nother at Orwelle to go yn to Flaunders to thentent to help them of Gaunt and Ypers the which wer at debate with them of Bruges for his quarel. But trewse taken betwyxt them brake this yorney.

King Edward knowing a pryvy practise that a Genuoyse of the garnison of Calays had for a great summe of mony with the French King for delyveraunce of Calays cam very secretely thither: and caussing as many of the French men to be let yn as might be welle over cum; slew them and brake al their purpose: And there was taken Geffray Charney very prive of the French Kinges counsel, and a great cause of thys conspiracy.

Geffray Charney delyverid for raunson toke in a castel the aforesaid Genuoyse whom King Edward had made knight: and for he had bene cause of his taking he put the Genuoyse to great tormentes.[13]

King Edward faught with a navy of the Spanyardes cummyng from Flaunders by causse they had afore done hys navy greate hurte; and vanquisshid them taking many great shippes of Castelle *[Castile]*.

The Englisch men of the garnison of Calays toke the castel of Gisnes.

The Englisch men toke a great parte of the counte of Bretayne wher Thomas Dagwort theyr capitayne a man to hy a corage to fly was slayne yn a skirmouche of the Frenchmenne. This Thomas Dageworth had often tymes over cum the French menne.[14]

Gualter Bente was gardian of Bretain after Dagworth did wonderus feates yn Britayne: But after he was put yn the tour of London by fals suggestion, as it was said.[15]

King Eduarde and his counsel wher much occupied by the space of a peace of viii. yeres procurid as is *[sic]* was spoken of afore by the messagers of Rome: and for the delyveraunce of King David of Scotland and Charlis de Bloys duke of Bretayn the which had beene in the space of these viii. yeres yn divers castelles on England yn prison.

In this tyme was a verygreat pestilence yn England and many noble men dyed of it beside the communes.

In this season at a parlament was Henry counte of Lancastre made duke: and Rafe Stafford counte.[16]

[e]   *MS:* Chales.

Henry duke of Lancastre made after a rode to Boloyne.

And this Henry was at a nother tyme yn wynter in Spruce [Prussia]: *f* but his yorney faillid to fight with the infideles.

Henry went thens to Cracow whither the Tartares enterid: and were departid a litle afore his cummyng.

Henry at his cummyng to Colayne [Cologne] fel by chaunce at hy wordes with the duke of Brunswik that gave hym gage of Bataile and receyvid it and had leve of King Eduarde to try it. The bataille was apointid at Parise before John King of Fraunce: and there they were armid an a horse bak redy to fight but King John toke up the quarel.[17] Henry laborid sore for the peace of viii. yeris afore spoken of yn so much that at the last by great difficulte it was concludid apon conditions at Avinion afore certayn cardinales and the counsel of Fraunce: But this peace cam to right smaul effect.

About this tyme John Beauchamp that was capitayne of Calays was taken aboute Arde goyng owt of Calays: wher the syre Beauin capitayne of the French band was slayn: but the French men beyng iiii. tymes doble as many as the Englische men had the victory.[18]

Clement was bisshop of Rome after Benedict. This Clement was a monk of Cluny*ℊ* ordre and archbisshop of Roan [Rouen]; and had beene before prior of a celle of the French ordre in Englande. He was a good clerk in divinite.[19]

In the meane whyle that King Davy was prisoner the lordes of Scotland by a litle and a litle wan al that they had lost at the bataille of Duresme: and there was much envy emong them who might be hyest for every one rulid yn his owne cuntery: and King Eduarde was so distressid with his afferes beyound the se that he toke litle regard to the Scottisch matiers.

At this tyme a baronet of France caullid Garenceris[20] cam with 50 men of armes yn to Scotland and brought with hym x.M. markes of the French Kinges treasor to be gyven emong the prelates and barons of Scotlande apon the condition that they should breke their trews with the King of England and make werre apon hym.

*h*About this tyme yn playne parlament the jugement of Mortymer that was erle of March by King Eduards gift was revokid at London. And so was the sunne of the sunne of Roger Mortymer restorid to therldom of Marche, and to al his possessions by the meanes of his

f Written above line.
ℊ Left margin: Clement bisshop of Rome sum tyme a Prior yn Englande.
h Left margin: Rogers Mortimers heir was restorid to the erledom of March.

great frendes that allegid that Mortimer dyed with oute answering to such thynges as wer layid agayne hym.

About this tyme King Edward was long deteynid by reason of a tretice of alliaunce betwixt the King of Navar that was the sunne of the erle of Ewerous [*Évreux*] and hym. The which alliaunce by tretice afore was ofirid when Henry duke of Lancastre was at Avinion: apon the which King Edwarde was with his navy apon the costes of Gascoyn the hole somer for performance of this alliaunce but his yorney faillid: for the King of Navar though [*sic*] to have more avantage at the French Kinges hand.

King Edward went with his hoste to Calays and rode thorough Artoys and Pykardy destroyng 700. paroches.

And apon this King John of Fraunce sumwhat to redubbe the rebuke of King Eduardes actes in his reaulme sent his Marescal to King Edwarde that he should apoint a day by gages: And King Edwarde assignid the place in the marches of Calays: but King John cam not nere it by viii. lieus.

At this season Eduard the prince of Wales was sent by King Edward with a 1000. men of armes and the erles of Warwike Oxford. Saresby, and Southfolk yn to Gascoyn the which with the Gascoynes rode over the hilles of Langedok with yn 2. dayes yorney of Avinion and brennid the suburbes of Narbone and destroyed Karkason [*Carcassone*] and the counteries about: and yn their returning to Burdeaux rode over the counte Ermeniak [Erminak][i] and cam to Burdeaux with out batail.

In the same tyme the Englischmen that wer in Britayne vanquisshid the vicunte of Roan and the syre Beaumaners. This Beaumaners had afore faught with the Englischmen by covenant 30. to 30. The englischmen at thebegynning had the better but at the ende they were vanquisshid.[21]

The lordes Percy and Neville gardians of the Englisch marches toke trewis with the lorde William Dugles at the tyme that he had conquerid the landes that the Englisch men had won of the Scottes.

Patrik erle of March that was patisid with Garaunceris the baron of Fraunce King John of Fraunce agent ther wold not consent to this trews: And so with other cam yn roode to the castel of Norham and imbuschid them self apon the Scottisch side of Twede: sending over a banaret with his baner and 400. men to forage: and so gathering prayes drove them by the castelle.

---

[i]   i.e. *Armagnac. Written above line.*

Thomas Gray conestable of Norham sunne to Thomas Gray that had beene 3. tymes besegid by the Scottes in Norham castel yn King Edwarde the secunde dayes: seing the communes thus robbid issuid out of Norham with few mo the [sic] 50. menne of the garnison and a few of the communes: and not knowing of Patrikes band be hynd were by covyn be set both before and behind with the Scottes yet for al that Gray with his men lightting apon foote set apon them with a wonderful corage and killid mo of them then they did of thenglisch men. Yet wer there vi. Scottes yn numbre to one Englisch man: and cam so sore on the communes of England that they began to fly and then was Thomas Gray taken prisoner.[22]

Patrik of Dunbar counte of Marche: and Thomas le Seneschal that caullid hym self counte of Angus one and twenty dayes after this preparid them self apon a nighte with scaling laders cumming to Berwik and with yn vi. dayes after tok be assaute one of the strongest toures of Berwik and enterid the toun.[23]

This tydinges was brought to King Edwarde at his very landing at Calays yn to England. Wherfore he taried at his parlament apointid at London but 3. dayes and with al spede cam to Berwike and enterid the castel: And then the burgeses tretisid with hym and the toune of Berwik was redelyverid ful sore[j] agayn the Scottes wylle to King Edwarde.

King Edward went to Rokesburg and there the xxvi. day of January anno D. 1355[24] Edward Bailliol King of Scottes resignid his corone and al his title of Scotland to King Edwarde: saying that the Scottes were ful of rebellion: and be cause he had no heyre nor any very nere of his linage: and that he was of King Edwardes blode wherfore he said he could not telle wher better to bestow his title and the corone of Scotlande better then apon hym.

Apon this King Eduarde went be yond Lambremore [Lammermuir] in Lownes [Lothian] destroying the countery on to Edinburg.

Then he repayrid yn to England and left the erle of Northampton gardian of the marches which toke a trews with the Scottes that was not wel kept.

John King of Fraunce toke by covyne the King of Navar that had afore treatid with King Eduard for alliaunce.

---

[j] MS corrected and unclear here.

[f. 220]

[48a][a] ... de Fraunce par treisoun, seaunt a manger, com ly Daufyn de Vien le fitz eyne le roy adonqes, li auoit prie a manger, le Count de Arcourt et autres seignours de Normendy decollez surmettaunt a eaux couyne de sa defesauns. Et fait asauoir qe a cel hour le fitz eyne du Roy de Fraunce estoit Daufyn de Vien, le quel Daufyn, Phelip le pier cesti Johan de Fraunce auoit achate au coroune de Fraunce, pur quoy cesti Roy Johan le dona a soun fitz.

...tail de ...tiers[a]

49. En lan de grace .Mile.CCC.lv.[b] et du regne le Roy Edward le tierce Dengleter apres la Conquest .xxx.e, Edward le eyne fitz du dit Roy Dengleter, et Prince de Galis, qi tretout lan auoit demure en Gascoigne sur la gerre soun pier, com auaunt est especifie, mouoit en host deuers Fraunce hors de Burdeaux le .vi. iour de Juylle, qy teint soun chemin a La Rule, et parmy Agenoys et Paragor et Lymosyne et en Berry ou plusours forteresces ly furont renduz. Il enueint a Remorentyne, vn vile en Saloigne, ou ly siris de Croun et monsire Bursigaud, vn chivaler trauaille, y furount enuoyez du Roy de Fraunce, qi pres estoit, pur surueoir le poair et la maner del ost au prince, la quel vile le dit prince prist par assaut. [c]Le sire de Croun et monsire Bursigaud, la vile gaigne, sez enmistrent dedenz vn toure fort qe y auoit, qi la tindrent hors, de quoy et de la vile ils estoint renduz, lour .lx.ᵐᵉ [d] dez cheualeris et esquiers en la grace de prince; de ou il se remua deuers la ryuer del Leyre, pur la auoir passe, en biaunce dauoir encontree le roi soun pier, qil quidoit qenfust aryuez en lez costiers de Fraunce ou de Normendy, sure la conquest de soun heritage de Fraunz; ou qe le Duk Henry de Lancastre poait auoir treit deuers ly, le quel Duk de Lancastre auoit la garde de Bretaigne, qi enuoiez estoit du Roy Dengleter meisme leste, si passage vst troue, ou de ge ou de pount, ou touz furrount rountis de Orliens a Touris, ou il teint soun chemyn par deuaunt Touris. En quel veage en le hour,

---

[a] *The sixteenth-century annotator who numbered the chapters failed to notice that a section of the text was missing here; he did not therefore number this fragmentary chapter separately from ch. 48, which precedes the lost folios.*

[a] *Left marg.*
[b] *sic.*
[c] *Marginal hand pointing to* Le sire de Croun.
[d] *Superscript* me *added by later hand.*

[f. 220]

[48a] ... of France by treason, as they were sitting at dinner, where the Dauphin de Vienne (the king's eldest son then) had invited them to dine, the Count of Harcourt and other Norman lords were beheaded, accused of plotting his destruction.[1] And it should be noted that at this time, the King of France's eldest son was the Dauphin of Vienne; Philip, the father of John of France, had bought the Dauphiné for the French crown, and therefore King John gave it to his son.

49. In the year of grace [1356],[1] the thirtieth of the reign of King Edward the third of England after the Conquest, Edward the eldest son of the King of England, and Prince of Wales, who had stayed in Gascony throughout the year in his father's war (as related above), moved out of Bordeaux towards France with his army, on 6 July.[2] He took the road to La Réole, and through Agenais and Périgord and the Limousin and into Berry, where many fortresses were surrendered to him. He came to Romorantin, a town in the Solange, where the lord de Craon and Sir Boucicaut, a hardened knight, had been sent by the King of France (who was nearby), to check the strength and nature of the prince's army. The prince took the town by assault. [When] the town was captured, the lord de Craon and Sir Boucicaut took refuge in a strong tower they had there, which they held separately; they were driven out of it and from the town, their sixty knights and squires [put] at the mercy of the prince.[3] From here, he moved on towards the river Loire, so as to cross it – in the hope of meeting his father the king, who he believed had landed on the coast of France or Normandy, for the conquest of his inheritance of France; or that Henry Duke of Lancaster had been able to come towards him (the Duke of Lancaster had the custody of Brittany, having been sent out by the King of England the same summer) – if he could find a crossing either by ford or by bridge. But all of them were destroyed, from Orleans to Tours, so he took the road round by Tours. On this expedition, some gentlemen of arms were captured at this time, nearly 200 French men-at-arms; the prince had reliable news from some of them that King John of France was approaching him nearby with his royal army, having crossed the Loire at Blois. Cardinal Périgord approached the prince, imploring for negotiations; he was answered courteously, that the prince would always be open to reason and ready to offer it. The prince got across the river Vienne in six day's journey, and at the time that he was getting ready to spend

estoint pris gentz darmes, pres .ij. centz homs darmis de ceux de
Fraunce, dez ascuns dez queux le prince auoit nouelis verrays qe le
Roy Johan de Fraunce ly aprochoit pres od soun ost real, qy passa
Leire a Bloys. Le Cardenal Peregor aprocha au prince, enpriaunt de
tretice; qi courtoisement fust respoundu, qe touz iours serroit prest a
prendre et a faire resoun. Le dit prince se trey par sez iournes outre la
ryuer de Viane, qauoit nouelis par prisoners, qe le Roy de Fraunce
passeroit la dit ryuer procheinement deuers Payteris, qe del hour qe
ly dit prince auoit fait passer tout la nuyte du Chastelle Arraud le
sumail, [*f. 220v.*] se trey en graunt hast od ses trois eschelis en batail a
trauers du pays, pur auoir auaunt venu la passe du Roy de Fraunce
de la dit riuer au pount de Chaueny, mes bon pece deuaunt qil pooit
le dit lieu aprocher, il aparceust qe le Roy estoit passe, mais vn graunt
route dez Fraunces estoit a dereir et a coste, o queux lez gentz le dit
prince auoit a faire, qe lez descoumfirent, ou furount prises dez
Fraunces, lez Countis de Ausoir, et de Juny, et od eaux plus de cent
homs darmis, cheualeris et esquieris, lez autres rechacez a Chaueny.
Cest iourne estoit le Samady le .xvij. iour de Septembre, le disme
Semain de cest veage. Le Dymange suaunt le prince se trey deuers
Payteris,[e] ou en chemynaunt, sez descouerours ly vindrent nouncier
qe lost le Roy de Fraunce, en counray dez batails, estoit pres venuz a
vn lieu Engles, ou en le hour, le dit prince descendy a pee, araya sez
bataillis. En quel lieu, le auaunt dit cardenal reueint autrefoitz au
prince, enpriaunt pur Dieux qil aresta sez gentz tanqe il auoit parle
od le dit Roy de Fraunce, pur saufete du sank Cristien, et qe oue leide
du Souerain, il luy serroit auoir pese resonable a soun honour, qi ly
respoundi, qe resoun prendroit il treuolountiers. Le cardenal sen a la,
qi tost reueint, qi troua le prince remue a pee en batail plus pres dun
quarter dun lieu, issy qe geris y auoit plus dun demy lieu Engles
entre lez .ij. ostes. Le dit cardenal ly pria, qe ordeiner voroit .ix. dez
soens pur treter en my lieu dez .ij. ostes de vn voy resonable de pese,
encountre autres .ix. de le lour, quoy fust ottroie et parfourny, mais
rien nen prist a affecte. Mais ceo ne fust fait com aparaunt fust, mais
pur taster le purpos de ly prince, et pur aloigner la bosoigne au
damage du dit prince en defaut de vitail et autres estofferis, et en
encressement de lour poair, qe touz iours enuindrent, tout enfist le
cardynal pur bien. La tretice fust proloigne tout la nuyte. Lendemain
au solail leuaunt, reueint ly cardynal, touz iours curious a destourber
la batail, enpressaunt longs trewis, en queux pooit estre trete final

[e]   *Left marg., in 16thc. hand* : Poytiers.

the night at Châtellerault, he had news from prisoners that the King
of France would cross the river near to Poitiers. *[f. 220v.]* He went
through the country in great haste with his three divisions in battle
order, to get there before the King of France crossed the river at the
bridge at Chauvigny; but a good while before he could reach the
place, he saw that the king had crossed, but that a large group of
Frenchmen were at the rear and on the riverside. The prince's men
had a go at them, and defeated them. Of the French, the Counts of
Auxerre and Joigny were taken, and with them, more than a hundred
men-at-arms, knights and squires; the others were driven back to
Chauvigny. This battle was on Saturday 17 September, the tenth week
of this expedition.[4] The following Sunday, the prince went towards
Poitiers; and on the way, his scouts came to tell him that the King of
France's army, formed up in battles, had come within an English
mile. Straightaway, the prince dismounted on foot and arrayed his
battles. Here, the cardinal came back to the prince once again,
imploring by God that, for the saving of Christian blood, he halt his
men until he [the cardinal] had talked with the King of France, and
that with the help of the Lord, he would obtain peace for him in
accordance with his honour. The prince replied to him that he would
very willingly listen to reason. The cardinal went off, and quickly
returned, to find the prince had moved nearer by quarter of a mile, in
battle order on foot, so that there was scarcely more than half an
English mile between the two armies.[5] The cardinal begged him that
he be willing to appoint nine of his men to negotiate with nine others
of theirs, in between the two armies, as a reasonable way forward to
peace. This was agreed to and carried out, but nothing was achieved
to any effect. However this was not done as it appeared, for the
cardinal did it all for the good [of the French], to test the prince's
resolve, and to draw out the business to the prince's detriment
through the lack of food and other supplies, and through the enlarge-
ment of their forces, which were arriving constantly.[6] The negotiations were prolonged for all the night. In the morning at daybreak,
the cardinal came back, ever anxious to prevent the battle, pressing
for a long truce in which it would be possible to negotiate a final
peace. Always, the prince told him that he would willingly agree to
whatever was within his authority and that he would not go any
further. The cardinal said that would return to the King of France,
and would let him know straightaway what he would be able to get
from him.[7] [The king] soon replied to the prince, that the affair could
turn out no other way than that each should try his best. The prince,

pese. Ly prince luy disoit touz iours, qen ceo qil auoit poair il se acorderoit uoluntiers, et ceo ne passeroit il my. Ly cardynal disoit qil reirroit au Roy de Fraunce, et ly lesseroit sauoir en le hour, a quoi il le puroit attreire; qi tost remaunda au prince, qe la bosoigne ny aloit en autre gise, mais qe chescun enfeist soun meilliour. Le prince, qi prest estoit en counray de batail, fist mounter a cheual touz lez soens; ses^f as costes deuaunt lez batails du Roy de Fraunce, pur choiser meilliour place a combatre, [*f. 221*] ou lez Fraunces quidoint qe ils sez vssent fuys, qi fortement sez hasterent; et nomiement lour auaunt garde de dieus mareschals, party en enuy, com fust dit, qi meutz enuailleroit pur parolis sours entre eaux. Le auauntgard du prince et soun reirgard assemblerent od lez marescheals, qe lour descomfirent. La batail du daufyn, fitz eyne du Roy de Fraunce, assembla od la batail du prince, qi bien tost furount areir botez. Et auxi la bataille du Duk de Orliens, freir au roi de Fraunce, qi a lour recoiller encontrerent oue la batail le Roy, qi descenduz estoit a pee, qi ala cheualerousement pur assembler sur la batail le Prince; del hidouse vieu de qoi, tot plain dez gentz de la batail le Prince sez retreierent as autres batails, qauoint descoumfitz lez lours, outre vn hay en vn autre chaumpe, lez quex aparceurent la arest, la couyn et le combatre de la batail le prince, sez hasterent deuers ly, qy assemblerent au coste oue tiel escry, qe moult reuygoura lours amys en graunt affray des enemys; issi qe par la especial grace du souerayne, la victoir demurra od le auaunt dit prince.

A quel batail de Payteris, le Roy Johan de Fraunce fust pris prisoner, et soun fitz Phelip, et .xiij. countis, et vn erceuesqe, et de barouns et de baneretis .Lxvi; la noumbre de gentz darmys prisis .ij.Mile. Et furount mortez, le Duk de Bourboun, et le Duk de Attenys, adonqes Conestable de Fraunce, et le Mareschalle de Cleremount, et vn evesqe, et viscountis plusours, barons et baneretz, et enuyroun .iij.Mile. homs darmis, a la chace et a la batail. Si estoit la noumbre de gentz darmis od cotis armours en lost de Fraunce: viij.Mile. Et en le ost le prince, fors .Mile.ix.C. et .Mile. et .D. archiers.

Willam seignour de Douglas, qi voloit faire pelerinage outre mere, passa hors Descoce, enueint en Fraunce en le hour qe le Roy Johan de Fraunce se adressa en ost deuers le dit Prince en Gascoigne. Sen ala od le dit roy, deueint cheualer de sez mayns, eschapa de la batail, reueint en soun pays, ascuns dez sez chiualers mortz a la bataile. Qy Willam deueint Count de Douglas, procheignement apres la

who was ready in battle formation, had all his men mount their
horses; they [crossed] towards the flanks of the King of France's
battles, to choose a better place to fight. [f. 221] The French thought
they had taken flight, and made great haste; and in particular, their
vanguard under the two marshals, partly due to ill-will, which had
been made worse by sour words between them, so it was said.[8] The
prince's vanguard and his rear-guard joined battle with the marshals,
and defeated them. The dauphin's battle (who was the eldest son of
the King of France), attacked the prince's battle, and was rapidly
pushed back. And likewise, the Duke of Orléans' battle, the brother of
the King of France; [this battle] rallied and joined up with the king's
battle, which was dismounted on foot, and chivalrously went to
attack the prince's battle. At this frightening sight, very many of the
men of the prince's battle fell back to the other battles, which had
beaten off [the attacks on] them, across a hedge in another field.
Seeing the prince's battle halted, and seeing its situation and the
fighting, these battles moved quickly towards him, attacking on the
flank with a great outcry that much revived their friends, to the great
dismay of the enemy; and so by the Lord's special grace, the victory
remained with the prince.

The King of France was taken prisoner at this battle of Poitiers,
and his son Philip, and thirteen counts, and an archbishop, and
sixty-six barons and bannerets; the number of men-at-arms taken was
2000. The Duke of Bourbon, the Duke of Athens, then Constable of
France, and the Marshal de Clermont, and a bishop, and many
viscounts, barons and bannerets, and around 3000 men-at-arms, were
killed in the pursuit and in the battle. And the number of
men-at-arms with coat armour in the French army was 8000; and in
the prince's army, 1900, and 1500 archers.[9]

Wishing to make a pilgrimage overseas, William lord Douglas
crossed from Scotland and arrived in France at the time that King
John of France was making his way with his army towards the said
prince in Gascony. He went with the king, became a knight at his
hands, escaped from the battle and returned to his own country,
[although] some of his knights were killed at the battle.[10] William
became Earl of Douglas, soon after the release of King David of Scotland. At this time, David de Bruce created William de Ramsay Earl of
Fife, mostly on account of [William's] wife, who he loved passionately, so it was said. The king claimed his right to grant this earldom
on account of a forfeiture, as he said, which Duncan Earl of Fife had
incurred in the time of King Robert de Bruce, his father, for the death

deliueraunce le Roy Dauid Descoce. Qi Dauid de Bruys en le hour, fist
Willam de Ramyssay deuenir Count de Fif, moult par enchesoun de
sa femme, qil amast paramurs, com len disoit. Quel countee, le Roy
dysoit soun droit a doner pur vn forfaiture, com disoit, qe Dunkan le
Count de Fyf auoit fait en le temps le Roy Robert de Bruys, soun pier,
de la mort dun esquier qi out a noun Michel Betoin, qil auoit fait tuer
en yre a la Ryuer; pur quoy le dit *[f. 221v.]* [Roy Dauid]⁸ suremist qe le
dit Count, pur pese auoir du Roy pur la forfet, auoit ordene par
endenture la reuersioun du Countee a soun dit pier le Roy, en cas qil
deueyoit saunz heir masl, qi ceo sesoit. Mais auoit le dit Count vn
feile de sa femme, la feile le Roy Dengleter la Countaise de
Gloucestre, quel feile estoit en Engleter, et deueroit auoir este vendu a
Robert Seneschalle Descoce, qe prist par amours a marry Willam de
Feltoun, vn cheualer de Northumbreland, qi la auoit en garde en le
houre; la quel claym droit hu countee, qe dedit celle taille.

Cest batail de Payteris auenu a la gyse, la sureveile de saint
Matheu, lan auaunt nome; le dit Prince se trey a Burdeux, od le dit
Roy de Fraunce prisoner, et od lez autres, pur lez mettir en sauf gard,
tanqe le Roy soun pier aueroit fait de eaux soun pleisir, qi bien
deueroit mercier Dieux de sa grace, qe a vn foitz il auoit et en le hour
prisoners .ij. roys coronez, le Roy de Fraunce, le plus pussaunt des
cristienes, et le Roy Dauid Descoce, qen cel hour auoit demure en
Engleter .x. aunz prisoner.

Meisme la seisoun, dedenz .ij. moys apres cest batail de Payters,
fust la cite de Basille rue tout a terre par terremote, et graunt noumbre
dez comunes de la cite mortez au cheyer, et plusours chasteaux
abatus enuyroun.

Meisme lan, le Duk Henry de Lancastre, qi gardeyn estoit de
Bretaigne en le hour depar le auaunt dit Roi Edward Dengleter, assist
la cite de Rems, de la saint Michelle tanqe apres la saint Johan le
Baptiste en my este, de ou il se delogea par vertu de trewis prisis en
Gascoigne, entre le dit Prince de Galis fitz le dit Roy Dengleter, et le
counsail de Fraunce, lez trewes a durreris .ij. aunz. Mais le Duk de
Lancastre auoit vn graunt soum dargent de ceaux de Bretaigne, dez
enherdauntz Charlis de Bloys, pur ses costages du dit assege. Ly dit
Prince de Galis amena le dit Roy Johan de Fraunce en Engleter a soun
pier, qi Roy Johan de Fraunce fust bon pece a Loundres, et puis remue
a Wyndesor.

⁸ *Supplied.*

of a squire named Michael Beaton, who he had had killed in a fit of
rage on the hunting field. [f. 221v.] King David claimed that because
of this, so as to have the king's pardon for the forfeiture, the earl had
arranged the reversion of the earldom to his father the king by indenture, in the event that he should die without male heir; and he had
died thus. However, this earl had a daughter by his wife, the
daughter of the King of England, the Countess of Gloucester.[11] This
daughter was in England, and she had been destined to sold be in
marriage to Robert the Steward of Scotland; but for love, she took for
her husband William de Felton, a knight of Northumberland, who
had her in his ward at the time. She claimed the right to the earldom,
which this entail had given away.[12]

The battle of Poitiers happened in this manner the day before the
eve of St Matthew [i.e. 19 September], in the fore-named year. The
prince went to Bordeaux, with the King of France prisoner, and with
the other [prisoners], to put them in safe-keeping until the king, his
father, should make known his intentions for them. The king owed
many thanks to God for his grace, for at one and the same time he
held two crowned kings prisoner: the King of France, the mightiest of
Christians; and King David of Scotland, who at that time had
remained a prisoner in England for ten years.

In the same season, within two months after the battle of Poitiers,
the city of Basel was all knocked to the ground by an earthquake; a
large number of the city's common people were killed in the collapse,
and many surrounding castles fell down.[13]

The same year, Duke Henry of Lancaster, who was keeper of
Brittany at the time for King Edward of England, besieged the city of
Rennes, from Michaelmas [29 September] until after St John the
Baptist in midsummer [24 June]. He decamped from there by virtue
of a truce made in Gascony, between the Prince of Wales, son of the
King of England, and the council of France, the truce to last for two
years. However, the Duke of Lancaster got a great sum of silver from
the men of Brittany, the adherents of Charles de Blois, for his
expenses in the siege.[14] The Prince of Wales brought King John of
France into England to his father; King John was in London for a
good while, and was then removed to Windsor.

Le Roy Dauid Descoce fust a la saint Michel suaunt deliuers pur raunsoun de .C.Mile. marcz dargent; sez ostages furount entrez a Berewyk. Le Count de Sothirland, et le fitz le dit Count, qi fitz estoit la sore le dit Roy Dauid, Thomas le Seneschal qi dez Escotz estoit nomez Count Dangous, Thomas de Murref baroun de Botheuille od autres .xx. fitz dez seignurs Descoce, estoint ostages.

Entour quel temps, vn cheualer nee du lang de Oke, qi se fist nomer le Ercheprestre, se assembla juuenceaux gentz darmes de plusours naciouns; mouerent guere en [f. 222] Prouince, gaignerent chastelis et viles enuyroun Auynioun, du quoi la court du saint pere, qy adonqes y endemura, estoit durement troeble, la quele ryot fust grauntement mese par lez dounes du pape Innocent.

La Royne Descoce et sore le dit Roy Edward Dengleter veint meisme la sesoune a Wyndesore, a parler od le Roy soun freir, et de boter en parlaunce greignour tretice; et fust delee sa mere la Royn Isabelle, qe morust a Herforthe meisme la sesoun, qe ne lauoit pas vieu .xxx. aunz. A quel lieu de Wyndesore, le dit Roy Edward teint sa graunt fest de joustes et reuelle le iour saint George com acoustomez estoit, ou le Roy Johan de Fraunce estoit en le hour en prisoun, et ou le Duk Henry de Lancastre fust naufre; com iousta oue vn chiualer, vn autre a trauers ly fery de sa Launce hu coste, moult perillousement, de quoy il gary.

As queux ioustes veint le Duk de Braban et de Lenburgh, qi freir estoit al Emperour Charlis de Bahayn, pur demaunder eyde encountre le Count de Flaundres, qi bon pece ly auoit guerroie pur la vile de Malyns et autres debatis entre eaux, qauoint espose .ij. sores, feilles Johan, Duk de Braban, qi nout nul fitz. Mais le dit Duk de Lenburhe auoit leyne espous, Johan la Countas de Henaw,[h] qy morust en Frise, qy Duk auoit la Douche du doune soun freir Lemperour par coustom del Empir.

La sesoun deuaunt vindrent dieus Cardynaux Peregor et Vrgen en Engleter, pur treter de la deliueraunce du Roy Johan de Fraunce, et de pese entre lez Roys, qi bon pece demurerent en Loundres, qe a vn voy de pese treterent quoi fust assentu du counsail le Roy, en maner qil agreast au comune de sa terre, par counsail dez queux, le chalange de soun droit de Fraunce fust comencee et perseuere. Quelis comunes desagreerent en playn parlement a Loundres au tail du dit tretice si ensy ne fust, qe autre addicioun ne fust aiouste. [i]Ceo fust qe le pape

[h] MS: le dit Duk de Lenburhe auoit leyne, la Countas de Henaw, espous Johan.
[i] Nota hic *in right margin, in late 15thc. hand.*

At Michaelmas following, King David of Scotland was released for a ransom of 100,000 marks of silver; his hostages were received at Berwick. The hostages were the Earl of Sutherland and the earl's son (who was the son of King David's sister), Thomas the Steward, who was called Earl of Angus by the Scots, Thomas de Murray, baron of Bothwell, along with another twenty sons of Scottish lords.[15]

Around this time, a knight born in the Languedoc, who called himself the Archpriest, brought together young men-at arms of various nations, and made war in [f. 222] Provence, taking castles and towns around Avignon.[16] The *curia* of the Holy Father, which was then resident there, was very troubled by this, but this concern was greatly reduced by Pope Innocent's gifts.

The Queen of Scotland, the sister of King Edward of England, came to Windsor in the same season, to speak with her brother the king, and to put forward a longer treaty for discussion; and she was with her mother Queen Isabella, who died at Hertford in the same season, who she had not seen for thirty years.[17] At Windsor, King Edward held a great feast with jousts and revelry on St George's day [23 March], as was customary. King John of France was there, being prisoner at the time, and Duke Henry of Lancaster was wounded there; as he jousted with a knight, another struck across him, hitting him in the side with his lance very dangerously, but he recovered.[18]

The Duke of Brabant and Luxemburg, brother of Emperor Charles of Bohemia, came to these jousts to ask for help against the Count of Flanders, who had been at war with him for a good while over the town of Malines and other points of contention between them. They had married two sisters, daughters of John, Duke of Brabant, who had no son. However, the Duke of Luxemburg had married the elder, Joan, Countess of Hainault, who had died in Frisia, and the Duke got the Duchy by the gift of his brother the emperor, by custom of the Empire.[19]

The previous season, the two cardinals Périgord and Urgen had come to England, to negotiate for the release of King John of France, and for peace between the kings. They remained in London for a good while, and negotiated a proposal for peace[a] to which the king's council agreed, on condition that it should be agreeable to the community of the land, by whose counsel, the challenge over his right to France had been begun and maintained. But, in full parliament in London,[20] the commons would not agree to the provisions of

---

[a]   *Lit.*: 'a way to peace'.

releissast, pur ly et sez successours, tout le contracte qe le Roy Johan
auoit fait par endenture et par attournement au patrounage le
Apostoil en le temps Innocent; et qe le Seint Pier cessast de chos, qen
le hour sentremist peniblement. Quoy com lez genz de lay Engles
disoint estoit grauntement countre la coroun, qar meisme le hour, *i*les
justicz le roy estoint personelement escomengez pur processe de vn
iugement, qils auoint fait en le bank le roy, encountre Thomas de Lile,
Euesqe de Ely, qe del ordre dez Jacobins estoit, qi ne respoundy my
fourmelement dun felouny qe ly fust par enditement surmis par sez
aduersairs, le counsail la Dame de Wake; pur quoy [*f. 222v.*] lez ditz
justises agarderent vn content solonc lour loys, pur quoy le roy seisist
lez temperautes le dit euesqe, qy sen ala a Auinioun del hour qil fust
attache, et baille al erceuesqe, enfist dure processe; issint qe le pape
sentremist du temperaulte, com disoint lez auauntditz gentz de lay,
en defesaunce du regaute le roy. Quel peticioun enuoye estoit au saint
pier, sure quel tretice od autres obstacles, lez ditz cardynaux
departerent hors Dengleter, qi desesparez estoint du tretice. Ia le
mainz, si pres lauoint chacez, qe lez .ij. roys estoint entrebaisez sure
condicioun dun fourme de pese, qe a vn terme limite del
aparfournicement ne poout estre tenu du part dez Fraunceis.

Meisme la sesoun lez plusours dez gentz Engles, qe vesqerent sure
la guere, lez trewis pris com auaunt est dit, sez mistrent en
Normendy, emblerent chasteaux, afforcerent manoirs, mouerent tiel
riote de guere hu pays, par suppuail dez gentz de commune
Dengleter, qi lez vindrent de iour en autre, contre defens le Roy. En
alerent espessement a meruail, tout saunz cheuetain de lour test
demene, qi grauntz mestries firent hu pays, truagerent apoy tout
Normendy, et lez costers dez plusours pais enuyroun; sez
purchacerent bons forteresces en Paitow, Aungeow, et en Humein, et
deuers douce Fraunce a .vi. lieus de Parys. Ils estoint esparplis en
tauntz dez lieus en diuers pais qe nuls ne pooit rementiuer lez punyes
ne lez faitz darmis qe lour aueindrent hu men temps. Mais taunt
firent, qe toutz gens Cristiens sez meruaillerent. Et si nestoint fors
comunes de coillet, ioens gentz, qe deuaunt le hour nestoint fors de
poy acount, qi durement deuindrent pussauntz dauoir et sachauntz
de cel guere, pur quoi lez ioens de plusours pays Dengleter sen
alerent. Lez comunes des vileins et lez laborours de Fraunce sez

---

j   Nota en lei [infoist?] ... escomange par pap... de ley engleterr... *in right margin,*
      in same late 15thc. hand.

the treaty as it was thus, without the addition of further terms. This was that the Pope should remit, for himself and his successors, the whole contract that King John had made by indenture and by attornment in favour of the Apostle, in the time of Innocent; and that the Holy Father, who was busily meddling with the matter at the time, should desist from it.[21] The English men of law said that this was greatly to the disadvantage of the crown, for at that time, the king's justices had been personally excommunicated for the judgement of a legal action which they had made in King's Bench, against Thomas de Lisle, Bishop of Ely. He was of the Dominican Order, and had not formally answered for a felony, which he was accused of in an indictment [brought] by his adversaries, the council of Lady Wake.[22] On account of this, [f. 222v.] the justices gave a verdict according to their laws, and therefore, the king had seized the temporalities of the bishop, who took himself off to Avignon as soon as he had been attached (and bailed by the archbishop), and set in motion a lengthy legal action; as a result, the pope intervened over the temporality, to the prejudice of the king's sovereignty, so the men of law claimed. This petition was sent to the Holy Father, and because of these discussions, along with other obstacles, the cardinals departed from England, having despaired of a treaty. Nevertheless, they had got so close to one, that the two kings had exchanged kisses on the terms of a form of peace, but with a time limit for its implementation, which on their part, the French were unable to keep to.[23]

In the same season, when the truce had been made (as aforesaid), many of the English who lived off the war set out for Normandy, took castles, fortified manors and caused other such warlike mayhem in the country, with the support of men of the community of England, who came to [join] them day by day, against the king's orders. They came in astonishing numbers, all of them on their own account without any leader, and inflicted great oppressions on the country, taking tribute from almost the whole of Normandy, and from the borders of many surrounding lands. They acquired good fortresses in Poitou, Anjou and Maine, and towards the fair Île de France, six leagues from Paris. They were scattered in so many places in different regions that no one could recount the fights and the deeds of arms which befell them in these times. And they achieved so much, that all Christian people marvelled. And yet they were nothing but a gathering of commoners, young men, who until this time had been of but little account, who came to have great standing and expertise from this war; and so the youths of many regions of England came [to join

assemblerent en routes apres ceo qe lour Roy Johan estoit pris a Payteris, despiserent lez gentilis homs et lez defolerent, ceaux qils pooint ateindre, abaterent lour mesouns, surmettaunt qe lez gentilis gentz ne ualoint rien, fors par extorsioun a reyndre la comune et lez poures gentz. Ils tuerent ascuns partz lez femmes et lez enfauntz dez gentilis homs, pur quoy lez gentilis homs sez assemblerent, et lez descoumfirent et lez enchacerent, et ameserent cel riote.

Meisme la sesoun lez comunes de Parys sez firent vn cheuetain, ly nomerent Prouost dez Marchaundes, leuerent sodeignement, sen alerent au palays le roy, ou le fitz le roy (qi dit fust Duk de Normendy et Daufyn de Vien) estoit en counsail, roumperent lez huses de sa chaumbre, tuerent deuaunt ly le Mareschal de Cleremount, *[f. 223]* le freir cely qi murust a Paiteris, detrencherent illoeqes plusours autres, suremettaunt a eaux qils auoint degaste par giser en bons viles la tresor de Fraunce, de eaux pris, saunz autre apertice faire darmys encountre les enemys; ia le mainz, le dist Mareschal auoit hu meisme la sesoun vn descoumfiture sure lez Engles en Normendy, ou Godfray de Harcourt estoit mort, qautre foitz auoit enherde as Engles. Le dit Prouost dez Marchaundez enmyst vn chaperoun de sa suyte sure la test le fitz le roy, ly amena deuant la comune, ou il lour fust encouenaunt de soy contener apres lour counsail, quel premesse, il ne teint point; se aloigna a plus tost qil pooit, enbrasa poair encountre eaux, pur qoy lez ditz comunes retindrent le Roy de Nauern, et ascuns Engles qi demurraunt estoint en Normendy. Qy Roy de Nauern estoit enprisone de le Roy de Fraunce, com deuaunt est dit, qi meisme la sesoun fust delyuers par le seignour de Pynkene, et de sez autres amys, qi de nuyt emblerent le lieu, ou le dit roy fust enprisone et ly amenerent en Normendy. Le dit roy, od plusours Engles, se enherda au dit comune de Parys, estoint dedenz la cite, de ou lez Engles isserent et soutzpristrent vn pount qe le Daufyn auoit fait adresser dez bateaux de nouel outre Seyn, a dieus lieus de amount Parys, pur destourber la vitail, ou au gaite soun Mareschal fust pris, se .iiij.^me ^k dez cheualers, et amenez a Parys dez ditz Engles, ou bien furount resceus et cheris, tanqe ils mouerent desordeinez riotes dez extorsiouns en la cite. Pur quoi lez comunes leuerent sure eaux, lez enchacerent hors de vile, suerent qi eschaperent as chaumps en batail. Lez Engles qauoint purpris et enforce Poisy, et autres forterescez enuyroun, estoint issus deuers Saint Clow; oyerent la

---

Superscript me *added by later hand.*

them]. The communities of the villeins and the labourers of France gathered together in bands after their King John had been taken at Poitiers, despising the noblemen and ill-treating those of them they managed to get their hands on, smashing their houses, claiming that the noblemen were worth nothing, except for oppressing the community and the poor men by extortion. In some places, they killed the wives and children of noblemen; and therefore the noblemen gathered themselves together, and defeated them and hunted them down, and subdued this rising.

In the same season, the commoners of Paris appointed themselves a leader, naming him Provost of the Merchants, and rose up without warning and went off to the palace of the king, where the king's son (called Duke of Normandy and Dauphin of Vienne), was in council. They broke down the doors of his chamber, killed the Marshal de Clermont in front of him [f. 223], whose brother had died at Poitiers, and slaughtered many others there, accusing them of having wasted the treasure of France, which had been taken from them [the commoners], by laying up in the best towns, without apparently doing any deeds of arms against the enemy, notwithstanding that the Marshal had in the same season [inflicted] a defeat on the English in Normandy, where Godfrey de Harcourt was killed, who had gone over to the English four times.[24] The Provost of Merchants put a cap of his livery on the head of the king's son, and brought him before the commune, where he was made to agree to conduct himself according to their counsel, a promise which he kept not at all. He got himself away as fast as he could, and organised a force against them; therefore the commoners retained the King of Navarre, and some of the English who had remained in Normandy. The King of Navarre had been imprisoned by the King of France, as was said before; and in the same season, he was freed by Lord de Picquigny, and by his other friends, who broke in to the place where the king was imprisoned at night, and took him to Normandy.[25] The king, along with many English, joined with the commune of Paris, inside the city; from there, the English made a sortie, and captured a bridge across the Seine which the Dauphin had had made from new out of boats, two leagues upstream from Paris, so as to disrupt the food supply. Here, his marshal was taken by ambush, and four of his knights, and brought to Paris by the English, who were well received and respected, until they provoked uncontrollable riots by their extortions in the city.[26] Because of this, the commoners rose against them, drove them from the town, and belligerently pursued those who escaped to the fields.

rumoure encountrerent lez fuauntz, enpristrent le chemyn deuers
ceaux de Parys qi issus estoint, currerent sure eaux et lez
descoumfirent, lez reboterent despitousement dedenz lour cite,
plusours de eaux mortez et noez en Seyne. Le Roy de Nauar eschapa
hors de Parys, pur quel riote, lez ditz comunes reenherderent meisme
la nuyte a Daufyn le fitz le Roy, qi pres estoit en ost. Ils detrencherent
en le houre lour Prouost dez Marchaundes, qils auoint leue en lour
cheuetayn, et od ly plusours autres de se mayntenours; pur quoi, le
dit Roy de Nauern od lez auauntditz Engles demurrauntz en
Normendy sez mistrent en ost deuaunt Parys, demaundaunt la batail
de Daufyn, qi ne voroit isser. En lour aler de illoeqes, ils pristrent de
assaut la vile de Creel. Le Roy de [f. 223v.] Nauern auoit couyn dez
gentz de Amyas, qauoint sure la nuyte purpris dieus ou trois portz de
la vile, et lez auoint lesse ouertz, enpense qe au soun dun clarion le dit
roy, qy pres estoit venuz la vile, vst entree. Mais com auenture de
gerre le aportoit. Meisme la nuyte le Count de saint Poel estoit entrez
la vile en la vespre, od quatre Cent homs darmes, qy oy laffray, com
ceaux qestoint de la couin quiderent le sodein entre du dit Roy, qi ia
nestoit pas prest, ou nauoit oy le enseigne, mouerent riot sez
esparplerent pur gayner, tanqe le dit count od lez soens, sez mistrent
as portez lez trouerent ouertz, lez cloierent, currerent sure lez
enbraceours, lez descoumfirent. Le dit roy failly de soun purpos,
destruyt le suburbe, se trey en Normendy. Les Engles purpristrent
plusours forterescez, enmysterent garnisoun, dount vn estoit entre
Beauuaisin et Pikardy, qe out a noune Maucounsail, quel lieu Leuesqe
de Noyoun et le Sire de Dawney assistrent; quatre centz homs darmes
de ditz Engles et le Sire de Pinkeny alerent rescoure le dit lieu,
enpristrent le dit euesqe, et od ly .iiij. barouns et .L. cheualeris,
descoumfirent lez autres. Maynt bele fait darmes aueindrent as
Engles cel sesoun en diuers lieus hu realme de Fraunce, qe ne sount
my en cestz recordez, pur lez causis susditz. Queux Engles de lours
testes propres sez auoint mys en plusours lieus hu realme de Fraunce
puis cest guere, qi gentz estoint de coillet, ieunes mesconuz de diuers
countres Dengleter, plusours sours dez archiers, et puis deuenus
chiualeris, lez vns capitayns, lez iournes dez queux ne purrount pas
touz estre especifiez en le hour qils auindrent pur diuersete deaux.

The English had seized and fortified Poissy, and other fortresses nearby, and were making a sortie towards Saint-Cloud. Hearing the tumult and meeting the fugitives, they took the road towards the Parisians who had made a sortie, charged against them and defeated them, driving them back pitylessly into their city; many of them died, drowned in the Seine. The King of Navarre escaped from Paris, and because of this disorder, on the same night the commoners rejoined the Dauphin, the king's son, who was nearby with his army. At the same time they slaughtered their Provost of Merchants, who they had appointed as their leader, and many of his supporters with him. Therefore, the King of Navarre, along with the English remaining in Normandy, came before Paris with an army, demanding battle with the Dauphin; but he did not want to come out. On their way there, they took the town of Creil by assault. The King of [f. 223v.] Navarre had an agreement with the men of Amiens, who took two or three of the town gates during the night, and left them open, thinking that at the sound of a trumpet the king, who had arrived near the town, would enter. But [the plot] was dashed by the fortunes of war. That same night, the Count de Saint-Pol had entered the town, in the evening, with 400 men-at-arms; he heard the commotion as those who were in the plot, expecting the king's imminent arrival – though he was either not ready, or had not heard the signal – started a riot and scattered in search of plunder, while the Count and his men, went to the gates and finding them open, closed them, charged against the conspirators and defeated them. Having failed in his purpose, the king destroyed the suburb, and took himself off to Normandy. The English captured many fortresses, and garrisoned them. One was between Beauvaisis and Picardy, called Mauconseil, and the Bishop of Noyon and Lord de Aunay besieged the place; 400 of the English men-at-arms and Lord de Picquigny came to relieve the place, taking the bishop, and four barons and fifty knights with him, and defeating the rest.[27] Many fine deeds of arms were achieved by the English at this time in different places in the kingdom of France, which have not been included in this account, for the reasons said above. These English had established themselves on their own account in many parts of the kingdom of France after this war. These were men who were gathered, as unknown youths, from different regions of England, many beginning as archers, and then becoming knights, and some of them captains, and it has not been possible to detail all of their battles at the time they took place, because of their variety.

50. Et pur ceo qe ascuns iournes notabilis estoient vbliez a escrier en le hour qils auindrent en proces du lyuer qi ia estoit par escript, pur ceo autre part est bon qils soient especifiez. Primerment la iourne de Gistres en Gascoyne, ou Hugh de Genefe fust cheuetain de la guere depar meisme le dit roy Dengleter Edward le tierce apres la Conquest, en lan de grace .Mile.CCC.xxxiij. au comencement de la guere de soun chalange de Fraunce, ou lez seneschals de diuers pays depar le Roy de Fraunce auoient assys Labbe de Gistres, le quel lez Gascoynes Engles auoint enforce. A rescous de quoy, le dit Hugh oue ascuns autres barouns Gascoines Engles, enuiroun .iiij.C. homs darmes, et .viij.C. seriauntz et archiers, vindrent adeuant lez Fraunceis, qi plus furont *[f. 224]* de mile homs darmes, qi bataillez estoint as champes. La ryuer de Ille estoit entre eaux, lez Engles estoint bataillez sure le gee de la dit riyuer. Ceaux qestoint assegez en lauaunt dit forteresce Englois isserent et eskirmygerent si tresabaundounment al assaute sure lez ditz enemys, qe saunz assent ou uolente dez cheueteins dez ditz Englois, lours seruauntz apoi touz saunz regard auoir, passerent pres a lour espaulis la dit Ryuer, launcerent ouesqes lez autres de si tre meruaillous apert couyn et enpris. Lez Fraunceys, quy trop pres dez hayes lour sembloit auoir tenu, remuerent et retreierent pur prendre plus large chaumps, oue quoy, lez auauntditz Engles qi ceo uirent, enpristrent a passer le dit riuer. Les ditz seruauntz dez Englois aparceurent la*ᵃ* uenu lours seignurs et la retrer dez Fraunceis, si crierent dun voice et curage, Alour, alour, ils sount descoumfitz. Oue qoi lez ditz Fraunceis, sen alerent descoumfiz taunt com cheueaux purroint coure. Et puis apres cel hour bon pece, enuyroun .xij. aunz, autres gros iournes auyndrent en Gascoigne, apres departir le Duk de Lancastre qi lieutenaunt estoit du Roi Dengleter illoeqes, com auaunt est dit, et deuaunt la uenu du fitz le roy, le Prince de Galis en la dit paijs, com de la iourne de Lymeloinge, au rescous de Lishinyane, ou Thomas Cok cheualer Englois fust seneschal, apres departir le dit Duk, qi Thomas od lez barounes Gascoines Engles furount .v.Cent. glayues, ou en chemynaunt lour vindrent a deuaunt .Mile. et .v.Centz. glayues de Fraunceis seneschalis du pays, en .iij. bataillis, sodeignement a cheualle. Lauauntgard as Fraunceis eschueront au pount dez launces, le a bout assembler, glasserount a reys dez Engleis, qi descenduz estoient a pee, costauntz si pres qe chescun Engloys qe vousist ferrir, ferry cheuealle mort oue la launce, les Fraunceis hors

---

ᵃ aparceurent la *written over an erasure;* aparceurent la *written in left margin.*

50. And as some notable battles were omitted from the writing at the time they occurred in the narrative of this book, which had already been written, so it is [only] right that they should be described in another part. Firstly, [there was] the battle of Guitres in Gascony, where Hugh de Geneva was the war leader for the King of England, Edward the third after the Conquest, in the year of grace [1341], at the beginning of the war over his claim to France.[1] The French king's stewards in various lands had besieged the Abbey of Guîtres, which the Anglo-Gascons had fortified. Hugh came to its relief with some other Anglo-Gascon barons, about 400 men-at-arms and 800 sergeants and archers, and came before the French, who numbered more [f. 224] than a thousand men-at-arms, arrayed in the fields. The river Isle was between them, and the English were in battle array on the ford at the river. Those besieged within the English fortress made a sortie and fought with such recklessness in their attack on the enemy, that without the agreement or command of the English leaders, their sergeants crossed the river nearly up to their shoulders with scarcely any heed, and charged alongside the others with wonderfully bold spirit and initiative.[2] The French, who thought themselves to be too near to the hedges to hold them, pulled back and retreated to take to a wider field, upon which, the English who observed this started to cross the river. Seeing their lords' advance and the French retreat, the English sergeants cried with one voice and one accord, 'Here we go, here we go, they're beaten'. With that, the French made off in defeat as fast as [their] horses could go. And then a good while after this time, around twelve years, other great battles took place in Gascony – after the departure of the Duke of Lancaster who was the lieutenant of the King of England there (as was explained before), and before the arrival in that country of the king's son, the Prince of Wales – such as the battle at Limalonges, at the relief of Lusignan, when the English knight Thomas Cok was seneschal, after the duke's departure.[3] Thomas, with the Anglo-Gascon barons, had 500 billhooks; on the way [to Lusignan], 1500 French billhooks [led by] the local seneschals suddenly came up against them, mounted, in three battles. The French vanguard avoided the points of the lances, attacking at the rear, slipping so close by the ranks of the English, who were dismounted on foot, that every Englishman who wished to, struck a horse dead with his lance, the French being thrown from their saddles to the ground. The second French battle charged through the English on horseback. Many of the English were knocked down, but got up again and rallied on foot, having killed

de selles trebouchez a terre. Lautre batail secound as Fraunceis assmblerent a cheual parmy lez Engles, plusours dez Engles abatuz, releuerent et sez relierent a pe, qi plusours dez cheueaux as Fraunceis auoint mortz au passer, queux Fraunceois escheus dez cheueaux, oue lez autres lour coumpaignons primes abatuz de lour auaunt garde, alerent as cheueaux dez Englois, lenpristrent apoi touz et mounterent. Lez Engleis pristrent vn bas more de antais as genolois. Lareirgard dez Fraunceis ses aresterent deuaunt eaux, et y endemurrerent tout le iour [*f. 224v.*] a cheualle, et a la nuyt sez departerount. Lez Englois qe plus nauoint a faire, alerent a pee lez launces en lour mains .iiij. lieus longes du pays a vn forteresce Englois. Hors de quel chastelle de Lissinyan estoint auenuz maint bel fet darmes au sires de Mountferaunt, tancom capitain y estoit, apres ceo qil estoit gaine de assaute dez Engles; quel chastel fust apres traiez de lour mains par vn castelain. Et puis autrefoitz com de la iourne de seint George, au rescous de Seint Johan le Angelin, ou Johan de Cheuerstoun, cheualer Engles et seneschal de Gascoigne, oue lez barouns du pays .ix.C. homs darmes, sez combaterent od lez Fraunceis, qi .xii.C. homs darmes estoint, qe uenoint de lassege encountre eaux, descenderent a pee, sez entre assemblerent apertement, qe bon pece dura la melle. Lez Fraunceis oue graunt pain estoint descoumfitz; lez mareschallis de Neel et de Oudenam, qi cheuetains estoint de Fraunceys, y estoint prisis, et plusours dez autres mortez et prises. Qi Mareschalle de Neel fust procheignement apres tue dez Engleis en batail en la guere de Bretaigne a Mauron pres boys de Onglis, ou plusours barouns de Bretaigne murerent, vn de meruaillous iournes qaueint en la guere de Bretaigne, hors pris la iourne de Lankaderet, ou Thomas de Dagworth cheualer Engles descoumfist meruaillousement lez barouns de Bretaigne.

51. Plusour iournes y aueindrent de cest gere, dount touz ne poount estre recordez. Mais puis qe lez trewes furount prisis en Gascoigne par le Prince de Galis fitz le dit Roy Dengleter, les auaunt ditz Engles des comunes continuerent la guere, com deuaunt en party est especifiez, en diuers pays hu realme de Fraunce, qe tout ne sount lez iournes recordez linielement en le hour qils aueindrent; vncore sount a especifier, quels gentz sez coillerent par cause dez ditz trewes, qils le fesount en la querel du Roy de Nauern, qi ia estoit deliuers de prisoun du chastel de Greuequer, qy par cause susdit auoit guere as Fraunceis. Qi roy, com auaunt est plus plainement dit, destruyoit plusours pays en Fraunce, moult par force dez ditz Engles, par ou, lez

many of the Frenchmen's horses as they passed. Those Frenchmen [who had been] parted from the horses, along with the others, their companions from their vanguard who had already been knocked down, went off to the English horses, took nearly all of them and mounted. The English took to a low mud wall, [crouched] on their knees. The French rearguard halted before them, and remained there all day [f. 224v.] on horseback; and at night-time, they left. The English, having nothing else to do, went on foot, their lances in their hands, for four long leagues through the countryside to an English fortress. Many fine feats of arms were achieved by the Lord de Montferrand from this castle at Lusignan, while he was captain there, after it had been won by an English assault. The castle was later betrayed out of their hands by a certain castellan.[4] And then [there were] other occasions, such as on St George's day [23 April], at the relief of Saint-Jean d'Angély, where John de Cheverston, an English knight and seneschal of Gascony, with the barons of the country and 900 men-at-arms, fought with the French. The French had 1200 men-at-arms, who came against them from the siege, dismounted on foot, and engaged with them boldly, and the mêlée lasted a good while. The French were defeated with great difficulty; Marshals de Nesle and d'Audrehem, the French leaders, were taken there, and many others killed or taken.[5] Marshal de Nesle was killed soon afterwards by the English, in battle in the Breton war at Mauron near the wood of *Onglis*, where many Breton barons died, one of the most marvellous battles that occurred in the Breton war – apart from the battle of *Lankaderet*, where Thomas de Dagworth, an English knight, marvellously defeated the barons of Brittany.[6]

51. Many battles took place in this war, and it has not been possible for them all to be recorded. However, after the truce in Gascony had been accepted by the Prince of Wales, son of the King of England, the English commoners continued the war, as was partly related before, in various lands of the realm of France. Not all the battles have been recorded chronologically at the time they took place; still to be recorded are [those of] the men who gathered together because of the truce. This they did in the cause of the King of Navarre, who had been freed from the prison of *Greuequer* castle by this time, and who, for reasons stated before, was at war with the French.[1] As has been more fully related previously, this king devastated many regions of France,

ditz Engles recouererent plusours forteresces plusours partz en
Fraunce, raunsonerent lez pays, par paroches, auoint lez punyes, la
foitz en perde, autrefoitz en gaign. Pres de Neneuers, Johan Waldbouf
Engleis, hors du chastelle de Courueu ly Orgliouse, coumbaty sez
cync quantisme homs darmes Engloys oue Lercheprestre, qe [f. 225]
capitain estoit du pays de Nenevers, qauoit .cc. homs darmes, et lez
descoumfirent, pristrent le dit Archeprestre et plusours autres. Qi
Archeprestre fust lessez aler a large sure sa foy, et a estre loial prisoner au dit Waldbouf, qi nul temps apres ne se uoloit entreir, teint
toutdiz autre tretice oue le dit Waldebouf, qi uoloit en condicioun
enherder au roy Englois, et qil bailleroit au dit Waldebouf vn bon
forteresce qil auoit. Mais ne voloit apres aprochier a luy saunz ostages
duraunt cest tretice. Le dit[a] Waldebouf cheuaucha sure autres
enemys, iousta de guere od vn Fraunces hors du chastel de Nostre
Dame de Cuchie a le demande dez Fraunceis, qi puis
entrecoumbaterent dez espeis et coulteaux. Le dit Waldbouf le
Fraunceois le enamena prisoner. Qi Waldbouf sei assura taunt en lez
losengeous parolis du dit Archeprestre, qil se mist en assuraunce de
sa bon foy, et a sa penible request dedenz vn soun chastelle a prendre
oue ly la soup, quel chastel il luy auoit en couenaunt a bailler sure lez
condiciouns taillez. Waldbouf fust traye, et retenu illoeqes prisoner
bon pece, et apres murdry en prisoun; surmettaunt sur ly, qil voloit
auoir suppris le dit chastelle par couyne dez autres prisoners Engleis,
lez ostages qestoint mys pur le dit Archeprestre, qestoint retenuz
prisoners en meisme la gise.

Deuaunt Troyes meisme la sesoun, estoint lez Engles par lour
desaray, descoumfitz par le Count de Wadmound, qi issist de la cite,
deuaunt quel, lez ditz Engles estoient enbussez; auoint enuoiez lour
descouerours a lez barrers de la cite, ne mistrent pas sagement lour
descouerours, tanqe saunz aparceiuaunce de eaux, lez enemys
venoient chacer curreours en mylieu lour enbussement, en vn villet,
ou estoint en mesouns desparplez, pur quoi relier ne purroient, mais
chescun a sauuere soy. Les vns furount prises; Johan de Daltoun,
cheualer, et autres sez departerent bien en maner; lez plusours des
quelis Englois oue autres garnisouns sez reassemblerent hors de
Bretaigne et de Normendy et dez autres forteresces qils auoient hu
paiis, pristrent de nuyt la cite Dausoir, y en troueroint
tresgraundismes auoirs, y en demurrerent bon pece. Lez citezeins,
oue le acorde dez seignours du pays, treiterent od eaux, qils lour

---

[a]   MS: dit *repeated erroneously.*

mostly by force of the English; because of this, these English recovered many fortresses in many parts of France, held these regions to ransom, parish by parish, and fought battles, sometimes losing, othertimes winning. From the castle of Corvol l'Orgeuilleux, near to the Nivernais, the Englishman John Waldboef fought with his forty-five English men-at-arms against the Archpriest, the [f. 225] captain of the Nivernais region, who had 200 men-at-arms.[2] They defeated them, and took the Archpriest and many others. The Archpriest was allowed to go free on his good faith, that he would be a loyal prisoner to Waldboef; but at no time afterwards was he willing to enter into or hold permanently to another agreement with Waldboef. He wanted to adhere to the English king on terms, and entrusted to Waldboef a fine fortress which he had, but he was subsequently unwilling to approach him without hostages while this agreement lasted. Waldboef rode against other enemies; and outside the castle of Notre Dame de *Cuchie*, at the request of the French, he jousted in war with a Frenchman, and then they fought with sword and dagger. Waldboef took the Frenchman prisoner. Waldboef trusted so much in the deceitful words of the Archpriest, that he accepted the assurance of his good faith, and at his humble request came to have dinner with him in a certain castle of his, the castle which he had entrusted to him in covenant under the terms agreed. Waldboef was betrayed, and detained there as a prisoner for a good while, and subsequently murdered in prison. He was accused of trying to capture the castle in a plot with other English prisoners, the hostages who had been given to the Archpriest, who had been detained in the same way.

In the same season, at Troyes, the English were defeated through their own disarray, by the Count of Vaudémont, when he sortied out from the city, which the English were lying in wait before.[3] They had sent their scouts up to the city barricades, but did not position them sensibly, so that the enemy came charging into the middle of the their ambush, without the the scouts spotting them. [This was] in a village, where they were scattered about in houses, because of which they were unable to rally, but it was every man for himself. Some were captured; [but] John de Dalton, knight, and others left in good order. The majority of these Englishman reassembled along with other garrisons from Brittany and Normandy, and from other fortresses which they had in the region, and took the city of Auxerre by night. There they found very great wealth, and they remained there for a good while. With the agreement of the lords of the region, the citizens

doneroint graunt soume dargent a voider la dit cite saunz ardoir de y cel; qi sez acorderent, firent ruer a terre graunt party de la mure, et sez departerent a lour [f. 225v.] forteresces enuyroun, qe plus eseez lour semblerent qe la cite, puisqe bonement ne purroint demurreir ensemble, chescun vorroit estre meistre; pur quoy ils pristrent assuraunce del argent. Et del hour qils estoint departiz a la maner, lez gentz du pais et de la cite allouerent genz darmes dez Allemaunz et dez estraungers pur mesime largent qils auoint fet fair coiller, et leuer des comunes, pur la dit pact as ops dez ditz Englois, qi sodeignment enboterent vn graunt poair dez gentz de armes, et firent reparailler la dit cite par meisme largent, plus fort qe deuaunt, saunz rien paier as ditz Engles.

Autrefoitz .c. glayues dez Engleis descoumfirent en Bourgoun au rescous du chastel de Brien, qen mains dez Engleis estoit, vn graunt poair dez gentz darmes du paiis .v. centz homs darmes qen vn chaump espesse du bleez plusours foitz assemblerent a pee, oue lez Fraunceis a cheual.

Johan de Foderinghay hors de la vile de Crael, oue autres capitaines Engleis, assaillerent vn forteresce en vn Abbey, qe Fraunceis auoint enforcez entre la dit Crael et Cumpyn; gaignerent la pail et lez fossez oue la bas court, ceaux dedenz treterent de condicioun oue ceaux de hors a lour sauuer lez vies. Le capitain dedenz veint hors, se rendy au penoun dun dez cheueteins Engleis, de quoy, lez vns dez autres Engleis auoient enuy, debaterent pur part de sa raunsoun, en quel estrif, il fust murdry, entre lour mains. Cely a qi il estoit renduz, sen departy sodeignement bien marry, lour disoit qe bien lour encouenoit. Ceaux dedenz lez forterescez, virent qe a mureir lour coueindroit, descenderent dun couyn auale vn degrez voitez oue tiel bruyt, cry et noys de chaier dez targes et bastouns oue autre rumour, criauntz diuers escries dez cheuetains du pays, qe lez Engles qestoint demurrez enpristrent tiel tresodeyn affray, pensauntz qils estoint traiez, quoi pur la retret du dit capitain, qi sen alast en la maner en curouce quoi pur la appertice du contenaunce et couyn dez enemys, sez recoillerent descoumfitz chescun cheiez sure autres en lez parfoundes fosses del eaw; .v. ou .vi. cheualeris Englois noyerent et plusours autres gentz. Lez autres qe purroint ateindre a cheual fuerent, et ensi lez gentz de la forteresce estoint rescous, qe nestoint lez plusours fors brigauntz et gentz du comune et du couyn Jakes Bonhom.

negotiated with them, to give them a large sum of silver to leave the city without burning it. They agreed to this, rased a large part of the wall to the ground and left for their [f. 225v.] surrounding fortresses, which seemed to them preferable to the city, for they could not willingly stay together, as each one wanted to be the master; therefore they took an assurance for the silver. And as soon as they had left in this manner, the men of the region and the city hired German and foreign men-at-arms with the same silver which they had had collected, and raised from the commoners, for the use of the English, according to the agreement. Very quickly, they brought in a great force of men-at-arms, and with the same money, had the walls of the city repaired, stronger than before, without paying anything to the English.[4]

Another time, at the relief of the castle of Brienne le Château in Burgundy, which was in English hands, 100 English billhooks defeated a great force of local men-at-arms, 500 men-at-arms who they attacked on foot many times, in a field thick with corn, with the French on horseback.

From the the town of Creil, John de Fotheringhay,[5] along with other English captains, attacked a fortress in an abbey which the French had fortified between Creil and Compiègne.[6] They gained the palisade and the ditches with the lower courtyard, and those within agreed to terms with those on the outside, to save their lives. The captain came out, and surrendered to the pennon of one of the English leaders, at which certain of the other English were jealous, arguing for part of his ransom; and in the strife, he was murdered at their hands.[7] The man he had surrendered to immediately departed, very angrily, telling them it served them right. Those within the fortress, seeing that they were going to die, came down a vaulted staircase with one accord, with such an uproar, outcry and clamour of shields and cudgels crashing down, and other noises, shouting various battle-cries of the local leaders, that the English who had remained took such sudden fright – thinking that they had been betrayed, both because of the withdrawal of the captain who went away in a rage in that way, and because of the enemy's boldness of bearing and trickery – that they fell back defeated, falling over each other in the deep ditches of water. Five or six English knights drowned along with many other men. The others who were able to get on horseback fled, and thus the men of the fortress were rescued, though they were mostly no more than brigands and common men and followers of Jacques Bonhomme.[8]

Hors de Espernoun, la forteresce *[f. 226]* qe James de Pipe Engles auoit gaigne, chiualers et esquiers Engleis, Johan Griffith cheuetain, cheuaucherent de guere pres de Cherres, ou Bek dez Vileins Fraunceis oue .lxxx. homs darmes et .xl. archers, vindrent assailer .vij. homs darmes et .xij. archers Engleis, qaloignez estoint de lour coumpaigni. Lez ditz Engleis descoumfirent lez ditz Fraunceis, pristrent le dit Bek et .xx. chiualers et esquiers fraunceis, par eide de ascuns lour compaignouns qestoient aloignez, qi lour suruinderent en le hour com les enemys estoint descoumfitz. Le dit Bek estoit plusours foitz pris duraunt cest guere.

Meisme la sesoun lan de grace .Mile.CCC.lix, lez Engles auoint enforce et gaigne la vile de Saint Wallery, et la perderent par assege du Count de Saint Poel, et du Sire de Feyns, qi Conestable estoit de Fraunce en le houre, et dez seignours du paiis. Monsire Phelip de Nauere, frer du dit Roy de Nauere, qi homageres estoit du Roi Dengleter, ou .vi.Centz. glayues dez Engleis dez garnysouns Engleis, venoient de Normendy et dautre part, pur rescoure le dit Seint Wallery; qi la trouerent perduz, cheuaucherount en Vermandays, ou pres de seint Quintyn le Count de Seint Poel, oue lez seignours du dit assege, qi nestoint pas desparpliez, oue .Mile. et .v.Centz. glaiues, trois .Mile. comunes armes, vindrent adeuant lez ditz Engles, si pres, geres plus loinz dun trete dun aublastre, demurrerent tout le iour deuaunt eaux saunz coumbatre; et a vespre, lez ditz Engles sez herbiserent en vn villet pres, qi lendemain a haut hour, sez departerent vers Sassoun, ardauntz le pays saunz nul destourber dez ditz Fraunceis.

Meisme la sesoun vn coumpaigny dez Engles enforcerent la vile de Veillye en la vale de Sessoun, de ou, ils gaignerent la Vile de Pountarsy, hors de quoi com cheuaucherent a rescoure le chastel de Sassoun, ou lour coumpaignouns Allemauns estoint assys, encountrerent sodeignement .C. homs darmes Bretouns, descenderent a pee de toutz partz. Lez Bretouns estoint descoumfitz; lez Engleis plusours nawrez, ascuns dez queux Engleis sez aresterent a cheueaux, saunz rien eider a lour coumpaignouns tanqe la bosoigne fust descomfist. Lez ditz Engleis ne tindrent pas purpos de la rescous, pur quoi le dit lieu fust rendu.

Plusours foitz aueint duraunt cest guere, qe le Fraunceis vindrent adeuaunt des Englois, qe sentredeparterent saunz coumbatre. Vn foitz en Auverne pres Nostre Dame de Puy, lez Fraunceis estoient *[f. 226v.]* .xx.Mile. coumbatauntz, dount .iiij.Mile. estoint cheualers et esquiers, Thomas de la Marche cheuetain, vindrent deuaunt

From Épernon, the fortress [f. 226] which the Englishman James de Pipe had won,[9] some English knights and squires, under their leader John Griffith, rode in war near to Chevreuse; here, the Frenchman the Bègue de Villaines, with eighty men-at-arms and forty archers, came up to attack seven English men-at-arms and twelve archers, who had been separated from their company. The English defeated the French, and took the Bègue and twenty French knights and squires, with the help of some of their companions who had become separated, who arrived just at the time when the enemy were defeated. The Bègue was taken many times during this war.[10]

In the same season in the year of Grace 1359, the English stormed and won the town of Saint-Valéry, and lost it by siege to the Count de Saint-Pol, and the lord of Fiennes (who was Constable of France at the time), and the local lords.[11] Sir Philip de Navarre, brother of the King of Navarre, who was a liegeman of the King of England, came to relieve Saint-Valéry with 600 English billmen from English garrisons in Normandy and elsewhere. Discovering it had been lost, they raided in the Vermandois, where near to Saint-Quentin, the Count de Saint-Pol came up against the English, along with the lords from the siege, who had not dispersed, with 1500 billmen and 3000 armed commoners. They came very near, scarcely further than a crossbow-shot, staying before them all of the day without fighting; and at eventide, the English lodged in a nearby village. The next day when the sun was high, they left for Soissons, burning the region without any hindrance from the French.

In the same season, a company of English fortified the town of Vailly in the Soissons valley, from where they gained the town of Pont-Arcy; as they rode out from there to relieve the castle of Sisonne, where their German companions were besieged, they unexpectedly encountered 100 Breton men-at-arms, and both sides dismounted on foot. The Bretons were defeated; [but] many of the English were wounded, and some of the English stayed on horseback, without doing anything to help their companions until the affair was brought to an end. The English did not stick to their aim of relieving [Sisonne], because of which the place was surrendered.[12]

Many times during this war, it happened that the French came up against the English, and they broke off from each other without fighting. One time in Auvergne, near Nôtre-Dame-de-Puy, the French, with [f. 226v.] 20,000 combatants, of whom 4000 were knights and squires, led by Thomas de la Marche, came up against 900 English billhooks, led by Hugh de Calveley, and broke off without

.ix.Centz. glaiues Engleis, Hugh de Caluerley cheuetain, sez departerent saunz coumbatre, et lendemain les fuerent; et lour envindrent autrefoitz adeuaunt eaux si pres, qe homs enruerent lez peres, sez endeparterent autre saunz auoir afair ensemble, fors en skirmuche.

Apres cest hour procheignement pur ceo qe lez counsaillis dez ditz Roys Dengleter et de Nauarre ne puroint acorder en tretez, le dit Roy de Nauarre estoit peise ou le Duk de Normendy, qi dit fust Daufyn de Vien, et fitz le Roy Johan de Fraunce, qen absence de soun pier, fust dit regent du paiis; et molt par cause de rescoure la Royne Blaunche, la sore du dit roi de Nauarre, qassegez estoit du dit Daufyn en Millein, la quel auoit este femme le Roy Phelip de Fraunce soun uncle; et auxi pur reauoir sez forteresces qe ly estoient detenuz, et par chaunge de auoir plus eises, tout auoint ils autrefoitz este acordez sure condicioun adeuaunt Parys, entreiurez sure le corps dieu, et rount, par le dit regent, com disoit li dit roys. Par cause de quel acorde, Poisy sure Seyn, qenforce estoit et tenu dez Engleis, et plousours autres forteresces estoint voidez et guerpis dez Engles plousours partz hu reame de Fraunce. Ja le meinz, le dit Roy de Nauarre nauoit geris greue as Engleis tout le meisme temps de cel sesoun suaunt. Pur cause de meisme lacord, Thomas de Holand cheualer, qe en Normendy estoit depar le Roy Dengleter, fist enforcer vn bon forteresce al eglise de Barflu, et endemurra illoeqes pur constreindre Costentyn. Qi Thomas morust hu paijs apres; lieutenaunt le Roy Dengleter de terres conquis, *b*estoit Count de Kent, del heritage sa femme.

Qi Roi de Nauarre auoit vn poy deuaunt eidez a destruyer vn graunt riot et couyn dez vileins comunes, qe leuez estoint oue Jakes Bonhom, de qy ils auoint fet lour cheuetain pur auoir guerroie lez gentils homs, com firent, com plus pleinement est deuaunt especifie. Renaud de Gulioun cheualer Fraunceis et capitain de Parys, fust descoumfist et pris pres de Staumpes, meisme la seisoun par lez Engleis, Gilbert de Rodom lour cheuetain, qi morust a la iourne. Lez Engleis nestoint fors .Liij. glaiues .Lxxx. archiers, lez Fraunceis estoint .vij. centz homs darmes et .iiij. centz brigaunz et archers armez. Qi Renaud de Gulion se disoit estre deliuers, deuaunt qil auoit par paie sa raunsoun, pur ceo qe soun *[f. 227]* gardein, vn faus Englois, sen ala oue li, pur qoi le dit Renaud estoit apelle de batail; li quel Renaud estoit autrefoitz pris prisoner pres de Paiters, ou estoit capitain en le

fighting; and in the morning they fled. And another time they came up so near against them, that men were throwing stones; but they broke off from each other without having any business together, except for skirmishing.[13]

Soon after this time, as the councils of the kings of England and Navarre were unable to reach agreement in negotiations, the King of Navarre was reconciled with the Duke of Normandy, who was called the Dauphin of Vienne, and was the son of King John of France, and who, in the absence of his father, was called regent of the country. [This was] mostly for the sake of the relief of Queen Blanche, the King of Navarre's sister, who was besieged by the Dauphin in Melun (she had been the wife of his uncle King Philip of France); and also to get back his fortresses that had been withheld from him, and to have more rest for a change.[14] All of this had been agreed on terms on another occasion at Paris, and mutually sworn on the body of God, and broken, by the regent, or so said the King [of Navarre]. Because of this agreement, Poissy-sur-Seine, which had been fortified and held by the English, and many other fortresses were evacuated and abandoned by the English, in many parts of the realm of France. Nevertheless, the King of Navarre did not do much harm to the English for all of the following season. Because of this same agreement, Thomas de Holland, knight, who was in Normandy for the King of England, had a fine fortress constructed at the church of Barfleur, and stayed there to control the Cotentin. This Thomas died afterwards in that country; the King of England's lieutenant in the conquered lands, he was Earl of Kent by his wife's inheritance.[15]

A little before, the King of Navarre had helped to put down a great rebellion and conspiracy by the common villeins, who had risen with Jacques Bonhomme, who they had made their leader to wage war on the noblemen, as they did, as is more fully described above.[16] Renaud de Gulioun, a French knight and captain of Paris, was defeated and taken in the same season near Étampes by the English, led by Gilbert de Roddam, who was killed in the battle.[17] The English had no more than fifty-three billmen and eighty archers, the French had 700 men-at-arms and 400 brigands[18] and armoured archers. This Renaud de Gulioun declared himself to be freed, before he had paid his ransom, because his [f. 227] warder, a false Englishman, went off with him; because of this, Renaud was challenged to a duel. On another occasion, this Renaud was taken prisoner near Poitiers, where he was

hour, la sesoun vn poy deuaunt la batail del dit lieu, par un seruaunt
de Gascoigne, qi oue .xxx. compaignouns descoumfirent .CC. homs
darmes Fraunceis au pris du dit Renaud.

52. Meisme lan del incarnacioun .Mile.CCC.lix., lauaunt dit Roi
Edward Dengleter le tierce puis la Conquest, od toutez lez grauntz de
soun realme, se adressa hors Dengleter; ses messagers reuenuz del
Apostoil, et fust a Sandwiche sure soun passage deuers sa guere de
Fraunce, a la Natiuite de nostre dame, qi durement fust tarie pur
defaut des niefes, par qoi ne purra aryuer a vn foitz, ne ou il auoit
enpense, pur qoi departi le passage, enuoia le Duk de Lancastre oue
sa retenu a Calais, pur hors treir de la vile le Markeis de Mise, oue
tout plein des Allemaunz qi illoeqes estoint venuz en eide du dit Roi;
qi ceo fist, oue queux, il se trei as chaumps cheuaucherent outre leau
de Soumme, assaillerent la vile du Dray, ou ils passerent lez fossez
parmy leau as reis dez mures, outre lours espaulis, en graunt defoul
de eaux, faillerent du pris de la dit vile, cheualers de lours mortz a
lassaute; sez reenalerent deuers Calays, pur ent sauoir du uenu du dit
roi. Le Count de la Marche, qi passe estoit la mere .vi. iours deuaunt le
dit roi, fist vn cheuauche outre Boloyne, ardy Lestapelis et repaira. Le
roi arriue a Calais le Lundy procheine deuaunt la Toucz Seintz, ou
demurra .viij. iours; departi soun host en .iij., vn party reteint oue soi,
vn autre party bailla a soun fitz eisne, le Prince de Galis, le tierce
party deuisast au Duk de Lancastre. Sen departi de Calays le Lundy
deuaunt la Seint Martin, ou le dit Duk de Lancastre li encountra le
Dimange, qi .v. simains, party en meschief de pain et de vin, auoit iu
as chaumps. Les .iij. hostes alerent diuers chemins. Le dit roi tient le
chemyn de Seint Thomers, pres de Arraz et delee Cambresi, par
Terrages, par Loignes, par Chaumpein, adeuaunt de Reyns. Le Prince
le fitz du dit roi, tient le chemyn de Monstrol, de Hedyn par Pountiue
et Pikardy, outre leau de Soumme, par Neel, par Haan, en Vermendas,
pres de ou, Baudewyn Daukyn, cheualer, meistre dez arblasteris de
Fraunce, fust pris en le hour, et autres cheualers Fraunceis, dez gentz
du retenu le Prince, com surecour voroit de nuyt lez loeges le Count
de Stafford, qi bien se defendy.

Entour quel hour, le viscount de Benoge, qi dit estoit Capitain de
Busche, Gascoyn Englois, vient hors de soun pays, de garnisoun en
garnisoun Englois, passa la ryuer de Seyn, par conduyt le Roi
[f. 227v.] de Nauarre, vient a Crael, a donqes tenuz dez Englois, hors
de quel vile, il eschalla de nuyt le chastel de Clermont en Beauuaisin;
quel vile de Crael, Johan de Foderinghay cheualer Englois auoit du

captain at the time, in the season a little before the battle at that place, by a Gascon sergeant with thirty companions, who defeated two hundred French men-at-arms when Renaud was taken.

52. In the same year of the incarnation, 1359, King Edward of England the third after the Conquest made his way out of England with all the magnates of his realm. His messengers had returned from the Pope, and, on the Nativity of Our Lady [8 September],[1] he was at Sandwich for his crossing to his war in France, which was greatly delayed by the lack of ships. Because of this, it was not possible to land all at one time, nor where he had planned, and for this reason, the crossing was divided up. The Duke of Lancaster was sent with his retinue to Calais, to lead the Margrave of Meissen away from the town, along with the many Germans who had come there to help the king.[2] He did this, and took to the fields with them, riding across the river Somme and attacking the town of Bray-sur-Somme, where they crossed the ditches through water up to their shoulders, to the base of the walls; to their great shame they failed to take the town, [some of] their knights [being] killed in the assault. They went away back towards Calais, to find out about the arrival of the king.[3] The Earl of March, who had crossed the sea six days before the king, made a *chevauchée* beyond Boulogne, burned Étaples and returned. The king landed at Calais on the Monday next before All Saints [28 October], remaining there for eight days. His army was divided into three parts; one part he kept with him, another part he put in the charge of his eldest son, the Prince of Wales, the third part he allocated to the Duke of Lancaster. He departed from Calais on the Monday before Saint Martin [4 November], when the Duke of Lancaster had met up him, on the Sunday, having been in the field for five weeks, sometimes in want of bread and wine.[4] The three armies went by different roads. The king took the road to St Omer, near to Arras and beside the Cambrésis, through the Thiérache, through the Laonnois, through Champagne, up to Reims. The prince, the king's son, took the road to Montreuil, to Hesdin, through Ponthieu and Picardy, across the river Somme, through Nesle, and Ham in the Vermandois. Near there, Baldwin d'Annequin, knight, master of the French crossbowmen, was taken at this time by men of the prince's retinue, along with other French knights, as they sought one night to overrun the lodgings of the Earl of Stafford, who defended himself well.[5]

At about that time, the Viscount of Benauges, an Anglo-Gascon called the Captal de Buch, came out of his country, [going] from one

baille du Roi de Nauarre, et sure condicioun iure a la susrendre au monestement du dit roy, qi souent auoit lez somouns, qi ne le uoloit faire, saunce vn graunt soume dargent, qy disoit qe le dit roy li deuoit, quel argent il prist dez Fraunceis en allouaunce du dit dett en lour bailla la dit vile. Ly dit Johan de Foderinghay enferma en le hour vn autre bon forteresce au Pount de Seynt Menseus sure la ryuer de Ese, ou il endemurra.

Le prince tient soun auaunt dit chemyn par Seint Quyntin, et par Retieris, ou lez enemys meismes arderoint lour vile pur destourber lour passage, lez gentz de qi conquistrent passage au Chastel Purcien, ou passa par Chaumpain, aprocha lost soun pier adeuaunt de Reyns. Le Duk de Lancastre tient le chemyn entre le roi et soun fitz, aprocherent ensemble le trois hostes par deuaunt de Reyns, iesoint tout enuiroun la cite en villetes vn moys, en temps de Noel. Hors de lost du dit prince, fust la vile de Curmousse eschale, et le chastel gaigne, la toure rue a terre par myne, par lez gentz du prince, Bartholomeu de Burghersche cheuetein. En lost du Duk de Lancastre y auoit ioustes de guere par coueunaunt taille, a demaund dez Fraunceis hors de Reyns, ou fust mort vn Fraunceis, et autres dieus naufrez de fere de glaiue. Hors del ost le roy, le Duk de Lancastre, lez Countis de Richemound et de la Marche, gaignerent dieus viles marches enforcez, Otry et Semay, sure leau de Ayne et la marche de Lorrein. Seignours et cheualers hors del ost le dit roy, firent de Reyns vn cheuauche pres de Parys; ses enbusserent et enuoierent lours discourreours pres lez portes de la cite, firent romour dedens lez suburbes, qe countenaunce ne firent ceaux dedenz de isser de la cite. Lez routis dez Engles furrount esparpliez en diuers lieus, ceaux qauoint demurrez de lour testez deuaunt la venu du roy, estoint en diuersis routis. Vn rout estoit apelle la Graunt Coumpaigny, qe tout lan auoint iu as champes en Burgoin, en Brie, en Chaumpein, et en Dairres,[a] et ou meilliours trouerent lez viures, quel Graunt Coumpaigni auoient eschallez la cite de Chalouns en Chaumpein de nuyt, mais ceaux de la dit Cite sez relierent en mylieu de lour vile a pount de la ryuer de Mairel, qe court parmy la cite, et lez tindrent de force hors du meilliour de la cite; pur qoi lour couenoit departir, voiderent sodeinement, qe plus ne purroit demurreir; quel compaigny sez desparplerent tost apres [f. 228] la venu du dit roi, et lour quistrent rescet. Autres routes estoient dez Englois, ascuns dez

[a]   r. Bairres?

English garrison to another; he crossed the river Seine, under safe conduct of the king [f. 227v.] of Navarre, and came to Creil, then held by the English, from which town, he took the castle of Clermont-en-Beauvaisis by escalade at night.[6] The English knight John de Fotheringhay had the town of Creil by the grant of the King of Navarre, and on sworn condition to surrender it at that king's command; he had frequently received such orders, but did not wish to do so, without a large sum of money, which, he said, the king owed him; this money he accepted from the French in allowance for the debt, and gave them custody of the town. Straightaway, John de Fotheringhay strengthened another good fortress at Pont-Sainte-Maxence on the river Oise, where he stayed.[7]

The prince took his road by Saint-Quentin, and by Rethel, where the enemy themselves burned their town to disrupt [his] crossing.[8] His men forced a crossing at Château-Porcien, from where they crossed through Champagne, and approached his father's army at Reims. The Duke of Lancaster took the road between the king and his son; the three armies came up together in front of Reims, and stayed in villages all around the city for a month, at Christmas time. The town of Cormicy was taken by escalade, and the castle was won, the tower brought to the ground by a mine, by the prince's men, coming from the prince's army, led by Bartholomew Burghersh.[9] There were jousts of war by indentured agreement in the Duke of Lancaster's army, at the request of the French from Reims, in which one of the French was killed, and another two wounded by blows from a bilhook. Coming from the king's army, the Duke of Lancaster, and the Earls of Richmond and March, won two fortified market towns, Autry and Cernay-en-Dormois, on the river Aisne and in the march of Lorraine.[10] Lords and knights from the king's army made a chevauchée from Reims almost to Paris. They hid themselves and sent their outriders close to the gates of the city, causing uproar in the suburbs, so that those within would not countenance sortieing out from the city. There were bands of the English scattered in various places; they had stayed on their own authority before the arrival of the king, in various bands. One band was called the Great Company, and they had remained in the field all year, in Burgundy, Brie, Champagne, and [Bar],[11] and wherever they could best find a living. The Great Company had scaled the walls of the city of Châlons in Champagne at night, but [the men] of the city rallied in the middle of their town at the bridge over the river Marne, which runs through the city, and held them out of the best [part] of the city by force. Therefore

queux eschallerount la vile de Attinye en Chaumpain en le hour du
venu du dit roi deuaunt Reyns. Le dit Roy de Engleter se delogea
depars adeuaunt de Reins, se trey pardeuers Chalouns, ou il auoit
tretice oue ceaux de Baires, lez queux faillerent, le roy alloigna lour
paiis.

James de Audeley, cheualer Englois, prist dassaut la forteresce de
Chanen, en la vale de Saxsoun sure Bretouns, Huwen Trevidige
capitein. Le dit James vient de soun chastel de Ferte en Bry, al host du
dit Prince pres de Chalouns, en compaigne de le Capitain de Busche,
qe venoit de Cleremount.

Le dit roy fist reparailler pount outre la riuer de Mairel, et outre
autres grandismes riuers, se trey pres de Troies, de ou le Markiz de
Mice et le Count de Nidow et autres seignours Dalmaigns, qi oue le
roi estoint venuz, sez departerent vers lour pays, en partie pur
destresce dez viures, et dout de quaresme aprochaunt, as queux estoit
fait duz allouaunce de lour costagez. Le roy passa la ryuer de Seyn
pres de Merrz, tient soun chemyn pres de Ceins et par Pounteny, et en
Burgoin. Soun fitz le Prince li suyst, et le Duk de Lancastre auxi; mais
pur defaute de foirre as cheueaux, soun dit fitz genchi la voy soun
pier, se logea a Eggliny pres de Auser, ou lost le dit prince fust plus
damagez dez enemys, qe nul autre part deuaunt de tout cel veage, ou
ascuns de sez cheualers et esquiers furount mortz de nuyt en lour
herbigages et lez vadletez forraiers prises as chaumps, qe deuaunt
toutez <autres>[b] le paiis lour estoit abaundounez, qe apain ne vierent
hom de guer hors de forteresces.

Pres de Regentz, vn forteresce qe lez Englois tenoient ioust Ausoir,
.v. esquiers Englois, ascuns del ost le dit Prince, qi desarmez estoient
fors lour bacynetz et escuez, qi nauoint qe vn soul haubergeon, et .iij.
archiers, estoient en vn molyn pur moldre bleez; lour vindrent
surecour .L. homs darmes, la route et penoun le sires de Hanget, lez
queux .v. descoumfirent lez .L., enpristrent .xi., pur quoi lez Fraunceis
meismes dez autres garnisouns le disoient la iourne de .L. countre .v.
en mokerie.

Le dit roy demurra a Golion en Burgoun, pres de Mountreal, pur
treitez du Duche de Burgoun, ou Roger de Mortimer, Count de la
Marche, et Marschal del host et le plus secre du dit Roy, se lessa
morir de feuir, le .xx.iiij. iour de Feuerer. Trewes de .iij. aunz sez
pristrent de Burgoin, rendaunt au .iij. termes au dit Roi Dengleter,

---

[b] MS: autres *erased;* parties *added in right margin, in a 15thc. hand.*

they were obliged to depart, leaving suddenly, for they could not stay any longer. The company disbanded soon after [f. 228] the king's arrival, and they sought for refuge. There were other bands of Englishmen, some of whom took the town of Attigny in Champagne by escalade at the time of the king's arrival before Reims.[12] The King of England broke camp from before Reims, and took himself to Châlons, where he had negotiations with [the men] of Bar; when these finished, the king left their country.[13]

James de Audley, an English knight, stormed the fortress of Chancu in the vale of Saxoun, under the Bretouns, Hugh Trevidige their captain. James came to the prince's army near to Châlons, from his castle of Ferté-sous-Jouarre in Brie, in the company of the Captal de Buch, who came from Clermont.

The king had the bridge across the river Marne repaired, and [bridges] across other great rivers, and took himself near to Troyes, where the Margrave of Meissen and the Count of Nidau, and other German lords who had come with the king, departed for their own country, in part because of the lack of supplies, and from respect for the approach of Lent. Due allowance was made to them for their expenses. The king crossed the river Seine near to Méry-sur-Seine, and took his road near to Sens and by Pontigny, and into Burgundy. His son, the prince, followed him, and the Duke of Lancaster as well; but for lack of fodder for the horses, his son turned from his father's route and encamped at Egleny near to Auxerre. Here the prince's army was more harmed by the enemy than in any other part of the whole expedition up to then. Some of his knights and esquires were killed at night in their lodgings, and foraying valets were taken in the field, where before every [part] of the country had been abandoned, so that they saw scarcely any fighting men outside of fortresses.[14]

Near to Regennes, a fortress held by the English, next to Auxerre, five English squires from the prince's army – who were unarmed except for their helmets and shields, having but a single mail coat – and three archers, were in a mill to grind some corn. Fifty men-at-arms came to attack them, the retinue and pennon of the lords of Hangest.[15] These five defeated the fifty, capturing eleven of them, and so the French from other garrisons themselves called it the Combat of Fifty against Five, in mockery.[16]

The king stayed at Guillon in Burgundy, near to Montréal, for negotiations with the Duchy of Burgundy, where Roger de Mortimer, Earl of March, and Marshal of the army, and the king's closest adviser, happened to die of fever, on 24 February.[17] A three year truce

.dieus.Centz.Mile. floreins, motouns, le florin a .iiij. s. desterlinges. La vile de Flaueny en Burgoun [f. 228v.] fort et bien ferme, qe pris estoit par Arlestoun Englois, fu rebaillez dez mains Nichol de Dagworth, pur ceo qe suppris estoit deinz le hour du comencement du tretice dez ditez trewes.

Pres de quel vile de Flaueny, le dit Dagworth auoit a faire la sesoun passez se treszisme dez Englois, countre .lxvi. glaiues Fraunceis. Lez Englois auoint pris vn estroit reu au bout de vn villet, fist treire charettes outre la voi, deuaunt et dereir, isserent a lour pleisir de lour forteresces, naufrerent, tuerent et pristrent dez Fraunceis. Norman Lesselyn, qi hors Descoce uenoit en eide dez Fraunceis, il fust pris, lez autres descoumfitz.

Meisme le hour Willam de Aldeburgh, Capitain de Honyflu en Normandy, fust pris dez Fraunceis a vn issu et sez gentz descomfitz. Thomas Fog, cheualere Englois, qi pres fust a vn soun forteresce, oy de la iourne, se mist dedeinz la dit Honyflu; la troua desgarny des vitaillis, cheuaucha od autres garnisouns Englois enuyroun, forria le pays pur vitailler la dit vile, encountrerent sodeignement .ij.Centz. et .l. homs darmes .ij.Centz. archiers et arblasters Fraunceis, qi en agait dez Englois furount assemblez, monsire Louys Darcourt et Baudren de la Huse cheuetains dez Fraunceois. Lez Englois estoient .xl. homs darmes, et centz archiers, auoint forteresces de hay; descenderent a pee de tout part, assemblerent apertement, lez Fraunceis furount descoumfitz, lez dieus cheuetains prises et od eaux plusours cheualers et esquieris et plusours mortz a la melle. Lowis Darcourt fust procheignement deliuers, par meismes lez Englois qi li prist<ent^c>, ly deueint Fraunceis. A Fregeuil sure la marche de Beauxs, vn forteresce Englois, vn chiualer Fraunceois, qauoit a noun le cheualer blaunche, demaunda du Conestable du dit lieu, batail personel de dieus Englois countre .ij. Fraunceis. La batail ottroie au lieu acorde, le cheualer oue soun esquier furrount descoumfistz par lez .ij. Englois, qi armez estoient tout vermail, et amenez prisoners ens susdit forteresce Englois.

Entour quel hour, Johan de Neuil chiualer Englois oue .xiij. glaiues descoumfist pres de Staumpes .L. homs darmes Fraunceis, de quels furount prises plusours. Outre le Heere en Berry, Gascoignes et

---

^c *There is an erasure and a short space in the MS at this point;* qi ane *is supplied in the right margin, in a 14thc. hand. Note also that the MS text reads* … prist<ent> ly deueint fraunceis a Fregeuil sure la marche de Beauxs … *without any punctuation, whereas the sense clearly requires a new sentence at* a Fregeuil.

with Burgundy was agreed, rendering to the King of England 200,000 *florins au moutons* over three terms, the florin at four shillings sterling.[18] The strong and well-fortified town of Flavigny-sur-Ozerain in Burgundy, *[f. 228v.]* which had been taken by the Englishman Harleston, was taken back from the hands of Nicholas Dagworth, because he was taken by surprise at the time of the beginning of the negotiations for the truce.[19]

In the past season, the same Dagworth had had some business near to this town of Flavigny, with his thirteen English against sixty-six French billmen. The English had seized a narrow street at the end of a village, and had had carts dragged across the road, before and behind; and they sortied out from their fortress at their pleasure, wounding, killing and taking the French. Norman Leslie, who had come from Scotland to the aid of the French, was taken, the others were beaten off.[20]

At the same time, William de Aldeburgh, captain of Honfleur in Normandy, was taken by the French in a sortie and his men defeated. Having heard of this battle, the English knight Thomas Fogg, who was nearby in one of his fortresses, took himself into Honfleur.[21] Finding it devoid of supplies, he rode out with other neighbouring English garrisons, foraging the country to supply the town. They suddenly encountered 250 French men-at-arms and 200 archers and crossbowmen, who had been assembled to guard against the English; Sir Lewis de Harcourt and Baudrain de la Heuse were the French leaders. The English, with sixty men-at-arms and a hundred archers, had the protection of a hedge; both sides dismounted on foot, and attacked boldly. The French were defeated, the two leaders were taken and many knights and squires with them, and many were killed in the mêlée.[22] Lewis de Harcourt was freed soon afterwards, by the same Englishmen who took him, who went over to the French. At Fresnay, an English fortress on the march of Beauce, a French knight, who took the name 'The White Knight', requested the constable of the place for a personal combat of two English against two French. The combat was granted at the place agreed, and the knight, with his squire, was defeated by the two English, who were dressed all in arms of vermilion; and they were taken into the foresaid English fortress as prisoners.[23]

At around that time, the English knight John de Neville, with thirteen billmen, defeated fifty French men-at-arms near Étampes, many of whom were taken.[24] Across the Cher in Berry, Gascons and English

Englois du garnisoun de Daubeny furent vn descoumfiture, dount plusours demurrerent prisouneris dez Fraunceis.

En quel temps, cheualers Fraunceis, Normaunz et Pikardz, oue autres comunes, as costages dez bons viles de Fraunce .iij.Mile. combatauntz firent vn arme en Engleter, en countenaunce a y demoreir en maner pur auoir retreit le dit Roy Dengleter hors de Fraunce, pur rescoure sa terre, lez queux Fraunceis arriuerent pres Wynchelse, le dymaunge en my qarresme [f. 229] lan susdit, y endemurrerent en la dit vile, vn iour et vn nuyt, a lour departir la arderent; et au retreir en lour niefs, perderent dieus niefs, qe secchez estoint a terre, enuyroun .iij. centz homs par comunes qe lour surcurrerent.

Pres de Parys Robert Lescot cheualer de la parti Englois fust pris et sez gentz descomfitz par lez Fraunceis, et ses forteresces perdu en le houre, quel il auoit enferme. Le prince de Galis, fitz du dit Roy de Engleter, com tient soun chemyn parmy Gastinoys, .v. cheualeris du pays oue .lx. homs darmes, et centz autres gentz du comunes, auoint de nouel enforce vn fort bastide adeuaunt de Tournelis, vn forteresce qe les Englois tenoient; deuaunt queux cheualeris, le dit prince se mist sodeignement tot enuiroun, se logea as chaumps hu boys, fist adresser engins et assautz, pur quoi les ditz cheualeris, monsire Jakes Degreuille et Hagenay de Bouille, oue lez autres toucz, sez renderent de tout au dit prince. Le dit Roi Dengleter, venaunt de Burgoun, perdy de soun ost .ij. cheualers ou .iiij. Almaunz, qi tuez estoint de nuyt en lours loeges, par Jwe de Vepount cheualer Fraunceois et sa coumpaigny. Et com le dit roi passa parmy Beaux, pres de Turry, le chastel se prist a ardre par fieu de eaux meismes de fortune, pur quoi ceaux dedenz en saillerount lez plusours, sez misterent en la grace du dit roi. Le chastelain tient la dungeoun .ij. iours, et puis se rendy au dit roi, qi fesoit abatre lez mures du dit chastel. Meisme la sesoun lez Englois du garnisoun de Nogent en Bry, .xxx. glayues, descoumfirent sure la ryuer de Marel cent homs darmes dez Fraunceis du garnisoun de Terry, et empristrent .lx.

Entour le Nowel deuaunt, James de Pipe cheualer Englois, fust suppris en la tour de Espernoun, quel il auoit dez Fraunceis gaigne. Ne fist pas mettre bon gayt, taunt se assura du force et hautesce de le dungeoun, et ou il auoit fait estopper vn fenestre bas, par couyn dun masoun Fraunceois qi la enmora faintement fust la forteresce perdu, parmy la dit fenestre, et le dit James pris en soun lite, et Thomas de Beaumound cheualer auxi, qi venoit la nuyt pur herbiser oue ly, com venoit dun pays en autre, sure conduyt; toucz dieus estoient et lour

from the garrison of Aubigny suffered a defeat, many of them remaining as prisoners of the French.

At that time, French, Norman and Picard knights, along with other commoners, 3000 combatants [in all], made an armed raid on England, paid for by the good towns of France, making semblance of staying there in order to get the King of England to withdraw from France, to rescue his own land. These French landed at Winchelsea, the Sunday in mid-Lent [f. 229] of the year aforesaid.[25] They remained there in the town for a day and a night, and burned it on their departure; as they withdrew to their ships, they lost two ships which were beached on dry land, and around 300 men, to the commoners who overran them.

Robert Scot, a knight of the English party, was taken by the French near Paris, and his men defeated; and at the same time the fortresses which he had fortified were lost.[26] As the Prince of Wales, the King of England's son, took his road through the Gâtinais,[27] five knights of the country with forty men-at-arms, and a hundred other men from the commoners, had fortified from new a strong *bastide* before Fournelis,[28] a fortress which the English had held. The prince came suddenly and surrounded these knights, set up camp in the fields in the woods, and had siege engines and storming-parties made ready; because of this the knights, Sir Jacques de Greville and Hageny de Bouille, along with all the others, gave themselves up unconditionally to the prince. Coming up from Burgundy, the King of England lost two or three German knights from his army, who were killed at night in their lodgings, by the French knight Ives de Vipont and his company. And when the king passed through Beauce, near to Toury, the castle [there] was accidentally set alight by those within it, because of which, most of them rushed out and put themselves at the king's grace; the castellan held the great tower for two days, and then surrendered to the king, who had the castles' walls knocked down.[29] In the same season, on the river Marne, 30 English billmen from the garrison of Nogent in Brie defeated 100 French men-at-arms of the garrison of Saint-Thierry, and took sixty.

Around the previous Christmas, the English knight James de Pipe was surprised in the tower of Épernon, which he had won from the French.[30] So much did he trust in the strength and height of the great tower that he did not have a proper watch organised; he had had a low-level window blocked up there, and due to the deceit of a French mason, who walled it up falsely, the fortress was lost because of this window. James was taken in his bed, and Thomas de Beaumont,

biens soutz conduyt du regent fitz le roy. Le dit James par cause qil
nauoit my parpaie sa raunsoun de lautrefoitz qe il estoit prisoner la
sesoun passe, com pris estoit pres de Graunsoures, entre ly et Otis de
Holand cheualer Englois, com uenoint de Eueruse du Roi de Nauern,
ou le dit Otis estoit naufrez dount morust, de quel primer pris, le
corps du dit James estoit deliuers hors dez mains dez enemys par lez
Engles, sez bienuoillauntz [f. 229v.] qi demurrerent en garnisoun hu
pays, qauoint espiez qil estoit acoustomez vne certain hour du iour
daler abatre hors du chastel de Dauneuyle ou fust demurraunt, sez
enbusserent pres, ly trouerent au point, et ly amenerent et ly disoint
rescous, ceaux qi ly auoint pris et en garde, as queux il estoit prisoner,
disoint qe cest rescous nestoit pas couenable, mes encountre sa
fiaunce, depuis qe il lour auoit assure de tenir loial prisoun, saunz
fraud, collusioun, ou mal engine, et ly suremistrent, et ly pursuerent
apertement, et luy disoient qe a sa couyne, informatioun, procurement, maundement et deuise, lez ditz Engles auoint fait cel agait
countre couenaunt de loial cheualerie; pur qoi apres acorderent dun
soume de raunsoun, la quel il auoit graunt purueu, et troue oue ly en
la dit toure.

Meisme la sesoun entour la Chaundelour, Robert Herle cheualer
Engles, qi gardein estoit de Bretaigne depar le Roy de Engleter, fust as
chaumpes countre lez Bretouns Gallows pres de Dowle, ou y auoit vn
ryuer entre ly et sez enemys; et com lez Engles aualerent, quidaunt de
auoir troue pount, qestoit round et cretyne de eau, Robert de Knollis
cheualer Engles, qi del autre part oue sa route, uenoit hors de
Bretaigne au maundement du dit gardein de sez forteresces, estoit
descouerour dez soens, ferry trestestousement cheual dez esperouns
soi septisme dez coumpaignouns, saunz scieu dez autres dez soens,
quidaunt pur la aualer qil vist dez Engles, qe le dit gardein fust la
ryuer passe. Si fust abatuz et pris dez enemys, mais en le houre fust
rescous dez soens qi uenoient apres, qe aragiez estoint del houre qils
aparceurent le meschief de lour cheuetain, qe oue lour apert
abaundone assembler, descoumfirent lez enemys, rescuerent lour
meistre.

[d]Lez auentures touz darmes qe auindrent a lez Engles toutz partz
duraunt cest guere, pur diuersite de els, ne rementif pas cest cronicle,

---

[d]   *Hand drawn in central margin, pointing to 'Lez auentures'.*

knight, as well, who had come to lodge with him for the night, as he came from one country to another, on a safe-conduct; both of them, and their goods, were under the safe-conduct of the regent, the king's son. James had not made full payment of his ransom from the other time he was prisoner, in the previous season, when he was taken near *Graunsoures*, along with the English knight Otes de Holland, as they came from the King of Navarre at Évreux; Otes was wounded, from which he died. As regards this first capture, James was freed from the hands of the enemy by the English, his well-wishers, [*f. 229v.*] who were staying in garrisons in the region. They had observed that at a particular time of the day, he was accustomed to wander out from the castle of *Auneuyle* where he was staying, to pass the time; they hid themselves nearby, found him at the right place, and led him off and declared him rescued. Those who had taken him and who had him under guard, whose prisoner he was, declared that this rescue was not valid, but contrary to his good faith, since he had assured them he would loyally keep to prison, without fraud, collusion, or deception. They accused him, and charged him publicly, claiming to him that it was at his instigation, information, procurement, orders and planning, that the English had carried out this ambush contrary to the code of loyal chivalry. Because of this, they afterwards agreed a ransom sum, for which he had [made] ample provision, and which was found with him in the tower.[31]

In the same season, at around Candlemas [2 February], the English knight Robert Herle, who was keeper of Brittany for the King of England, was in the field against the Welsh Bretons near Dol.[32] Here there was a river between him and his enemys; but when the English moved down, thinking they had found a bridge, though it was broken and flooded with water, the English knight Robert de Knollys, who was on the other side with his band (having come out of Brittany from his fortresses at the keeper's command), spotted the men and spurred on his horse in a very headstrong fashion with seven of his companions, without the knowledge of his other men – for having seen the English moving down, he thought that the keeper had crossed the river. He was knocked down and taken by the enemy, but he was rescued straightaway by his men who came after him, who were so enraged then, seeing their leader's trouble, that they threw aside caution and attacked, defeated the enemy and rescued their master.[33]

Not all the feats of arms which befell the English everywhere during this war are related in this chronicle, because of their variety,

mais soulement lez plus notables, qe trop prolinxt matir serroit a tout countier.

Fait asauoir qe le dit Roi Dengleter vient la semain penouse meisme la sesoun susdit parmy Beaux, ou lez mousters furount apoy toucz enforcez et estuffes dez vitailles du pays, dez queux lez vns furrount gaignez par assaute, ascuns renduz com lez engins furrount adressetz, par queux tout lost dez viures fust grauntment refreiscez.

En quel temps, le capitain de Busch,[e] par congie du dit Roi Dengleter, sen ala deuers Normendy oue .xx. glaiues Englois et Gascouns, pur parler oue le Roi de Nauarre, a qi estoit bien [f. 230] uoillaunt, encountra pres de Drewes sodeignement oue .xxiiij. homs darmes, cheualers et esquiers Fraunceois, qenbussez estoient pur autres garnisouns Englois; descenderent a pee de toz partz, sentrecombaterent apertement. Lez Fraunceis furrount descomfitz, et Bek de Villeins lour cheuetain pris, soi quart dez cheualeris; lez autres prises et mortz.

53. Le dit Roi Dengleter se logea adeuaunt Parys, le Mekerdy en la Semayn de Pasch, lan de grace Mile.CCC.lx., en lez procheyns villetes dehors lez suburbes de Seintclou, atrauers al eau de Seyne para-mount de Paris, y endemora .v. iours; et a soun departir, se moustra en batail pardeuaunt le fitz du Roi de Fraunce, qi regent estoit du pays, qi dedenz la cite estoit oue graunt noumbre des gentz darmes. Le Prince de Galis, le fitz eyne du dit Roi de Engleter qauoit lauaunt garde et le Duk de Lancastre en autre batail, tindrent pres deuaunt lez forburs de solail leuaunt iesqes mydi, enfirent buter le fieu. Lez autres batails du roy tindrent vn poy plus loinz. Pilerin de Vadencourt, cheualer Fraunceis, fust pris as barreirs de la cite, com soun cheual qe naufrez estoit dun sete ly engetta. Cheualers nouelis dubbez la iourne du retenu le dit Prince, sez enbusserent desoutz lez suburbes au departir dez ditz batails, ou sez tenoient tanqe lez vns isserent de la cite, ferrerent cheueaux dez esperouns, iousterent de guere. Richard de Baskiruille le fitz, cheualer Englois, fust porte a terre; sailly en peez, naufri de soun espey dez cheueaux dez Fraunceys, se defendy apertement tanqe rescous estoit, et soun cheual, dez autres sez compaignouns, qi abaundounnement enbuterent lez Fraunceis issuz, dedenz lour forteresces. Le Count de Tankiruille enueint hors de la cite en le houre, requist tretice du counsail le dit Roy Dengleter, qe ly

[e]   *MS:* Dusch.

but only the more notable, as it would be too wordy a matter to recount them all.

It should be noted that in Holy Week [29 March-4 April] in the same season, the King of England came through the Beauce, where the monasteries were nearly all fortified and stocked with the region's food; some of them were won by assault, others surrendered when siege engines were set up, and through this, the whole army was amply resupplied with food.

At this time, by licence of the King of England, the Captal de Buch took himself towards Normandy with twenty English and Gascon billhooks, to talk with the King of Navarre, to whom he was well [f. 230] inclined. Near to Dreux he suddenly encountered twenty-four men-at-arms, French knights and squires, who were waiting in ambush for other English garrisons; both sides dismounted on foot and fought each other boldly. The French were defeated and their leader, the Bègue de Villaines, was taken, and four knights with him; the others were taken or killed.[34]

53. The King of England set up camp before Paris on the Wednesday in Easter Week [8 April][1] in the year of grace 1360, in the villages outside the suburbs of Saint-Cloud, across the river Seine above Paris, remaining there for five days; and on his departure, he arrayed himself in battle order before the King of France's son, the regent of the country, who was in the city with a great number of men-at-arms. The Prince of Wales, the eldest son of the King of England, who had the vanguard, and the Duke of Lancaster with another battle, held close by the *faubourgs* from sunrise until midday, and put them to the flame. The king's other battles kept a little further off. The French knight Pelerin de Vadencourt was taken at the city's barricades, when his horse was wounded by an arrow and threw him. [Some] knights of the prince's retinue, newly dubbed that day, hid themselves down by the suburbs when these battles had departed, where they stayed until some men made a sortie out from the city, [then] spurred on their horses, for jousts of war.[2] The English knight Richard de Baskerville the younger was knocked to the ground; jumping to his feet, he wounded the French horses with his sword, and defended himself boldly until he was rescued, with his horse, by his other companions, who recklessly pushed back the French who had sortied out, back into their fortress. At this time, the Count of Tancarville[3] sent a message from the city, requesting negotiations with the King of England's council; he received the reply that their said lord would

fust respoundu, qe lour dit seignour prendroit toutdiz resoun toutez houres. Le dit roy sen departy, le fieu enbote par tout enuiroun soun chemyn, se logea pres de Monthery, et soun host enuiroun. Le Dymaunge, le .xiij. iour Dauerille, pur defaute de feur as cheueaux, couenoit faire vn tresgraundisme iourne deuers Beaux. Le temps estoit si tresmeruaillous mauueis, de plu, de greil et de neggie oue tiel freidour, qe plusours feblis vadletz et cheueaux periroint mortz as chaumps, enlesserent plusours chariotis et somaille com en vn fortune du pier temps de froid, vent et de moil, qe en cel sesoun auoit este vieu de memoir.

Entour quel temps, lez gentz monsire *a*James Daudele, dez garnisouns de Ferte et de Nogent en Bry, eschallerent le chastelle de Huchi en Valoys, pres de Sesson, apres solail leuaunt *[f. 230v.]* com lez gaites estoient aualez, le quel est[oit]*b* trebien vitaille, et plein dez gentils femmes. Vndz homs darmes, chiualers et esquyers, et .viij. archiers Galoisdu retenu le sires de Spenser auoint vn bele poignez en Beaux, com lost le dit roy estoit herbigez en villetez, qe warderent lez moliners en vn molyn pur moldir blez dehors lost, pres de Bonevaille, qestoient espiez des garnisouns Fraunceis enuyroun, qe lour uindrent surcour .xxvi. glaiues .xij. archiers dez Bretouns Fraunceis. Descenderent a pee de touz partz sentrecombaterent apertement; lez Fraunceis furount descoumfitz, .iij. homs darmez de lour mortz et .xx. prises prisoners, toutz naufres pres de mort de touz dieus parties. Ascuns des ditz Englois furount fiauncez a les ditz enemys duraunt la melle, qe rescous estoint des ditz Galois, qe trebien illoeqes firent.

Le dit Roy Dengleter demurra en Beux pres Orliens .xv. iours, pur tretice de pes, qe le counsail de Fraunce ly emparlerent, Labbe de Cluny, monsire Hugh de Genef, le messager du Pape, mediatours. Lez Engles del ost du dit roy auoint lez punyes, lez vns en perd, lez autres en preu. Cheualers en la compaignie du Duk de Lancastre countrefirent lez pilours, vadletz, forraiours saunz glaiues, currerent disaraiement pur treyn, encharnicement et corage doner a lez enemys dauoir afaire oue eaux, puisqe ils auoint plusours de lour foraiours pris, lez ioures passez. Lez vns dez queux, Eadmound Pirpount, Baudewyn Malet, cheualers, outre mesure countrefirent la countenaunce en tiel daunger dez Fraunceis qe y ne pooit autrement estre, qe a meschief ne lour couenoit estre suppris; si furount prisis et fiaunces.

---

a   Marginal hand, pointing to 'James'.
b   MS: estb; estoit *added in left margin.*

always listen to reason at all times. The king took his leave, and putting fire to everything around his route, set up camp near to Montlhéry, with his army around him. On Sunday 13 April, it was agreed to make a very long day's march to the Beauce, due to a lack of fodder for the horses. The weather was so tremendously bad, with rain, hail and snow, and such was the cold, that many weakened squires and horses died in the field, and many carts and pack horses were abandoned in the misfortune of the worst weather, with cold, wind and wet, that had been seen in this season in living memory.[4]

At around this time, sir James de Audley's men, from the garrisons of la Ferté-sous-Jouarre and Nogent in Brie, took by escalade the castle of Oulchy in Valois, near to Soissons, after sunrise [f. 230v.] when the lookouts had been stood down. The place was very well supplied, and full of noble ladies. Some men-at-arms, knights and squires, and eight Welsh archers, of the Lord Despenser's retinue had a fine fight in the Beauce, when the king's army was quartered in villages. They were away from the army, near to Bonneval, guarding the millers in a mill, to get some grain milled; they were spotted by the French garrisons round about, who came to attack them with twenty-six billmen and twelve archers, French-Bretons. Both sides dismounted on foot and fought each other boldly; the French were defeated, three of their men-at-arms killed and twenty taken prisoner, and everyone on both sides was wounded near to death. Some of the English were put on their faith to the enemy during the mêlée, and were rescued by the Welsh, who did very well there.[5]

The King of England remained in the Beauce near Orleans for fifteen days, for peace talks which the council of France had proposed to him, with the Abbot of Cluny and Sir Hugh de Geneva,[6] the Papal envoy, as mediators. The English of the king's army had some battles, some to their loss, others to their profit. [Some] knights in the Duke of Lancaster's company disguised themselves as pillagers, valets and foragers without polearms, deceitfully running about in disarray, to embolden the enemy and give them courage to have a go at them, since they had taken many of their foragers in the previous days. Some of them, Edmund Pierpoint and Baldwin Malet, knights, carried this pretence beyond reason, in such danger from the French that it could not be otherwise but they should come to grief; and so they were taken and paroled.

Cheualers del host du prince du retenu du Count de Salisbires, monsire Brian de Stapleton et autres, com warderent lez forreiers, auoint afair oue lez Fraunceois pres de Yanville et les descoumfirent, pristrent lez vndz.

En vengeaunce del ariuail qe lez Fraunceis firent a Wenchelse, lez admiraux dez Fipportez et du north nauy Englois, od .Mile. homs armez, .Mile.v.C. archiers, arriuerent en Lisle de Dans, dedenz .xv. iours apres la Pasche meisme la sesoun, assaillerent et gaignerent la vile del Lure, et larderent, et plus vssent fait, si nussent estez destourbez par maundement le roy lour seignour, par caus de trewes.

Lem doit sauoir,[c] qe le .vij. iour de Maij, lan susdit pres de Chartres; tail de pes fust treite et assentuz du dit Roy Dengleter, et de soun counsail entour ly dun part, et de le susdit Regent, et del counsail de Fraunce et de la comune dautre part, en maner *sub compendio*. [d]Toutes acciouns, demaundes et querelis lesseitz exteintes et relessez, lez auaunt ditz couenantes acompliez, qe le *[f. 231]* auaunt dit Roi Dengleter, aueroit la Duche de Gyen entier, a la aunciens merches, et le paijs de Roergus, lez countees de Pountyne, de Gienes, oue lez apurtenaunces, Calays oue la seignoury enuiroun, quitement saunz appendaunce, entendauntz, appeles, resortes, demaundes ou subieccioun nul au coroune de Fraunce, fraunchement oue toutez regaltes regauls pur touz iours; et qil aueroit pur raunsoun du Roi de Fraunce, trois miliouns dor; et qe lez auaunt ditz roys serrount par comune ascent countre toutez gentz entrealliez, sure sensures serementz, assuraunces toutz qe purrent estre deuisez a tenir lez auauntditz couenaunces; et qe laccioun et la querel de Bretaigne entre Montfort et Charlis de Bloys serroit a iuge, par lez bons descrecions dez ditz roys, et si se ne agre as ditz parties, qe lez roys ne lour heires ne sentremettrount de eide, ne suppuail. Le Roi de Fraunce lessera la liaunce de ceaux Descoce outriement, et le Roi Dengleter ostera mayn de ceux de Flaundres, et serrount lez .ij. roys assous del Apostoil de lour sermentz du dit alliaunce; al parfournisement dez quelis couenaunces, fust treite qe les fitz eisnez dez ditz roys, le Prince de Galis dun part, et le Duk de Normandy dautre, en lez almes lour piers serroient iurez sur le corps Dieu. Et le Roy de Nauarre et .xx. autres persouns de Fraunce, et le Duk de Lancastre et autres .xx. Dengleter, a la choise dez auaunt ditz counseils serrount auxi iugez. Lez .ij. eisnz fitz dez ditz Roys affermerent lez tretices assentuz, comprisez et

[c] MS: no'. *in right margin, in same hand as main text.*
[d] *Marginal hand, pointing to 'toutes'.*

While they were guarding foragers, Sir Brian de Stapleton and other knights from the prince's army, in the retinue of the Earl of Salisbury, had some business with the French near to Janville and defeated them, capturing some of them.

The admirals of the Cinque Ports and the English northern fleet landed on the Isle of *Dans*, in revenge for the landing the French made at Winchelsea, with 1000 men-at-arms, 1500 archers, in the quinzaine of Easter [5–19 April] in the same season; they attacked and won the town of Leure, and burned it, and would have done more, if they had not been prevented by command of their lord the king, by reason of the truce.

It should be known that on 7 May in the same year, near Chartres, a peace treaty was negotiated and agreed by the King of England, and his council around him on the one part, and the regent and the council of France and the commune on the other part, in the manner of the summary below.[7] All actions, claims and complaints were desisted, ended and remitted, and the aforesaid agreements were put into effect, that the [f. 231] King of England should have the Duchy of Guienne in its entirety, at its ancient borders, and the region of Rouergue, the counties of Ponthieu, Guines, with its appurtenances, and Calais with the neighbouring lordship, quit without dependency, services owed, appeals, legal recourses, claims or any subjection to the French crown, freely with full royal sovereignty for all time; and that he should have three million in gold for the King of France's ransom; and that the kings should ally with each other against all men by common assent, under censure of sworn oaths, and all the guarantees that could be devised to keep these agreements; and that the action and dispute over Brittany between Montfort and Charles de Blois should be adjudicated at the discretion of the kings, and if this was not agreeable to the said parties, that neither the kings nor their heirs should intervene with either help or support. The King of France was to abandon the alliance with the Scots completely, and the King of England was to remove his hand from the Flemish, and the two kings would be absolved by the Pope from their oaths for these alliances; and it was agreed that the eldest sons of the kings, the Prince of Wales on the one part, and the Duke of Normandy on the other, should swear to the fulfilment of these covenants on their fathers' souls over the sacrament. And also to be sworn were the King of Navarre and twenty other French persons, and the Duke of Lancaster and twenty other English, chosen by the councils. The two eldest sons of the kings confirmed the treaties that had been agreed,

escriptz, par lour serementz, sure le corps nostre seignour sacre. Le Duk de Normande et regent de Fraunce, qe maladez estoit denpostym, le iura a Parys en presence de vaillaunz cheualres Englois, pur ceo y enuoiez, par queux le dit regent tramist au dit Prince de Galis tresnoblis precious reliqes du seintisme croice, de la coroune des espines, de quoi Dieux fust corone en la croice, oue autres noblis jueaux, en signifiaunce qe sure la croice la dit coroune a test, nostre seignour fist pees, salut et tranquillite perdurable au lygne humain. Le dit Prince de Galis fist meisme le serement en la graunt Moustier de Louiers, le .xv. iour de Maij, lan susdit, en presence dez noblis cheualers Frounceis pur la cause y enuoiez. Le Roy de Nauarre ne voloit faire le serement, mes vient parler ouesqe le Roi de Engleter pres de Nemburgh de ou le dit Roy Dengletere prist soun chemyn deuers Huniflu, ou se mist sure mere deuers Engleter, sez fitz et plusours seignours oue ly, lessa le <duk>^e de Warwyk en Normendy gardein dez trewes.

Le Duk de Lancastre et le Count de Stafford, oue le remenaunt del host dez Englois, passerent [f. 231v.] Seyn au Pount de la Arche, deuers Calays, qen partye estoient ensaulez del anuyouse trauail de cel veage qe auoit dure .ix. moys, ou auoint enuyrounez le plus de Fraunce en qanqe en lour fust, queraunt batail, dauoir derenez le droit lour siris, qe ne trouerount nul part countenaunce a ceo faire, mais uesquerent le temps sure le paijs, alafoitz meutz, autrefoitz com purroint trouer, com en paijs destrut et cheuauchez auaunt lour venu dez Englois auaunt nomez, qe de lour testes propres auoint contenuz la guere meruaillousement. Et ensi lez trois hostes dez Englois departiz, en espoir du pes tretez, oue trewes a durer tanqe la seint Michael procheyn a vn ane, dedenz quel temps la pes purparlez serroit affermez, et ensi la guere estanche, le iour et lan susditz, quel guere auoit en le hour duree vint et qatre aunz.

54. Meisme la sesoun, lan de grace .Mile.CCC.lx., entour la seint Johan, Katarine de Mortymer, vn damoisel de Loundres estoit si priue de monsire Dauid de Bruys, qe dez Escotois fu dit roy, par aquaintaunce qe il auoit de lye tancom prisoner estoit, qe il ne pooit desporter sa presence. En absence de sa moillier, la sore le Roi

---

^e   MS: duk *partially erased.* Count *added in right-hand margin, in later hand.*

settled and written down, by their oaths on the body of our holy lord. The Duke of Normandy, regent of France, who was ill with an abcess, swore to this at Paris in the presence of worthy English knights, sent there for the purpose; and through them, the regent sent to the Prince of Wales [some] very noble precious relics of the holy cross, of the crown of thorns, with which God was crowned on the cross, with other noble jewels, to signify that on the cross, with that crown on his head, our lord brought peace, salvation and eternal tranquility to the human race. The Prince of Wales himself took the oath in the great minster at Louviers, on 15 May of the aforesaid year, in the presence of noble French knights sent there for that reason. The King of Navarre was not willing to take the oath, but came to talk with the King of England near le Neubourg, from where the King of England took the road towards Honfleur, where he took to the sea towards England, with his sons and many lords; the [earl] of Warwick was left in Normandy as keeper of the truce.

The Duke of Lancaster and the Earl of Stafford crossed *[f. 231v.]* the Seine at Pont-de-l'Arche, towards Calais, with the remainder of the English army. They were somewhat dishevelled from the arduous work of that expedition, which had lasted nine months, while they had traversed as much of France as they could, seeking battle, to prove the rights of their lord.[8] They could not find any means of doing this, other than to live off the country for that time, sometimes well, sometimes on whatever they could find, when in regions that had been ravaged and raided before their arrival by the English mentioned previously, who had carried on the war outstandingly, on their own authority.[9] And so the three English armies departed,[10] in expectation of the peace treaty, with a truce to last until next Michaelmas for a year, within which time the agreed peace [terms] were to be ratified. And so the war came to an end, on the day and year abovesaid; and at the time, this war had lasted twenty-four years.

54. In the same season, in the year of grace 1360, around St John's day [24 June], Katherine de Mortimer, a young lady of London, became so intimate with David de Bruce (who was called the king by the Scots), through the acquaintance he had with her while he was prisoner, that he could not do without her presence. In the absence of his wife, the sister of the King of England, who was staying with her brother at the

Dengleter, qe en le hour demurra oue soun dit freir, cheuaucha
toutdiz enuyroun oue ly, quel especialte desplesoit as ascuns
seignours Descoce. Vn vadlet Escotois qe out a noun Richard de
Hulle, al abette dez ascuns grauntz Descoce, se feigna a parler oue la
dit Katerine des busoignes deuers le roy, com ils cheuaucherent de
Melros, pres de Soltre, la ferist de vn cotel parmy le corps mort
treboucha a terre, du cheual, qi Richard estoit bien mountez et
eschapa. La chos fait a la gise, le dit roy, qe deuaunt estoit en la route,
reuient au cry, fesoit graunt doel du despite, et perd qil auoit de sa
amy; la fist aporter a Neubotil, ou apres, honourablement la fist
enterer.

Entour quel temps, le Roi Despayn, qe fitz fust du bon Roy
Alphonsus,[a] estoit gouerne par Jues, ne amoit pas sa mulier, amoit
paramours vn Juesse; pur lamour de qei, il fesoit Juys cheualres et
Compaignouns de la Bend, la quel compaigny, soun pier auoit ordene
pur encharnycement doner a cheualery, car en soun temps, nuls ne
portast la Bend si ne fust cheualer esproue sure Sarazins. Pur quoi,
ascuns cheualres Cristiens de la dit compaignie auoint despit, qe lez
Jues estoint ensy chirrez en parigaute as Cristiens, et pensoient qe ceo
estoit encountre lour paternalis custumes; si disoient au dit roy, qe
ceo estoit desordene chos, qe tiels mastins [f. 232] serroint
compaignouns de tiel honest, honourable et digne compaigny. Le roy
lour respoundy en curous et disoit qils estoient homs com autres et
noun pas mastins, mais sount piers de eaux. Ceo, disoient lez
cheualres, et ceo sumes nous prestez par noz corps en le hour a
prouer. Depar Dieux, fesoit ly Roy, et soit si verroms qe vous le ferrez.
Lez Cristiens estoient .xxx., lez Juys .lxij., qe oue gree du dit Roy, oue
bones espeis, launceroint ensemble desarmez en vn pleyn, present le
roy. Lez Cristiens decouperent lez Juys mortz toucz, qi roy estoit
moult sauuage, se delitoit de tout en foly de juuent, pur quoi
plusours dez soens sez enherderent a soun freir bastard, a qy il auoit
guerre, et si auoit fait tuer autres de sez tiels freirs. Le dit Roy
Despaigne auoit hu guerre oue le Roy de Arragoun la quel fust peise
entre eaux par tail de pees, qi Roy Despayne, se trei en soun pays,
vesqi   desordeinement,   quel   guerre   de   Arragoun   saunz
aparceiuaunce de ly, ly fust renouele sodeinement plus fere qe
deuaunt. Et pur ceo, tout soit pes par sen, la proprete terrien plus a

---

[a]   *MS:* Alphosus.

time,[1] he always rode everywhere with her; and this special treat-ment was displeasing to some Scottish lords. At the instigation of certain Scottish magnates, a Scottish valet, named Richard de Hull, pretended to talk with Katherine about business concerning the king, as they were riding from Melrose, near to Soutra, and stabbed her to death with a dagger through her body, throwing her from her horse to the ground. Richard was well mounted and so escaped. The deed was done in this way, and the king, who was on the road ahead, turned back at the outcry, grieving greatly for the harm, and loss which he had borne from his mistress. He had her carried to Newbottle, where afterwards, he had her honourably buried.[2]

Around that time, the King of Spain,[3] who was the son of the good King Alfonso, was ruled by Jews. He did not love his wife, but passionately loved a Jewess; and for the love of her, he made Jews knights and Companions of the Band, the company which his father had established to give encouragement to chivalry, for in his time, no one might wear the Band, unless he was a knight proved against the Saracens.[4] Because of this, some Christian knights of that company were scornful that the Jews were thus honoured in parity with Chris-tians, and considered that this was contrary to their ancestral customs; so they said to the king that it was an unseemly thing, that such dogs [f. 232] should be companions of such an honest, honour-able and worthy company. The king replied to them in anger and said that they were men like others and not dogs, but their equals. 'Both those points', said the knights, 'we are ready to contest with our bodies at once'. 'By God!', said the king, 'and we will make sure that you do'. There were thirty Christians, sixty-two Jews, with good swords, but unarmoured, and with the king's agreement they charged together on a plain, with the king present. The Christians cut down all the Jews dead, at which the king was greatly enraged, and consoled himself wholly with the follies of youth; because of this, many of his men joined with his bastard brother, with whom he was at war, as he had had his other such brothers killed.[5] The King of Spain had been at war with the King of Aragon, and this was settled by a peace agreement between them. The King of Spain took himself back to his own country, living decadently; and without him forseeing it, the war with Aragon was suddenly renewed, more bitterly than before.[6] For even though, rationally, peace should be everything, the worldly quality that is most to be desired of all reasonable aspirations, as the sovereign benefit in this world and something to be exhorted by the sovereign, yet the manner in which

voloir en toutis desires resonablis, com la souerayn benefice du siecle
et chose amonestement du souerayn, vncor la maner fait moqult a
consydereir, qe ou le foundement et desires de pes sourd
fraunchement de vertu en plesaunce de Dieu, saunz encharnisement,
norisement ou constremement de nul accidence, particuler de nul
plesaunt desire ne voloir charnel, mais vertuousement en
droiturelement au profite du comune; cel pese ne purra estre, qe ne
soit <dez ditz [unz?]>[b] bon. Mais ou le desioint soit duble, et le point
pris en contrair lez ditz vertuez, la nest pas taunt a preisere, mais
grauntement a douter le effecte de la matire, com qi sent soun droit et
le lesse a pursuire pur perresce, et a eschuer desese, en desir et espoir
autre part greindre plesaunce a auoir; ou le lesse pur defaute de
tresor; ou pur pesaunce dez cuers dez gentz a lasseitz, ou enveillez.
Cel estauntisement de guere ne est pas souent trop profitable al issu,
qar plusours sez quident chaufer qe lez ardrent, qe lez casueletes du
siecle sont si muables, qe plusours foitz hom quide eschuer vn
pesaunce, si engist en vn greindre. Et si nest pas vieu qe par tresor
soulement soient eschuez lez guerres, quel tresor en suffisauntye ne
doit estre desesparez en roys, ne si de vn ne soit eidez, qe y ne trouera
autres qe ly eidera, si defaut de vertu ne le destourbe; ceo est a dire,
com defaut de sen, hardement et de largesce; defaut de sen, qe qy ne
voet pas si Dieux luy moustre sa grace en auauncement *[f. 232v.]* de sa
querel, et ne le pursu pas en mesure par resoun, oue douce acoil dez
soens, oue tiel hardement, qe ne soit exteint au point pur dout de
meschief, ou desplesaunce lez propretes duraunt guere, suffraunce
dez queux en maner apport honour, profit et ioy; issi qe la main soit
ount a doner, as ceaux qe le deseruient, en encharnicement as autres
de ceo fair, chos terrien plus eidable a guerroier. Qe qi chace
estaunticement de guerre, autrement fors com a Dieu plerra, ne
nenpensez ia, qe la iette ne bestournera, qant meutz auoir le quidera.
Et si purra estre, qe Dieux ne vouchera sauf, pur ordesce de pecchie,
qe hom yet sez benefices, en maner com il tollist a Moyses la entre de
la Terre de Promissioun, pur ceo, qen vain gloir, il prist longa du
poeple de Israel, qe suremistrent en sa pussaunz lez miracles qe lour
moustra en sez mains, de quoi, il se glorifia; pur quoi perdi la dit
entree, chos qe plus desirat. Et pur ceo, bien doient les roys arrettier
lour bienfaitez a Dieu, et au bon executioune de lour poeple, le bien

[b]   MS: dez ditz unz *erased.* profitable *added in right-hand margin, in 15thc. hand.*

it is acquired should be considered at length; for where the foundation and the desire for peace arises freely from virtue, to the delight of God, without enboldenment, nourishment or constraint by any other influence, and relating not to any idle fancy nor carnal desire, but virtuously and rightfully for the profit of the community, then such peace can only be to the good. Yet where those desiring [peace] have double standards, and take up this position contrary to those virtues, it is not to be valued so much; and the result of the matter is to be greatly feared – such as when someone is conscious of his rights but gives up pursuing them through idleness, and so as avoid discomfort, in the desire and hope of gaining greater gratification from another quarter; or who gives them up through lack of wealth; or from the heaviness of men's heart through weariness; or from old age. Such a curtailment of war is not often very profitable in the end, for many who intend [just] to warm themselves get burned; for the circumstances of the world are so changeable, that many times a man who thinks he has avoided one burden, is caught up with a greater one. And if it appears that wars cannot be avoided through wealth alone, then a king should not despair of a sufficiency of wealth; or that if he is not supported by someone, that he shall not find others there to support him, so long as a lack of virtue does not impede him; that is to say, a lack of good sense, courage and generosity. And it is a lack of good sense, if he does not see whether God is showing him grace in the furthering [f. 232v.] of his dispute; or that he should not pursue it in moderation, with reason, and with the cheerful agreement of his people, with a courage that should not be quenched when it came to the point through fear of trouble, or destruction of property during war. The endurance of such things in this manner brings honour, profit and joy; and so the [king's] hand should be ready to give to those that deserve it, as an encouragement to others to do this, which is the most helpful thing in this world for the waging of war. He who would seek the curtailment of war, other than when pleasing to God, should never imagine that the throw of the dice will not go against him, even when he supposes he has the advantage. And it may well be, that because of the stain of sin, God shall not deign to grant that man should enjoy his benefactions, in the the same way that he barred Moses from entering the Promised Land, because, in his vainglory, he accepted the praise of the people of Israel, who attributed to his power the miracles that were shown to them through his hands; and for which, he glorified himself. Because of this, he lost his admission [to the Promised Land], that thing which he desired

estre dez queux en est lour tresor, le qil tient en due gouernail dez
roys, com del execucioune du gouernement de la comune, qar souent
le poeple port coup dez pecchez dez roys; pur quoi bien sez doient
engarder, qe lour singulertez ne face destruccioun general et comune,
com maintfoitz y ad este vieu, issi qe lour estat soit gouernez deuers
Dieu par vertu, et au poeple par moralite.

55. Hom doit sauoir qe meisme lan del Incarnacioun, .Mile.CCC.lx.,
entour la seint Michel, le dit Roy Johan de Fraunce, fust deliuers a
Calays hors de prisoun le Roy Dengleter sure lez condiciouns einz
parlez. Qi roi auoit demurre prisouner trois aunz en Engleter a
Loundres a Wyndesor, et a Somertoun, paya a soun passer vn milioun
dor, lessa honourablis hostages pur le aparfournicement du
remenaunt dez ditz couenauntez treitez; cest assauoir sez dieus fitz,
lez Countis Daungeow et de Paiters; soun freir Duk Dorliens; soun
cosyne, Duk de Burboun; lez Countis de Bloys, de Alasoun, de Saint
Poelle, de Harcourt, de Porcien, de Valentinoys, de Brein, de
Waddemound, de Fores; et le viscount de Beaumount; les seignours
de Coucy, de Fenys, de Preux, de Saintvenaunt, de Garensers, de
Mountmaracy, de Haunget; le Daufyn Daineryne; mesires Peres de
Alensoun, Willam de Cinoun, Lowys de Harcourt, Johan de Ligny. Et
fust outre acorde, qe si lez .xvi. prisoners prisis a Paiters ouesqe le dit
Roy de Fraunce vousissent demurrer en hostage pur la dit cause, qils
fussent quitz deliuers sure la dit treit; et si noun, ils demurascent a
raunsouner, et autres [f. 233] couenablis ens mys, lez nouns dez queux
prisoners sount Phelip, fitz du dit roi, Count de Berry; lez Countis de
Longuille, de Tankiruille, de Juny, de Poncieu, de Saucer, de
Dawmartyn, de Ventatour, de Salebruch, Daucer, de Vendom; lez
sires de Cynoun, Derualle; le Marschal de Oudenam; et le sire de
Aubigny. Et auxi acorde fust, qe dieus des greignours burgeis de
chescun vile dez meillours cites de Fraunce demurassent en hostage a
le Roi Dengeleter, tanqe a le parfournisement de la dit treit, cest
assauoir de Parys, Amyas, Saintomer, Arras, Tournay, Lille, Doway,
Beauvoys, Reynes, Chalouns, Troys, Chartres, Orliens, Tullous,
Liouns, Tours, Roan, Came, et Compyn. Cest tail et condiciouns et
maner de peise a la gise treitez, fust acordez et affermez par assent
general dez grauntz de toutz dieus lez Realmes et en parlement

most.[7] And therefore, kings well-ought to ascribe their good deeds to God, and to the good undertaking of their people, in whose well-being is their wealth; and this lies within the proper rule of kings, through their undertaking of the government of the community, because the people often suffer the blows for the sins of kings. Because of this, [kings] well-ought to ensure that their particular powers do not bring about general and communal destruction, as has been seen many times, so that their estate may be ruled under God by virtue, and for the people by morality.

55. Everyone should know that the same year of the Incarnation, 1360, at around Michaelmas [29 September], King John of France was released at Calais from the King of England's prison on the terms previously discussed. The king had remained as a prisoner for three years in England, at London, Windsor and Somerton,[1] and paid a million gold at his crossing, leaving honourable hostages for the fulfilment of the remainder of the negotiated agreements;[2] that is say, his two sons, the Counts of Anjou and Poitiers; his brother, the Duke of Orleans; his cousin, the Duke of Bourbon; the Counts of Blois, Alençon, Saint-Pol, Harcourt, Porcien, *Valentinois*, Brienne, Vaudémont, Forez; and the Viscount of Beaumont; the lords of Coucy, Fiennes, *Preux*, *Saint Venaunt*, Garencières, Montmorency, Hangest; the Dauphin *D'Aineryne*; and Sirs Peter de Alençon, William de [Craon],[3] Lewis de Harcourt and John de Ligny. And it was agreed furthermore, that if the sixteen prisoners taken at Poitiers with the King of France should be willing to remain as hostages for the same reason, they should be released quit [of ransom] under the same treaty; and if not, they should stay to be ransomed, and other [f. 233] suitable men put in their place, the names of these prisoners being Philip, the Count of Berry, the king's son; the Counts of Longueville, Tancarville, Joigny, Ponthieu, Sancerre, Dammartin, Ventadour, Saarbrucken, Auxerre, Vendôme; the lords of Craon and Derval; the Marshal d'Audreham; and the lord of Aubigny.[4] And it was also agreed that two of the senior burgesses from each town of the greater cities of France should remain as a hostage of the King of England, until the fulfilment of the treaty, that is to say from Paris, Amiens, Saint-Omer, Arras, Tournai, Lille, Douai, Beauvais, Reims, Chalons, Troyes, Chartres, Orléans, Toulouse, Lyons, Tours, Rouen, Caen and Compiègne. This agreement, and the conditions and the manner of the peace in the form negotiated, was agreed and confirmed by the

publy; et au uoloir de lez dieus Roys a ceo entreiurez, a la executioun
de la aparfournicement de quel treit, Johan de Chaundos, cheualer,
fust enuoyez depar le Roy Dengleter, eiaunt commissioun suffisaunt,
a deliuerer lez chasteaux et fermetes conquysis diuersis partz hu
realme de Fraunce, qi ceo fist, com comaunde li fust loyalment du
Roy de Engleter, solonc lez condiciouns acordez. Lez Engles qe de
lour testes propres auoint contenu cest guere de Fraunce, sez
associerent ensemble, oue diuers naciouns, estoint appellez la Graunt
Compaigny, voiderent Fraunce, au comaundement le Roi Dengleter,
gaignerent la vile de Saint Spirit, mouerent guere en Prouynce,
vesqerent de prai meruaillousement.

Le Duk Henry de Lancastre morust en Marce, et enterez a
Laycestre, lan de grace .Mile.CCC.lxj, qi Henry estoit sage, glorious et
prus, et ensa iuuent reueillous en honour et armys, et deuaunt soun
descesse, durement bon Cristien. Il auoit as heyres .ij. feilles, le Duk
Willam de Beyuer et count de Henaw, de Seland et de Holand, qi pius
deueint franetik,[a] auoit la primer, Johan fitz du dit Roy Dengleter
Count de Richemound auoit la secound.

56. Le dit Roy Dengleter fist edifier de nouel vn chastel en lentre sur
Temys meisme cel ane, en le Isle de Schiphey. En meisme lan susdit,
fust le Roy de Lettow pris, par lez seignours de Spruz qe par
enbussement ly suppristerent, al issu qe lost dez Cristiens isserent sa
terre apres la Pasche, com testousement il lour pursuy. Cel ane aueint
vn general mortalite dez gentz en Engleter, qe plus qe par tout lan
durra ascun part, la secound pestilence de mortalite dez genz qaueint
en le temps cesty Roy Edward le tierce.

Le Roy de Cypre prist de assaute le iour de seint Bartholomeu en
Aust, meisme la sesoun, la [f. 233v.] vile de Satally en Turky, et la
garny dez Cristiens.

Lionel, Count de Hulster del heritage sa femme, et fitz du dit Roy
de Engleter, passa en Ireland meisme la sesoun, a destreindre les
Irroys, qe durement greuerent lez Englois du pays a lour gise.

Ly Roy de Denemark guerroya lez Estirlings durement sure mere
cel sesoun, qauoit reconquys Scon, et mout de Swetherik, sure le Roy
de Norway.

---

[a]   *Marginal hand, pointing to 'deueint franetik'.*

general assent of the magnates of both the realms and was announced in parliament;[5] and at the will of the two kings, who were mutually sworn to this, John de Chandos, knight, was sent on behalf of the King of England, to undertake the implementation of the treaty, having a sufficient commission, to deliver the conquered castles and strongholds in various parts of the kingdom of France. This he did, as he had been loyally commanded by the King of England, according to the agreed conditions. The English who had continued this war of France on their own account, banded themselves together with various nations; they were called the Great Company. They left France, at the command of the King of England, gained the town of Pont-Saint-Esprit, and made war in Provence, living marvellously from pillaging.[6]

Duke Henry of Lancaster died in March in the year of grace 1361, and was buried at Leicester. This Henry was wise, glorious and worthy; and intent on honour and arms in his youth, and very much the good Christian before his death. He had two daughters as his heirs; William, Duke of Bavaria and Count of Hainault, Zeeland and Holland, who afterwards went mad, had the first; John, Earl of Richmond, son of the King of England, had the second.[7]

56. The King of England had a castle built from new on the mouth of the Thames in that same year [*i.e.* 1361], on the Isle of Sheppey.[1] In the same year, the King of Lithuania was taken by the lords of Prussia, who surprised him by ambush, as the Christian army departed from his land after Easter, when he pursued them too headily.[2] That year, there occurred a widespread mortality of men in England, which lasted for more than a year in some parts, the second mortal pestilence of men which had occurred in the time of King Edward the third.[3]

On St Bartholomew's day in August [24 August], in the same season, the King of Cyprus took the [*f. 233v.*] town of Satalia in Turkey by assault, and garrisoned it with Christians.[4]

Lionel, Earl of Ulster by his wife's inheritance, and son of the King of England, crossed to Ireland in the same season, to restrain the Irish, who were greatly harming the English of the country in their usual fashion.[5]

Edward eysne fitz du Roy Dengleter, et prince adonqes de Galis,[a] prist meisme cel an en espouse, par dispensacioun, la feil le Count de Kent, le vncle soun pier. Ele auoit este autrefoitz mariez, ele estoit durement gentil femme, et richiz heire soun pier, et de soun vncle le seignour de Wake. En my Jeneuer meisme lan de grace .Mile.CCClxj., chey en plusours countees entour Loundres, vn tempest de vent, qe abatist mousters et cloichers, les arbres hu bois et gardyns, descouery lez mesouns meruailousement, lestoil Comata aparust cel sesoun.

Le auaunt dit Roy de Lettow eschapa meisme la sesoun de prisoun par myne, et par couyn dun renegat Lettow, qe norriz estoit od lez ditz seignours de Spruce, par enchesoun de quel eschap, la sesoun procheigne, lez ditez seignours firent vn graunt arme par nefe en Lettow assistrent le chastel de Coun sure le Memil, le pristrent de assaute par beaux fetz darmis.

Meisme la sesoun vn rout de la Graunt Coumpaigny, qe comence estoit duraunt la gerre le Roy Dengleter, descoumfirent en Auuern le poir de Fraunce, lez plusours seignours reprisis, qe autrefoitz prisoners estoint au Roi Dengleter. Jaqis de Burboun mort et le Count de Salbrog et plusours autres a la iourne.

Meisme la sesoun en quarresme, vn rout dez Bretouns, coumpaignouns de la Graunt Route, furount descoumfitz en Limosin a la Garet, par Willam de Feltoun, cheualer Englois, seneschal adonqes du pays, depar le Roy Dengleter.

La sesoun suaunt, lan de grace .Mile.CCC.lxij. vn rout dez Gascouns, coumpaignouns de la Graunt Rout, qe esparpliez estoient ou meutz troueroint a viure, estoient descoumfitz en Auuern, par le Bastard Despayn. Le gouernour de Bloys descoumfit vn autre rout de Gascouns de meisme la coumpaigny, en Berrye.

Vn rout dez Englois oue Robert Dyer furount descoumfiz par Bertrem de Gleukin Bretoun, pres de Ho en Normendy meisme la sesoun.

Entour quel temps, chey la Duche de Burgoyne od le counte, a Johan Roy de Fraunce, del heritage sa mere, qe sore estoit a le duk, mort le issu soun freir.

---

[a]   *Marginal hand, pointing to 'prince adonqes de Galis'.*

In that season, the King of Denmark fought hard on the sea against the Easterlings, who had reconquered Skåne, and much of Sweden, from the King of Norway.[6]

In that same year, Edward, eldest son of the King of England, and at that time Prince of Wales, took as his wife the daughter of the Earl of Kent, his father's uncle, by [papal] dispensation. She had been married previously, and she was a particularly noble woman, and the rich heiress of her father, and of her uncle, Lord Wake.[7]

In the middle of January of the same year of grace 1361 [i.e. 1362], a tempest of wind occurred in many counties around London, which knocked down churches and bell-towers, the trees in the woods and gardens and laid bare houses astonishingly.[8] The Comet star appeared that season.[9]

In the same season, the aforementioned King of Lithuania escaped from prison through a mine, and by the connivance of a certain renegade Lett, who had been fostered with the lords of Prussia.[10] By reason of this escape, in the season following, those lords made a great armed expedition into Lithuania by ship, besieging the castle of Kaunas on the Memel, and taking it by assault through fine deeds of arms.

In the same season, a band of the Great Company, which had started up during the King of England's war, defeated the forces of France in Auvergne; many lords, who had previously been prisoners of the King of England, were re-captured. Jacques de Bourbon was killed at the battle, and the Count of Saarbrück and many others.[11]

In the same season in Lent, a band of Bretons, companions of the Great Band, were defeated in Limousin at le Garet, by the English knight William de Felton, then seneschal of the country for the King of England.[12]

In the following season, the year of grace 1362, a band of Gascons, companions of the Great Band, who had split away so as to find a better living, were defeated in Auvergne, by the Bastard of Spain.[13] The governor of Blois defeated another band of Gascons from the same company, in Berry.

A band of English under Robert Dyer were defeated by the Breton Bertrand de Guesclin, near to La Hogue in Normandy, in the same season.

At around this time, the Duchy of Burgundy, along with the county, fell to King John of France through the inheritance of his mother, who was the sister of the duke, her brother's progeny being dead.

Le dit Roy de Fraunce fist treiter oue le Graunt Rout, qauoint riote en sa terre, puis la guere peise de Roy Dengleter, pur graunt soume dargent a voyder soun realme, qe ceo firent *[f. 234]* treierent en diuers pays, ou trouoint lez gueres, plusours de eaux au Roi de Arragoun, encountre le Roy Despayne qe guere auoint ensemble.

Cel sesoun dona le dit Roy Dengleter a Edward soun fitz, Prince de Galis, la Duche de Gyene, a tenir de ly par haute seignourye, homage, resortz, et appelis regalis.

57. Entour la seint Michelle, meisme lan de grace .Mile.CCC.xij.,[a] morust a Auynioun Innocent le pape, apres mort de qi, y out graunt dissencioun entre le College de Cardinalis pur la eleccioun de papee, qe graunt temps ne purroient acorder pur enuy, qe nuls ne vorroit qe autres y fust pape; qe au darayn choiserent vn moyne noir, vn pouer Abbe de Seint Victoir, pres de Marcil, qe quidoit qe lez messagers qe ly porterent lez nouels de sa eleccioun vssent bourde od ly, taunt se meruailla. Il fust sacree et nome Vrban; il fist constitucioun, qe nul auaunce de Seint Eglis passast .C. li. de extent, fors ceaux qe vssent estat en escolis, et ceaux a .CC. li.; et lez doctours de ciuile, de decretz, de diuinite, ne passasent .CCC. li.

Johan, Royn Descoce, et sore le Roy Dengleter, espous Dauid de Bruys, morust meisme la sesoun, et enterrez a Loundres a Freirs Menours ioust sa mere.

Apres, meisme la saint Martyne, le dit Roy Dengleter auoit general parlement a Loundres ou ordene estoit par estatut, qe lez loys de soun realme fussent pledez en Engles, ou deuaunt, estoient en Frmaunceis, puis le temps le conquerour Willam; au meisme le parlement, enfist le dit roy sez dieus fitz dukis. Lionel, Count de Hulster, qe adunqes estoit en Ireland, Duk de Clarrens; ly autre, Johan, Duk de Lancastre; et a lours heyres masls. Soun tierce fitz Eadmound, Count de Kauntbrige. Ordeyna le stapille de laynes a Calays, ou meisme le iour de seint Brice le sessauntisme ane de sa natiuite, pardonoit de sa grace as toucz sez suzgis, qanqe ils ly estoient duys, toutes dettes et arrerages apurtenauncz a sa regalte, saunz suyt de party, tresoun et homycid, en signifiauns de grace

---

[a]   MS: .CCC.xij. (Mile *supplied*).

The King of France negotiated with the Great Band, which had run riot in his land since the war had been settled with the King of England, to clear out of his realm for a great sum of money; and this they did, [f. 234] taking themselves to various countries where they could find wars, many of them [joining with] the King of Aragon, against the King of Spain, who were at war together.[14]

In that season, the King of England granted the Duchy of Guienne to Edward his son, the Prince of Wales, to hold of him by high lordship, homage, jurisdiction and royal appeals.[15]

57. At around Michaelmas [29 September], in the same year of grace 1362, Pope Innocent died at Avignon. After his death, there was great dissension within the College of Cardinals over the election of the pope, as they were unable to reach agreement for a long time due to envy, for none of them wished that any of the others there should be pope; so in the end, they chose a black monk, a poor abbot of St Victor, near to Marseilles. He thought that the messengers who brought him the news of his election were playing a trick on him, so greatly was he astonished. He was consecrated and named Urban.[1] He made an ordinance that no promotion within the Holy Church should exceed £100 in value, except for those who were in the schools, and for these £200; and the doctors of civil law, of decretals and of divinity should not exceed £300.

Joan, Queen of Scotland, and sister of the King of England, wife of David de Bruce, died in the same season, and was buried at London at the Friars Minor beside her mother.[2]

Afterwards, around Martinmas [11 November], the King of England held a general parliament at London where it was decreed by statute, that the laws of his realm should be pleaded in English, where before, they had been in French, since the time of William the Conqueror. At the same parliament, the king made his two sons, dukes. Lionel, Earl of Ulster, who was then in Ireland, was made Duke of Clarence; the other, John, was made Duke of Lancaster; and their heirs male. His third son, Edmund, was made Earl of Cambridge.[3] The wool staple was established at Calais, while on St Brice's day itself [13 November], the sixtieth year of his birth,[4] he pardoned, by his grace, all his subjects of whatever dues they owed him, and all debts and arrears pertaining to his regality, except for cases of conspiracy, treason, and homicide, as a sign of temporal

temperele, com est lan de grace espirituel, chescun synkqauntisme
ane del Incarnacioun.

Deuant Nowel meisme la sesoun, chey vn graunt iourne de batail
en Gascoigne, entre le Count de Foys, et le Count de Hermynak, le
Count de Foys auoit la victoir, par eide de vn route de la Graunt
Compaignye, plusours Engles, le count de Hermynak et le siris de la
Bret prisis, plusours mortz et pris du party de Hermynak.

Le Roy Dauid Descoce assist, meisme la sesoun, le chastelle de
Kyndromy en Marre, pur extorsiouns qe le Count de Marre [f. 234v.]
et lez soens auoint fait enuiroun au poeple, com luy surmist le roy,
quel chastel ly estoit renduz, et puis engagez oue la countee pur mile
liuers du dit count au dit roy apaier, al issu de .v. auns sure pein de lez
perdre, quel mouement moult sourdy pur vn apel de batail, qe
Willam de Keth appella le dit count en la court le dit roy; sure quoy
furent armez en lices a Edinburgh, la querel illoeqes p<ris e>n^b mayn
du roy, qi plus sembloit bien uoillaunt au dit Willam qe au dit count,
tout estoit il son cosyn prochein.

Procheinement meisme la sesoun sourdy vn debate entre le dit Roi
Dauid Descoce et Willam Count de Douglas, qauoit la sore le count
de Marre en espouse, pur diuersis mouementz qe au dit count
sembloit, qe le dit Roy ne ly moustra pas si bon seignoury, com voroit;
enbrasa couyne, fist graunt retenu, prist le chastel de Driltoun, enmist
garnisoun, quel chastel fust au roi par voi de garde. Le dit count, par
ascent du Seneschal Descoce et du Count de la Marche, lour seaux
pendauntz au peticioun maundez au dit roy, fist sa querel, qe le dit
roy lour auoit fait rountre lez condiciouns as queux estoient iurez sur
le corps Dieux au Roy Dengleter pur paiement du raunsoun du dit
roy lour seignour, qoi fust leuez du subside des comunes et^c degaste
par mauuais counsail, amendiz de quoi demaunderent et gouernail
de meilliour counsail. Pur quoi le dit roy cheuaucha sure le dit count;
et com le roy estoit en vn pais, le dit count cheuaucha en vn autre,
sure ceaux qestoient entour le roy, enprisona lez gentz le roy ou lez
poast prendre. Trenuita a Ethirkenyn, prist le viscount Dangous, oue
vn rout dez gentz darmys venauntz deuers le roy, lez maunda en
diuers lieus en prisoun. Le dit roy trenuta de Edinburgh, vst apoy
suruenuz le dit Count de Douglas a Lanerc ou auoit la nuyt iu, mais
eschapa a graunt pain, ascuns des soens prises. Le Seneschal Descoce
se peisa oue soun seignour le roy, saunz su ou gre de sez alliez. Le

---

^{b} The MS is illegible due to staining at this point; the reading given is conjectural.
^{c} The final column of the text, from here, is badly stained.

grace, just as it is the year of spiritual grace, each fiftieth year of the Incarnation.

Before Christmas in the same season, a great day of battle occurred in Gascony, between the Count of Foix and the Count of Armagnac. The Count of Foix had the victory, with the help of a band of the Great Company, many of them English; the Count of Armagnac and the Lord of Albret were taken, and many of Armagnac's party killed or taken.[5]

In the same season, King David of Scotland besieged Kildrummy castle in Mar, because of the extortions which the Earl of Mar [f. 234v.] and his men had committed round about against the people – so the king accused him. The castle was surrendered to him, and along with the county, was then pledged by the earl for a thousand pounds for the term of five years, on pain of forfeiting them, to appease the king. This event arose mainly from an appeal of battle, by which William de Keith appealed the earl in the king's court. On account of this, they were armed in the lists at Edinburgh, and there the quarrel was taken into the king's hand, who seemed more well-disposed to William than to the earl, for all that he was his close cousin.[6]

Soon afterwards in the same season a dispute arose between King David of Scots and William Earl of Douglas, who had the Earl of Mar's sister as his wife, for it seemed to the earl for various reasons, that the king did not show him such good lordship as he wished.[7] He joined a plot, formed a great retinue, seized Dirleton castle and put in a garrison, which castle was the king's, by way of wardship.[8] With the assent of the Steward of Scotland and of the Earl of March, with their seals attached to a petition sent to the king,[9] the earl made his complaint, that the king had made them break the conditions on which they were sworn on the body of God to the King of England for the payment of the ransom of the king their lord, which had been raised by a subsidy from the commons and wasted by bad counsel; they demanded the amending of this and governance by better counsel. Therefore the king rode against the earl; and as the king was in one region, the earl rode into another against those on the king's side, imprisoning the king's men wherever he was able to take them. Advancing to Inverkeithing, he took the sheriff of Angus, who was going to the king with a band of men-at-arms, and sent them to prison in various places.[10] The king marched through the night from Edinburgh, and almost caught the Earl of Douglas at Lanark where he had stayed the night; but he escaped with great difficulty, while some of his men were taken. The Steward of Scotland made his peace

Count de Douglas autresy a par ly, le Count de la Marche fesoit auxi. Et cest riot pur le temps ensi enmesez, le dit Dauid prist en espouse dame Margaret de Logy, vn dame qautre foitz auoit este marie, qe oue ly auoit deuaunt demurrez. Cest matremoigne fust fait soulement par force damours, qe toucz veint.

with his lord the king, without the knowledge or agreement of his allies.[11] The Earl of Douglas did likewise for himself, and the Earl of March as well. And with this unrest having been thus put down for the time being, David took to wife Lady Margaret de Logie, a lady who had been married previously, and who had been living with him before. This marriage was made only through the force of love, which overcomes everything.[12]

APPENDIX

[I] A letter describing the defeat of a Scottish raiding party in June
[1340].[1]

Trescher sire, endroit des nouelles vers noz parties, veillez sauoir qe
le Counte Patrike et le Counte de Sotherland vyndrent en les parties
Dengleterre le .xxviij. iour de Juyn dirreine passe et praierent la terre
tancqe a deus lieus de Bamburghe et pristrent bien a deus .Mille.
grosses bestes et pleuseurs persons, et quant ils auerent pris lour
praies et auerent ars la terre, ils se treierent vers les parties de Dunbar;
et bien a quatre lieus deinz la terre Descoce les compaignons de
Rokesburgh les encountrerent et descenderent a pie et combaterent
ouesqi eux issint qe par la grace de Dieu, ils feurent a celle heure
descomfitz, et plus de la moyte de lour gentz feurent pris et mortz, et
as toux les persons et bestes qils auoient pris et praiez en Engleterre a
celle iourne, feurent rescutz, et a grant peyne les deus Countes
eschaperent. Et vereme<nt>, sire, le poigne feut dure et fort, et il ny
auoit nul hom du pays, sicome monsieur Thomas de Grey, et
monsieur Robert du Manoirs, qi vyndrent illoeqes auant qils feurent
tout outrement discomfitz et mys a meschief, mes taunt soulement
les compaignons de Rokesburghe et les gentz du meen qe sount
demurantz en le Chastel de Werke en la compaignie Johan de
Coupelande. Et sachez sire qe iai afforte le Chastel de Werke od dicz
hommes darmes a mes coustages tantqe iai autres nouelles de mon
seigneur. Et sire, meisme le iour auantdit Alisaundre de Rameseye
oue deus Centz hommes darmes ouesqe lui auoient fait vne
enbuschement a deus lieus de Rokesburgh, et quant mes
compaignons feurent venuz a lostiel et feurent assis a manger, ils
debrissent lour enbuschement et vyndrent deuant Rokesburgh, et
volerent auoir ars la ville; mes mercie en soit Dieux la ville feut
recuse, et partie de lour gentz feurent pris et mortz, et ils se
returnerent saunz nulle manere de gayne a celle heure. Et par ce qe
les chiuaux mes compaignons feurent recrus, et ils feurent las de
trauail, ieo ne voilleie mye soeffrer, qe nulle issue feut fait sur eux
adonqes. Et sire endroit de les trois freres qe sount appellez Johan

[I] Beloved Sir, regarding the news from our parts, you might wish to know that Earl Patrick and the Earl of Sutherland came into the parts of England on the 28 June last past, and plundered the land as far as two miles from Bamburgh and took a good 2000 fat beasts and many people; and when they had taken their plunder and burned the land, they took themselves towards the parts of Dunbar; and a good four miles within the land of Scotland, the companions of Roxburgh encountered them, and dismounted on foot and fought with them, so that by the grace of God, they were defeated at that time. More than half of their men were taken or killed, and all the people and beasts which they had taken and plundered in England on that journey were rescued, and the two earls escaped only with great difficulty. And truly sir, the fight was long and hard, and no man of the region was there, except Sir Thomas de Gray and Sir Robert de Manners,[3] who arrived there before [the Scots] were completely defeated and put to mischief, but only the companions of Roxburgh and the men of the retinue who were staying in Wark castle in John de Coupland's company. And sir, you should know that I have strengthened Wark castle with ten men-at-arms at my expense until I have had other news from my lord. And sir, on that same day, Alexander de Ramsey,[4] and two hundred men-at-arms with him, had laid an ambush two miles from Roxburgh, and when my companions had got to their quarters and had sat down to eat, they broke from their ambush and came before Roxburgh, and they would have burned the town, but thanks be to God, the town was rescued, and some of their men were taken or killed, and they returned without any manner of gain at that time. And because my companions' horses were exhausted, and they were tired from the fight, I was unwilling to allow a sally to be made against them then. And sir, regarding the three brothers who are called John Kerr, Thomas Kerr and Henry Kerr, who were the greatest enemys I had in the forest, or in William Douglas' company, you

Ker, Thomas Ker et Henri Ker, qe feurent les plus grants enemys qe ieo auoi en la foreste, ou en la compaignie William Douglas, voillez sauoir sire, qe Johan Ker est mort par iouster de guerre de vne coupe qe vn de mes vadletz liu ferst parmy le corps, et parmy son haketone et hauberioun et les autres dous freres Thomas et Henri sount en ma garde et a ma voluntie sicome prisons pris de guerre. Et sire, endroit daucune secre busoigne dounc vous sauez qe feut parle en la chambre monsieur Henri de Ferers en la presence de lui et de vous, ne purroit mye estre exploite tanqe en ora[a] par enchaison qe lour host ad este gisant toute foiz en la foreste, mes verment sire, si la busoigne purroit estre mene a fyn, il ne y aueroit si grant exploite sur la guerre, si ne feut par bataille.

[II] A letter from Sir Thomas Gray to William de Bohun, Earl of Northampton, the king's lieutentant on the Scottish Marches, regarding a ransom dispute. Not dated.[2]

A mon' seigneur le Counte de Northantoun, Conestabill de Angletere, e liu tenaunt nostre seigneur le Roy les Marches des Scocies. Moustre si ly plest Thomas Gray, qe il estoit pleger par le encre Alayn de Hetoun et William seigneur de Duglas, en defaute de qel encre le dit Thomas este constreynt de se entre en prisoun, de qoi y prie a soun dit seigneur de remedi.

---

[a]   MS: oea.

might wish to know sir, that John Kerr is dead by jousting of war from a blow which one of my squires struck him through the body, and through his haketon and haubergeon;[5] and the other two brothers, Thomas and Henry, are in my guard and at my will as prisoners taken in war. And sir, regarding a certain secret business that you know was discussed in Henry de Ferrer's chamber that time, in the presence of him and you, it has not been possible to accomplish it up to now because their army has remained in the forest all the time. But truly sir, if the business could be brought to an end, no exploit so great could be had in the war, except by battle.

[II] To my lord the Earl of Northampton, Constable of England, and lieutenant of our lord the king on the Scottish Marches. If he pleases, Thomas Gray explains that he was pledged by a written agreement between Alan de Heton and William, Lord Douglas, in default of which agreement, Thomas is constrained to put himself in prison, for which he prays his said lord for remedy.

NOTES

Prologue [1]

1. 'Conuersacioun' can also mean 'behaviour, way of life', which would fit equally well here.

2. This a punning reference to the Grey friars (known as 'cordeliers' from the thin cords they used to tie their grey habits). Note that by the fifteenth century, and possibly before, the Gray family was using the symbol of a cloak as one of its badges, along with a ladder; both devices appear on Sir Ralph Gray's tomb at Chillingham, of *c.* 1450: Heslop and Harbottle, 'Chillingham Church', 131.

3. The 8th letter of the alphabet [H] after the 19th [T], followed by the 12th [M] after the 14th [O], and the 1st [A] and the 18th [S] spells 'Thomas'; the 7th [G] and 17th [R] letters, followed by the 1st [A] and 3rd vowels [I/Y] spells 'Gray' (as noted by James, *Catalogue, Corpus Christi*, 305). As the MS uses 'I' and 'Y' interchangeably, and invariably spells the name as 'Gray', we may assume that this was the spelling intended, rather than 'Grai'. Note that the modern letters 'I' and 'J' were not distinguished by medieval grammarians; thus 'I' was the 19th letter of the medieval alphabet, 'R' the 17th, etc.

Prologue [2]

This section is heavily annotated by a hand of the sixteenth century, perhaps that of John Leland (see above, lviii). The following notes have been made, in both margins, near the appropriate text: 'Thom. de otreburn', 'Sibilla', 'gualterus', 'Beda', 'Monachus Cesrensis [*sic*]', 'Polycronicon', 'Alfredus' [apparently a misunderstanding of the text's 'Egbright'], 'W. de Malmesbery, Henry de Huntindon, Roger de Houden, Mariotus Scotus', 'Vicar de Tilmouth', 'futur...', 'Vilissimi', 'Scala Cronica!', '1355', 'Brutus'. These annotations were added after the cropping of the MS; 'Thom. de otreburn' is written over three lines, with 'o-treburn' split to fit on the cropped page.

1. This is taken from Geoffrey of Monmouth, 17, which refers to 'the fortress-town of Mount Agned, which is now called the Castle of the Maidens' (*oppidum montis Agned, quod nunc Castellum Puellarum dicitur*).

2. Gray may have been referring here to a specific work, such as Guido delle Collonne's standard work, the *Historia destructionis Troiae*, or Benoît de Sainte-Maure's *Roman de Troie*; or – perhaps more likely – to the generic 'Matter of Troy', the large body of material which had been written on the subject since the twelfth century. See Ingledew, 'The Book of Troy', 666.

3. *Recte* Walter of Oxford; in the *Scalacronica*'s discussion of the historicity of King Arthur, Gray refers to 'the *Gest Bretoun* [which] was recounted in Breton until Walter, archdeacon of Oxford, translated it into Latin' (*la Gest Bretoun estoit dit en Breton tanqe Gauter Archedeken de Oxenford le translata en Latin*): MS 133, f. 83r.; therefore, the reference here to Walter of Exeter was simply a slip-up (possibly already present in the copy of the *Historia regum Britannie* used by Gray) for confu-

sion between the Latin soubriquets 'of Exeter' (*Exonie*) and 'of Oxford' (*Oxonie*) was not uncommon (cf. Marlborough, p. xviii). Gray is referring to the 'certain very old book in the British language', *i.e.* Breton – or perhaps Welsh (*quendam Britannici sermonis librum uetustissimum*), belonging to one Walter, archdeacon of Oxford, which Geoffrey of Monmouth claimed to have used as the source for his *Historia regum Britannie* (Monmouth, 1, 129, 147), written *circa* 1136. Gray obviously gleaned the reference from the *Historia regum*, and seems to have misunderstood it, for according to the *Historia regum*, Walter simply owned the book, and it was Geoffrey himself who actually translated it (Monmouth, 1). See Gransden, *Historical Writing*, i, 202–3.

4. The MS 'keile' is puzzling, as no medieval writer of that name is now known; Nennius would be a much more likely candidate for naming alongside Gildas.

5. Gray's *de gestis Anglorum* is clearly a reference to Bede's *Historia Ecclesiastica*. Durham's copy of this work was bound together with other historical works, in a compilation which was put together in its present form in the late middle ages (Durham Cathedral Library, MS B.ii.35); the title page of this compilation refers to the work as *Beda de gestis Anglorum*. A 1395 catalogue of the books of Durham Priory also refers to *liber Bede de gestis Anglorum* (*Catalogi veteres*, 65). Gray's use of this unusual title for Bede's work is unlikely to be co-incidental; it therefore seems likely that Gray made use of a Durham copy of the *Historia Ecclesiastica*, perhaps that in B.ii.35 itself.

6. The monk of Chester was Ranulf Higden, author of the *Polychronicon*, a 'universal history' of the world (though focussing on England). His was the most widely read Latin history in later medieval England. Higden was an older contemporary of Gray's. For him and his work, see Taylor, *Ranulf Higden*.

7. The author of the *Historia aurea* (*i.e.*, the 'Golden History') is usually identified as John of Tynemouth. The reference to Tillmouth, on the Tweed in Norhamshire, near to the Gray's manor of Heton, must be a slip, for Tillmouth was not a vicarage, and nor was there a castle: Galbraith, 'Historia Aurea'; NCH, viii, 124–7. Gray may have used the copy owned by the Priory of Durham: above, xx.

8. As the quote concerning 'seint Edward' is in Latin, the Sibyl was presumably referring to a Latin work; the standard Latin life of Edward the Confessor was that of Ailred of Rievaulx. This does indeed contain a lengthy relation of a vision experienced by Edward on his deathbed, but this prophecy concerns the immediate aftermath of Edward's death, and makes no mention of the Scots (cf. Ailred of Rievaulx, col. 771–4). In fact, Gray's quote appears to have been derived from Henry of Huntingdon's *Historia Anglorum*, which, in its account of the troubles of the reign of Æthelred, includes the following passage: 'quidam uir Dei ... predixit etiam quod non ea gens [*i.e.* the French] solum uerum et Scotorum, quos uilissimos habebant, eis ad emeritam confusionem dominaretur' (Huntingdon, 338–41). No such prophecy appears in the *Polychronicon*, which Gray states was his main source for late Anglo-Saxon history.

9. This is a direct translation of one of the *Prophecies of Merlin*, popularised (and doubtless concocted) by Geoffrey of Monmouth in his *Historia regum* ('Cadualadrus uocabit Conanum ...', 77). The line quoted by Gray is not derived from any known Middle English version of the *Brut*, but has the distinctive metre of fourteenth-century English alliterative verse. Gray was probably referring to an

alliterative verse translation of the *Brut*, or at least of the *Prophecies of Merlin*, which has not survived.

10. A Franciscan friar called Thomas de Oterbourn (described as 'a professor of holy writ' – *sacrae paginae professori*) was licensed to hear confessions in the diocese of Durham in 1343, presumably the same Thomas Oterborne who became lector of the Franciscans at Oxford, probably before 1350: *Richard of Bury, Register*, 28; Little, *Grey Friars in Oxford*, 174–5. This is likely to be the friar of Gray's vision. His chronicle does not appear to have survived (clearly, it is unlikely to be the chronicle attributed to Thomas Otterbourne, printed in 1732 by Thomas Hearne as *Duo Rerum Anglicarum Scriptores Veteres viz. Thomas Otterbourne et Johannes Whethamstede*, which goes down to 1420 – though see Little, 'Authorship of Lanercost', 276–7); however, Otterburn appears in Gray's vision as the supporter of the ladder which gives him access to his sources; and the Sibyl's words to her student suggest that his work is to be used as a model for producing his own chronicle, rather than as a direct crib (*ibid.*, 278–9). Perhaps the most likely explanation is that Otterburn's chronicle was one of the first histories which Gray read as a prisoner in Edinburgh, and which first fired his enthusiasm for the idea of writing his own; but when he actually started to work, he relied on other sources.

11. *Poepla* can also mean 'make known, make famous', which would also fit the context here.

Chapter 32

1. The coronation was actually on 19 Aug.

2. Edward was actually thirty-five, being born 18–19 June 1239. Most of the details of Edward's coronation are also to found in the *Brut* chronicle, couched in similar – though not identical – terms: *Brut*, ed. Brie, 179–80 (and see Cleopatra D.III, f. 141v., for the French text).

3. King Alexander did not do homage to Edward at the coronation, as Gray implies; in fact, he did not do homage until the autumn parliament of 1278: Prestwich, *Edward I*, 357. This was actually three years after the death of his wife Margaret, a daughter of Henry III, who died in Feb. 1275; their eldest son, called Alexander – and not Edward – died in Jan. 1264, and was indeed aged twenty; their younger son was indeed named David, but he was aged only eight at his death in June 1281.

4. *i.e.* Simon de Montfort, Earl of Leicester.

5. Gray is muddled here; Llewelyn did not rebel a second time after binding himself for 50,000 marks. Gray's account is very close to that of Langtoft, 232–5, who makes the same mistake.

6. Dafydd ap Gruffydd was granted the manor of Frodsham, Cheshire, in September 1278, for life (and not in heredity) having previously held it at will. *CPR 1272–81*, 278. This grant is mentioned by Langtoft, 234, 235, one recension of which relates that the manor was given in fee (*ibid.*, 235). The *Historia aurea*, however, makes no mention of Frodsham.

7. In fact, it was Dafydd who first set the war in motion, storming Hawarden castle in a surprise attack on 22 Mar. 1282: Prestwich, *Edward I*, 182–3. The *Historia aurea*, Lambeth, f. 214, gives an account of Dafydd's attack on Hawarden which Gray does not follow.

8. For a modern account, see Smith, *Llywelyn ab Gruffudd*, 536–42.

9. 11 Dec. 1282: Prestwich, *Edward I*, 193–4. Gray's account of Llewelyn's death is abbreviated from the *Historia aurea*, Lambeth, f. 214.

10. Pecham was consecrated on 19 Feb. 1279.

11. This celebrated tournament took place in 1279. See Barker, *Tournament*, 66–7. Gray's account is derived from the *Historia aurea*, Lambeth, f. 214.

12. Dafydd was captured on 21 June 1283: Prestwich, *Edward I*, 195–6.

13. Alexander's second wife, Yolande de Dreux, whom he married in Oct. 1285, was not the daughter of the Count of Flanders, but a member of a distinguished French noble family. The same error is made by the *Historia aurea* (Lambeth, f. 215) – clearly the source of Gray's mistake – *Rishanger*, 118–19, and Guisborough, 233 (which compounds the error by describing the Count of Flanders as a duke).

14. Gray's chronology is wrong here, for the expulsion of the Jews took place in 1290, after the king's return from Gascony in Aug. 1289: Prestwich, *Edward I*, 343–6. Gray seems to have been following a different source from the *Historia aurea* (which mentions the fifteenth only, and not the tenth: Lambeth, f. 215), such as Guisborough, 227, whose lengthy account of the expulsion ends with a note on taxation very similar to Gray's (note that Higden's brief notice makes no mention of taxation at all: *Polychronicon*, viii, 270).

15. See Prestwich, *Edward I*, 318–26. The whole affair is described in considerable detail in the *Historia aurea*: Lambeth, ff. 214–15.

16. Thomas Weyland abjured the realm after being indicted and arrested in September 1289 for harbouring two murderers; a number of his fellow justices, including the two named by Gray, were convicted of misconduct and fined, though not exiled, and it appears that their misdeeds were in fact comparatively minor. Brand, 'Edward I and the Judges', 31–40. For Beckingham and Mettingham, see *ibid.*, 38.

17. Acre fell in May 1291; Eleanor of Castile had died in the previous year, in Nov. 1290.

18. Alexander died 19 Mar. 1286. Gray is here largely following the chronology of the *Historia aurea*, which relates the death of Alexander almost immediately before describing the death of his granddaughter Margaret, the 'Maid of Norway', without giving any indication of the date of Alexander's death: Lambeth, f. 215.

19. Margaret, the 'Maid of Norway', died *c.* 26 September 1290. 'Meistre Weland' may perhaps be identified with Weland de Stiklaw, a clerk in the service of Alexander III: Crawford, 'North Sea Kingdoms, North Sea Bureaucrat'. The agreement between the two countries referred to by Gray is presumably the Treaty of Birgham, sealed at Birgham (on the Scottish side of the Tweed, up from Norham) on 18 July 1290, which does not, however, contain a clause specifying that Edward of Caernarvon should spend alternate years in each realm. *Documents*, ed. Stevenson, i, 162–73; Prestwich, 'Edward I and the Maid of Norway', 165–72.

20. This curious story that Edward planned to marry Blanche was widely reported by contemporary English chroniclers: see Ormrod, 'Love and War in 1294', 143–52. The closest account to Gray's is that of Langtoft, 260–5. Although the *Historia aurea* has a detailed account of the dispute with France (Lambeth, ff. 216–217), it makes no mention of Edward's marital plans.

21. Hugh de Manchester and William de Gainsborough are mentioned in the *Historia aurea*'s account (Lambeth, ff. 216v.–217), but not the detail that they were

held by the Count of Artois. Langtoft, 270–1, does record this detail, reporting that they were held for a week.

22. Madog ap Llewelyn and Morgan ap Maredudd, two of the leaders of the Welsh revolt which broke out at the end of September 1294: see Prestwich, *Edward I*, 219–24.

23. Bellegarde was a *bastide* in Gascony: Prestwich, *Edward I*, 385.

24. In fact, while Cynan ap Maredudd was executed at Hereford, Madog and Morgan were both spared, and indeed, Morgan subsequently entered Edward's household: Prestwich, *Edward I*, 224.

25. The Count of Flanders was Guy, not Robert.

26. In fact, from 1290 to 1301 the Archdeacon of Richmond was Gerard von Wippingen: Neve, *Fasti Ecclesiae Anglicanae*, 25. The identity of John de Glantoun is not clear.

27. This is another of Gray's chronological muddles, for the death of Margaret took place in 1290, and the Flanders campaign in 1297.

Chapter 33

1. This is a cross-reference to an account of Pictish origins previously related in the *Scalacronica*, and derived from Geoffrey of Monmouth; Broun, *Irish Identity*, 85.

2. Fordun's version of this tale locates the stone at 'Themor', *i.e.* Tara: Fordun, 23; Bower, i, 64.

3. 'La laund Porry' is probably to be identified with Cape Wrath, called *Am Parph* in Gaelic: Broun, *Irish Identity*, 90n.

Chapter 35

1. Cf. Bower, ii, 298, 'Cruthne filius Kynne Judicis qui cepit maonarchium in regnum Pictorum' (Cruithne son of Judge Kynne who founded the monarchy in the kingdom of the Picts).

2. The unfeasibly long reigns of Gede and Taren are found in other king-lists: Anderson, *Kings and Kingship*, 271, 279 (king lists F and I; and cf. *ibid.*, 265, king list D, where Gede is described as ruling for just fifty years, though Taren is still said to have ruled for 100). Fordun, 152–3 (copied by Bower, ii, 296–8) expressed his reservations on the matter and commented that the reader could always investigate the truth of the matter himself.

3. Bower, ii, 302, has 'ducentis annis xxvi, novem mensis et sex diebus' (226 years, nine months and six days) here. Given the *Scalacronica*'s habitual mangling of numbers, the discrepancy is probably an error on the part of Gray or his scribe.

Chapter 36

1. Three other king lists record that Tirg macDungald ruled for twelve years: Anderson, *Kings and Kingship*, 267, 274, 283 (king lists D, F and I). All three identify 'Tirg' as Girg, and add the details of his conquests and reformation of the church, though I specifies that he conquered Bernicia, rather than Hibernia (see also the note in Bower, ii, 468–9). D and F (though not I) also, like the *Scalacronica*, record Athe mac Kenneth as having been killed by Girg *filio* Dungal, and then name Girg *Mac* Dungal as having ruled for twelve years. According to Fordun, 159, who dates his 'coronation' to 875, Girg 'reigned for almost eighteen years'; intriguingly, Bower, ii, 318 here inserts a caveat (in a marginal aside), 'or twelve years, as I have

read in an old chronicle'. Gray's allusion to the 'cronicles of Scotland' probably reflects the lack of corroboration for these claims to conquest in English chronicles.

2. Duncan (acceded Nov. 1034; killed Aug. 1040) was the son of Crinan the hereditary abbot of Dunkeld; his claim to the kingship came through his mother, Bethoc. The MS has 'Betowe *fitz* Malcolme mac Kynech' (Bethoc *son* of Malcolm macKenneth), when the sense – and indeed historical accuracy – requires 'Betowe *feile* Malcolme Mac Kynech' (Bethoc *daughter* of Malcolm macKenneth). Gray's confusion (or possibly that of his source) may have stemmed from misreading 'Betowe' as a placename.

3. The *Scalacronica* has a full and splendid – if somewhat fanciful – account of Malcolm Canmore's death in its narrative of the reign of William II of England: *Scalacronica*, Stevenson, 21. Canmore, who acceded to the kingship in Mar. 1058, was killed in battle at Alnwick, Northumberland, on 13 Nov. 1093.

4. Gray (or possibly his source) has garbled the chronology here, for it was Earl Henry who pre-deceased his father, King David – Malcolm did not pre-decease his father Henry. Note also that the lordship of Garioch did not actually convey any comital title.

5. In fact, Kerrera, where Alexander II died on 8 July 1249, is an island in Oban Bay, in Argyll. He succeeded to the kingship in Dec. 1214, so in fact he reigned for thirty-four years.

6. Alexander III, who broke his neck in a fall from his horse whilst riding in the dark to see his wife on 19 Mar. 1286. In fact, Alexander was succeeded by his three-year-old granddaughter, Margaret, the 'Maid of Norway', whom Gray – or his source – neglects to mention. It was her death without heirs in September 1290 that led to the 'Great Cause'. Gray gives an account of Alexander's death along with that of Margaret, above, 13.

7. This refers to the eighty-odd years of peace between Alexander II's invasion of England in 1215–17 and the outbreak of war in 1296.

8. There are a few minor errors in this summary account of the 'Great Cause': the John de Balliol who was a claimant in 1291 was the son and heir of John de Balliol and Dervorguilla; Isabella's husband was Robert, not Peter, de Bruce; and Ada's husband was Henry de Hastings, not John – the John de Hastings who was a claimant in 1291 was their grandson.

9. *Lanercost*, 157, records that the bridge was knocked down when the river Teviot flooded disastrously in Aug. 1294, also causing great damage in Scotland.

10. Alnwick was granted to Bek, in 1295, who sold it to Percy in 1310; according to Gray's contemporary, the Durham Priory chronicler Robert Graystanes, Vesci granted Alnwick to Bek on the understanding that he would pass it on to his bastard son John, as he had no legitimate issue: *Historiæ Dunelmensis*, ed. Raine, 91. Doubt has been cast on the veracity of Gray's and Graystanes' accounts by Bean, 'The Percies' Acquisition of Alnwick', 309–14. However, in 1323, at York, Gray's father was a witness to a deed by Vesci's heir, Gilbert Aton, confirming Bek's grant of Alnwick to Percy (*Percy Chartulary*, ed. Martin, 232); he would therefore have had some knowledge of the affair, particularly as Vesci's widow, Isabella, was the sister of his patron, Henry de Beaumont, and he was the probable source of this information.

Chapter 37

1. For the hearings, see *Great Cause, passim*.

2. The proceedings opened on 10 May 1291, at Norham church. It should be noted that many of Gray's dates and details are wrong; in particular, the proceedings were resumed at Berwick on 3 Aug. 1291: *Great Cause*, i, 11–13; and see Duncan, 'The Process of Norham'.

3. The petitions were submitted at Berwick castle on 3 Aug. 1291. Gray omits the names of Robert de Pinkeny and Roger de Mandeville, who also put in claims; and King Eric II of Norway, who put in his claim in June 1292 (the petitions are all printed in *Great Cause*, ii, 132–43). On 12 Aug., the hearings were adjourned until 2 June 1292. It was actually William de Vesci, the brother of John, who put in a claim, as John had died in Feb. 1289; *CP*, xii/2, 280. For John, see above, 11. The *Historia aurea* gives an almost identical list, except that Robert de Bruce comes before John Comyn, and Patrick Golightly is omitted altogether: Lambeth, f. 215.

4. This is another error; the number of auditors was 104, of whom 40 were nominated by Bruce, 40 by Balliol and Comyn, and 24 by Edward, and they had been nominated at the beginning of the process, at Norham: *Great Cause*, i, 12–13. Gray copied this error, including the reference to Michaelmas, from the *Historia aurea*: Lambeth, f. 215v. It would appear that John of Tynemouth – or his source – mistook forty auditors from *each* realm to mean forty auditors from *both* realms.

5. The final judgement was actually given on 17 Nov. 1292, at the hall of Berwick Castle: *Great Cause*, i, 278.

6. Bruce married Isabella de Clare in 1240; she was the youngest daughter of Gilbert de Clare (d. 1230), and was therefore the aunt, not the sister, of Gilbert, Earl of Gloucester (d. 1295, Gilbert de Clare's grandson): Altschul, *The Clares*, 33, and table ii. Warenne's support for Balliol may similarly be explained by the fact that the latter had married his daughter Isabella, in 1279: *NCH*, vi, 73. Bek's support may have been due to Balliol's grant, pre-emptively styling himself as 'heir of the kingdom of Scots', of the manors of Wark on Tyne and Penrith, in Nov. 1290, which could only take effect if Balliol did in fact succeed to the kingdom: *Documents*, ed. Stevenson, i, 203–4; Fraser, *Antony Bek*, 57, 89–90. Note that this information about Gloucester, Warenne and Bek is not derived from the *Historia aurea*; Gray seems to have used another source to supplement his account.

7. For a genealogy, see *Great Cause*, fig. 4.

8. There does not appear to be any documentary evidence that Bruce was ever 'a young bachelor of King Edward's chamber'. This is perhaps a contemporary English smear, intended to impugn Bruce's loyalty, mistakenly reported by Gray as fact.

9. This accords with the date given for Balliol's inauguration by the *Historia aurea* (Lambeth, f. 216), Fordun, 321, and Guisborough, 238–9. See also *Great Cause*, ii, 259.

10. In fact, John had four sisters (as well as two elder brothers, who were both dead by the time of the 'Great Cause'): Margaret, who is 'stated to have married ... Multon', presumably Thomas de Multon of Gilsland; Cecily (omitted by Gray), who married John de Burgh; Ada, who married William de Lindsay, and whose daughter Christina married the Sire de Coucy; and Eleanor (or Mary), who married John Comyn of Badenoch. *NCH*, vi, 73; Stell, 'Balliol Family', 153, 158. The Balliols held the Northumbrian barony of Bywell, and the lordship of Barnard Castle in Durham, until 1293.

11. This was Edward Balliol who was installed as King of Scots by the English 'Disinherited', after their victory at Dupplin Moor, 1332; above, 111.

Chapter 38
1. 26 Dec. 1292, in the castle hall at Newcastle: *Great Cause*, ii, 260–3.

2. This was Roger Bartholomew, who lodged his appeal with Edward on 7 Dec., just a week after Balliol's inauguration: Barrow, *Bruce*, 51–2. Bartholomew was a burgess of Berwick, and so Gray's reference to 'un gentil hom' is somewhat puzzling, as burgesses were not generally considered to be *gentil*. However, this may perhaps reflect Gray's sensitivity about his own family's standing, as his probable great-grandfather, Sir John Gray, had served as mayor of Berwick; above, xxiii.

3. The *Historia aurea* (Lambeth, f. 217v.), and also Guisborough, 264–5, include the detail of the composition of the Scottish council, and record the envoys as the bishops of St Andrews and Dunkeld, and John de Soules and Ingram de Umfraville (for whom, see below, 220, n. 7). See Barrow, *Bruce*, 63–5; Watson, *Under the Hammer*, 20–1.

4. The *Historia aurea* (Lambeth, f. 217v.) records that Edward demanded 'three castles, Berwick, Edinburgh, Roxburgh'. Guisborough, 270, records the same, albeit listing the three in a different order.

5. Wark on Tweed, Northumberland. Easter Sunday was on 25 Mar. in 1296.

6. This is not derived from the *Historia aurea*, which records merely that 'a certain knight, Robert de Roos, lord of Wark castle, deserted to the Scots, notwithstanding the faith which he had sworn to the King of England' (*... miles quidam Robertus de Roos, dominus castri de Werk, non obstante fidelitate quam regi Anglie iurauerat, ad Scotos transfugit*: Lambeth, f. 218 – the same passage occurs *verbatim* in *Rishanger*, 155–6; and *Trivet annales*, 342), before describing the subsequent battle at Pressen, a couple of miles south of Wark, between Robert and his brother William. Gray's account is corroborated by Guisborough, 271, which states that Roos was 'moved by love for a certain woman of Scottish race, whom he proposed to take in marriage'. Gray presumably owed his information about Christine de Mowbray to his father. Sanquhar was a barony in Dumfries.

7. The Scots attacked on Easter Monday, 26 Mar. 1296; the 'siege' of Carlisle lasted little more than a day: Summerson, *Carlisle*, i, 193–4. Gray's account is a summary of that of the *Historia aurea*: Lambeth f. 218. See also, Guisborough, 272–4; *Rishanger*, 156.

8. Berwick was captured on 30 Mar.: Prestwich, *Edward I*, 470–1.

9. The detail concerning the delivery of the letter is taken from the *Historia aurea*, Lambeth f. 218v., which includes the letter's text. The letter was presented to Edward at Berwick on 5 Apr. 1296, and copied by the notary John of Caen; the notorial copy is printed in *Anglo-Scottish Relations*, ed. Stones, 140–5. Guisborough, 275–6, names the Scottish friar as Adam Blunt, and also includes a copy of the letter (note that the *Historia aurea*'s version is derived from a slightly different text).

10. The *Historia aurea* makes no mention of this raid, which took place in Apr., after the fall of Berwick: Barrow, *Bruce*, 71. The burning of Hexham Priory is noted by *Rishanger*, 159; *Lanercost*, 174, relates a lurid atrocity story about the burning alive of a group of young school boys in Hexham Abbey on this occasion.

11. Earl Patrick had been one of the 'competitors' in the Great Cause; above, 33. His wife was Marjorie, the daughter of Alexander Comyn, Earl of Buchan (*NCH,*

vii, 77), and the Comyns were Balliol's main supporters. In fact, despite Gray's commendation, there appears to have been some doubt over Patrick's initial loyalty to the English crown; although he declared his homage and fealty to Edward at Wark castle on 25 Apr., the sheriff of Northumberland had already taken the trouble to confiscate his lands, though he got them back at the end of the year: *Anglo-Scottish Relations*, ed. Stones, 136–9; *CCR 1296–1302*, 9. Indeed, Langtoft, 303, claimed that Patrick came 'to the king's peace' only after the capture of Berwick. Note that Gray's account of the earl and his wife's treachery is largely independent of the *Historia aurea* (Lambeth, f. 218v.) which notes only that Earl Patrick came to Edward at Jedburgh, after the Scots had taken Dunbar by deception ('fraude') on the feast of St Mary (25 Mar.). The *Scalacronica* appears to be the only reference to Patrick's 'black beard', but Gray's father served with him in 1302 (*Rot. Scot.*, i, 52), so there is no reason to doubt it. For an account of the earl's career, see *NCH*, vii, 69–77.

12. 27 Apr. 1296. For modern accounts, see Barrow, *Bruce*, 72; Prestwich, *Edward I*, 471–3. Spott is a couple of miles south of Dunbar.

13. The list of prisoners captured in Dunbar castle matches that in the *Historia aurea*, except the latter gives the number of squires (*scutifers*) captured as eighty-three; Lambeth, f. 218v.

14. It is normally assumed that the chair in which the stone was placed was intended to be used for coronations. It is, however, more likely to have been used as Gray describes, by the priest (*Rishanger*, 163, also states that the chair was used by the priest). It may also have been used when the newly crowned king disinvested himself of the regalia. See Binski, *Westminster Abbey*, 135–9.

15. This is derived from the rather detailed account in the *Historia aurea* (Lambeth, f. 219). The sealed record of homage is the 'Ragman Roll'; most of the fealties recorded on it are dated 28 Aug. 1296, at Berwick, though it is hardly likely that all the 1500-odd landholders (not just magnates) recorded on it were physically present in Berwick on that day: Barrow, *Bruce*, 75–7. Edward was at Berwick from 22 Aug. to 16 September 1296: Safford, *Itinerary of Edward I. Part II*, 93–4.

16. Warenne was appointed keeper of Scotland on 3 September 1296, although Edward was in Berwick on that date, and did not reach Newminster until 29 Sep.: *Rot. Scot.*, i, 27; Safford, *Itinerary of Edward I. Part II*, 94–5. Gray's father took out letters of protection for serving with Earl Warenne in Scotland, in June 1297: *Rot. Scot.*, i, 47. Warenne himself is therefore probably the ultimate source for this remark. Newminster was a Cistercian abbey near Morpeth, Northumberland. The appointment of Warenne, Cressingham and Ormsby is noted by the *Historia aurea*, Lambeth, f. 219, though without the detail of Edward's coarse opinions.

17. In fact, Edward led an expedition to Flanders, not Gascony, leaving England on 23 Aug. 1297.

18. Wallace's victim is usually described as the sheriff of Lanark (Fordun, 328; Bower, vi, 82; *CDS*, ii, no. 1597), though as the sheriff of Lanark was sometimes referred to as sheriff of Clydesdale, the difference is immaterial. The killing took place at Lanark, in May 1297: Barrow, *Bruce*, 83. A William de Heselrigg witnessed a charter relating to the vill of Hazelrigg (a few miles east of Bamburgh, Northumberland), in 1292 x 1296, along with his like-named son. The son was probably the William de Heselrigg who held land in Akeld, near Wooler, and who certainly died soon after the start of the Scottish wars: MacDonald, 'Laing Charters

Relating to Northumberland', 108–9; *CDS*, iii, no. 633; *NCH*, xiv, 227; *NCH* xi, 231. The man killed at Lanark was probably the son.

19. This Thomas de Gray was the author's own father, who was undoubtedly the source of the story.

20. The battle was fought on 11 September 1297; for a modern account, see Barrow, *Bruce*, 86–9. Gray's father may well have been present, for he received letters of protection for service in Scotland with the Earl of Warenne in June 1297, and further letters in June 1298: *Rot. Scot.*, i, 47; *Scotland in 1298*, ed. Gough, 44. Note that Wallace's invasion of Northumberland took place after Stirling Bridge, and also took in Cumberland: McNamee, 'William Wallace's Invasion of Northern England'.

21. The *Scalacronica*'s account of the battle is essentially the same as that of the *Historia aurea*, Lambeth f. 220v. This also includes the detail regarding the unfortunate Cressingham, 'whom the Scots skinned, and divided up his skin into little bits' (*quem Scoti excoriantes, pellem eius in particulas diuiserunt*). The same story is also related by Guisborough, 303 (in very similar phrasing to the *Historia aurea*), and *Lanercost*, 190; nevertheless, Gray adds the qualifier 'it was said', suggesting he considered the tale to be of doubtful veracity. Cressingham's appointment as the chamberlain of Scotland is mentioned by Gray, above, 21.

22. There is a place called Hutton, a few miles north-west of Berwick, on the way to Duns; presumably, Hutton Moor was near there.

23. Edward was actually in Flanders; he returned to England on 14 Mar. 1298 (see n. 17, above). The Prince of Wales was, of course, the future Edward II.

24. Robert Wishart, Bishop of Glasgow, and William Douglas submitted to the English at Irvine, Ayr, at the end of June 1297, before the battle of Stirling Bridge: Barrow, *Bruce*, 84–5; *Knighton*, ed. Lumby, i, 376–7. Douglas was in Berwick by 24 July, when a letter describes him as 'still very intractable (*sauvage*) and very abusive'; another letter states that he was being kept in irons, and requested the king not to release him until he could be sure how Douglas would behave. He was dead by Jan. 1299. *Documents*, ed. Stevenson, ii, 204–5 and note; *Knighton*, ed. Lumby, i, 371; *CDS*, ii, nos. 960, 1054–5.

25. Gray's father served with fitz Roger in the garrison of Berwick soon after this, receiving letters of protection in Jan. 1299: *CDS*, v, no. 2198. For fitz Roger, see *CP*, iii, 274–5. John fitz Marmaduke (d. 1311), lord of Horden, was a prominent baron in the palatinate of Durham who served the Crown extensively on the Scottish Marches: Offler, 'Murder', 195–7; Fraser, *Antony Bek, passim*. According to Guisborough, 324–5, he was regarded as excessively cruel even by Edward I.

26. Although the town of Berwick was taken, the castle held out. Berwick and Roxburgh were relieved in Feb. 1298: Prestwich, *Edward I*, 478–9; Watson, *Under the Hammer*, 50.

27. *Rishanger*, 385, quotes Wallace himself as saying, 'Hy haue pult ou into a gamen, hoppet yif ye kunnet' (I have put you into a ring, hop if you can). The most detailed contemporary account of the battle is that of Guisborough, 325–8. For modern accounts, see Barrow, *Bruce*, 100–4; Prestwich, 480–1.

28. The 'Falkirk Roll of Arms' lists twenty-six bannerets in Bek's battle, including the earls of Angus and Dunbar, but not Warwick or Oxford: Blair, 'Northern Knights at Falkirk', 78–92.

Chapter 39

1. Balliol was released from papal custody in the summer of 1301, and resided at Bailleul-en-Vimeu, in Picardy; he died in France around Dec. 1314: *Documents*, ed. Stevenson, ii, 402–4; Stell, 'Balliol Family', 160.

2. Note that Gray here refers to 'the *land* of Scotland' (*la terre Descoce*), rather than the '*kingdom* of Scotland', which accords with Edward I's line that Scotland was not to be treated as a kingdom.

3. Printed *Anglo-Scottish Relations*, ed. Stones, 162–75. The bull was dated 27 June 1299, but was not actually delivered to Edward until the autumn of 1300: Prestwich, *Edward I*, 490–1. For the Scottish input into its content, see Barrow, *Bruce*, 61, 116.

4. This was announced in a letter dated 7 May 1301, and presented to Boniface VIII on 2 July; printed *Anglo-Scottish Relations*, ed. Stones, 192–219. The text of a slighty different version of this letter was copied into the *Historia aurea*: Lambeth, ff. 222–223v. The English and Scottish propaganda campaigns at the papal *Curia* are examined in Prestwich, *Edward I*, 490–2, 495. The parliament at Lincoln was held 20–30 Jan. 1301.

5. Gray's chronology is confused here, for the siege of Caerlaverock took place in July 1300, while Wallace was captured and executed in Aug. 1305, eleven months after the siege of Stirling castle. The *Historia aurea* does not mention Caerlaverock; it does have a brief account of Wallace's execution, though without any account of his capture: Lambeth, f. 224v. Menteith, a Scot, was keeper of Dumbarton, though he had only come into Edward's peace in 1304; he was awarded £100 for his efforts: *Documents*, ed. Palgrave, i, 295; Barrow, *Bruce*, 136–7. According to Langtoft, 419, Menteith captured Wallace in bed with his lover.

6. Walsingham, i, 99, refers to Edward 'committing the custody of that land [*i.e.* Scotland]' to Segrave after All Saints Day 1302. Segrave, from a Warwickshire/Leicestershire magnate family, was certainly serving as royal lieutenant south of the Forth, and justiciar of Lothian by Apr. 1303: *CCR 1302–7*, 25. For his career, see *CP*, xi, 605–8.

7. Ingram de Umfraville was the youngest son of Robert de Umfraville, lord of Chollerton, Northumberland, brother of Gilbert de Umfraville, Earl of Angus and lord of Prudhoe and Redesdale (d. 1245): *NCH*, xii, 100. Ingram made his career in Scotland after marrying the daughter of Ingram de Balliol, and adhered to the Scots until 1306, at which point his Balliol connection brought him to the English allegiance: King, 'War, Politics and Landed Society', 14–15. *Lanercost*, 204, also describes him as a Scot, despite his Northumbrian origins. His career is outlined – in rather purple prose – in Hodgson, *History of Northumberland*, II, i, 31–4; and rather more soberly in Blair, 'Baronys and Knights of Northumberland', 53–4. Robert de Keith was the hereditary Marshal of the King of Scots. He was appointed warden of the Forest of Selkirk in Aug. 1299, but was captured in a skirmish in Galloway in Aug. 1300, shortly after the fall of Caerlaverock castle; a royal writ of 10 Aug. ordered Keith to be moved from Carlisle castle to Nottingham castle, as the king had heard that he was 'among his worst enemies, and of bad repute': *SP*, vi, 30; *Rishanger*, 441; *CDS*, ii, no. 1147. He was released in 1304, but subsequently adhered to Robert Bruce, becoming one of his closest advisers, and appending his seal to the Declaration of Arbroath: *SP*, vi, 30–2; Barrow, *Bruce*, 284–5. Robert de Hastang was appointed sheriff of Roxburgh, with the keeping of the castle in September 1296, and retained the office until Oct. 1305. He was subse-

quently granted Robert de Keith's lands in Lothian by Edward II, in Mar. 1312. *Rot. Scot.*, i, 30; *CFR 1272–1307*, 529; *CDS*, iii, no. 258. These 'great encounters' presumably took place between Keith's appointment as warden in Aug. 1299 and his capture in Aug. 1300.

8. In September 1302, Gray's father took out letters of protection until Christmas for service with the Earl of March (*Rot. Scot.*, i, 52); he may still have been serving with him the following Feb., at the battle of Roslin.

9. The term 'battle' here refers to the division of the army under Segrave's direct personal command: see the note on the translation of military terms, lxiii above.

10. 24 Feb. 1303. According to Guisborough, 351–2, Segrave was captured by the Scots, but was subsequently rescued by the second English division (*turma*), presumably, the vanguard referred to by Gray. Fordun, 334, describes the Scots as defeating three English divisions, while Guisborough also refers to a third English division, led by Robert de Neville, though his account suggests that the third English division had some success. For modern accounts of the battle, see Watson, *Under the Hammer*, 170–1; Barrow, *Bruce*, 126.

11. Ralph Manton, cofferer of the Wardrobe. He had held this post since 1297: Tout, *Medieval Adminstrative History*, vi, 30. For his role in Scotland, see Watson, *Under the Hammer, passim*.

12. Edward arrived in Scotland, at Roxburgh, on 16 May 1303. Note that as Gray generally reckoned the start of the year from the Annunciation (25 Mar.), the battle of Roslin took place in Feb. 1302 by this reckoning, and therefore 'the year following' was 1303, by modern reckoning.

13. This is a reference to Gray's own father, who was obviously the source for this account of the ambush of Audley's force.

14. Comyn and his followers formally submitted on 16 Feb. 1304: Watson, *Under the Hammer*, 185–8.

15. Soules died in France in *c.* 1310: Barrow, *Bruce*, 155; M'Michael, 'de Soulis', 180.

16. 'The Lion' was the heraldic device used by Scottish kings; Oliphant was claiming to hold Stirling for the Scottish crown. This claim may have been connected with his request to Edward I that he might send a messenger to John de Soules, in exile in France (as Gray notes), as the guardian of Scotland who had appointed him, asking whether he should surrender the castle or defend it to the last: Barrow, *Bruce*, 126–8.

17. The castle surrendered on 24 July; Edward had arrived at Stirling on 22 Apr., so Gray's estimate of the duration of the siege is slightly exaggerated, though the castle may have been blockaded by the English before the siege was formally underway. The most detailed contemporary account is that of *Flores*, iii, 118–20, 315–20; for modern accounts, see Prestwich, *Edward I*, 501–2; Watson, *Under the Hammer*, 188–91.

18. The chronology is wrong, for the battle of Courtrai was fought two years earlier in 1302, on 11 July. For an account of the battle, see DeVries, *Infantry Warfare*, 9–22.

19. This curious and highly implausible story is not contained in any other chronicle, and it is unlikely to have any basis in fact: Prestwich, *Edward I*, 130. However, it may reflect court gossip at the time, which Gray's father could have been familiar with through his contact with Henry de Beaumont.

20. The battle was fought on 18 Aug. 1304, two years after Courtrai. Although the Flemings were indeed defeated, it was a close-run affair, and the French suffered heavy casualties: DeVries, *Infantry Warfare*, 32–48.

21. The Count of Flanders in question was Guy of Dampierre, not Robert. Robert of Béthune succeeded Guy in 1305.

22. Guisborough, 366, and *Lanercost*, 203 give the date as iv. ides of Feb. (*i.e.* 10 Feb.), as do Fordun, 340, and Bower, vi, 312. Gray must have taken the date from the *Historia aurea*, which also gives iv. kalends of Feb. (Lambeth, f. 224v.). However, he must also have referred to another source which gave him the year 1306, a source which dated the start of the year from Christmas, or 1 Jan. – for Gray usually dates the start of the year from the Annunciation (25 Mar.), by which reckoning, 27 Jan. was still 1305.

23. John Comyn was the son of John Comyn of Badenoch (one of the claimants to the Scottish kingship in 1291–2: above, 33) and Eleanor (or Mary) the youngest sister of John Balliol (the marriage is noted by Gray, above, 35). He was therefore descended from Earl David of Huntingdon, and indeed, arguably had a better claim to the kingship than Bruce himself.

24. See Introduction, xlv above. Dalswinton was a Comyn castle.

25. Duncan, Earl of Fife, was certainly in Edward's ward at about this time, for in Nov. 1306, the king obtained dispensation for him to marry Mary de Monthermer: *Vetera monumenta*, ed. Theiner, 177; and see 246, n. 11, below. Isabella was Duncan's aunt, not his mother, and was married to John Comyn, Earl of Buchan: *SP*, iv, 11–12; Barrow, *Bruce*, 151–2.

26. The order for the construction of this cage is printed in *Documents*, ed. Palgrave, i, 358–9. Gray's father may have watched this spectacle himself, as he was serving at Berwick for much of 1306: *CDS*, v, nos. 415, 492 (p. 210), 510, 2621.

27. In fact, Valence did not become Earl of Pembroke until Nov. 1307.

28. Barbour, II, line 211, identifies Mowbray as Philip de Mowbray, and Philip was certainly present at the battle, for he lost a horse there: *CDS*, v, no. 472, p. 211. Alexander de Abernethy, banneret, was serving with Valence with a retinue of 4 knights and 22 esquires, and Adam de Gordon with 8 esquires; David de Brechin was the keeper of Aberdeen castle: *CDS*, v, no. 492, pp. 210, 215–16. Barbour's account gives a particularly prominent role to Ingram de Umfraville, as one of the Scots advising Aymer de Valence (for Ingram, see above, 220, n. 7). Gray's father was later to encounter Adam de Gordon and Philip de Mowbray's brother, Alexander, as enemies, at Norham castle; above, 83, 81.

29. 19 June 1306. According to Guisborough, 368, and Barbour, II, lines 195–470, Valence waited until the evening, when the Scots had already retired to make camp (though Barbour, II, line 308, does add the detail that a third part of the Scots' army was foraging at the time). Gray's father may have been at the battle, as he was serving in Henry de Beaumont's retinue at this time, and Beaumont was in Valence's company: *CDS*, v, nos. 492 (p. 210), 420; *CCR 1302–7*, 376.

30. According to Guisborough, 368, Bruce ordered all his mounted men-at-arms to wear linen shirts over their arms, so that, 'it was not possible to recognise anybody or what arms they bore'. Haliburton was presumably one of the Haliburton family who were the lords of Dirleton, Lothian.

31. Randolph was captured in Ettrick Forest by James Douglas, probably in the summer of 1308: Barbour, IX, lines 677–762. He returned to the Scottish allegiance, attending Bruce's first parliament in Mar. 1309, as Lord of Nithsdale. He was

created Earl of Moray by Bruce in 1312: Barrow, *Bruce*, 186; *SP*, vi, 291–4. Gray mentions his death in 1332, as guardian of Scotland: above, 109.

32. Gray's account is derived from the *Historia aurea* (Lambeth, f. 224v.), which provides a very similar account to Guisborough, 368 – both of which are mistaken. In fact, it was Kildrummy castle in Aberdeenshire where Bruce's wife, Elizabeth de Burgh, took shelter, and which was besieged in Aug. However, Elizabeth had already fled to the sanctuary of St Duthac at Tain, Ross, where she was captured by the Earl of Ross: Barbour, IV, lines 39–183; Fordun, 342. Dunaverty was the castle in Kintyre, besieged in the same September by Sir John de Botetourt and Sir John Menteith: *CDS*, ii, nos. 1833–4.

33. Atholl's mother was Isabella, daughter of Richard of Dover, who was the son of one of King John's bastards; her mother was Maud, daughter of Malcolm, Earl of Angus: *CP*, i, 305. Atholl's elevated gallows is also reported by Guisborough, 369, and *Flores*, iii, 134–5.

34. This is clearly a reference to the famous Feast of the Swans, held to celebrate Edward of Caernarvon's knighting, 22 May 1306 (for which, see Bullock-Davies, *Menestrellorum Multitudo*, pp. ix–xli). Intriguingly, those knighted at the feast included one Thomas de Grey (*ibid.*, 186); however, this cannot have been the chronicler's father, who was already a knight by July 1302 (above, xxvi). In fact, Edward of Caernarvon arrived in Scotland in early July, shortly after Methven, but before the sieges of Kildrummy and Dunaverty: Haines, *Edward II*, 16–18.

35. Kildrummy was besieged by the Prince of Wales in Aug.–Sep. 1306 (see above, n. 32).

36. According to Guisborough, 369, Seton and his wife were captured at Loch Doon castle. Seton was the son of a Yorkshire knight, and the second husband of Christina, Bruce's youngest sister: Barrow, *Bruce*, 148. Seton was executed, while his wife was sent to Sixhills Priory in Lincolnshire: *CPR 1301–7*, 503.

37. Although Christopher de Seton was indeed drawn and hanged at Dumfries (Guisborough, 369), Gray appears to have confused him here with John de Seton (another English knight in the Scottish allegiance) who captured Sir Richard Siward, sheriff of Dumfries, at Dumfries castle, shortly after the killing of John Comyn in Feb. 1306. Note also that Gray is mistaken in saying that the sheriff of Dumfries was killed. John de Seton was drawn and hanged at Newcastle in Aug. 1306, after being captured in Siward's castle at Tibbers. *CDS*, ii, no. 1811; *Anglo-Scottish Relations*, ed. Stones, 130.

38. Edward ordered Gaveston's exile on 26 Feb. 1307, requiring him to leave the country by 30 Apr.: *Fœdera*, I, ii, 1010; *CCR 1302–7*, 526–7. The circumstances are examined by Hamilton, *Piers Gaveston*, 34–6. Note that although Gray refers to Gaverston's 'divers crimes et vices', he makes no explicit reference to any homosexual relationship between Gaveston and Edward; the nearest he comes to it is in his final assessment of Edward II's character, where he writes that, '[Edward] loved too much a certain person in particular', above, 95, though he also writes of Hugh Despenser the younger that Edward 'loved and trusted [him] completely', above, 91. The most recent discussion of Edward's sexual proclivities is Haines, *Edward II*, 42–3.

39. In fact, Edward I did not reach Scotland at this time; he got as far as Lanercost Priory in Cumberland by 29 Sep. 1306, where he fell ill, remaining there until the following Mar., to the great expense of the canons. Moorman, 'Edward I

at Lanercost Priory', 161–74. Gray's father was employed to take money to the king at Lanercost in Oct. 1306; above, xxv.

40. Aymer de Valence was appointed king's lieutenant and captain for Yorkshire, Northumberland and Lothian on 5 Apr. 1307; a similar appointment was made for Henry Percy covering Lancashire, Westmorland, Cumberland, Ayr, Wigton, Dumfries and Galloway on the same day: *CPR 1301–7*, 426.

41. *Lanercost*, 205, relates that the brothers invaded by ship on 10 Feb. 1307, with the support of an Irish sub-king (*regulo*), but were defeated by Dungal Macdouall, a nobleman of Galloway, and executed at Carlisle on 17 Feb. However, a writ from the English Crown to pay Macdouall a reward of £40 for thê deed is dated 3 Feb.: *CDS*, v, no. 492 (xvi), p. 216. According to Fordun, 342, the brothers were captured at Loch Ryan, Wigtonshire. Alexander Bruce was the dean of Glasgow, and had been a student at Cambridge; he obviously made an impression there, for writing in Edward III's reign, the Lincolnshire poet Robert Manning of Bourne (a fellow student) recorded his admiration for Alexander's scholastic abilities. Manning, i, pp. xii–xiii; Barrow, *Bruce*, 143.

42. The battle was fought *c.* 10 May 1307: Barrow, *Bruce*, 172.

43. Monthermer, possibly of Northumbrian origin, was in the household of Gilbert, Earl of Gloucester. After the latter's death in Dec. 1295, Ralph attracted the affections of his widow, Joan of Acre, the second daughter of Edward I, by Eleanor of Castile. They married clandestinely early in 1297, to Edward's great displeasure, but he subsequently forgave them, and Ralph was styled Earl of Gloucester while she lived. In fact, by the time of these events, Ralph would no longer have been known by this title, as Joan had just died, on 23 Apr. 1307: *CP*, v, 708–12.

44. This reference to 'lez croniclis de sez gestis' suggests that Gray made use of a lost 'life' of Bruce: see above, xlvii.

45. Edward died on 7 July. He had actually reigned thirty-four years, seven months and *seventeen* days, but his age at his death is given exactly right.

46. Edward's first wife was Eleanor of Castile (d. 1290), daughter of Ferdinand III of Castile; his second wife was Margaret of France (d. 1318), daughter of Philippe III, and half-sister of Philippe IV.

47. Despite similar claims about Edward's hostility in *Flores*, iii, 125 (which erroneously referes to the Earl of Warwick) and *Rishanger*, 227, it would appear that Bigod's surrender of the earldom was an amicable deal, brought about on account of the earl's dire financial straits: see Morris, 'Roger IV Bigod and Edward I', 89–99. In fact, it was Edward II who granted the earldom to Thomas, creating him Earl of Norfolk in Dec. 1312, having granted Roger Bigod's lands to Thomas and his brother Edmund in July 1310: *CP*, ix, 596–7.

48. Edmund, along with his brother Thomas, was granted the lands of Roger Bigod in 1310; he was created Earl of Kent in July 1321. Edward III granted him the honour of Arundel, Sussex, in Feb. 1327, shortly after his coronation: *CP*, vii, 142–8. For Gray's description of Kent's execution in 1330, see below, 103–5.

49. In order of age, Eleanor married Henry, Count of Bar; Joan married Gilbert de Clare, Earl of Gloucester, and after his death, Ralph de Monthermer (as Gray describes above; and see n. 43); Margaret married John, Duke of Brabant; Elizabeth married John, Count of Holland, and then the Earl of Herford; and Mary became a nun.

Chapter 40

1. Innocent V, elected Jan. 1276, died in June.

2. Adrian V, elected July 1276, died in Aug.

3. Adrian V was succeeded by John XXI, elected Sep. 1276, died May 1277. The *Historia aurea* (Lambeth, f. 213) gives John's correct number, and gives his reign as 8 months.

4. The account of the papacy is particularly muddled at this point; in fact, John XXI was succeeded by Nicholas III, without another John intervening. Nicholas III did reign for three years, being elected in Nov. 1277, and dying in Aug. 1280. Whether the errors are Gray's, his clerk's, or his copyist's is impossible to determine, but given that the same phrase 'il auaunsa uolountiers lez grantz clerks' is applied to two separate Pope Johns, it is likely that the confusion arose as Gray conflated the separate accounts scattered through the *Historia aurea*.

5. Honorius IV, elected Apr. 1285 (in succession to Martin IV, who is missed out of Gray's account), died Apr. 1287.

6. Nicholas IV, elected Feb. 1288, died Apr. 1292.

7. As Gray refers to 'winter thunder' (*foudre yuernail*), he obviously means St Margaret of Scotland, whose feast day is 16 Nov.

Chapter 41

1. Celestine V was elected in July 1294 (two year's after Nicholas' death), and resigned just six months later. Clearly, Gray's chronology is wrong.

2. Celestine resigned 13 Dec. 1294; Boniface was elected 24 Dec., and died in Oct. 1303.

3. Benedict XI was elected in Oct. 1303 and died in the following July. The Latin verse is quoted *verbatim* from the *Historia aurea* (Lambeth, f. 224v.). Gray's account of Benedict is translated directly from the same source, although he does add the reference to the goliard.

4. Bek was created patriarch on 26 Feb. 1306 by Clement V: Fraser, *Antony Bek*, 165.

5. In fact, Clement V was Pope for nine years: he was elected in June 1305 and died in Apr. 1314.

6. Clement was succeeded by John XXII (not XXI, as the MS records), who actually reigned for less than twenty years, being elected in Aug. 1316, and dying in Dec. 1334.

7. Note that Gray here repeats *verbatim* his comment on John XXI, 'il auaunsa uolountiers lez grantz clerks' (above, ch. 40). Given his evident confusion over which John reigned when, he may not have been sure which particular John had the reputation for advancing learned clerks.

Chapter 42

1. In fact, Albrecht of Habsburg was Emperor at Edward I's death; Henry VII was elected Emperor in Nov. 1308, and crowned in Jan. 1309, after Albrecht was murdered in May 1308: *NCMH*, 526–7, 530.

2. Henry VII died 24 Aug. 1313, of malaria, at Buonconvento near Siena. For his career, and death, see *NCMH*, 529–37.

3. Ludwig of Bavaria was elected in Aug. 1316. For his election, career, and the dispute with the papacy, see *NCMH*, 527–50.

4. The antipope Nicholas (V) was elected in May 1328, and submitted to Pope John in July 1330.

5. Ludwig had two wives, Beatrix of Glogau and Margaret of Holland. His eldest son, by Beatrix, was also called Ludwig, and became Margrave of Brandenburg in 1323; he only gained Tyrol in 1341, when he married the daughter of the Duke of Carinthia. The Emperor Ludwig granted Zeeland, Holland and Hainault to his wife Margaret in Jan. 1346; it was she who in turn granted them to their eldest son, William, in Jan. 1349, after Ludwig's death. Their younger son, Ludwig of Rome, married Kunigunde of Poland. See genealogy in Thomas, *Ludwig der Bayer*, 394; NCMH, 538, 547, 579.

6. Ludwig died in Oct. 1347. Gray refers to Ludwig's negotiations with Edward in 1338, above, 123–5.

Chapter 43

1. This is a very brief summary, albeit with a rather favourable spin, of the famous assessment of Edward's character in the *Polychronicon* (viii, 298), repeated *verbatim* by the *Historia aurea*: Lambeth, f. 225. Edward's physical strength was noted by other chroniclers: the 'Short Version' of the *Brut* described him as 'a hand-some man and strong in body and limb' (*Anonimalle, 1307–1334*, 81).

2. Edward and Isabella were in France from May to July 1313; they were at St Germain-des-Prés on 6 June. The scandal over the King of France's daugh-ters-in-law did not break until Apr. 1314, while Isabella was at the French court on a separate diplomatic mission. Hallam, *Itinerary of Edward II*, 99; Brown, 'Isabelle's Mission', 53; Haines, *Edward II*, 92, 309, 310.

3. Blanche of Navarre married Edmund of Lancaster in 1275 or 1276, his second wife; Joan, her daughter by her first marriage to Henri of Navarre, married Philippe IV.

4. Philippe and Gautier d'Aunay, knights of the French royal household, were accused of adultery with Marguerite of Burgundy, wife of Louis of Navarre (King Philippe's eldest son, the future Louis X), and her cousin Blanche, wife of Charles, Count of La Marche (Philip's youngest son, later Charles IV). Blanche's older sister Jeanne (wife of Phillipe, later Philippe V) was accused of abetting the affair. In fact, while the unfortunate d'Aunay brothers were indeed flayed alive, Marguerite and Blanche were merely imprisoned, while Jeanne was eventually cleared. Hallam and Everard, *Capetian France*, 362; Brown, 'Isabelle's Mission', 53; Haines, *Edward II*, 310.

5. Gray's source was probably his father, for Henry de Beaumont, and Beaumont's sister Isabella de Vesci, accompanied the queen on this trip: CPR 1313–17, 85–6. The *Scalacronica's* is the most detailed contemporary English account of the affair. *Louth Park Chronicle*, 22–3, has a brief notice, though it mentions only two wives, and correctly records that they were imprisoned rather than put to death; nor does it include Gray's detail that one of the knights sought refuge in England. Murimuth, 22, records only that 'on account of adultery with Sir Philip d'Aunay which was imputed to her', Louis' wife was 'suffocated'. Gray's tale about Phillippe d'Aunay's unwitting judgement of his own sons is also related by a Flemish chronicler, writing at the end of the fourteenth century: Brown, 'Isabelle's Mission', 75. The episode is examined by *ibid.*, 74–7. Note that no other source mentions the brother's flight to England.

6. Philippe IV's eldest son, Louis X, ruled 1314–16. Apart from his daughter, Jeanne, he did have a posthumous son, Jean I, who lived for just five days.

7. Phillippe V, ruled 1314–22. Faucogney, a Burgundian lord, was actually married to Phillippe's daughter, but quarrelled with his brothers-in-law over the inheritance and was courted as a potential ally by Edward III: Sumption, *Trial by Battle*, 293.

8. 1 Feb. 1328.

9. Above, 101–3.

10. For Robert de Artois' military endeavours against the French, in the allegiance of Edward III, see above, 131–3.

11. Edward II's coronation was on 25 Feb. 1308.

12. Bickerton had good reason to hold a personal grudge against Gray, for in 1306 the latter had petitioned Edward I for the lands of 'Walter de Bickerton of Kincraig', following Bickerton's forfeiture as an adherent of Bruce; he had held his lands in the county of Fife (*Documents*, ed. Palgrave, i, 303, 300).

13. Gray had also petitioned for the lands of one 'Alexander Fraser, the son of Andrew Fraser' in 1306 (*Documents*, ed. Palgrave, i, 303–4).

Chapter 43a

1. Gaveston was married to Margaret, second of the three daughters of Gilbert de Clare, Earl of Gloucester, and Joan, Edward II's elder sister; he was created Earl of Cornwall on 6 Aug. 1307.

2. This is an extremely summarised and telescoped account of the period between the start of the royal expedition to Scotland in September 1310, and the killing of Piers Gaveston on 19 June 1312. Lancaster's particular responsibility for Gaveston's death is emphasised by the *Vita Edwardi*, 27–8; see also Maddicott, *Lancaster*, 127–30.

3. Banaster's revolt broke out on 22 Oct. 1315, and he was executed on 12 Nov. A disgruntled retainer of Lancaster, Banaster raised the king's standard, which presumably accounts for Gray's assertion that he was acting with the king's connivance, although there is no evidence that was in fact the case. *Vita Edwardi*, 64–6; Maddicott, *Lancaster*, 174–7.

4. Guillemin de Fiennes was knighted in 1311 whilst serving at Roxburgh (*CDS*, iii, p. 406; Barrow, *Bruce*, 195). According to Barbour, X, lines 473–494, Fiennes was severely wounded in the face during an assault on the great tower, and surrendered on terms which allowed him and the garrison to return to England, where he died of his wound. See also *Lanercost*, 223; *Vita Edwardi*, 48.

5. Barbour, X, lines 511–777, relates that one William Francis, who claimed to be the son of a former keeper of the castle, revealed a path to the Scots which ran down the crag from the castle, which he had used in his youth when courting a girl in the town.

6. Gray's account differs somewhat from that of the *Historia aurea*, which explicity states that the castle was taken through Piers Libaud's 'treason' (*prodicionem*); nor does the *Historia* mention that Libaud was the sheriff, or Thomas Randoph's role in the attack, and it's account of Libaud's execution by Bruce differs in detail: Lambeth, f. 226v.; Galbraith, 'Extracts', 210. The *Vita Edwardi*, 48, describes Libaud as Piers Gaveston's cousin, and similarly accuses him of betraying the castle; Barbour, X, lines 327–40, 761–71, has it that the English garrison suspected him of treachery while the castle was still being besieged by the

Scots, and imprisoned him. Libaud had been convicted of treason by Bruce by Mar. 1316: *RRS, Robert I*, no. 84.

7. This sentence ('King Edward … Bishop of St Andrews') is a summary of the *Historia aurea*'s brief account of Bannockburn (Lambeth, f. 225v.; *Illustrations*, ed. Stevenson, 2). Gray follows the *Historia aurea* which mistakenly identifies the Bishop of St Andrews in the exchange of prisoners; in fact, it was Robert Wishart, Bishop of Glasgow. A detailed account of Hereford's capture and exchange is given by Barbour (XIII, lines 401–412, 679–697).

8. Precisely which 'chronicles' Gray is referring to is not clear, as from here on Gray's account of Bannockburn appears to be largely independent of any other surviving accounts. Much of it is certainly derived from the reminiscences of his father, and it may be that the reference to 'chronicles' was intended to disguise Gray's reliance on an oral source, which he may have felt did not command sufficient authority.

9. This is the same William Oliphant who had defended Stirling castle 'for the Lion'; above, 47. He had been released from prison in England in Dec. 1308, and had the keeping of the town of Perth by Oct. 1311. *Rot. Scot.* 61, 105; Barrow, *Bruce*, 194–5. According to *Lanercost*, 220–1, Perth fell on 8 Jan. 1313.

10. This refers to David de Strathbogie, Earl of Atholl, whose loyalties were somewhat flexible, but who was in the Scottish allegiance from the autum of 1312 to Oct. 1314: *SP*, i, 428–9. According to Barbour, XIII, lines 486–504, Atholl returned to the English allegiance after falling out with Robert Bruce's brother Edward; the latter was married to Atholl's sister, Isabella, but disliked her intensely and kept the sister of Sir Walter Ross as a mistress. Gray's is the only account of the taking of Perth to name Atholl as the leader of the Scottish forces; other accounts name Robert Bruce as leader.

11. Barbour, X, lines 825–6, gives the deadline as 'mydsomer the neyst yer to cum'; however, this appears to be a misunderstanding, perhaps due to the unusually short period of notice. Edward appears to have been informed of the terms only at the end of May 1314. *Bruce*, ed. Duncan, 402.

12. Accounts of a single combat between Bruce and an English knight at this stage of the battle feature in several accounts: Barbour (XII, lines 25–67); and the *Vita Edwardi*, p. 51; but all name Bruce's victim as Henry de Bohun. The continuator of Trevet's chronicle (*Trivet continuatio*, 14) also lists Bohun amongst the English who died at the battle.

13. Deyncourt's death is noted by Barbour, XII, lines 577–86; *Trivet continuatio*, 14, also includes Deyncourt in its list of the English dead.

14. Thomas Gray is named by *Trivet continuatio*, 15, in a list of English *barones et baneretti* captured at Bannockburn.

15. Alexander de Seton was a Scottish knight who had wavered between the English and Scottish allegiances. He may have been the Alexander de Seton who swore allegiance to Robert Bruce at Cambuskenneth in 1308 or 1310, but he was in the English allegiance soon after. Following Bannockburn, he served with Edward Bruce in Ireland, and became one of Robert Bruce's closest advisers, appending his seal to the 'Delaration of Arbroath' in 1320. *SP*, viii, 563–70; Barrow, *Bruce*, 151, 223, 28. For his defence of Berwick against the English in 1333, see above, 115.

16. Note that the *Scalacronica* is the only source to mention Alexander Seton, and Robert Bruce's apparent reluctance to fight. However, Gray's father would have been well placed to know about events in the Scottish camp, for he spent the

night there, as a prisoner. Barbour, XII, lines 171–99, does portray Bruce as offering his men the chance to withdraw during the night; the absence of any mention of Seton here does not necessarily invalidate Gray's account, for Barbour had a particular propagandist agenda, and is hardly likely to have highlighted the fact that his hero secured the greatest triumph of his career only at the prompting of a renegade from the English army.

17. Edward's reluctance to leave the field of battle, and his fighting spirit, 'in the manner of a lion ... and in the manner of a spirited knight' is confirmed by Trokelowe, 86. Interestingly, Gray's description of the king's handiness with a mace echoes the descriptions typical of medieval romances, praising the martial prowess of chivalric heroes (Kaeuper, *Chivalry and Violence*, 135–49).

18. Barbour (XIII, lines 299–327) gives a very similar account of Argentine's conduct, quoting his speech: 'Schyr sen it is sua that ye thusgat your gat will ga, havys gud day for agayne will I, yeit fled I never sekyrly, and I cheys her to bid and dey than for to lyve schamly and fley'. However, the *Vita Edwardi*, 53–4, while confirming that Argentine had the command of the king's rein, records that he was killed going to the aid of the Earl of Gloucester, 'thinking it more honourable to perish with so great a man than to escape death by flight'. As the *Vita* describes the king's flight from the battlefield as following on from Gloucester's death, this is difficult to reconcile with the accounts of Gray and Barbour. For Argentine's renown, see King, 'Helm with a Crest', 33–4; Barker, *Tournament*, 127–8.

19. Notwithstanding this conspicuously scrupulous conduct, March defected to the Scots shortly afterwards; he was present at the parliament held by Bruce at Ayr in Apr. 1315. *NCH*, vii, 79. Given his account of how his father quarrelled with Henry de Beaumont at Bannockburn, it is interesting that Gray entirely omits the detail supplied by the *Historia aurea*, that Beaumont (along with the Earl of Pembroke, Hugh le Despenser, John de Cromwell and others) got to Dunbar, and also escaped to Berwick by sea (Lambeth, f. 225v.).

20. In ascribing Edward Bruce's motives to regal ambition, Gray here follows the *Historia aurea*, which describes Edward as 'aspiring to the name of king' (*ad nomen regium aspirans*, Lambeth, f. 225v.). Fordun (348), and following him, Bower (vi, 412–13), also attributes the Scottish invasion of Ireland to Edward Bruce's ambition. Otherwise, the *Scalacronica*'s account of Edward's invasion is largely independent of the *Historia aurea*. For modern accounts of the Scottish invasion of Ireland, see McNamee, *Wars of the Bruces*, 169–86; Haines, *Edward II*, 289–97.

21. See above, xlviii.

22. The battle of Faughart, near Dundalk, 14 Oct. 1318. Note that *lieu* can mean either 'league' or 'mile', and either might be meant here. Scottish sources (above, xlviii) mention that reinforcements were just a day's march away (and six leagues could easily have been managed by a medieval army in one day). The most detailed English accounts of the battle are in *Lanercost*, 238, and the 'Continuation' of Nicholas Trevet: Duffy, 'Nicholas Trevet', 314–15.

23. This section ('At the same time ... Richmond was killed') is derived from the *Historia aurea*'s much more detailed account of Arundel's ineffective attack on Scotland: Lambeth, ff. 225v.–226; Galbraith, 'Extracts', 208. Gray's father served on this expedition (see above, 28). Richmond was a former constable of Norham castle; he may have been acquainted with the elder Gray, as both witnessed a deed of Anthony Bek, Bishop of Durham, at Norham in Aug. 1310 (*CPR 1334–8*, 78).

24. The MS has 'Bewyk' here, and it is probable that the scribe accidently omitted the abbreviation sign which would have indicated 'Berewyk', his usual spelling of the place-name Berwick on Tweed. Thus *Scalacronica*, Stevenson, 143, cautiously amends 'Bewyk' to 'Berewyk' (followed by *Scalacronica*, Maxwell, 58); however, there is a Bewick in Northumberland (spelt 'Bewyk' in royal letters patent of 1335; *CPR 1334–8*, 79), near Eglingham, south-west of Alnwick, and it is possible that the skirmish occurred here. Bridlington, 56, dates the skirmish to 6 June 1319. A detailed account of it is given by Barbour, XV, lines 425–538, who makes no reference to any treachery on the English side; nor does Neville's brother Ralph, captured in the same skirmish, in his petition for aid towards paying his ransom; *Northern Petitions*, 178–9.

25. Marmaduke was murdered in Dec. 1318; Bridlington, 57; according to Bridlington, Neville justified his actions on the grounds that fitz Marmaduke was 'a faithless traitor to the king and to the realm'. The dispute probably related to Marmaduke's role in arranging the payment of money to buy-off Scottish invasions; there may well also have been a political aspect to the affair, for fitz Marmaduke had been an adherent of Thomas of Lancaster. The background to the affair is examined in detail by Offler, 'Murder', 193–211. Richard fitz Marmaduke's father, John, is referred to above, 41.

26. Horsley was a prominent Northumbrian knight who served as constable of Bamburgh castle from 1315 to 1327, and would have been well known to the elder Gray.

27. May 1317; in fact, Pembroke was not on his way to the *curia* when he was taken, but was returning from it, after a diplomatic mission there for the king. Lamouilly had indeed served with the English, with Pembroke himself, according to Murimuth, 26. He is recorded in the garrison of Berwick in 1312, and had provided Edward I with gunpowder at the siege of Stirling in 1304. *CDS*, iii, pp. 400, 419; Prestwich, *Edward I*, 155, 501; Phillips, *Valence*, 111–15. It is not unlikely that Gray's father had been acquainted with him.

28. The precise meaning of this isolated statement is difficult to gauge. Presumably it is a veiled reference to the infamous conspiracy of Gilbert de Middleton, which Gray describes shortly afterwards, but there is no evidence that the Scots actually were implicated in this affair; Prestwich, 'Gilbert de Middleton', 183–5. Gray would have been aware of this, and he may have been trying to further blacken the reputations of those involved in the rebellion, to further John de Coupland's nefarious schemes for the retrospective forfeitures of their sons and grandsons: see above, xlii–xliii.

29. The Soules conspiracy is examined by Penman, 'The Soules Conspiracy'. For William de Soules, see M'Michael, 'De Soulis', 187–9. Gray's father may have been acquainted with Soules while the latter was in the English allegiance (1306–14), for they were both witnesses to a grant of land by Bishop Anthony Bek in Aug. 1310: *CPR 1334–8*, 78.

30. The robbery took place 1 Sep. 1317, near Rushyford, nine miles south of Durham on the road from Darlington. Of the many chronicle accounts of the infamous robbery of the cardinals, Gray's is the only one which mentions Swinburne's role in the affair (he does not feature in the *Historia aurea*'s detailed account, for instance – cf. Lambeth, f. 226). In fact, Swinburne was not related to Middleton, but Gray's error is readily explicable, for although Middleton's mother was married to one Nicholas de Swinburne, Nicholas was one of the Swinburnes of West

Swinburn, whilst Adam was a Swinburne of East Swinburn, an entirely separate and apparently unrelated family. However, both Swinburne and Middleton were knights of the royal household, and the former was indeed arrested in Aug. 1317, just a month before the robbery. Disaffection at Swinburne's arrest may well have been one of the factors that spurred Middleton to rebellion. As Gray's father was a retainer of Henry Beaumont, the *Scalacronica*'s account is particularly valuable, as it undoubtedly reflects the Beaumonts' perception of Middleton's motives. For the background to this affair, see King, '*Schavaldours*', 125–8; Prestwich, 'Gilbert de Middleton', 179–94.

31. The *Historia aurea* names Middleton's captors as William de Felton and Thomas de Eton (Lambeth, f. 226). Gray presumably heard of Horncliffe's role in the affair from his father. His account is confirmed by the rewards subsequently granted to Felton, Heton and Horncliffe by the crown (*CPR 1317–21*, 75, 310–11; *Northumberland Petitions*, 137).

32. Wark castle was taken by the Scots on 21 May 1318 (SAL, MS 121, f. 20).

33. This was the chronicler's father.

34. In fact, Gray was only constable for eight years. He was appointed in 1319, after the belated consecration of Bishop Louis de Beaumont, and was replaced before the coronation of Edward III in Feb. 1327. Above, xxix, xxxii.

35. This is undoubtedly the best known passage from the *Scalacronica*; for comment, see King, 'Helm with a Crest', *passim*. William Marmion was undoubtedly already known to Gray before he turned up at Norham with his gold-crested helm, having served in Scotland with Henry Beaumont in 1309–10 (*CDS*, v, nos. 2709, 2737, 2774); their names appear together in the Durham *Liber vitae* (*Facsimile*, f. 68), in a list headed by Henry de Beaumont, in what is clearly a group entry for Beaumont's knightly retinue.

36. Cryn should probably be identified with Crabbekyn, the nephew and partisan of the infamous Flemish pirate and engineer John Crabb (for whom, see Balfour-Melville, 'Two John Crabbs', 32–4). He was in his uncle's company in 1315, when they plundered a ship belonging to Alice, Countess Marshal, but was not mentioned in Nov. 1319, when the Count of Flanders promised to break Crabb on the wheel for his crimes (*CDS*, iii, nos. 417, 673). Crabb was certainly in Scottish service at Berwick at this time.

37. The North Yorkshire manor of Northallerton belonged to the bishops of Durham. Gray's account is greatly abbreviated from the *Historia aurea*, which describes the incident at some length (adding the interesting detail that Deyville's men dressed as lay brothers of Rievaulx abbey) dating it to *c*. 11 Nov. 1317, and linking it to the capture of Gilbert de Middleton (Lambeth, f. 226; Galbraith, 'Extracts', 208). Deyville, a Yorkshire knight, was hanged after the battle of Boroughbridge as an adherent of Thomas of Lancaster; for an account of his career, see de Ville, 'Jocelin Deyville'.

38. *Circa* 11 Nov. 1315; Bridlington, 48. Jack le Irish was one of the 'English born in Ireland', and a valet of the royal household, who served in the Marches from 1314 to 1316: King, 'Jack le Irish'. 'Schavaldour' was a term coined to describe English men-at-arms on the Marches when they were engaged in criminal activity, during Edward II's reign; like le Irish, virtually all those so-described in strictly contemporary documents were knights or valets of the royal household: King, '*Schavaldours*', *passim*.

39. Again, Gray's chronology is muddled, as this appears to be a reference to

the Westminster parliament of July–Aug. 1321, during which an army of Edward's opponents marched on London, 'et ensi auoit chescun bataille cote armures de vert drape dount le droit quarter estoit glawke ou bendes blaunches parount ceo est appellee le parlement del bende', Cleopatra D.iii, f. 154 (translated 'and euery bataile hade cote armur of grene cloþe; and þerof þe right quarter was yalwe, wiþ white bendes; wherfore þat parlement was callede þe parlment wiþ þe whit bende', *Brut*, 213). See also Trokelowe, 109; Haines, *Edward II*, 127–8. The *Historia aurea*'s account of this parliament (Lambeth, f. 227) makes no mention of the rebel army or its livery; Gray may have heard the story from his father, without getting the precise context, which would explain the confused chronology.

40. Variously named as John of Powderham, John Poydras or John Tanner, he appeared at Oxford and made his claim in mid-June 1318, and was hanged around 24 July. Childs, 'Edward II, John of Powderham and the Chronicles', 194–63.

41. 12 September 1319. For other accounts of the battle, sarcastically referred to by Barbour as 'the Chapter of Myton', as so many priests were slain there, see Barbour, xvii, lines 531–88; *Historia aurea*, Lambeth ff. 226v.–227; *Lanercost*, 239; *Vita Edwardi*, 96.

42. Gray's chronology is confused; Tickhill was besieged in Jan. 1322, while Knaresborough had been attacked in Oct. 1317. Maddicott, *Lancaster*, 305–9, 207. Both castles are in West Yorkshire.

43. Knaresborough was held by the then royal favourite Roger de Amory; Lilleburn seized the castle on behalf of Damory's bitter enemy Thomas of Lancaster, on 5 Oct. 1317, and surrendered it on terms on 29 Jan. 1318. *CIM 1307–49*, no. 392; *Sempringham*, 334. Lilleburn was a prominent Northumbrian knight, holding land at Lilburn in the north of the county (*NCH* xiv, 435). He was probably acquainted with Gray's father; both were amongst the witnesses for a deed of John de Penrith, in *c.* 1316: MacDonald, 'Laing Charters Relating to Northumberland', 110. For his career as a royal household knight, then as a Lancastrian rebel, and his subsequent reconciliation with the king, see King, 'Lordship, Castles and Locality', 224–6. Neither Knaresborough nor Lilleburn are mentioned in the *Historia aurea*.

44. The battle of Boroughbridge was fought on 16 Mar. 1322, and Lancaster was captured on the following morning; according to *Lanercost*, 243, Harclay arrayed his troops in a *schiltrom* formation, 'in the manner of the Scots'. For modern accounts, see DeVries, *Infantry Warfare*, 86–99; Haines, *Edward II*, 140.

45. See above, 85.

46. Lancaster was executed 22 Mar. 1322; Maddicott, *Lancaster*, 311–12. The reference to jeering relates to an incident early in Oct. 1317, when Edward was returning from York to London (and not on the way to York, as Gray states), after an abortive attempt to muster a royal expedition against the Scots, an attempt undermined by Lancaster's hostility to the court. Edward had to be dissuaded from besieging Pontefract, by the Earl of Pembroke. *Fœdera*, II, i, 479; *Flores*, iii, 180–1; *Vita Edwardi*, 82; Phillips, *Valence*, 125–30; Maddicott, *Lancaster*, 208–10.

47. Harclay, from an obscure family of Westmorland knights, made his fortune as one of the few English commanders to have any real success in defending the Marches against the Scots, particularly his defence of Carlisle in 1315. He was captured around the turn of 1316, and ransomed for at least 2000 marks; *CDS*, iii, no. 697. Barbour, XVI, lines 516–26, names his captor as Sir John de Soules. He was created Earl of Carlisle 25 Mar. 1322, for defeating Lancaster at Boroughbridge; he

was executed 3 Mar. 1323 for negotiating an unauthorised peace treaty with Robert Bruce; differing versions of this are printed in *Anglo-Scottish Relations*, ed. Stones, 308–15, and *RRS, Robert I*, no. 215. Harclay's career, and his unauthorised negotiations with the Scots, are detailed by Summerson, i, *Carlisle*, 230–56.

48. The levy of a footman from every town was a revival of a scheme originally planned for the abortive royal campaign of 1316, put forward again in the York parliament of May 1322: Powicke, *Military Obligation*, 152–3.

49. Penrith was a Cumberland knight and household knight, who had been appointed warden of the March for Northumberland in June 1322, and served in the garrison of Newcastle from then until his death, which occurred on 29 July (*CPR 1321–4*, 128; BL, Stowe MS 553, ff. 58, 101v.). He was acquainted with Gray's father (see n. 43, above).

50. Hobelars were lightly armed and armoured horsemen, riding light horses, or 'hobbies'; McNamee, *Wars of the Bruces*, 23–4, 155–7.

51. For discussion of the victualling of this campaign, see Prestwich, 'Military Logistics, 276–88.

52. This battle took place 14 Oct. 1322. Although this passage is not very clear, it is apparent from other accounts (Barbour, XVIII, lines 348–568; *Lanercost*, 247; Bridlington, 79) that the English took up a defensive position on top of a steep hill – this is presumably what Gray means by 'vn forteresce dun mountaigne'. There are plenty of hills in the area (near to Sutton Bank, N. Yorks.) which would fit the description. Barrow, *Bruce*, 243–4; McNamee, *Wars of the Bruces*, 100–1.

53. The Lord of Sully is identified by Fordun, 350, as Henry de Sully; Sully was Butler of Philip V of France, and an envoy of Charles VI: *Fœdera*, II, i, 507, 511. In Nov. 1324, Bruce was recorded as owing 4400 marks to James Douglas, for the redemption of 'Robert Bercham, William Bercham, Elye Inyllage, knights of France, and their valets', captured by Douglas at Byland, whom Bruce had released as a gesture of friendship to the king of France (*Registrum Magni Sigilli*, ed. Thomson, i, app. 1, no. 38).

54. Sealed at Bishopsthorpe, near York, on 30 May 1323, to take effect from 12 June: *Fœdera*, II, i, 521; *RRS, Robert I*, no. 232. For analysis, see Barrow, *Bruce*, 249–50; Haines, *Edward II*, 273–4.

55. Gray's chronology is badly muddled here, as Despenser was exiled during the Westminster parliament of May to Aug. 1321: Haines, *Edward II*, 127–9.

56. Despenser's piracy was notorious, and was widely reported in contemporary chronicles, *e.g.*, *Vita Edwardi*, 115–16; *Brut*, ed. Brie, 214; *Anonimalle, 1307–34*, 100; 'Annales Paulini', 300; and the *Historia aurea* (Lambeth, f. 227). The subsequent cost to the realm of England resulted from the fact that Edward III had to pay compensation to the Genoese when he wished to procure their services as boatbuilders; Haines, *Edward II*, 420, n. 270.

57. Edmund of Woodstock, Earl of Kent, was Edward's half-brother, born to Edward I's second wife, Margaret of France. For his career, see *CP*, vii, 142–8; and see above, 57.

58. *i.e.* the future Edward III, then twelve years old. He was created Duke of Acquitaine on 10 September 1325: *CPR 1324–7*, 173–4; *Fœdera*, II, i, 607–8.

59. Edward married Phillippa at York on 24 Jan. 1328, a year after his accession as king.

60. Rumours of a plot against Isabella's life, organised by Edward, were later recorded by Walsingham, 179. See also Haines, *Edward II*, 171, 172.

61. In fact, Caerphilly castle held out for Edward, under Despenser's retainer, the Northumbrian Sir John de Felton, a younger son of Sir William de Felton: *CPR 1324–7*, 344; *CPR 1327–30*, 10; SAL, MS 122, f. 40; *NCH*, vii, 113; Fryde, *Tryanny and Fall*, 184–5, 191. As a fellow Despenser retainer, Gray's father is likely to have been well aware of this.

62. The 'foreigners' were the men-at-arms from Hainault.

63. Mar was described as a 'page of the chamber' (*pueris camere*) of Edward II by Bridlington, 96 (cf. *CP*, viii, 404–5).

64. This is another chronological error, for Walter Stapledon, Bishop of Exeter, was murdered on 15 Oct. 1326, long before Queen Isabella's arrival in London – although according to the 'Annales Paulini', 316; Baker, 23; and Murimuth, 48, the Londoners did send his decapitated head to her. The murder is examined in detail by Buck, *Walter Stapledon*, 217–23.

65. Despite Gray's claim that the manner of Edward's death was not known, the *Historia aurea* records that Edward was moved from Kenilworth to Berkeley, and then on 21 Sep., he was killed 'by the insertion into his bottom of a red-hot iron through the middle of a horn thrust right inside': *Hemingburgh*, ii, 298 (a very similar account of Edward's death is provided by the *Polychronicon*, viii, 324, albeit slightly different in detail). It is not clear whether Gray's unwillingness to repeat this story stems from incredulity or tact.

66. The 'certain person' whom Edward 'loved too much' is presumably a reference to Piers Gaveston, though Hugh Despenser the younger may have been in Gray's mind. A similar comment, that Edward was 'ardently attached to a certain favourite', was made by Ranulf Higden in his assessment of his character, reproduced *verbatim* in the *Historia aurea*; *Polychronicon*, viii, 298; Lambeth, f. 225. Much the same sentiment is expressed in Bridlington, 91.

67. This passage appears to be Gray's own composition, reflecting his own opinions (or perhaps those of his father), for there is nothing similar in the *Historia aurea*; however, there is an interesting parallel in the Long Version of the *Brut* chronicle, in a passage relating to the battle of Boroughbridge, which ascribes the 'vnkyndenesse' displayed at that battle to the mixed racial origins of the English. *Brut*, ed. Brie, i, 220 (for the French text, see Cleopatra D.iii, ff. 156v.–157).

68. John of Eltham, whose death Gray records, above, 123; Eleanor (not Isabella), married Reginald, Count of Guelders, May 1332; and Joan, who married David Bruce in July 1328, which is also recorded by Gray above, 101.

Chapter 44

1. The coronation was actually on 1 Feb. 1327. The *Historia aurea* also gives 2 Feb.: Lambeth, f. 228(b)v.

2. Lancaster and Kent were appointed captains of the king's army in the Marches of Scotland on 6 June 1327: *Rot. Scot.*, i, 213; Nicholson, *Edward III*, 22.

3. 7 June. The Long Version of the *Brut* confirms that the trouble was started by the English: *Brut*, ed. Brie, i, 250. According to Le Bel, 42–5, it blew up over a game of dice, and involved archers from the diocese of Lincoln. See also Nicholson, *Edward III*, 21.

4. 'lieus' must here mean 'miles' rather than 'leagues'; clearly, Edward's army could not have marched twenty-six leagues (nearly eighty miles) in one day.

5. As it appears in the MS, the place-name 'Anandredalle' must be an error. It is probably meant to refer to Allendale, which lies next to Tynedale, and is near to

Haydon Bridge: Barrow, *Bruce*, 373n. Alternatively, it may possibly refer to Bywell St Andrews, a village on the north bank of the Tyne, a couple of miles east of Corbridge.

6. Le Bel, i, 61–3, provides a detailed account of this episode. Rokeby was from a family which held lands in the honour of Richmond, north Yorkshire. He was granted annuity of £100 on 28 Sep. 1327, pending the provision of his lands (*Fœdera*, II, ii, 717). For an overview of his career, which ended with him serving as justiciar in Ireland, see Frame, 'Thomas Rokeby', 274–96.

7. Barbour, XIX, lines 778–804, confirms that the Scottish force was commanded by the earls of March and Angus. John Stewart of Bonkhill was not in fact created Earl of Angus (by Robert Bruce) until 1329; he is first styled as earl in a charter of June of that year: *CP*, i, 153; *SP*, i, 169–70. Gray refers to Stewart as 'calling himself' Earl of Angus because, from the English perspective, Gilbert de Umfraville, lord of Redesdale and Prudhoe in Northumberland, remained the rightful Earl of Angus.

8. Gray's detail concerning Edward's tears is confirmed by *Lanercost*, 260.

9. The Northumbrian Robert de Manners was lord of Etal, just a couple of miles from the Gray family *caput* at Heton, Northumberland. He had replaced Gray's father as constable of Norham castle after Mortimer's coup against Edward II, and was in turn replaced by Gray himself in 1345/6 (see above, xxxvii). Manners died in 1355, the year Gray started work on the *Scalacronica*; and the two of them were well acquainted, for as well as being near-neighbours, they served on various crown commissions, and witnessed many charters and deeds together: *Rot. Scot.*, i, 713–14, 717; *Northumberland and Durham Deeds*, pp. 22, 23, 93, 94, 103, 196, 217; NRO, ZSW 2/26. For the Manners family, see *NCH*, xi, 443–7. See also, above, 127, 134, and app.

10. Fordun, 353, records that 'in the same siege at Norham, William de Monealto, knight, John de Claphame and Robert de Dobery, and others, were killed through their own incompetence'. This is probably William Mowat, hereditary sheriff of Cromarty, who forfeited lands in Angus to Edward I for supporting Bruce's rebellion in 1306, and had his seal attached to the Delaration of Arbroath, in May 1320, but who had gone over to the English by May 1321, having previously served with Edward II in 1312. Bower, vii, 2, 170n., 185n.; *Documents*, ed. Palgrave, i, 317; *CPR 1317–21*, 595.

11. The 'Short Version' of the *Brut* chronicle has it that the Scots were driven away from Alnwick by force, and that they also besieged Warkworth, where they suffered heavy losses: *Anonimalle, 1307–34*, 138.

12. William de Denum was a Northumbrian lawyer. A petition of *c.* 1321 from 'les poures gentz de Northumberland' requested his appointment as a justice of assize in the county, describing him as an 'homme de lei'; a petition of *c.* 1319 described him and a colleague as local men of law (*gentz de lei et du pais*): *Northumberland Petitions*, 115–16. Denum was acquainted with Gray's father (*RPD*, ii, 1170–1), and was appointed to a commission to inquire into the abduction of John de Rayton in 1332 – the perpetrator of which was apparently to be Gray himself: *CPR 1330–34*, 387; above, xxxiv.

13. This parliament was held 31 July–6 Aug. 1328. Edward had already married Philippa on 24 Jan.

14. There was in fact no dowry paid for Joan; the financial arrangement was, rather, that Bruce should pay £20,000 to the English. The treaty and its negotiation are discussed by Nicholson, *Edward III*, 42–56; Haines, *Edward II*, 279–81.

15. Charles IV, died 1 Feb. 1328.

16. Philip of Valois succeeded on 29 May 1328; Cassel was fought on 28 Aug. 1328. For an account of the battle, see DeVries, *Infantry Warfare*, 100–11.

17. The submission of the rebels at Bedford took place in Jan. 1329; Sir Thomas Wyther and Sir William Trussell were also excluded from the king's pardon, as well as Beaumont and Roscelyn. *Calendar of Plea Rolls of London*, ed. Thomas, 85–6; Haines, *Edward II*, 207–9.

18. A general pardon was issued on 28 Mar. 1329 to twenty-eight individuals 'who aided the king in the late rebellion' (*CPR 1327–30*, 475), including a number of marchers such as Thomas de Heton, knight (named by Gray as one of the captors of Gilbert de Middleton in 1317: see above, 81); Thomas son of Thomas de Featherstonehaugh; Peter de Featherstonehaugh; Roland de Vaus; John de Lilleburn, knight (who held Knaresborough castle for Thomas of Lancaster in 1317; above, 87); and Robert de Ogle (who distinguished himself at the relief of Lochindorb castle, 1336; above, 123). Presumably, these marchers were pardoned for their service at Rothwell.

19. The Winchester parliament was 11–21 Mar. 1330. The plot against Kent is described in detail by Baker, 43–4; and the *Brut*, ed. Brie, 263–7. See also Haines, *Edward II*, 211–12, 233.

20. *i.e.* Kent was merely beheaded (on 19 Mar.), and pardoned the full ritual barbarities of a traitor's execution. Nevertheless, according to Knighton, ed. Lumby, i, 452, he suffered the indignity of being executed by a 'criminal ribald from the Marshalsea'. See also *CP*, vii, 146–7.

21. The *Scalacronica*'s account of Edward's coup is not derived from the *Historia aurea*, which gives only the most cursory summary of these events (*Hemingburgh*, ii, 302). As Gray served with William Montague in Flanders in 1338–9 (above, xxxv), and as Montague is particularly prominent in his account, his source was almost certainly Montague himself. Detailed accounts of this dramatic event are also provided by the Long Version of the *Brut* (Cleopatra D.iii, ff. 175r.–76r., rendered into Middle English in *Brut*, ed. Brie, 269–71) and Baker, 45–6. For a modern account, see Shenton, 'Edward III and the Coup of 1330', 13–34.

22. The *Brut* names the constable as William de Eland. However, Baker comments that Eland 'had been *speculator* in the castle for many years', the meaning of 'speculator' not being entirely clear: Shenton, 'Edward III and the Coup of 1330', 19.

23. Note that Gray's account makes no reference to the caves under Nottingham castle; nor does he mention any underground passages, though both the *Brut* and Geoffrey le Baker state that Edward's party entered the castle via a tunnel. The *Brut* describes 'vn aley qe le tende hors del garde desouthe terre, iusqes al Chastelle vers le west', Cleopatra D.iii, f. 175v. ('a alie þat stracches out of the ward, vnder erþe, vnto the castel, þat goþe into þe weste', *Brut*, ed. Brie, 270), through which Eland led Montague and company 'par le dit aley qe ils entrerent le Chastell and monterent a la tour' ('by þe forsaide way vnder the erþ, so til þat þai comen into the castel, and went vp into the Toure [þere þat þe Mortymer was in]'). Baker refers to a 'certain secret underground passage, that began at a distance outside the castle and ended in the middle at the kitchen or hall of the main tower, where the queen was lodged'. Gray's account suggests that Montague's party entered into the Middle Bailey, and climbed the stairs up to the Upper Bailey (*i.e.*, the *tour* referred to by the *Brut*): Drage, *Nottingham Castle*, 50–1. There is a

collapsed underground passage leading out from the Middle Bailey (*ibid.*, 51), but if Gray's account is correct, Montague may have gained access to the castle through a postern gate at the bottom of the ditch separating the Middle and Upper Baileys (for a plan of the castle as it would have been in 1330, see *ibid.*, 45). However, it remains difficult to reconcile the *Scalacronica*'s account with those of Baker and the *Brut*.

24. The meaning of this curious phrase can be gleaned from the *Brut*, which quotes Turpington as crying: 'Ha traitours, pur nient auez vous ceste chastel pris, vous murrez vnqore a male mort' ('A, traitoures! hit is al for nought þat ye beþ comen into þis castel. Ye shul dye yitte in euel deþ euerychon').

25. For Edward's complicity in the Disinherited's plotting, see Nicholson, *Edward III*, 77.

Chapter 45

1. There is a wide range of contemporary estimates of the strength of the Disinherited's forces. Typical of the confusion is Lanercost, 267, which reports that 'in total there were no more than 1500, all told, or according to others, 2800'; Wyntoun, v, 400–1, gives a figure of 'but 1500 fighting men'; Bridlington, 102–3, 106, gives 500 men-at-arms and 1000 footmen and archers; *Melsa*, ii 362, 364, similarly gives a total of 1500, including 500 armoured men; the Long Version of the *Brut*, ed. Brie, 275, gives 500 men-at-arms and 2000 archers; the Short Version, *Anonimalle, 1307–34*, 148, also gives a total of 2500 men; Capgrave, *De illustribus Henricis*, 168, and *Chronicle*, 201, numbers them at 2000. Given that Gray mentions only men-at-arms, his figure is not out of line with other reports.

2. The landing and battle at Kinghorn was on 6 Aug. 1332: Nicholson, *Edward III*, 83. Alexander de Seton 'the son' was the son of the Alexander de Seton who, according to Gray, defected from the English army the night before Bannockburn (above, 75) and who was to defend Berwick against Edward III in 1333 (above, 115). For the son, see *SP*, viii, 567, 569; his death is recorded by Fordun, 354, and Wyntoun, v, 404–5.

3. Thomas Randolph, Earl of Moray, was appointed guardian of Scotland after Robert Bruce's death, during the minority of David II. He actually died on 20 July, more than two weeks before the landing of the Disinherited; Nicholson, *Edward III*, 79. Gray mentions his capture at Methven in 1306: above, 53–5. The detail about the staffs is confirmed by the Long Version of the *Brut*, ed. Brie, 276, which states that 500 'stafes' were found in a chamber in the abbey; according to Bridlington, 104, the Disinherited remained at the abbey for two days.

4. This was Donald, Earl of Mar, previously described by Gray as being fostered by Edward II, 93 above.

5. In similar vein, Wyntoun, v, 400–1, comments that the Disinherited set out with so few men that people wondered how they dared to undertake such an enterprise, unless they had support in Scotland.

6. The Long Version of the *Brut*, ed. Brie, 276–7, quotes an edifying speech by Edward de Balliol at this point, without mentioning Henry de Beaumont; it also quotes a speech made by Fulk Fitzwarin, after the initial fight when the Disinherited crossed the river Earn.

7. This was Roger de Swinnerton the son, according to both versions of the *Brut*: Cleopatra D.iii, f. 178v. (note that the English translator mistranslated this

passage; cf *Brut*, ed. Brie, 277); *Anonimalle, 1307–34*, 150. Swinnerton's drowning is
noted by the *Historia aurea*: Hemingburgh, ii, 304.

8. The disastrous impact of the Scottish rearguard, commanded by the
guardian, the Earl of Mar, is confirmed by Bower, vii, 76; Wyntoun, v, 412–13; and
the Long Version of the *Brut*, ed. Brie, 278. According to the *Brut*, Mar was enraged
by Robert Bruce, commander of the vanguard, who accused him of treachery as
the Scots were preparing to advance, provoking him to advance in disorder.

9. Bridlington, 106–7, Wyntoun, v, 412–13, Fordun, 355, all confirm that thou-
sands of Scots died in the crush; Fordun also attributes the English victory to
'divine revenge'. The battle of Dupplin Moor took place on 11 Aug. 1332. For
modern accounts, see Nicholson, *Edward III*, 75–90; Rogers, *War, Cruel and Sharp*,
27–47; DeVries, *Infantry Warfare*, 112–20.

10. Balliol was enthroned 24 September 1332: Nicholson, *Edward III*, 93–4. Note
that the *Historia aurea* gives the date as 27 Sep.: Hemingburgh, ii, 306.

11. Gray's account is greatly expanded from the *Historia aurea*, which merely
notes the fact of Moray's capture at Roxburgh, with the added detail (omitted by
Gray) that he was held at Durham: Hemingburgh, ii, 306.

12. The York parliament lasted 4–11 Dec. 1332, and was then prorogued until 20
Jan. 1333, due to the non-appearance of various magnates and prelates. It ended on
27 Jan. The deliberations of this parliament are summarised in *Rot. Parl.*, ii, 67.
Lanercost, 270, names Henry de Beaumont and the Earl of Athol amongst those sent
to this parliament by Balliol.

13. This is a reference to the 'Great Cause' of 1291–2; in fact, John Balliol did
homage to Edward I on 26 Dec. 1292, a month after his inauguration at Scone on 30
Nov., St Andrew's Day: *Great Cause*, ii, 259–63.

14. Edward had a notorial copy made of the letter by which John formally
renounced his homage; according to this, it was delivered at Berwick on 5 Apr.
1296, 'by two friars (the warden of the Franciscans of Roxburgh, and his
companion)', though the notorial record of the 'Great Cause' relates that it was
delivered to Edward in March, while he was still in Northumberland. *Anglo-Scottish Relations*, ed. Stones, 140–5; *Great Cause*, ii, 288. This detailed material relating
to the 'Great Cause' is not derived from the *Historia aurea*; it may perhaps be
derived from memoranda circulated at this parliament during the debate over
possible English intervention in Scotland (the parliament is discussed by
Nicholson, *Edward III*, 105–6).

Chapter 46

1. This was Thomas, described by Wyntoun, vi, 6–11, and Bower, vii, 90, as
Seton's heir: *SP*, viii, 568. Seton had already lost his son Alexander in battle at
Kinghorn, when the Disinherited had landed there in the previous year: above,
109. Another of his sons, William, was drowned in the Tweed during this siege,
while attempting to attack some English ships: Bridlington, 113; Fordun, 357;
Wyntoun, v, 4–5. This is the same Alexander de Seton who defected from the
English on the eve of Bannockburn, and who – as Gray relates it – persuaded Bruce
to stand and fight: above, 75.

2. The indenture recording these terms, sealed at Berwick on 15 July, is printed
in *Fœdera*, II, ii, 864–5.

3. The battle of Halidon Hill, 19 July 1333. The *Historia aurea* provides a list of
magnates in the Scottish battle formation, which Gray chose not to reproduce:

Hemingburgh, ii, 308–9. Versions of this list were also included in *Knighton* (ed. Lumby, 468–70); the 'Long Version' of the *Brut* (*Brut*, ed. Brie, i, 283–5); and the 'Anonimalle' version of the *Brut* (*Anonimalle, 1307–34*, 164–6); these lists are discussed in *ibid.*, 59–60, 68–73. Detailed contemporary accounts are provided by the *Anonimalle* chronicler (*Anonimalle, 1307–34*, 163–8).

4. Presumably this is a reference to the later siege, when Dunbar was successfully held against the English by the Countess of March, 'Black Agnes'.

5. This is probably a sarcastic reference to Edward's well-attested enthusiasm for the tournament: King, 'Helm with a Crest', 27–8.

6. In May 1334: Penman, *David II*, 51–3.

7. 12 June 1334; see Nicholson, *Edward III*, 158–62, for the terms of this agreement (printed in *Foedera*, II, ii, 888), which stipulated the handing over of considerable Scottish lands to the King of England.

8. John Randolph, Earl of Moray, was the younger brother of Thomas Randolph, who been killed at Dupplin Moor; and indeed, Gray notes the death of the Earl of Moray at that battle. The phrase 'vn enfaunt parcru' suggests that John was in his late teens. For his career, see *SP*, vi, 295–7

9. See Nicholson, *Edward III*, 168–9.

10. Talbot was captured on 8 Sep. 1334, near Linlithgow, and ransomed for 2000 marks; his captors were William de Keith (mentioned above, 115), recently appointed steward of Balliol's household, and Godfrey de Ross, Balliol's sheriff of Ayr: Fordun, 357; Wyntoun, vi, 84–5; *Melsa*, ii, 372; Capgrave, *Chronicle*, 204; Nicholson, *Edward III*, 169. John de Stirling was a Scottish knight who had settled in Northumberland, having married the daughter of Adam de Swinburne (mentioned by Gray in connection with Gilbert de Middleton, above, 79) by Feb. 1329: *Feet of Fines, Northumberland*, no. 223; *CP*, xii/1, 407–8. Gray was personally acquainted with him, as they served on royal commissions together; they were also both witnesses to a deed of Alan de Heton. *CPR 1361–4*, 65, 204; NRO, ZSW 2/29. Note that the Northumbrian John de Felton, also personally known to Gray, was captured on the same occasion, but the *Scalacronica* omits to mention this.

11. Dundarg, a coastal castle in Aberdeenshire, associated with the earldom of Buchan, surrendered 23 Dec. 1334: Fordun, 357. According to Wyntoun, 72–3, Fordun, and Bridlington, 121, Beaumont was given safe-conduct to leave the country, which accords with Gray's account. However, both Fordun and Bridlington add that the surrender terms also required him to work towards a peace settlement with Edward III. Bower, 118, also claims that Beaumont agreed never to return (though earlier, 94–6, he repeats Fordun's account, *verbatim*). Whatever the terms, Beaumont was in fact ransomed by the Scots, as the king subsequently lent him 400 marks towards his ransom; and he certainly served in the English campaign in the following summer, with a retinue of 92 men-at-arms. *CPR 1334–8*, 165; *CCR 1337–9*, 302; Nicholson, *Edward III*, 185–6, 249.

12. The Earl of March gave a receipt for 100 marks on 13 May 1334, given to him in part payment for a gift from the king of 600 marks: *NCH*, vii, 83–5. This is perhaps the silver for which the Northumbrian criminals greeded.

13. Walsingham, 196, records that March sent letters to the king renouncing his homage when the latter was returning towards Berwick, having laid waste to Lothian. *Melsa*, ii, 374, records March's defection, but offers no explanation other than that he 'lapsed into perjury'. No other account mentions the assault on the

earl in Northumberland. March's change of allegiance is discussed by Nicholson, *Edward III*, 190–1.

14. Edward de Bohun was a younger brother of the Earl of Hereford; their mother was Elizabeth, a daughter of Edward I by his first wife, Queen Eleanor of Castile. *CP*, vi, 469. Bohun had been granted Annandale by Edward Balliol in September 1334, in settlement of a dispute over the lordship with Henry Percy: *Rot. Scot.*, i, 280–1; Nicholson, *Edward III*, 150–1, 170.

15. *i.e.* Gilbert de Umfraville, the English claimant to the earldom of Angus.

16. According to Murimuth, 54, at the time of Edward II's death, 'it was commonly said that he was killed by the order of Sirs John Mautravers and Thomas de Gorneye as a precaution'.

17. Guy, Count of Namur (in what is now Belgium), was a cousin of Queen Philippa. According to *Lanercost*, 282, his force included 'seven or eight knights, and 100 men-at-arms'. Fordun, 359, dates the battle to 30 July [1335]. *Lanercost* and Bower, vii, 112–14, confirm that the count was released without ransom, due to Moray's 'regard for Philip, the illustrious King of France', though his English prisoners were ransomed. The details of Gray's account of the battle correspond with Bower, and Wyntoun, vi, 52–5, though both state that Namur was initially ambushed at Burgh Muir, just outside Edinburgh, before fleeing to the site of the castle. *Lanercost*, 283, echoes Gray's critiscism of Namur for being foolhardy. The incident is described in detail by Nicholson, *Edward III*, 212–14.

18. Aug. 1335. Gray here follows the *Historia aurea* (*Hemingburgh*, ii, 311). *Melsa*, ii, 375, relates that Presfen had 30 men-at-arms with him; Bridlington, 123–4, puts the English at 200 horse and foot, including William's brother Michael. Both describe Presfen as constable of Roxburgh, but he was actually constable of Jedburgh: *Rot. Scot.*, i, 271, 275, 280. In Oct., William was rewarded by the king with lands near Berwick valued at £107 'in time of peace': *Fœdera*, II, ii, 923. Presfen was Gray's father-in-law.

19. Gray's chronology is out of sequence here, as William de Burgh, Earl of Ulster, was killed on 6 June 1333, at Le Ford (now Belfast). According to *Knighton*, ed. Lumby, i, 467, he was killed by some of his followers who were in league with the Scots, as he was preparing an expedition to join Edward III at Berwick: Frame, *English Lordship*, 144–5; *CP*, xii, 179.

20. The Earl of Ulster's mother was Elizabeth, the daughter of Gilbert de Clare, Earl of Gloucester, by his second wife, Joan of Acre, a daughter of Edward I. Ulster's only daughter and heir Elizabeth married Lionel, the second surviving son of Edward III, in 1342, while they were both minors. It was from this marriage that Richard, Duke of York, derived his claim to the English throne in 1460. *CP*, xii, 177, 180–1.

21. David Strathbogie, Earl of Atholl, was killed in battle in the forest of Culblean, 30 Nov. 1335, near the river Dee in Aberdeenshire. The most detailed account is that of Wyntoun (vi, 64–71); see also Nicholson, *Edward III*, 232–5. For David's career, see *SP*, i, 430–2.

22. Roscelyn, a retainer of Henry of Lancaster, was killed in early June 1336, during a successful expedition to capture and re-fortify Dunnotar castle, fifteen miles south of Aberdeen: Wyntoun, vi, 60–3; Sumption, *Trial by Battle*, 158. For Roscelyn's association with Henry de Beaumont as an opponent of the Mortimer regime, see above, 103.

23. John of Eltham, Edward's younger brother, died at Perth on 13 Sep. 1336;

CPR 1334–8, 447, 574. Gray's reference to him dying a 'fine death' is presumably an implicit refutation of Fordun's claim that John was stabbed to death by the king, following an argument (Fordun, 361), a story repeated by other Scottish chroniclers. These stories are discussed by James, 'John of Eltham', 63–80. The *Historia aurea* mentions John's death at Perth without comment, though it does add that John was 'honourably buried' at London: *Hemingburgh*, ii, 312.

24. Edward arrived in Berwick by 26 June 1336.

25. Lochindorb castle, in Moray. The countess was Catherine, widow of David Strathbogie, Earl of Atholl, who had been killed at Culblean, and the daughter of Henry de Beaumont, the patron of Gray's father.

26. A contemporary newsletter provides a detailed account of the *chevauchée* (Ellis, *Original Letters*, i, 34–9); see also Rogers, *War Cruel and Sharp*, 16–19. Robert de Ogle had poached deer with Gray in his youth, and was appointed to a commission of array with him in Oct. 1353; and his son was named in the chain of remainders on an entail created by Gray in 1366/7: *CPR 1330–4*, 202; *Rot. Scot.*, i, 762; 'Chancery Enrolments, Hatfield', 279–80.

27. In fact, Edward returned to England before coming to Bothwell (in Oct. 1336), in order to attend a Great Council called to discuss the collapse of negotiations with Philip VI of France: Rogers, *War, Cruel and Sharp*, 119–23. Gray's father – and perhaps Gray himself, with him – may have been at Bothwell with the king, for 'Thomas de Grey senior' took out letters of protection for service in Scotland with Henry Percy, on 23 Sep. 1336: *CDS*, v, no. 3525.

28. The parliament was held at Westminster, 3–16 Mar. 1337. The *Historia aurea* (*Hemingburgh*, ii, 312–13) mentions the parliament, but only in relation to Edward's promotions to the nobility, concerning which it makes no adverse comment. Gray appears to have been alone amongst contemporary chroniclers in criticising this mass creation of earls. Edward III's patronage in these years is discussed by Bothwell, 'Edward III and the "New Nobility" ', 1111–40; and *idem*, 'Edward III, the English Peerage, and the 1337 Earls', 35–52.

29. The details of these taxes are not quite accurate. No taxes were granted at the Mar. 1337 parliament; a subsidy was negotiated at a great council in July, and three fifteenths and tenths were granted at the parliament at Westminster in Sep. 1337. The wool tax involved the purchase of wool by the crown for sale abroad. Jurkowski *et al.*, *Lay Taxes*, 40–2; Harriss, *King, Parliament and Public Finance*, 232–52; Rogers, *War Cruel and Sharp*, 137–8.

30. Moray died in 1338 from dysentry, during Lent: *Lanercost*, 296.

31. *Lanercost*, 292, dates the attack on Carlisle to mid-Oct. 1337, and confirms that Lords Percy and Neville came to the town's relief. Fordun, 362, relates that Moray was diverted from the siege of Edinburgh by 'the power of the English army, and by the fraudulent and deceitful intervention of certain Scots', but does not mention any battle. Bower, vii, 130, puts the siege in October. In an account of the exploits of William Douglas, both Bower, vii, 138, and Wyntoun, vi, 116–19, record that he was badly wounded while charging an English army at Crighton Dean, though neither relate this to the siege of Edinburgh.

32. Dunbar castle, defended by 'Black Agnes', Countess of March, was besieged by the English from Jan. to June 1338: see Nicholson, *Scotland*, 136–7.

33. Fordun, 362, dates the start of the siege to 13 January 1338. William Montague, Earl of Salisbury, held the barony of Wark in Northumberland, and Gray himself served with him in Flanders in 1339, just a year after the siege of

Dunbar, so it may have been Salisbury himself who was the source of this story. On the other hand, as it portrays him in a rather unflattering light, it may just have been gossip going round the earl's retinue behind his back.

34. The battle took place on 9 Nov. 1337; Guy was the illegitimate half-brother of the Count of Flanders: Sumption, *Trial by Battle*, 216.

35. Again, the Earl of Salisbury may be the source for the rancour within Edward's court; while Gray's qualification ('com fust dit') might suggest that he was reporting contemporary rumour, it may just reflect his caution regarding the earl's self-justifications. The explanation Gray gives for the failure of the English siege of Dunbar castle certainly reads like a piece of special pleading, and Salisbury was one of the leaders of the English forces there. As Gray notes above, Salisbury had been one of the envoys on Burghersh's diplomatic mission to Germany: *Fœdera*, II, ii, 985.

Chapter 47

1. According to Scottish sources (Wyntoun, 148–51; Bower, vii, 148), the Scots were a raiding force led by Alexander Ramsey, and they defeated the English Marchers by a feigned flight. Robert Manners (d. 1355) – if this is not his like-named son (d. *c*.1347) – was the lord of Etal (see above, 235, n. 9).

2. The meeting took place on 5 Sep. 1338; Gray's account is not based on the equally short notice in the *Historia aurea*, which places it 'near Cologne': *Hemingburgh*, ii, 316. A much more detailed account is provided by *Knighton*, ed. Martin, 8–11; see also Lucas, *Low Countries*, 290–2; Sumption, *Trial by Battle*, 243–4. The Emperor, Ludwig of Bavaria, was married to Margaret of Holland, a sister of Edward's queen, Philippa of Hainault. For the financially crippling payments promised to Edward's allies, see Rogers, *War Cruel and Sharp*, 133–6.

3. Middelburg, on the island of Walcheren; the ships were captured on 21 Sep. 1338. Southampton was raided on 5 Oct., with the raiders withdrawing on the following day. Sumption, *Trial by Battle*, 247–8.

4. Edward was commisioned as an imperial vicar at the meeting at Coblenz on 5 September (above, n. 2).

5. Reginald, Count of Guelders (he did not become Duke until the following year, 1339), was married to Edward's sister, Eleanor; William, Margrave of Juliers, had become Count of Juliers in 1336, and would be created Earl of Cambridge in 1340; he was married to a sister of Queen Philippa.

6. Honnecourt was attacked on 10 Oct. 1339: Sumption, *Trial by Battle*, 283.

7. Edward formally assumed the title of King of France on 26 January 1340, though his new regnal year was dated from 25 January. His son, John of Gaunt, was born in March.

8. Edward crossed over to England on 21 Feb. 1340. Note that neither the *Historia aurea* (*Hemingburgh*, ii, 348) nor the *Polychronicon*, viii, 334, refer to any storm on this occasion. Gray subsequently refers to Edward being in danger of drowning in a tempest when returning to England in Nov. 1340: below, 134. Possibly he was reporting the same incident on both occasions.

9. Apr. 1340: Sumption, *Trial by Battle*, 311–12. Gray himself had served in Flanders with the Earl of Salisbury, shortly before the earl was captured. *Knighton*, ed. Martin, 26, puts Salisbury's capture in a rather kinder light, relating that he and Suffolk attacked on their own initiative 'because of their great zeal and manifest boldness', and were only captured because they were unable to withdraw with

honour. *Lanercost*, 332, records their capture without comment, but Murimuth, 105, shared Gray's opinion, stating that they were captured 'due to their own stupid audacity'. Jean le Bel similarly portrays the earls as reckless: Le Bel, i, 168–9. For a curious French account of the incident, see Rogers, *Wars of Edward III*, 81–2.

10. The siege lasted for most of June 1340, ending on the 23rd: Sumption, *Trial by Battle*, 317–18.

11. The *Scalacronica*'s brief outline of the battle of Sluys bears no relation to the much longer account in the *Historia aurea*: Hemingburgh, ii, 355–9.

12. According to Le Bel, 180, the dukes of Brabant and Guelders, the Count of Hainault and the Margrave of Juliers met with Edward at Vilvoorde, separately from the Flemish town councillors. The *Historia aurea* makes no mention of any meetings at all, and nor do any other chronicles: Lucas, *Low Countries*, 404. The siege of Tournai began on 1 Aug. 1340.

13. Robert of Artois had fled to England in 1334, after falling out with Philip over his claim to the County of Artois: Sumption, *Trial by Battle*, 170–1.

14. The letter was dated 26 July, and offered the alternatives in reverse order to that recorded by Gray, *i.e.*, personal combat, failing which, a combat between teams of 100 knights (led by the respective kings, a stipulation which Gray omits), failing which, a set-piece battle: *Fœdera*, II, ii, 1131. The *Historia aurea* gives an accurate summary of the letter, in the right order: Hemingburgh, ii, 361.

15. Philip's reply, dated 30 July, must have been circulated amongst the English forces, for it is quoted in full in the original French in Avesbury, 315–16, and in Latin translation in the *Historia aurea*: Hemingburgh, ii, 362–3.

16. 26 July 1340. For a modern account of the battle, see Sumption, *Trial by Battle*, 341–4.

17. The terms of the truce are printed in *Fœdera*, II, ii, 1135–7.

Chapter 48
1. Benedict XII, elected Dec. 1334, in succession to John XXII.

2. This raid took place on 28 June 1340: PRO, SC 1/54/30 (printed in Appendix, below; calendared in *CDS*, v, no. 809). A differing account is provided by some recensions of Murimuth's chronicle; according to this, the 'nobiles marchiones', who had been assigned a large sum of money for the custody of the Marches, failed to make any effective resistance to the Scots, who therefore managed to amass a huge haul of booty. It was left to the 'populares ... marchie' to attack them on their way back to Scotland, which they did with considerable success, taking over eighty prisoners: Murimuth, 109n.; King, 'Pur Salvation du Roiaume', 25.

Leland's Abstract, 1340–56
1. Bodleian Library, Oxford, GB 0161 MS Top. gen. c. 1, pp. 803–14; printed in John Leland, *De rebus Britannicis collectaneorum* (6 vols., Oxford, 1715), ii, 558–66. I would like to thank Matt Holford for kindly checking Leland's MS.

2. This is probably a reference to the chronicler himself, though it may be to his father instead; above, xxxvi. A letter describing this raid is printed in the Appendix, below.

3. For Manners, see above, 101, 127; for Coupland, above, xlii–xliii, 207.

4. Note that this is one of very few allusions in the later part of the *Scalacronica* to any form of divine punishment being inflicted within this world – or indeed, any other.

5. Edward crossed to England on the night of 30 Nov. 1340; see above, 242n.

6. The battle of Morlaix, 30 Sep. 1342.

7. For Moray's capture, see above, 121; for Salisbury and Suffolk, above, 129. Algeciras in Grenada, on the Straits of Morocco, was besieged by Alfonso XI of Castile, falling in Mar. 1344, after a two year siege.

8. This account of affairs in Brittany appears somewhat garbled (perhaps due to a misundertanding by Leland). Quimper was taken by Charles de Blois by assault in May 1344; it was then besieged by John de Montfort, in Aug. 1345, but relieved by Blois. Montfort died of an illness on 26 September. Sumption, *Trial By Battle*, 433–4, 471.

9. *i.e.* Philippe VI, King of France.

10. The battle of Crécy, 26 Aug. 1346.

11. For Gray's account of Gilbert de Middleton, see above, 81. Selby was a Northumbrian knight, lord of Seghill, north of Morpeth, and so may have been known personally to Gray. For his career, see *NCH*, ix, 58–63.

12. The battle of Neville's Cross, 17 Oct. 1346. Coupland was known personally to Gray; above, xlii–xliii. For his career, see King, 'War, Politics and Landed Society', 154–73.

13. This was Geoffroi de Charny, a French nobleman, councillor of Philippe VI and Jean II, and writer on chivalry; for his career, see *The Book of Chivalry of Geoffroi de Charny*, ed. R.W. Kaeuper and E. Kennedy, 3–18. His attempt to recapture Calais by bribery, on 31 Dec. 1349, and the fate of the Genoese Aimery de Pavia, are described in ibid., 10–14.

14. Dagworth was ambushed and killed on the forest road from Auray to Vannes, in the south of Brittany, on 20 July 1350: Sumption, *Trial by Fire*, 57.

15. The Yorkshire knight Sir Walter Bentley, for whom see, Sumption, *Trial by Fire*, 29–30, 134.

16. Parliament at Westminster, Feb. 1351. Henry Grosmont was created Duke, and Ralph de Stafford Earl of Stafford in March.

17. Henry departed England in the winter 1351 and returned the following summer; for an account of the expedition and the dispute with Brunswick, see Fowler, *King's Lieutenant*, 103–10.

18. Ardres, 8 June 1351; the French captain who was slain was Eduarde de Beajeu. Sumption, *Trial by Fire*, 81.

19. Benedict XII, elected in Dec. 1334, died Apr. 1342. Clement VI was elected May 1342, and died Dec. 1352.

20. The Sire de Garencières: see above, xxxix–xli.

21. This is the famous 'Combat of the Thirty' at Ploermel in Brittany in 1351, a set-piece combat between thirty English knights and thirty of their French counterparts. Detailed accounts also appear in Wyntoun, vi, 208–21, and Bower, vii, 282–4, who obviously relished such a conspicuous English defeat. It is intriguing to note that both Wyntoun and Bower record the incident as a digression in their accounts of events in 1355, as does Gray. It is possible that all three accounts were derived from the same source; certainly, Wyntoun and Bower relied on a common source: Bower, vii, 475n.

22. This is, of course, the occasion which gave Gray the enforced leisure time to write the *Scalacronica*: see above, xxxix–xli.

23. The Scots captured Berwick *c.* 1 Nov. 1355.

24. 26 Jan. 1356 by modern reckoning.

Chapter 48a

1. On 5 Apr. 1356, at a banquet at Rouen castle following a council of the leading magnates of Normandy, held by the Dauphin in his capacity as his father's Lieutenant in Normandy. King Jean burst in, and arrested the Count of Harcourt, the lord of Graville and Guillaume de Mainemares, for plotting with Charles, King of Navarre, who was also arrested on the same occasion. Harcourt, Graville and Mainemares were beheaded later that day; Navarre was imprisoned. Sumption, *Trial by Fire*, 205–8.

Chapter 49

1. The MS gives the year as 1355, but the regnal year is correct, and this is undoubtedly a simple scribal error, for Gray had already started work on his chronicle by the time of the battle.

2. The same date is given by the *Brut*, ed. Brie, ii, 307. Note that this is the first occasion that Gray dates by the day of the month, rather than by the ecclesiastical calendar: *Scalacronica*, Maxwell, 121n.

3. Romorantin was captured on 30 Aug., its tower on 3 Sep.: Rogers, *War, Cruel and Sharp*, 357–8.

4. The French numbered 700 according to a newsletter from the Prince of Wales himself; John of Reading records that 100 French men-at-arms were killed, and another 100 captured; a newsletter from Bartholomew Burghersh gives a figure of 240 French men-at-arms killed or captured there; while the *Anonimalle Chronicle* puts French casualties at 800. All confirm Gray's date for this battle. Barber, *Life of the Black Prince*, 58; Reading, 124; Rogers, *Wars of Edward III*, 163; *Anonimalle, 1333–81*, 37.

5. *Anonimalle, 1333–81*, 37, states that the two armies stood for all of Sunday and the following night at a distance of an archer's shot between them; accordingly, 'lieu' must here mean 'mile' rather than 'league'.

6. The same charge is made by the *Eulogium*, iii, 223. Baker, 144, whilst not explicitly accusing the cardinal of deliberately aiding the French, similarly comments that while the negotiations were in progress on the Sunday, the French army increased in size by '1000 men-at-arms and huge multitude of commoners'.

7. *i.e.* the cardinal would let the French king know what concessions he could expect to gain from the prince.

8. According to Baker, 144–5, the two marshals, Arnoul d'Audrehem and Jean de Clermont, argued over precedence, while Chandos Herald, lines 1121–56, ascribes their falling out to a disagreement over tactics.

9. Burghersh's newsletter (Rogers, *Wars of Edward III*, 164) gives 8000 men-at-arms (and 3000 infantry) for the French, but 3000 men-at-arms, 2000 archers and 1000 sergeants for the English: Baker, 143, also gives 8000 men-at-arms for the French, but 4000 men-at-arms (curiously referred to as *togati*), 1000 sergeants and 2000 archers for the Black Prince. Reading, 124, numbers the French at just 7000 men-at-arms, but tallies closely with Gray for the English, numbering them at 1900 men-at-arms 'and about the same of archers'. However, *Anonimalle, 1333–81*, 38, describes King Jean's battle having 8000 men-at-arms, while Chandos Herald, lines 736–8, 931–1060, who refers to a 'list' as his source, gives a total of 10,400 men-at-arms in four battles for the French army. For a discussion of the numbers, see Rogers, *War, Cruel and Sharp*, 377. Note that if Gray was indeed using

a newsletter as his source, as seems probable, this would appear to be where it ended.

10. William Douglas had spent his childhood in exile in France, and held lands in Normandy: Brown, *The Black Douglases*, 210–11.

11. Gray's account of Fife's marriage is somewhat muddled; the earl had married Mary de Monthermer, daughter of Ralph de Monthermer; it was actually Mary's mother, Joan of Acre, who was Countess of Gloucester and a daughter of Edward I. *Vetera monumenta*, ed. Theiner, 177; *CP*, v, 708–12, ix, 140–2; *SP*, iv, 12–13. Note that this is not the William Ramsay who was present when Gray was captured in 1355 (see above, xl).

12. Felton was certainly married to an Isabella at his death, in Sep. 1358; and he had a son with the unusual – and suggestive – name Duncan, whose mother was described in a papal petition of 1351 as being kin to Edward III: *Wills and Inventories*, ed. Raine, 29; *CIPM*, x, no. 444; *Calendar of Papal Registers, Petitions*, i, 210; *Calendar of Papal Registers, Letters*, iii, 428; Penman, *David II*, 58, 102–4; Boardman, *Early Stewarts*, 13. It should be noted that Gray was personally acquainted with Felton, having poached deer with him, fought against the Scots alongside him, and through his dealings with him when the latter served as escheator and sheriff of Northumberland. See above, xxxiv; app. above; *CPR 1343–5*, 220, 252, 275; *CFR 1337–47*, 364–5, 381.

13. 18 Oct. 1356. See Mayer-Rosa and Cadiot, 'The 1356 Basel Earthquake', 325–333, which confirms the basic accuracy of Gray's account.

14. Fowler, *King's Lieutenant*, 161–5. The siege was conducted on behalf of John de Montfort, the English-backed claimant to the Duchy of Brittany, against his rival French-backed claimant, Charles de Blois. The truce was sealed at Bordeaux, 23 Mar. 1357 (printed in *Fœdera*, III, i, 349); Lancaster delayed in implenting it as he had not been party to the negotiations. The 'great sum of silver', recorded by *Knighton*, ed. Martin, as 100,000 *écus*, was paid by the defenders of Rennes to buy off Lancaster.

15. The treaty concerning David's release was sealed at Berwick on 3 Oct. 1357; *RRS, David II*, no. 148; *Rot. Scot.*, i, 811–14; Penman, *David II*, 188. Gray would have been personally familiar with the terms of this treaty, as one of the hostages, John, son and heir of John Gray, was put in his custody; *Rot. Scot.*, i. 814. Gray refers to Thomas Steward as 'called Earl of Angus by the Scots', because Gilbert de Umfraville, lord of Redesdale and Prudhoe, laid claim to the earldom. See above, 235, n. 7.

16. 'The Archpriest' was Arnaud de Cervole, a defrocked clergyman and notorious *routier*, who came from a family of minor Gascon nobles; Sumption, *Trial by Fire*, 359–60.

17. Isabella of France died on 22 Aug. 1358, as the *Eulogium*, iii, 227, noted; Joan, Queen of Scotland, had visited her on 26 June, and stayed for some time, perhaps until her death. Bond, 'Last Days of Isabella, Queen of Edward II', 461–2. Gray later notes that Isabella was buried in the Greyfriars church in London (at Newgate); above, 201.

18. According to the *Eulogium*, iii, 227 (which claims that such a *hastilude* had not been seen since the time of King Arthur), Lancaster was wounded in the leg. Lancaster's wound was also noted by Reading, 130, but curiously not in Knighton's account of the jousting, despite the latter's evident interest in Lancaster's career; *Knighton*, ed. Martin, 158.

19. Wenceslaus, Duke of Luxemburg, had acquired Brabant when his father-in-law, John, Duke of Brabant, died in 1355, precipitating a dispute over the inheritance with his brother-in-law, Louis de Mâle, Count of Flanders, who was aligned with the French; Wenceslaus had been heavily defeated by Louis at the battle of Asse, 17 Aug. 1356: Nicholas, *Medieval Flanders*, 226. The Duke of Brabant's presence was noted by *Knighton*, ed. Martin, 158, but not his request for aid.

20. At Westminster, Feb. 1358. Unfortunately, there is no surviving roll for this parliament.

21. This was the annual tribute of 1000 marks pledged by King John when he surrendered the kingdom of England to Pope Innocent III, and received it back as a fief of the papacy, in 1213. In 1358, Innocent VI attempted to obtain payment of the tribute, which was then decades in arrears; cf. *Knighton*, ed. Martin, 158; Lunt, *Financial Relations of the Papacy*, 68–70. The tribute was finally repudiated in May 1366.

22. According to Lady Wake's petition in parliament, Lisle's men had burned her houses, and killed one of her servants, Willima de Holme: *Rot. Parl.*, ii, 267. The case is discussed in detail by Aberth, *Criminal Churchmen in the Age of Edward III.*

23. This refers to the draft treaty drawn up in May 1358, after negotiations lasting for more than a year, now known as the First Treaty of London: see Rogers, 'Anglo-French Peace Negotiations', 199–203.

24. Harcourt was killed in a skirmish with a French raiding party in the Cotentin, in Nov. 1356 (Sumption, *Trial by Fire*, 270), more than a year before the killing of Marshal de Clermont.

25. Jean de Picquigny, the hereditary *vidâme* of Amiens, freed Charles of Navarre from the castle of Arleux, near Cambrai, before dawn on 9 Nov. 1357, after eighteen months of imprisonment; Sumption, *Trial by Fire*, 294–5. For Navarre's imprisonment, see above, 141.

26. This sortie took place on 14 July 1358, two days after the bridge had been constructed. In fact, the Anglo-Navarrese forces failed to capture the bridge, though they did indeed capture the Dauphin's marshal: Sumption, *Trial by Fire*, 341.

27. The attacks on Creil, Amiens and Mauconseil took place in Aug. and Sep. 1358: Sumption, *Trial by Fire*, 366–8. For a detailed account of the battle at Mauconseil, see Froissait, v, 122–5, who dates it to 21 Aug. He lists eight prominent lords who were captured (including the bishop), adds that 'a good hundred' knights and squires were also taken, and that 1500 men were killed.

Chapter 50

1. This battle, at the Benedictine abbey of Guitres, in Saintonge, Gascony, took place on 26 Aug. 1341: Sumption, *Trial by Battle*, 381–2. The year given in the manuscript, '.Mile.CCC.xxxiij.', is clearly wrong, as England and France were not actually at war in 1333 (and see n. 3, below). Hugh of Geneva was a distinguished Savoyard nobleman who had fought for Edward since 1337.

2. *i.e.*, the sergeants in Hugh de Geneva's relief force crossed the river without the command of Hugh's captains, and charged alongside the abbey's garrison.

3. Cok was a prominent retainer of the Duke of Lancaster, and was appointed seneschal of Aquitaine in Jan. 1347, at Lancaster's instigation: Fowler, *King's Lieutenant*, 184. The battle at Limalonges took place in May 1349: Sumption, *Trial by*

Fire, 49–50. This renders Gray's dating of the battle at Guitres even more problematic, as working back twelve years from Limalonges would put Guitres in *c.* 1337.

4. Bertrand de Montferrand, a Gascon nobleman retained as captain of Lusignan castle at the expense of the English crown, after its garrison surrendered to the Earl of Lancaster in Oct. 1346; it was recaptured by the French in the autumn of 1350, when its castellan surrendered, but only after a siege of some weeks. Sumption, *Trial by Battle*, 544, 547; *idem*, *Trial by Fire*, 43, 66.

5. This battle was actually fought on 1 Apr., not St George's day, in 1351. Nevertheless, Saint-Jean d'Angély capitulated to the French at the end of Aug., as the French blockading forces remained undeterred by the English victory: Sumption, *Trial by Fire*, 76–8, 83.

6. Mauron was fought on 14 Aug. 1352: Sumption, *Trial by Fire*, 94–5. For Guy de Nesle, the Marshal, son of Jean de Nesle, lord of Offémont, and a favourite councillor of King Philip VI, see *ibid.*, 52. *Lankaderet* is presumably a garbled reference to the battle of La Roche-Derrien, June 1347; Gray's accounts of this battle, and of Dagworth's death in a skirmish in 1350, are summarised in Leland's abstract, above 136, 138.

Chapter 51

1. Note that Charles of Navarre was actually sprung from Arleux castle, not *Greuequer*: see above, 247, n. 25.

2. For the Archpriest, see above, 151.

3. 12 Jan. 1359: Sumption, *Trial by Fire*, 383.

4. Auxerre was captured on 10 Mar. 1359 by a force led by Robert Knollys. In fact, the failure of the town's inhabitants to stump up the promised ransom appears to have been due to impoverishment, rather than bad faith: Sumption, *Trial by Fire*, 384–5.

5. Fotheringhay, a Northamptonshire man, was Charles of Navarre's marshal, and held Creil in his name from Sep. 1358 with a very large garrison: Sumption, *Trial by Fire*, 343, 366, 369–71.

6. This was actually a farmhouse at Longeuil belonging to the Benedictine monks of Saint-Corneille, Compiègne; it was attacked after Auxerre had fallen in Mar. 1359: Venette, 90–2, 258.

7. According to French accounts, this captain was Guillaume l'Aloue (who may have served with Bertrand de Guesclin); they also state that he was killed fighting the English, rather than after surrendering to them: Venette, 91, 258; Wright, *Knights and Peasants*, 82.

8. 'Jacques Bonhomme' was a French nickname for the stereotypical peasant; but in the contexts Gray uses the term he is probably referring specifically to peasant rebels, from its association with the *Jacquerie*, the rebellion of 1358: above, 155; and see Wright, *Knights and Peasants*, 12, 82 and *passim*.

9. Épernon was captured in Jan. 1358: Sumption, *Trial by Fire*, 304–5. Pipe's career is reviewed in *ibid.*, 300–1, and see above, 179–81.

10. The Bègue de Villaines was a minor nobleman from the Île de France, who had previously attacked Paris while it was under the sway of Étienne Marcel: Sumption, *Trial by Fire*, 316. For another of the 'many times' on which the Bègue was taken, see below, 183.

11. Saint-Valéry was captured in Oct. 1358, by Anglo-Navarrese forces

supporting Charles of Navarre; it fell to the French in Apr. 1359. Sumption, *Trial by Fire*, 367–8, 418.

12. The 'English' forces were men from the mercenary Companies, nominally in the employ of Charles of Navarre; one of their leaders was Sir Robert Scot, mentioned in Gray's account of Edward III's expedition of 1359–60 (above, 179). Similarly, the 'Germans' in Sisonne were mercenaries, commanded by Frank Hennequin, who was probably a Hainaulter, though contemporaries believed he came from Cologne. Vailly was taken in the autumn of 1358, Sisonne was recaptured by the French in the autumn of 1359. Sumption, *Trial by Fire*, 405–10.

13. Aug. 1359: Sumption, *Trial by Fire*, 416. Sir Hugh de Calveley was a Cheshireman, and captain of the Companies, who went on to have a long, famous and very prosperous career: see Bridge, 'Calveley and Knollys'.

14. Sumption, *Trial by Fire*, 418–21. Melun is twenty-five miles south-east of Paris, on the Seine.

15. Thomas was the son of the Lancashire knight Robert de Holland; he made a very successful and profitable military career, and was a founder Knight of the Garter. In 1340, he clandestinely married 'la plus amoureuse' Joan of Kent, daughter of Edmund, Earl of Kent and youngest son of Edward I. Joan became Countess of Kent on the death without heirs of her only brother in 1352, and Thomas assumed the title of Earl of Kent shortly before his own death. Wentersdorf, 'Maid of Kent'. He died 26 Dec. 1360: *CIPM*, x, no. 657.

16. See above, 155; and see 248, n. 8.

17. Gilbert de Roddam may have been one of the Northumbrian Roddams, from Roddam near Wooler (for whom, see *NCH*, xiv, 282–3), and thus perhaps personally known to Gray.

18. The word 'brigan' was a French term coined in the mid-fourteenth century, referring to footsoldiers wearing a brigandine, a protective leather coat with steel plates sewn into it. Although the term already appears to have acquired its modern sense of 'bandit' by 1377 (Wright, *Knights and Peasants*, 89–91), Gray is clearly using it in its original military sense here.

Chapter 52

1. This date is confirmed by Knighton (ed. Martin, 168).

2. The Germans needed to be removed from Calais because they were rioting, and fighting with the English garrison – and because there were insufficient supplies in the town to feed them. *Knighton*, ed. Martin, 168; Froissart, v, 190–1, Fowler, *King's Lieutenant*, 201.

3. For Lancaster's brief *chevauchée*, see *ibid.*, 201–2. 'Dray' is an error for 'Bray'.

4. Reading, 133, also gives 4 Nov. for Edward's departure from Calais, though the *Eulogium*, iii, 228, records that he landed in Calais on 27 Oct., and that his expedition set out on the following Saturday (*i.e.* 2 Nov.). According to *Anonimalle, 1333–81*, 44, Edward met with Lancaster after he had set out, some twenty miles from Calais. Froissart, v, 194–5, states that they met up four leagues (*lieves*) from Calais.

5. According to Knighton (ed. Martin, 170), this incident took place on 26 Nov.; Knighton puts the strength of d'Annequin's party at sixty men.

6. 18 Nov. 1359. Jean de Grailly (d. 1377), known as the Captal de Buch, was from one of the leading noble families of the Bordelais, who were staunch supporters of English rule in Gascony. He was a founder Knight of the Garter, had

figured prominently in the English victory at Poitiers, and had been serving with Charles of Navarre before coming to Creil. Sumption, *Trial by Fire*, 85–6, 242, 422.

7. Fotheringhay was paid 24,000 royals (1 royal was worth 3s 10d sterling) to vacate Creil, in Nov. 1359; he did not bother to go very far, as the castle of Pont-Sainte-Maxence was just eight miles downstream. Sumption, *Trial by Fire*, 422. For Fotheringhay's capture of Creil, see above, 157, 165.

8. *i.e.* the crossing of the river Aire.

9. According to *Knighton*, ed. Martin, 172, the town was captured on 20 Dec. 1359, and the castle on 6 Jan.; the tower, having been undermined, was demolished two days later. Froissart, v, 220–3, 410–12, has a lively account of the undermining of the tower. Burghersh was serving in the Black Prince's retinue: *Register of the Black Prince*, iii, 371.

10. According to *Knighton*, ed. Martin, 170–2, Cernay-en-Dormois was taken on 28 Dec., and Autry on 1 Jan. Fowler, *King's Lieutenant*, 203–4. The Earl of Richmond was John of Gaunt, Edward's third son.

11. 'Dairres' is probably a scribal error for 'Bairres'.

12. The assault on Châlons was led by Sir Peter de Audley, perhaps a younger brother of James de Audley, who subsequently died in his bed at his castle at Beaufort, early in 1360: Froissart, v, 152–6, 182. Attigny was taken by a company led by the Hainaulter Eustache d'Aubricourt: Froissart, v, 213.

13. Rogers, *War, Cruel and Sharp*, 409n., suggests that *faillerent* should be taken to mean that the negotiations were 'completed' successfully, rather than that they 'failed'. Certainly, *Anonimalle, 1333–81*, 45, reports that the men of Bar paid a ransom to the English.

14. One of those captured at about this time was the young Geoffrey Chaucer: *Chaucer Life Records*, ed. Crow and Olson, 23–8.

15. This may have been Jean, Sire de Hangest, who was at the battle of Mauron (Sumption, *Trial by Fire*, 94), alluded to by Gray, above, 161.

16. This was a mocking reference to set-piece combats, beloved of chivalric commentators such as Froissart, such as the Combat of the Thirty. King, 'Helm with a Crest', 30.

17. 27 Feb., according to the contemporary 'Wigmore Chronicle', which had Mortimer connections: printed in Taylor, *Historical Literature*, 290.

18. The agreement, dated 10 Mar., is printed in *Fœdera*, III, i, 473. The *florin au mouton* was a French gold coin, first minted in 1355; at the exchange rate specified by Gray, this would have been equivalent to £40,000 sterling, a vast sum of money.

19. Froissart, v, 224–5, 416, relates that Flavigny had been taken by the English squire John de Arleston, when Edward first arrived in Burgundy; and sufficient supplies were found in the town to feed the English army for a whole month.

20. The second son of Sir Andrew Leslie, Norman was fairly prominent in Scottish government circles; he had come to France in May 1359, as an ally of Robert the Steward's faction, on an embassy to secure a Franco-Scottish treaty against England, and also to the papacy at Avignon, for the grant of an ecclesiastical tax to help pay David II's ransom. Along with his elder brother Sir Walter Leslie, he was a keen crusader, and may have been killed at the capture of Alexandria in 1365. Bower, vii, 312; Penman and Tanner, 'An Unpublished Act of David II'; MacQuarrie, *Scotland and the Crusades*, 81–4; *SP*, vii, 270–1.

21. Fogg had been appointed by Henry, Duke of Lancaster, as his lieutenant in

the castles of Domfront, Bois-du-Maine, Messei and Condé-sur-Noireau, on the Norman-Angevin border, in 1355: Fowler, *King's Lieutenant*, 156, n. 50.

22. *Knighton*, ed. Martin, 172–4, gives the French force as 240 lances (*lanceati*), and the English as twenty-seven lances and about 100 archers. Venette, 96–7, locates the battle at Pont-Audemer, and relates that the English attacked from ambush. Fogg subsequently received £800 from the English Crown in part payment of his share of the ransoms, and the revenues of his castles; *CPR 1361–4*, 126.

23. This appears to have been a case of life imitating (chivalric) art, for Chrétien de Troyes' *Perceval, Le Conte du Graal* includes an episode with a *Chevalier Vermeil* (*Le Roman de Perceval*, ed. Roach, lines 938–1130). The fact that Chrétien's Red Knight was actually rather disreputable does not seem to have especially concerned his English would-be imitators.

24. This was the son (and subsequently heir) of Ralph, Lord Neville, of Raby. He inherited his father's lands and title in 1367. *CP*, ix, 502.

25. Actually, Friday 13 Mar. 1360, in the third week of Lent: Sumption, *Trial by Fire*, 436–7.

26. Robert Scot was a leader of the mercenary companies. See n. 249, above.

27. An area south of Paris, south-west of Nemours.

28. 'Tournelis' is probably an error for 'Fournelis'.

29. According to Venette, 101, the castle was accidentally set on fire when its keeper had a neighbouring house burned down as a defensive measure; and many townsmen were within the castle, most of whom died in the flames.

30. For Pipe, see above, 167.

31. For Gray's conception of the 'couenaunt de loial cheualerie', see King, 'Helm with a Crest', 33–5.

32. Robert de Herle, *chevaler*, received letters of protection for service in Brittany for one year on 22 Nov. 1359: PRO, C 76/38, m. 4.

33. Sir Robert Knollys was a Cheshireman, and one of the English whom Gray described as coming to France, 'as unknown youths, from different regions of England, many beginning as archers, and then becoming knights, and some of them captains' (above, 157), for Knollys probably started his career as an archer in the company of Sir Hugh Calveley. Walsingham, i, 286, comments '… Robert Knolles, from being a poor and lowly valet, was soon made a leader of knights'. See also Bridge, 'Calveley and Knollys', 166–70.

34. For the Bègue de Villaines, see above, 167.

Chapter 53

1. According to *Knighton*, ed. Martin, 176, Edward reached Paris on the Monday after Easter (*i.e.*, 6 Apr.).

2. *Knighton*, ed. Martin, 176, relates that there were thirty newly dubbed knights, and that they rode to the gates of Paris openly, to seek combat 'under the law of arms', and that they were met by sixty men from the city, whom they defeated.

3. As Gray wrote this, he could not have foreseen that his own grandson, John de Gray, would be created Count of Tancarville by Henry V: *CP*, vi, 136–8.

4. 13 Apr. 1360 was actually a Monday. *Anonimalle, 1333–81*, 46, describes the day as 'le mauveys lundy': Sumption, *Trial by Fire*, 444.

5. 'Some of the English were put on their faith to the enemy …', *i.e.* they surren-

dered and promised to pay ransoms. Note that according to the laws of war, having being put on their faith, they would still have been liable for these ransoms, even after having been rescued: Keen, *The Laws of War*, 164–8. This contrasts with the dispute over James Pipe's ransom (above, 181), because Pipe was accused of having deliberately arranged his 'rescue' in advance, contrary to his promise not to escape, which clearly amounted to a breach of faith.

6. Hugh de Geneva had previously been in English service; for Gray's description of his exploits at the abbey of Guitres in Aug. 1341, see above, 159.

7. This was the Treaty of Brétigny, sealed on 8 May 1360. Printed in *Fœdera*, III, i, 486–94; discussed by Rogers, 'Anglo-French Peace Negotiations'.

8. Note that this corroborates Clifford Rogers' thesis that Edward III was deliberately seeking battle with the French on this and other campaigns: *idem*, *War, Cruel and Sharp*, 412–13 and *passim*.

9. This refers to the 'English' of the Great Company, who had wreaked enormous devastation in many parts of France in 1358–9, sometimes nominally in the service of Charles of Navarre, but without the authority of the English Crown.

10. *i.e.*, the three battles commanded by the Prince of Wales, the Duke of Lancaster and the King himself, respectively.

Chapter 54

1. David's wife, Joan, was estranged from her husband, and had retired to the English court.

2. Bower relates that Thomas Stewart, Earl of Angus, was imprisoned for suspected involvement in the plot (amongst other misdeeds). According to his account, Katherine (whom he describes as Welsh) was killed when David was returning from England, and he names her murderers as Richard Holly and 'Dewar'. He adds that David 'loved her more than all other women'. Bower, vii, 319–21; Penman, *David II*, 245–6, 247.

3. *i.e.* Pedro I 'the Cruel', King of Castile. Alfonso XI ('le bon Roy Alphonsus') is mentioned by Gray in connection with the siege of Algeciras, above, 135.

4. The Order of the Band was a chivalric order of knights founded by Alfonso XI in 1330. It was not in fact necessary for knights to prove themselves against the Moors to qualify for membership: Boulton, *Knights of the Crown*, 46–95.

5. Pedro's bastard brother was Enrique of Trastámara, the son of Alfonso's mistress, expelled from Castile on his brother's succession in 1350 (and see below, 254, n. 13). Stories such as that repeated by Gray were assiduously circulated around Europe by Enrique's supporters, in a highly successful propaganda campaign intended to blacken Pedro's reputation. This evidently reached English circles, as Froissart (vi, 201–2) reports that stories of Pedro's cruelty influenced the English councillors of the Black Prince. Russell, *English Intervention*, 17–18, 38–9, 61.

6. Hostilities had broken out in 1356. Gray is presumably referring here to the peace treaty sealed at Terrer in May 1361, which broke down in the summer of 1362. In fact, Pedro may well have foreseen the renewed outbreak of war, as it was his invasion of Aragon in June 1362 that precipated it. Russell, *English Intervention*, 24–7.

7. Cf. Deuteronomy, 3:23–8. Note that this is the only direct allusion to any biblical story in the later part of the *Scalacronica* (though it is not impossible that the missing section contained a similar allusion).

Chapter 55

1. Gray's father had had joint custody of Somerton castle, Lincolnshire (where King Jean was held) with Henry de Beaumont in 1322 (*CFR 1319–27*, 133; *CPR 1321–4*, 143; *CIM 1307–49*, no. 939).

2. The terms for John's release were sealed at Calais on 24 Oct. 1360: *Fœdera*, III, i, 514–18.

3. The treaty names 'Monsire Guillaume de Craon' here, instead of 'Mesire Willam de Cinoun': *Fœdera*, III, i, 515. Note that it has not been possible to identify the Count of *Valentinois*, the lords of *Preux* and *Saint Venaunt*, or the Dauphin *D'Aineryne*.

4. Note that Gray actually names only fifteen prisoners, omitting the Count of Eu: cf. *Fœdera*, III, i, 515; see also Given-Wilson and Bériac, 'Edward III's Prisoners of War', 818–19. Note that the *Scalacronica* again has 'le sire de Cynoun', instead of 'le sire de Craon'.

5. This was the parliament held at Westminster 24 Jan.–18 Feb. 1361, for which writs were issued on the preceding 20 Nov., *i.e.*, a month after the sealing of the agreement; unfortunately, no rolls from it survive. Walsingham, i, 294; Reading, 147–8; and the *Brut*, ed. Brie, 313 (which misdates the year to 36 Edward III – in fact, it started on the first day of 35 Edward III), all confirm that the treaty 'was put forþ and showed' at this parliament.

6. Pont-Saint-Esprit is on the Rhône, 25 miles upstream from Avignon, and was stormed on the night of 28–29 Dec., 1360: Fowler, *Mercenaries*, 28–32. Avignon and Provence were nominally part of the Empire, and therefore outside of the kingdom of France.

7. Duke Henry died on 23 Mar. at Leicester, and was buried in the collegiate church he had founded there. His eldest daughter Maud (who died shortly after her father, in Apr. 1362) married Duke William in early 1352, who lost his sanity in 1357. The younger daughter Blanche married John of Gaunt on 19 May 1359. Fowler, *King's Lieutenant*, 117–21, 174–5, 218. For's Henry's piousness, see *ibid.*, 187–96.

Chapter 56

1. *i.e.* Queenborough castle, Kent; building work was still going on in the year of Gray's death, 1369. The castle does not appear to have been known as 'Queenborough' until the adjoining new town was so-named in 1367, in honour of Queen Philippa. Brown *et al.*, *History of the King's Works*, 793–804.

2. This was Kestutis, the pagan Prince of Lithuania, captured in the spring of 1361; for the circumstances, see Urban, *Teutonic Knights*, 176. Gray's informant about affairs in Lithuania must have been one of the English crusaders who went to Prussia at this time, perhaps a retainer of the Scropes of Masham, North Yorkshire. Geoffrey le Scrope died in Prussia in 1362; his uncle William le Scrope was at Satalia, in the company of the Earl of Hereford: *Scrope and Grosvenor*, i, 123, 146, 188, 166.

3. Other contemporary accounts of the second pestilence are conveniently translated in Horrox, *The Black Death*, 85–8.

4. The King of Cyprus was Peter I of Lusignan, who took Satalia in 1361.

5. Lionel, Edward's second surviving son, was appointed king's lieutenant in Ireland on 1 July 1361, being married to Elizabeth, daughter and heiress of William

de Burgh, earl of Ulster; he was created Duke of Clarence in Nov. 1362. For the background, see Otway-Ruthven, *Medieval Ireland*, 284–6.

6. The King of Denmark was Valdemar IV; the 'Easterlings' referred to by Gray were the Swedes, who had captured Skåne from the Danes in 1332. *NCMH*, 720–2.

7. Edward's wife was Joan of Kent. She had previously been married to William Montague, Earl of Salisbury, which marriage was annulled due to her previous clandestine marriage to Sir Thomas Holland. Holland died in Dec. 1360 (above, 169), and Edward Prince of Wales secretly married her in the following spring, apparently for love. After obtaining papal dispensation for consanguinity, they were publicly married in Oct. 1361. Wentersdorf, 'Maid of Kent'.

8. As Gray usually dates the start of the year from the Annunciation (25 Mar.), this should be Jan. 1362 by modern reckoning. This storm was widely reported in contemporary chronicles, including *Knighton*, ed. Martin, 184; the *Eulogium*, iii, 229; *Louth Park Chronicle*, 40–1, which describe it in identical terms, and date it to 15 Jan.

9. Venette, 108, also records this, describing 'a very large and brilliant star, hitherto unknown and rather like a comet' which appeared in Lent.

10. Kestutis escaped from Marienburg castle, the headquarters of the Teutonic Knights, in mid-Nov. 1361: Urban, *Teutonic Knights*, 177.

11. This was the battle of Brignais, 6 Apr. 1362. Jacques de Bourbon was the Count of La Marche; he died of his wounds a few days after the battle. Fowler, *Mercenaries*, 46–52. The Count of Saarbrück was captured, not killed: Froissart, vi, p. xxvii, n. 4.

12. See Sumption, *Trial by Fire*, 475. Felton was the eldest son of the Northumbrian William Felton (above, 246n.), by his first wife. *NCH*, vii, 122. He subsequently died a futilely heroic death on the Black Prince's Spanish campaign of 1367: Chandos Herald, lines 2725–58; Froissart, vii, 23; *CIPM*, xi, no. 200.

13. 3 June 1362, at Montpensier, near Vichy. The 'Bastard of Spain' was Enrique of Trastámara (see above, 252, n. 5), who was in French service at this time, having temporarily taken refuge in France following the (shortlived) peace agreement between Castile and Aragon of May 1361. Fowler, *Mercenaries*, 54–5; Sumption, *Trial by Fire*, 480–2.

14. These negotiations were conducted by Arnould d'Audrehem, Marshal of France, who sealed a treaty with the captains of the Great Company on 23 July 1362. In fact, this agreement was ineffective in removing the companies from France. Fowler, *Mercenaries*, 55–61. The 'King of Spain' referred to here is Pedro I of Castile.

15. 19 July 1362; the Black Prince was given the title of Prince of Acquitaine. *Fœdera*, III, ii, 667–70; Barber, *Black Prince*, 171, 175–8.

Chapter 57

1. Guillaume de Grimoard, elected 28 September 1362, and consecrated as Urban V on 6 November. Innocent VI died on 12 September.

2. Joan died on 14 Aug. 1362; she was buried at the Franciscan church near Newgate; and see above, 246, n. 17.

3. The parliament was held at Westminster, 13 Oct.–17 Nov. 1362; the king's sons were awarded their new titles on 13 November. Edmund was Edward's fourth surviving son, as Gray would have been well aware. The reference to 'soun [Edward's] tierce fitz Eadmound' must be either a careless slip, or was intended to

mean 'a third son', [i.e., in addition to the previous two]. Northumberland's knights of the shire for this parliament were Sir Thomas Surtees and Roger Widdrington, again (see above, xlix).

4. Edward was born 13 Nov. 1312, so this was actually his fiftieth birthday. The parallel with the fifty-year Papal Jubilee suggests that this may be another slip, either on Gray's part, or his scribe's.

5. This was the battle of Launac on the plain north-west of Toulouse, 5 Dec. 1362. The Castilian chronicler Lopez de Ayala confirms the presence of English *routiers*, naming the Cheshire knight Sir John Amory amongst the Count of Foix's captains: Fowler, *Mercenaries*, 63–6.

6. Mar's pledge of his lands to the king may have preceded the siege, arising from David's judgement of his dispute with Keith; and the siege may have resulted from Mar's failure to observe the terms of the pledge. Duncan, 'Laws', 262–4; and see also Penman, *David II*, 274–7. Thomas, Earl of Mar, was a grandson of Christina de Bruce, Robert I's sister.

7. A contemporary account of this rising, in early 1363, is provided by Fordun, 381–2, copied almost *verbatim* by Bower, vii, 324–6. For modern accounts, see Penman, *David II*, 283–95; Boardman, *Early Stewarts*, 17–19; Duncan, 'Laws', 264–5. Note that this is an interesting early example of the use of the phrase 'good lordship' (*bon seignoury*).

8. Dirleton, in Lothian, was held by the Haliburton family; John de Haliburton, lord of Dirleton, had been killed at the battle of Nesbit, 1355, at which Gray was captured. Fordun, 372.

9. Fordun, 381, relates that, 'indentures were drawn up, strongly confirmed with all of their seals', though according to Fordun, this was an agreement between the rebels, to try to prevent any of them backing out of the plot; however, such a document, drafted as a petition for reform and presented to the king, would have served to publicly bind in opposition to the king all those who sealed it, so Gray and Fordun may both be right. The Steward was Robert Stewart, David's heir-presumptive, who would succeed him as Robert II in 1371.

10. The sheriff of Angus was Sir Robert de Ramsay, one of the witnesses of Stewart's oath of 14 May (see following note): Bower, vii, 330; Boardman, *Early Stewarts*, 18.

11. Stewart publicly swore an oath to be faithful to David, and renouncing 'whatever contracts, bonds and oaths that I have made and maintained with Patrick, Earl of March and Moray, William, Earl of Douglas ...', on 14 May 1363. Bower, vii, 330.

12. The marriage probably took place in spring 1363, probably just before Stewart's oath of 14 May. Margaret was the daughter of Malcolm Drummond, and widow of John Logie (*SP*, vii, 32–4). The reference to 'the force of love' has been taken as an invocation of *fin amour*, and thus indicative of Gray's enthusiasm for chivalric culture; however, given its context in a description of David's troubled relations with his magnates, it is perhaps rather a sardonic aside to the effect that David was not a man to let affairs of state stand in the way of his amorous endeavours. King, 'Helm with a Crest', 28–9. In similar vein, Bower, vii, 332, writing in the fifteenth century, commented that David 'chose a most beautiful lady ... perhaps not so much for the excellence of her character as a woman as for the pleasure he took in her desirable appearance'.

Appendix

1. PRO, SC 1/54/30. The letter's author was clearly a figure of authority in Roxburgh; the Northumbrian William de Felton, then constable of Roxburgh castle (PRO, E 101/22/40), and a veteran of the Scottish wars, is the obvious candidate. I owe this suggestion to the kindness of Dr Andrew Ayton.

2. PRO, DL 34/1/21. The letter presumably found its way into the Lancastrian archives when Henry Bolingbroke married Mary de Bohun, the daughter and co-heiress of William's son Humphrey (*CP*, vi, 472–4).

3. Robert Manners is mentioned in the *Scalacronica*, above, 127, 134.

4. The death of Alexander Ramsey, at the hands of Sir William Douglas, is mentioned in the *Scalacronica*, above, 134.

5. *i.e.* the blow pierced both Kerr's quilted jerkin (haketon) and the mail shirt (haubergeon) he was wearing under it. Such armour would usually have been sufficient to keep Kerr alive: King, 'Prisoners and Casualties', 268–9. The reference to 'jousting of war' is presumably figurative, referring to a *mêlée*, rather than an actual formal joust.

BIBLIOGRAPHY

Aberth, J., *Criminal Churchmen in the Age of Edward III. The Case of Bishop Thomas de Lisle* (Pennsylvania, 1996).

'Adæ Murimuth continuatio chronicarum', *Chronica A. Murimuth et R. de Avesbury*, ed. E.M. Thompson, Rolls Series 93 (1889).

Ailred of Rievaulx, 'Vita sancti Edwardi regis', *Patrologiæ cursus completus: Patrologia Latina*, ed. J.P. Migne, cxcv.

Altschul, M., *A Baronial Family in Medieval England: The Clares, 1217–1314* (Baltimore,1965).

Anderson, M.J., *Kings and Kingship in Early Scotland* (Edinburgh, 1973).

Anglo-Scottish Relations, 1174–1328, ed. E.L.G. Stones (2nd edn, Oxford, 1970).

'Annales Paulini', *Chronicles of the Reigns of Edward I and Edward II*, ed. W. Stubbs, Rolls Series 76 (2 vols., 1882–3), vol. i.

Anonimalle Chronicle, 1307–1334, The, ed. W.R. Childs and J. Taylor, Yorkshire Archaeological Society Record Series cxlvii (1991).

Anonimalle Chronicle, 1333–81, The, ed. V.H. Galbraith (Manchester, 1927).

Balfour-Melville, E.W.M., 'Two John Crabbs', *Scottish Historical Review* xxxix (1960).

Barber, R., *Edward, Prince of Wales and Aquitaine. A Biography of the Black Prince* (London, 1978).

—— (tr.), *The Life and Campaigns of the Black Prince* (2nd edn, Woodbridge, 1997).

Barbour's Bruce, ed. M.P. McDiarmid and J.A.C. Stevenson, 3 vols., Scottish Text Society, 4th ser., xii, xiii, xv (1980–5).

Barker, J.R.V., *The Tournament in England, 1100–1400* (Woodbridge, 1986).

Barrow, G.W.S., *Robert Bruce and the Community of the Realm of Scotland* (3rd edn, Edinburgh, 1988).

Bean, J.M.W., 'The Percies' Acquisition of Alnwick', *Archaeologia Aeliana*, 4th ser., xxxii (1954).

Binski, P., *Westminster Abbey and the Plantagenets: Kingship and the Representation of Power, 1200–1400* (New Haven, 1995).

Blair, C.H.H., 'A Book of North Country Arms of the Sixteenth Century', *Archaeologia Aeliana*, 3rd ser., iii (1907).

——, 'Northern Knights at Falkirk, 1298', *Archaeologia Aeliana*, 4th ser., xxv (1947).

————, 'Knights of Northumberland 1278 and 1324', *Archaeologia Aeliana*, 4th ser., xxvii (1949).

————, 'Baronys [*sic*] and Knights of Northumberland, 1166–*c*.1266', *Archaeologia Aeliana*, 4th ser., xxx (1952).

Boardman, S., *The Early Stewart Kings. Robert II and Robert III, 1371–1406* (Edinburgh, 1996).

Bond, E.A., 'Notices of the Last Days of Isabella, Queen of Edward II, Drawn from an Account of the Expenses of her Household', *Archaeologia* xxxv (1853).

Book of Chivalry of Geoffroi de Charny, The, ed. R.W. Kaeuper and E. Kennedy (Philadelphia, 1996).

Bothwell, J., 'Edward III and the "New Nobility": Largesse and Limitation in Fourteenth-Century England', *English Historical Review* cxii (1997).

————, 'Edward III, the English Peerage, and the 1337 Earls: Estate Redistribution in Fourteenth-Century England', *The Age of Edward III*, ed. J.S. Bothwell (Woodbridge, 2000).

Boulton, D'A.J.D., *The Knights of the Crown. The Monarchical Orders of Knighthood in Later Medieval Europe, 1325–1520* (2nd edn, Woodbridge, 2000).

Bower's Scotichronicon, ed. D.E.R. Watt *et al.* (9 vols., Aberdeen and Edinburgh, 1987–98).

Brand, P., 'Edward I and the Judges: The "State Trials" of 1289–93', *Thirteenth-Century England I*, ed. P. Coss and S. Lloyd (Woodbridge, 1986).

Bridge, J.C., 'Two Cheshire Soldiers of Fortune of the Fourteenth Century: Sir Hugh Calveley and Sir Robert Knollys', *Journal of the Architectural, Archaeological and Historic Society for Chester*, ns xiv (1908).

Broun, D., *The Irish Identity of the Kingdom of Scots in the Twelfth and Thirteenth Centuries* (Woodbridge, 1999).

Brown, E.A.R., 'Diplomacy, Adultery and Domestic Politics at the Court of Philip the Fair: Queen Isabelle's Mission to France in 1314', *Documenting the Past. Essays in Medieval History Presented to George Peddy Cuttino*, ed. J.S. Hamilton and P.J. Bradley (Woodbridge, 1989).

Brown, M., *The Black Douglases. War and Lordship in Late Medieval Scotland, 1300–1455* (East Linton, 1998).

Brown, R.A., *et al.*, *The History of the King's Works. Vol. II: The Middle Ages* (1963).

Bruce, The, ed. A.A.M. Duncan (Edinburgh, 1997).

Brunne, Robert Manning of, *The Story of England*, Rolls Series 87 (2 vols., 1887).

Brut, The, ed. F.W.D. Brie, Early English Text Society, 1st ser., 131, 136 (2 vols., 1906, 1908).

Buck, M., *Politics, Finance and the Church in the Reign of Edward II. Walter Stapledon* (Cambridge, 1983).

Bullock-Davies, C., *Menestrellorum multitudo. Minstrels at a Royal Feast* (Cardiff, 1978).

Calendar of Documents Relating to Scotland, ed. J. Bain *et al.* (5 vols., Edinburgh, 1881–1988).

Calendar of Plea and Memoranda Rolls of the City of London, 1323–64, ed. A.H. Thomas (Cambridge, 1926).

Campbell, J., 'England, Scotland and the Hundred Years War in the Fourteenth Century', *Europe in the Late Middle Ages*, ed. J.R. Hale, J.R.L. Highfield and B. Smalley (London, 1965).

Capgrave, John, *The Chronicle of England*, ed. F.C. Hingeston, Rolls Series 1 (1858).

———, *Liber de illustribus Henricis*, ed. F.C. Hingeston, Rolls Series 7 (1858).

Catalogi veteres librorum ecclesiæ cathedralis Dunelm, Surtees Society vii (1838).

Catalogue of the Harleian Manuscripts in the British Museum, A (London, 1808).

Chaucer Life Records, ed. M.M. Crow and C.C. Olson (Oxford, 1966).

Childs, W.R., ' "Welcome, My Brother": Edward II, John of Powderham and the Chronicles, 1318', *Church and Chronicle in the Middle Ages: Essays Presented to John Taylor*, ed. I. Wood et G.A. Loud (London, 1991).

Chronica Johannis de Reading et Anonymi Cantuariensis, 1346–67, ed. J. Tait (Manchester, 1914).

Chronica monasterii de Melsa, ed. E.A. Bond, Rolls Series 43 (3 vols., 1866–8).

Chronicle of Jean de Venette, The, tr. J. Birdsall and R.A. Newhall (New York, 1953).

Chronicles of the Picts, Chronicles of the Scots and other Early Memorials of Scottish History, ed. W.F. Skene (Edinburgh, 1867).

Chronicon de Abbatie de Parco Lude. The Chronicle of Louth Park Abbey, ed. E. Venables, tr. A.R. Maddison, Publications of the Lincolnshire Record Society, i (1891).

Chronicon de Lanercost, ed. J. Stevenson, Bannatyne Club lxv (Edinburgh, 1839).

Chronicon domini Walteri de Hemingburgh, ed. H.C. Hamilton, English Historical Society Publications (2 vols., 1849).

Chronicon Galfridi le Baker de Swynebroke, ed. E. M. Thompson (Oxford, 1889).

Chronicon Henrici Knighton, ed. J.R. Lumby, Rolls Series 92 (2 vols., 1889–95).

Chronique de Jean le Bel, ed. J. Viard and E. Déprez (2 vols., 1904–5).

'Chroniques de Sempringham', *Le Livre de Reis de Brittanie*, ed. J. Glover, Rolls Series 42 (1865).

Cockayne, G.E., *et al.* (ed.), *The Complete Peerage*, rev. and ed. V. Gibbs (12 vols., London, 1910–59).

Controversy between Sir Richard Scrope and Sir Robert Grosvenor, The, ed. N.H. Nicholas (2 vols., London, 1832).

Crawford, B.E., 'North Sea Kingdoms, North Sea Bureaucrat: A Royal Official who Transcended National Boundaries', *Scottish Historical Review* lxix (1990).

Crown Surveys of Lands 1540–1, with the Kildare Rental begun in 1518, ed. G. Mac Niocaill (Irish Manuscripts Commission, 1992).

Dean, R.J., and Boulton, M.B.M., *Anglo-Norman Literature: A Guide to the Texts and Manuscripts* (Anglo-Norman Text Society, 1999).

de Ville, O., 'Jocelin Deyville: Brigand, or Man of his Time?', *Northern History* xxxv (1999).

DeVries, K., *Infantry Warfare in the Early Fourteenth Century* (Woodbridge, 1996).

Documents and Records Illustrating the History of Scotland, Preserved in the Treasury, ed. F. Palgrave (Record Commission, 1837).

Documents Illustrative of the History of Scotland, 1286–1306, ed. J. Stevenson (2 vols., London, 1870).

Drage, C., *Nottingham Castle. A Place Full Royal*, Transactions of the Thoroton Society xciii (Nottingham, 1989).

Duffy, S., 'The 'Continuation' of Nicholas Trevet: A New Source for the Bruce Invasion', *Proceedings of the Royal Irish Academy* xci (1991).

Duncan, A.A.M., 'The "Laws of Malcolm MacKenneth" ', *Medieval Scotland. Crown, Lordship and Community*, ed. A. Grant and K.J. Stringer (Edinburgh, 1993).

———, 'The Process of Norham, 1291', *Thirteenth-Century England V*, ed. P. Coss and S. Lloyd (Woodbridge, 1995).

'Durham Records, Calendar of the Cursitor's Records, Chancery Enrolments. Roll of Richard de Bury, Bishop of Durham', *The Thirty-First Annual Report of the Deputy Keeper of the Public Records* (London, 1870).

'Durham Records, Calendar of the Cursitor's Records, Chancery Enrolments. Roll of Thomas de Hatfield, Bishop of Durham', *The Thirty-Second Annual Report of the Deputy Keeper of the Public Records* (1871).

'Durham Records, Calendar of the Cursitor's Records, Inquisitions Post Mortem. Pontificate of Thomas de Hatfield', *The Forty-Fifth Annual Report of the Deputy Keeper of the Public Records* (London, 1885).

Edward I and the Throne of Scotland, 1290–1296; An Edition of the Record Sources for the Great Cause, ed. E.L.G. Stones and G.G. Simpson (2 vols., Oxford, 1978).

Ellis, H., *Original Letters, Illustrative of English History*, 3rd ser. (4 vols., London 1846).

Eulogium historiarum, ed. F.S. Haydon, Rolls Series ix (3 vols., 1858–63).

Feet of Fines, Northumberland, 1273–1346, Newcastle upon Tyne Record Series xi (1932).

Fleta, vol. iv, ed. G.O. Sayles, Selden Society xcix (1983).

Flores historiarum, ed. H.R. Luard, Rolls Series 95 (3 vols., 1890).

Fœdera, conventiones, litteræ, et cujuscunque generis public acta, etc., ed. T. Rymer (4 vols. in 7 parts, Record Commission edn, 1816–69).

Fowler, K., *The King's Lieutenant. Henry Grosmont, First Duke of Lancaster, 1310–1361* (1969).

———, *Medieval Mercenaries* (Oxford, 2001).

Frame, R., *English Lordship in Ireland, 1318–61* (Oxford, 1982).

———, 'Thomas Rokeby, Sheriff of Yorkshire, Justiciar of Ireland', *Peritia* x (1996).

Fraser, C.M., *A History of Antony Bek, Bishop of Durham, 1283–1311* (Oxford, 1957).

Froissart, Jean, *Chroniques*, ed. S. Luce *et al.* (15 vols., Paris, 1869–1975).

Fryde, N., *The Tryanny and Fall of Edward II 1321–6* (Cambridge, 1979).

Galbraith, V.H., 'Extracts from the *Historia Aurea* and a French *Brut*', *English Historical Review* xliii (1928).

———, 'The *Historia Aurea* of John, Vicar of Tynemouth, and the Sources of the St. Albans Chronicle, 1327–77', *Essays in History Presented to Reginald Lane Poole*, ed. H.W.C. Davis (Oxford, 1927).

'Gesta Edwardi de Carnarvon auctore canonico Bridlingtoniensi', *Chronicles of the Reigns of Edward I and Edward II*, ed. W. Stubbs, Rolls Series 76 (2 vols., 1882–3), vol. ii.

Given-Wilson, C., *Chronicles. The Writing of History in Medieval England* (London, 2004).

Given-Wilson, C., and Bériac, F., 'Edward III's Prisoners of War: The Battle of Poitiers and its Context', *English Historical Review* cxvi (2001).

Gransden, A., *Historical Writing in England, c.550 to c.1307* (London, 1974).

Gransden, A., *Historical Writing in England, c.1307 to the Early Sixteenth Century* (London, 1982).

Greenwell Deeds, ed. Joseph Walton, *Archaeologia Aeliana*, 4th ser., iii (1927).

Greenwell, W, and Blair, C.H.H., 'Durham Seals. Part II', *Archaeologia Aeliana*, 3rd ser., viii (1912).

Haines, R.M., *King Edward II. His Life, His Reign and its Aftermath, 1284–1330* (Montreal, 2003).

Hallam, E.M., *The Itinerary of Edward II and his Household, 1307–28*, List and Index Society Publications, ccxi (1984).

Hallam, E.M., and Everard, J., *Capetian France, 987–1328* (2nd edn, Harlow, 2001).

Hamilton, J.S., *Piers Gaveston, Earl of Cornwall, 1307–12. Politics and Patronage in the Reign of Edward II* (Detroit and London, 1988).

Harriss, G.L., *King, Parliament and Public Finance in Medieval England to 1369* (Oxford, 1975).

Heslop, D., and Harbottle, B., 'Chillingham Church, Northumberland:

The South Chapel and the Grey Tomb', *Archaeologia Aeliana*, 5th ser. xxvii (1999).

Higden, Ranulf, Polychronicon Ranulphi Higden monachum Cestrensis, ed. C. Babington and J.R. Lumby, Rolls Series 41 (9 vols., 1865–86)

Historiæ Dunelmensis scriptores tres, ed. J. Raine, Surtees Society ix (1839).

Hodgson, J., *A History of Northumberland* (7 vols. in 3 parts, Newcastle upon Tyne, 1820–58).

Hodgson, R.W., 'Deeds Respecting the Manor of Offerton', *Archaeologia Aeliana*, 1st ser., ii (1832).

Horrox, R. (ed.), *The Black Death* (Manchester, 1994).

Huntingdon, Henry of, *Historia Anglorum*, ed. D. Greenway (Oxford, 1996).

Illustrations of Scottish History from the Twelfth to the Sixteenth Century, ed. J. Stevenson, Maitland Club (Edinburgh, 1834)

Ingledew, Francis, 'The Book of Troy and the Genealogical Construction of History: The Case of Geoffrey of Monmouth's *Historia regum Britanniae*', *Speculum* lxix (1994).

James, M.R., *A Descriptive Catalogue of the Manuscripts in the Library of Jesus College, Cambridge* (London, 1895).

———, *A Descriptive Catalogue of the Western Manuscripts in the Library of Corpus Christi College, Cambridge* (2 vols., Cambridge, 1905).

James, T.B., 'John of Eltham, History and Story: Abusive International Discourse in Late Medieval England, France and Scotland', *Fourteenth-Century England II*, ed. Chris Given-Wilson (Woodbridge, 2002).

Johannis de Fordun. Chronica gentis Scotorum, ed. W.F. Skene (Edinburgh, 1871).

'Johannis de Trokelowe Annales', *Johannis de Trokelowe et Henrici de Blaneforde chronica et annales*, ed. H.T. Riley, Rolls Series xxviii (1866).

Jurkowski, M., Smith C.L., Crook, D., *Lay Taxes in England and Wales, 1188–1688* (Kew, 1998).

Kaeuper, R.W., *Chivalry and Violence in Medieval Europe* (Oxford, 1999).

Keen, M.H., *The Laws of War in the Late Middle Ages* (London, 1965).

King, A., 'A Helm with a Crest of Gold: The Order of Chivalry in Thomas Gray's *Scalacronica*', *Fourteenth-Century England I*, ed. N. Saul (Woodbridge, 2000).

———, 'Jack le Irish and the Abduction of Lady Clifford, November 1315; The Heiress and the Irishman', *Northen History* xxxviii (2001).

———, 'Lordship, Castles and Locality: Thomas of Lancaster, Dunstanburgh Castle and the Lancastrian Affinity in Northumberland, 1296–1322', *Archaeologia Aeliana*, 5th ser., xxix (2001).

———, 'War, Politics and Landed Society in Northumberland, c.1296–c.1408', unpublished Ph.D. thesis (University of Durham, 2001).

———, ' "According to the Custom Used in French and Scottish Wars":

Prisoners and Casualties on the Scottish Marches in the Fourteenth Century', *Journal of Medieval History* xxviii (2002).

————, ' "Pur Salvation du Roiaume": Military Service and Obligation in Fourteenth-Century Northumberland', in *Fourteenth-Century England II*, ed. C. Given-Wilson (Woodbridge, 2002).

————, '*Schavaldours*, Robbers and Bandits: War and Disorder in Northumberland in the Reign of Edward II', *Thirteenth-Century England* IX, ed. M. Prestwich *et al.* (Woodbridge, 2003).

————, 'Thomas of Lancaster's First Quarrel with Edward II', *Fourteenth-Century England III*, ed. Mark Ormrod (Woodbridge, 2004).

————, 'Scaling the Ladder; the Rise and Rise of the Grays of Heton, *c*.1296–*c*.1415', *North-East England in the Later Middle Ages*, ed. R. H. Britnell and C. Liddy (Woodbridge, 2005).

King, A., and Marvin, J., 'A Warning to the Incurious: M.R. James, the *Scalacronica* and the Anglo-Norman Prose *Brut* Chronicle' – forthcoming.

Knighton's Chronicle, 1337–96, ed. G.H. Martin (Oxford, 1995).

Knowles, C.H., 'The Resettlement of England after the Barons' War, 1264–7', *Transactions of the Royal Historical Society*, 5th ser. xxxii (1982).

Leland, J., *De rebus Britannicis collectaneorum* (6 vols., Oxford, 1715).

Liber vitae ecclesiae Dunelmensis: A Collotype Facsimile of the Original Manuscript, ed. A.H. Thompson, Surtees Society cxxxvi (1923).

Little, A.G., *The Grey Friars in Oxford*, Oxford Historical Society xx (1891).

————, 'The Authorship of the Lanercost Chronicle', *English Historical Review* xxxi (1916).

Lucas, H., *The Low Countries and the Hundred Years War, 1326–47* (Michigan, 1929).

Lunt, W., *Financial Relations of the Papacy with England, 1327–1534* (Cambridge, MA, 1962).

MacDonald, A., 'Calendar of Deeds in the Laing Charters Relating to Northumberland' *Archaeologia Aeliana*, 4th ser., xxviii (1950).

McFarlane, K.B., *The Nobility of Later Medieval England. The Ford Lectures for 1953 and Related Studies* (Oxford, 1973).

McNamee, C.J, 'William Wallace's Invasion of Northern England in 1297', *Northern History* xxvi (1990).

————, *The Wars of the Bruces. Scotland, England and Ireland, 1306–28* (East Linton, 1997).

M'Michael, T., 'The Feudal Family of de Soulis', *Transactions of the Dumfriesshire and Galloway Natural History and Antiquarian Society*, 3rd ser., xxvi (1947–8).

MacQuarrie, A., *Scotland and the Crusades, 1095–1560* (2nd edn, Edinburgh, 1997).

Maddicott, J.R., *Thomas of Lancaster 1307–22. A Study in the Reign of Edward II* (Oxford, 1970).

————, 'The County Community and the Making of Public Opinion in

Fourteenth-century England', *Transactions of the Royal Historical Society*, 5th ser. xxviii (1978).

Marlborough, Thomas of, *History of the Abbey of Evesham*, ed. J. Sayers and Leslie Watkiss (Oxford, 2003.

Mayer-Rosa, D., and Cadiot, B., 'A Review of the 1356 Basel Earthquake', *Tectonophysics* liii (1979).

Middleton, A.E., *Sir Gilbert de Middleton* (Newcastle upon Tyne, 1918).

Mirror of Justices, The, ed. W.J. Whitaker and F.W. Maitland, Selden Society vii (1893).

Monmouth, Geoffrey of, *Historia regum Britannie, I: Bern Ms*, ed. N. Wright (Woodbridge, 1985).

Moorman, J.R.H., 'Edward I at Lanercost Priory, 1306–7', *English Historical Review* lxvii (1952).

Morris, M., 'The "Murder" of an English Earldom? Roger IV Bigod and Edward I', *Thirteenth-Century England IX*, ed. M. Prestwich *et al.* (Woodbridge, 2003).

Neve, J. le, *Fasti Ecclesiae Anglicanae, 1300–1541. VI, Northern Province* (London, 1963).

Neville, C.J., *Violence, Custom and Law. The Anglo-Scottish Border Lands in the Later Middle Ages* (Edinburgh, 1998).

New Cambridge Medieval History VI, c.1300–c.1415, The, ed. Michael Jones (Cambridge, 2000).

Nicholai Triveti annales, ed. Thomas Hog, English Historical Society (1845).

Nicholas, D., *Medieval Flanders* (Harlow, 1992).

Nicholson, R., *Edward III and the Scots. The Formative Years of a Military Career, 1327–35* (Oxford, 1965).

———, *Scotland. The Later Middle Ages* (2nd edn, Edinburgh, 1978).

Nicolai Triveti annalium continuatio, ed. Anthony Hall (Oxford, 1722).

'North Country Deeds', ed. W. Brown, *Miscellanea II*, Surtees Society cxxvii (1916).

Northern Petitions, Illustrative of Life in Berwick, Cumbria and Durham in the Fourteenth Century, ed. C.M. Fraser, Surtees Society cxciv (1981).

Northumberland and Durham Deeds from the Dodsworth MSS. in Bodley's Library, Oxford, Newcastle upon Tyne Record Series vii (1929).

Northumberland County History (15 vols., Newcastle upon Tyne, 1893–1940).

Northumberland Petitions. Ancient Petitions Relating to Northumberland, ed. C.M. Fraser, Surtees Society clxxvi (1966).

Offler, H.S., *Medieval Historians of Durham* (Durham, 1958)

———, 'A Note on the Northern Franciscan Chronicle', *Nottingham Medieval Studies* xxviii (1984)

———, 'Murder on the Framwellgate Bridge', *Archaeologia Aeliana*, 5th ser., xvi (1988).

Ormrod, M., 'Love and War in 1294', *Thirteenth-Century England VIII*, ed. M. Prestwich *et al.* (Woodbridge, 2001).

Otway-Ruthven, A.J., *A History of Medieval Ireland* (2nd edn, London, 1980).

Parliamentary Writs, ed. F. Palgrave (2 vols. in 4 parts, London, 1827–34).

Paul, J.B. (ed.), *The Scots Peerage* (9 vols., Edinburgh, 1904–14).

Percy Chartulary, The, ed. M.T. Martin, Surtees Society cxvii (1909).

Penman, M., 'A Fell Coniuracioun agayn Robert the Douchty King: The Soules Conspiracy of 1318–20', *The Innes Review* l (1999).

———, *David II, 1329–71* (East Linton, 2004).

Penman, M., and Tanner, R., 'An Unpublished Act of David II, 1359', *Scottish Historical Review* lxxxiii (2004).

Phillips, J.R.S., *Aymer de Valence, Earl of Pembroke, 1307–24. Baronial Politics in the Reign of Edward II* (Oxford, 1972).

Pierre de Langtoft, le règne d'Edouard Ier, ed. J.C. Thiolier (Créteil, 1989).

Powicke, M., *Military Obligation in Medieval England* (Oxford, 1962).

Prestwich, M.C., 'Isabella de Vescy and the Custody of Bamburgh Castle', *Bulletin of the Institute of Historical Research* xliv (1971).

———, 'Colonial Scotland: The English in Scotland under Edward I', in *Scotland and England 1286–1815*, ed. R.A. Mason (Edinburgh, 1986).

———, *Edward I* (London, 1988).

———, 'Edward I and the Maid of Norway', *Scottish Historical Review* lxix (1990).

———, 'Gilbert de Middleton and the Attack on the Cardinals, 1317', *Warriors and Churchmen in the High Middle Ages*, ed. T. Reuter (London, 1992).

———, *Armies and Warfare in the Middle Ages. The English Experience* (London, 1996).

———, 'Military Logistics: The case of 1322', *Armies, Chivalry and Warfare in Medieval Britain and France*, ed. M. Strickland (Stamford, 1998).

Raine, J., *The History and Antiquities of North Durham* (London, 1852).

Regesta Regum Scottorum V: The Acts of Robert I, 1306–29, ed. A.A.M. Duncan (Edinburgh, 1988).

Regesta Regum Scottorum VI: The Acts of David II, 1329–71, ed. Bruce Webster (Edinburgh, 1982).

Register of Bishop Philip Repingdon, 1405–19, The, ed. M. Archer (3 vols., Lincoln Record Society lvii, lviii, lxxiv, 1963–82).

Register of Edward the Black Prince (4 vols., HMSO, 1930–33).

Registrum magni sigilli regum Scotorum. The Register of the Great Seal of Scotland, ed. J.M. Thomson *et al.* (11 vols., Edinburgh, 1882–1914).

Registrum palatinum Dunelmense, ed. T.D. Hardy, Rolls Series lxii (4 vols., 1873–8).

Richard D'Aungerville of Bury. Fragments of his Register and other Documents, ed. G.W. Kitchin, Surtees Society cxix (1910).

'Robertus de Avesbury de gestis mirabilibus regis Edwardi Tertii', *Chronica A. Murimuth et R. de Avesbury*, ed. E.M. Thompson, Rolls Series 93 (1889).

Rogers, C.J. (ed.), *The Wars of Edward III. Sources and Interpretations* (Woodbridge, 1999).

———, *War Cruel and Sharp. English Strategy under Edward III, 1327–60* (Woodbridge, 2000).

———, 'The Anglo-Norman Peace Negotiations of 1354–60 Reconsidered', *The Age of Edward III*, ed. J.S. Bothwell (Woodbridge, 2000).

Le Roman de Perceval ou le Conte du Graal, ed. W. Roach, Textes Littéraires Français lxxi (1956).

Rotuli hundredorum (2 vols., Record Commission, 1812–18).

Rotuli Parliamentorum (6 vols., London, 1767–77).

Rotuli Scotiæ, ed. D. Macpherson (2 vols., Record Commission, 1814–19).

Russell, P.E., *The English Intervention in Spain and Portugal in the Time of Edward III and Richard II* (Oxford, 1955).

Safford, E.W., *Itinerary of Edward I. Part II: 1291–1307*, List and Index Society cxxxii (1976).

Saul, N., 'The Despensers and the Downfall of Edward II', *English Historical Review* xcix (1984).

Scalacronica, by Sir Thomas Gray of Heton, Knight, ed. J. Stevenson (Edinburgh, 1836).

Scalacronica. The Reigns of Edward I, Edward II and Edward III, tr. H. Maxwell (Glasgow, 1907).

Scotland in 1298. Documents Relating to the Campaign of Edward the First in that Year, and especially to the Battle of Falkirk, ed. H. Gough (Paisley, 1888).

Scott, J., *Berwick-upon-Tweed. The History of the Town and Guild* (London, 1888).

Shenton, C., 'Edward III and the Coup of 1330', *The Age of Edward III*, ed. J.S. Bothwell (Woodbridge, 2000).

Smallwood, T.M., 'An Unpublished Early Account of Bruces' Murder of Comyn', *Scottish Historical Review* liv (1975).

Smith, J. B., *Llywelyn ab Gruffudd. Prince of Wales* (Cardiff, 1998).

Stell, G., 'The Balliol Family and the Great Cause of 1291–2', *Essays on the Nobility of Medieval Scotland*, ed. K.J. Stringer (Edinburgh, 1985).

Summerson, H.R.T., *Medieval Carlisle: The City and the Borders from the Late-Eleventh to the Mid-Sixteenth Century*, Cumberland and Westmorland Antiquarian and Archaeological Society, Extra Series, xxv (2 vols., 1993).

Sumption, J., *The Hundred Years War. Trial by Battle* (London, 1990)

———, *The Hundred Years War. Trial by Fire* (London, 1999).

Tate, G., *The History of the Borough, Castle and Barony of Alnwick* (2 vols., Alnwick, 1868–9).

Taylor, J., *The Universal Chronicle of Ranulf Higden* (Oxford, 1966).

———, *English Historical Literature in the Fourteenth Century* (Oxford, 1987).

Thiolier, J.C., 'La *Scalacronica*: Première Approche (MS 133)', *Les*

manuscrits français de la bibliothèque Parker. Actes du Colloque 24–27 mars 1993, ed. N. Wilkins (Cambridge, 1993).

Thomas, H., *Ludwig der Bayer (1282–1347): Kaiser und Ketzer* (Graz, Vienna, Cologne, 1993).

Thomæ Walsingham, historia Anglicana, ed. H.T. Riley, Rolls Series 28/i (2 vols, 1863).

Tout, T.F., *Chapters in Medieval Adminstrative History* (6 vols., Manchester, 1920–33).

Tuck, A.J, 'Northumbrian Society in the Fourteenth Century', *Northern History* vi (1971).

Urban, W., *The Teutonic Knights. A Military History* (London, 2003).

Vetera monumenta Hibernorum et Scotorum historiam illustrantia, ed. A. Theiner (Rome, 1864).

La Vie du Prince Noir by Chandos Herald, ed. D.B. Tyson (Tübingen, 1975).

Vita Edwardi Secundi, ed. Noel Denholm-Young (London, 1957).

Wardrobe Book of William de Norwell, 12 July 1338 to 27 May 1340, The, ed. M. Lyon, B. Lyon and H. S. Lucas (Brussels, 1983).

Watson, F., *Under the Hammer: Edward I and Scotland, 1296–1306* (East Linton, 1998).

Watson, G.W., 'Ormond and Kildare', *Miscellanea Genealogica et Heraldica*, 5th ser., viii (1932–4).

Wentersdorf, K.P., 'The Clandestine Marriages of the Fair Maid of Kent', *Journal of Medieval History* v (1979).

Wilkins, N., *Catalogue des manuscrits français de la bibliothèque Parker (Parker Library), Corpus Christi College, Cambridge* (Cambridge, 1993).

Willelmi Rishanger, chronica et annales, ed. M.T. Riley, Rolls Series, 28/ii (1865).

Wills and Inventories of the Northern Counties of England, Part I, ed. J. Raine, Surtees Society ii (1835).

'Woodman Charters', tr. H.H.E. Craster, *Archaeologia Aeliana*, 3rd ser., v (1909).

Wright, N., *Knights and Peasants. The Hundred Years War in the French Countryside* (Woodbridge, 1998).

Wyntoun, Andrew of, *The Original Chronicle of Andrew of Wyntoun*, ed. F. J. Amours, Scottish Text Society (6 vols., 1903–14).

INDEX

Places in Britain are identified by medieval county; places in France by medieval province; places in the Low Countries by medieval county or duchy.

Suffixes: A refers to the Appendix, L to Leland's Abstract (pp. 134–41), n. to the Notes (or to footnotes in the Introduction).

Abbreviations: Abp – archbishop; Bp – bishop; br – brother; Ct – count; Cts – Countess; d. – died; D. – duke; E. – earl; eldr – the elder; da. – daughter; gds.-grandson; K. – king; kt – knight; m. – marriage, marries; Q. – Queen; s. – son, sons; yngr – the younger

Ralph, lord (d. 1331), xxx, xxxii, 85,
230n.
Ralph, lord (d. 1367), xxxiii, xxxix, xlii,
119, 140L, 241n.
at siege of Dunbar, 125
at Neville's Cross, 137L
Robert de, 77, 230n.
Neville's Cross, battle of (1346), xxxviii,
137L
Newcastle on Tyne, xxxviii, xli, 37, 97,
101
Edward Balliol does homage to
Edward III at, 117
John Balliol does homage to Edward I
at, 35
riots at, 89
Newminster abbey (Northumb.), 39,
218n.
Nicholas III, Pope (1277–80), 59
Nicholas IV, Pope (1288–92), 59
Nicholas V, anti-Pope (1328–30), 63
Nidau, Ct of, 175
Norfolk, E. of – see Edward I, his s.
Thomas; Bigod
Nogent (Champagne), 179, 185
Norham, xxviii, xxxvii, xl, xliii, l, 31
castle
attacked by Scots, xxix, 81–5, 101,
140–1L
Constables of – see Gray, Thomas,
eldr; Gray, Thomas, yngr;
Manners
church, 216n.
used as fortress by Scots, 85
Normandy, Normans, 15, 35, 136L, 155,
169, 183
kts of, raid Winchelsea, 179
plundered by the commoners of
England, 153
Norsemen, 27
Northallerton (N. Yorks.), 85, 231n.
Northumberland, xxii, 79, 117
barons of, 41
burned by Scots, 115
burned by William Wallace, 41, 219n.
criminals of, waylay E. of March, 119
false men of, connive with Scots, 81
knights and squires of, 103, 236n.
raided by David II, 134L
support of, for Gilbert de Middleton,
79–81
Northampton, execution at, 85
E. of – see Bohun, William de
Norway, 13; see also Margaret, Q. of

Norway; Margaret of Norway; Eric II;
Haakon VI
Nôtre-Dame-de-Puy (Auvergne), 167
Nottingham, 105
castle, 105–6, 236–7n.
constable of, 105, 236n.
Noyers, John de, Ct of Joigny, 145, 195

Ogle, Robert de, Northumb. kt, xxxiv,
xxxviii n., 123, 236n., 241n.
Old Byland, battle of (1322), xxix, 89,
233n.
Oliphant, William de, xxiv, 47, 73, 221n.,
228n.
Orkney, 19, 29
Orleans, 143, 185, 195
Philip, D. of (1344–74), 147, 195
Orleton, Adam, Bp of Hereford
(1317–27), 95
Ormsby, William de, royal justice, 39
Orwell (Suff.), 93, 129, 138L
Otterburn, Thomas de, chronicler, 7,
210n., 212n.
Oulchy castle (Île de France), 185
Oxford, 71
E. of – see Vere

papacy, the, xlv
curia, the, 13, 43, 79, 151
popes – see Adrian; Benedict; Boniface;
Celestine; Clement; Honorius;
Innocent; John; Nicholas; Urban
Paris, 91, 129, 139L, 195
attacked by Charles II, 157
captain of – see Gulioun
commoners of rebel, 155
faubourgs of, burned by English, 183
raided by the English, 173
Parker, Matthew, Abp of Canterbury
(1559–75), liv n., lvi–lviii
parliament, 9, 37, 39
Lincoln (1301), 45
Norham (1291), 31
Scottish parliaments
Scone (1322), 79
Scone (1333), 117
Westminster (1321), 85, 91, 231–2n.,
232n., 233n.
Westminster (1327), 95
Westminster (1330), 107
Westminster (1337), 123
Westminster (1351), 138L, 244n.
Westminster (1355), 141L
Westminster (1358), li, 151–3

William de, claimant to Scottish
    kingship, 31, 33, 215n., 216n.
  John de (bastard s. of William), 31
Villaines, the Bègue de, frequently
    captured French nobleman, 167, 183
Vipont, Ives de, French kt, 179
Vortiger, K. of Britain, 95

Wake, Thomas Lord, 199
  Blanche, his wife, 153
  campaigns against Scots (1327), 97
  goes into exile, 103
  retains his Scottish inheritance, 101
Waldboef, John, English *routier*, 163
Wallace, William, 41–3
  almost kills Thomas Gray, eldr, xxiv, 41
  capture and execution of, 45
Walter, archdeacon of Exeter [*recte*
    Oxford], 5, 210–11n.
Wales, the Welsh, 91
  a deceitful Welshman, 93
  at war with England, 9–11, 13, 15
  in English service, 17, 185
  Prince of – *see* Llewelyn; Edward II;
      Edward, Prince of Wales
  Welsh Bretons, 181
Warenne, John de, E. of Surrey, 33, 39, 41,
    119, 216n.
  keeper of Scotland, 39, 41, 218n.
  Thomas Gray, eldr, serves with, xxiv,
    218n., 219n.
Wark on Tweed (Northumb.), 37
  castle, xxxv–xxxvi, 81, 207A
Warkworth (Northumb.) – *see also* fitz
  Roger
  castle, xxix, 235n.
Warwick, 71
  E. of – *see* Beauchamp

Wear, river, 97
Wearmouth (Durham), 5
Weland, Master, Scottish clerk, 13, 213n.
Westminster, 55
  abbey, 9, 21, 39, 57
Weyland, Thomas de, royal justice, 13,
    213n.
'White Knight', the, 177
Widdrington, Roger, xliii, xlix, 255n.
William I, K. of England (1066–87), 7, 201
Winchelsea (Sussex), raided by French,
    173, 251n.
Winchester, parliament at, 103
  E. of – *see* Despenser, Hugh le, eldr
Windsor, 135L, 195
Wishart, Robert, Bp of Glasgow, 41, 55,
    219n., 228n.
Witton Underwood (Northumb.), 117
wool, xli, 39 – *see also* sheep
  wool staple established at Calais, 203
Wotton, Nicholas, antiquarian, lix
Wyntoun, Andrew, Scottish chronicler,
    xl–xli

Yarmouth (Norf.), 93
Yolande de Dreux, Q. of Scotland, 11, 13,
    213n.
York, 13, 65, 89, 91, 99, 215n.
  Abp of – *see* Zouche, William
  executions at, 87
  parliament at, 101, 113
  soldiers drunkenly brawl at, 97, 234n.
Ypres, men of, 131, 138L

Zeeland, County of, 65, 91
Zouche, William de la, Abp of York
    (1342–52), 137L
  William, Lord, 101

Printed and bound by CPI Group (UK) Ltd, Croydon, CR0 4YY

09/06/2025